BEYOND COLONIALITY

BLACKS IN THE DIASPORA

Herman L. Bennett, Kim D. Butler, Judith A. Byfield, and
Tracy Sharpley-Whiting, editors

BEYOND COLONIALITY

Citizenship and Freedom in the
Caribbean Intellectual Tradition

Aaron Kamugisha

Indiana University Press

This book is a publication of

Indiana University Press
Office of Scholarly Publishing
Herman B Wells Library 350
1320 East 10th Street
Bloomington, Indiana 47405 USA

iupress.org

First paperback edition 2022
© 2019 by Aaron Kamugisha

Manufactured in the United States of America

First paperback edition printing 2022

Cataloging information is available from the Library of Congress.

ISBN 978-0-253-03626-1 (hdbk.)
ISBN 978-0-253-06263-5 (pbk.)
ISBN 978-0-253-03627-8 (web PDF)

For my sister, Kemi Kamugisha
And in memory of my mother and grandmother,
  Stephanie Kamugisha (1948–2013) and
  Dorin St. Hill (1919–2008)

Contents

Acknowledgments

THE THOUGHTS THAT I articulate in *Beyond Coloniality* have occupied my mind for well over a decade, and the conversations that have inspired me to think that a work like this is possible have been many. I am grateful to many friends and colleagues who have shared their thoughts with me on this journey: Jacqui Alexander, Kamau Brathwaite, Timothy Brennan, Mark Campbell, Gena Chang-Campbell, Chris Cozier, Lewis Gordon, Peter Hudson, Pablo Idahosa, Chike Jeffers, Samia Khatun, Robin Kelley, Kamala Kempadoo, Aisha Khan, George Lamming, Neil Lazarus, David McNally, Melanie Newton, Raj Patel, Annie Paul, Jemima Pierre, Richard Pithouse, Heather Russell, David Scott, Ato Sekyi-Otu, Nitasha Sharma, Maziki Thame, Greg Thomas, Todne Thomas, Krista Thompson, Alissa Trotz, Rinaldo Walcott, Alex Weheliye, and Elleni Centime Zeleke. In particular, Paget Henry, Percy Hintzen, and Patrick Taylor have been superb mentors and friends.

Over the past few years, parts of this book were presented in several locations around the world. Thanks to Andrew Smith (University of Glasgow), Elleke Boehemer (Oxford University), Minkah Makalani (University of Texas at Austin), Peter Hudson and Jemima Pierre (at the symposium "Black Folk in Dark Times" hosted by Vanderbilt University), Katherine McKittrick (Queen's University), Lawrence Hamilton (University of Witwatersrand), and Melanie Newton (University of Toronto) for invitations to deliver my work and to the entire Department of African American Studies at Northwestern University for a memorable postdoctoral fellowship year in 2007–8. I would like to thank Marilyn Lake at the University of Melbourne, Sue Thomas at Latrobe University, and Karina Smith at Victoria University for giving me the opportunity to present my work in Melbourne; and in New Zealand, to Tony Ballantyne at the University of Otago and Charlotte McDonald at Victoria University of Wellington—all in a very memorable month of May 2015. Kuan Hsing-Chen was a gracious and thoughtful host at National Chiao Tung University in Taiwan, as were Chris Taylor and Kris Manjapra at a special symposium, "Global Capitalism, through the Caribbean Prism" at Harvard University, and Mike Niblett at Warwick University. I am indebted to many colleagues and friends in South Africa, from three separate trips over the last five years. Victoria Collis-Buthelezi and Ruchi Chaturvedi's invitation to be the inaugural guest of their ongoing Other Universals symposium was a wonderful encounter I will not forget. Many, many thanks to Richard Pithouse, Michael Neocosmos, and Vashna Jagarnath in

Grahamstown and Isabel Hofmeyr, Eric Worby, and Dilip Menon in Johannesburg. At the University of Giessen, Lea Hulsen and Jens Kugele facilitated a first visit to Germany through a fascinating intellectual encounter at the University of Giessen, while Robin Kelley was a great host at the University of California, Los Angeles.

At the University of the West Indies, I would like to thank my colleagues Joan Cuffie, Halimah Deshong, Therese Hadchity, Tonya Haynes, Kristina Hinds, Gabrielle Hosein, Yanique Hume, Tennyson Joseph, Maureen Warner Lewis, Rupert Lewis, Don Marshall, Tracy Robinson, Christianne Walcott, Tara Wilkinson-McClean, and Dale Webber. Thanks especially to Hilary Beckles, for his support of my work and scholarly example. I would also like to acknowledge the School for Graduate Studies and Research of the University of the West Indies, Cave Hill campus, for their generous assistance in funding this research, and the staff in the West Indian collections at the library of the University of the West Indies, St. Augustine, for their assistance in utilizing the C. L. R. James Archive.

I have had a number of memorable collaborations with colleagues on a series of edited collections. Thanks to Alissa Trotz for our special issue of *Race and Class* (2007) "Caribbean Trajectories: 200 Years On"; Peter Hudson for the *C. L. R. James Journal* (2014) issue on "Black Canadian Thought"; Jane Gordon, Lewis Gordon, Paget Henry, and Neil Roberts for *Journeys in Caribbean Thought*; and most of all, Yanique Hume for our collaborations that produced *Caribbean Cultural Thought* and *Caribbean Popular Culture*. I have also benefitted from a number of invitations by colleagues to contribute to their edited collections and participate in the intellectual life of journals under their editorship. For this, I would like to thank especially Hilary Beckles, Michael Bucknor, Paget Henry, Brian Meeks, Heather Russell, Jeremy Pontying, and David Scott. The invitation by Antoinette Burton and Isabel Hofmeyr to participate in the 10 Books That Changed the British Empire project introduced me to a world of intellectual historians whose work I had not encountered and for which I am deeply grateful. Thanks to Sylvia Wynter, a key inspiration behind this study, for the gift of her work and the memory of our conversations about what it will mean to exist within a different world.

For reading chapters and for their discerning feedback, I am indebted to Tonya Haynes, Christian Høgsbjerg, Peter Hudson, Aisha Khan, Katherine McKittrick, Richard Pithouse, Heather Russell, and Todne Thomas and I especially thank David Austin, Percy Hintzen, Mimi Sheller, and Rinaldo Walcott for reading the entire manuscript and for their generous and scrupulous comments. I appreciate the dedication Indiana University Press has shown to this project; special thanks are in order to my editor Dee Mortensen, and also David Miller, Robert Sloan, Julia Turner, and Paige Rasmussen for expertly guiding my project through to publication.

Parts of this book have been published in different forms in *Race and Class* 49, no. 2 (2007), *Small Axe* 34 (2011), *Small Axe* 49 (2006), and *Rihanna: Barbados World-Gurl in Global Popular Culture*, edited by Hilary Beckles and Heather Russell (University of the West Indies Press, 2015). I'd like to thank the Institute of Race Relations, Duke University Press, and the University of the West Indies Press for their permission to reprint parts of these articles, which appear in a substantially revised form in this book. Thanks also to the University of California Press for permission to republish portions of the poems "Lost Body" and "A Salute to the Third World" by Aimé Césaire and to Kamau Brathwaite for permission to quote from his lecture "Middle Passages." I am forever grateful to Leandro Soto for our many conversations about art and life and for permission to reproduce his painting *Sirens en el mar Caribe* on the cover of this book.

Among my many friends, thanks go especially to Damien Appelwaite, Kyesha Appelwaite, Stan Armstrong, Jason Carmichael, Kerri Catlyn, Ayola Mayers, Sade Mayers, Robert Harewood, Paul Simpson, Alberta Whittle, and Rose Whittle, for the companionship and laughter without which life would be so dreary and, quite simply, scarcely worth living. The considerate and thoughtful advice offered by Steven Butcher, Sergio Catlyn, Ryan Davis, Robin Douglas, Anton Hunte, Brian Lashley, Michelle Workman, and Shemeika Williams will never be forgotten.

This book is in part dedicated to the memory of my mother and grandmother, Stephanie Kamugisha and Dorin St. Hill, for their care and wisdom. To Arlette, thank you so much for making me understand the importance of artistic courage in this world. To all my in-laws, foremost Uji Oboh, thank you for everything over this last decade. Kemi, my sister, this book is for you and for the time and conversations we have shared over all my life. To my niece and nephew, Asha and Tega, thank you for your presence in my world.

Alana, I thank you for your confidence, grace, and happiness and for revealing to me the true meaning of love.

Bathsheba, Barbados,
August 2018

BEYOND COLONIALITY

1 Beyond Caribbean Coloniality

The contemporary Caribbean—an area of experience that so many of its dispossessed citizens have given their lives and hearts to in the hope of social transformation—is in a state of tragedy and crisis, destroyed and corrupted by a postcolonial malaise wedded to neocolonialism. This state of affairs is hardly unique and may well be seen as the condition of much of the postcolonial world, two generations after the promise of the Bandung Conference, which pointed to a horizon of true self-determination for people emerging from colonialism, and fifty years after the Tricontinental Conference of Solidarity of the Peoples of Africa, Asia and Latin America, the greatest summit ever held in the region against empire.[1] Ato Sekyi-Otu's reading of Frantz Fanon in his *Fanon's Dialectic of Experience*, perhaps the most discerning interpretation of the last century's most influential anticolonial thinker, captures our condition in the most prescient manner: "After all, what is our situation? An omnivorous transnational capital that requires local political agencies to discipline their populace into acquiescing to its draconian measures; a free market of material and cultural commodities whose necessary condition of existence is the authoritarian state; the incoherent nationalism of dominant elites who are in reality transmitters and enforcers of capital's coercive universals: that is our historical situation."[2]

Sekyi-Otu's return to Fanon in order to comprehend, as an African intellectual, "three blighted decades of postcolonial existence" shares the intent and practice of this meditation on the contemporary Caribbean.[3] The story about the Caribbean's retreat from a moment striving for revolutionary coherence in the 1970s to the decline and lethargy of our time is often tied to the advent of global neoliberalism, a global story in which we are all enmeshed. My claim, here though, is that the term *neoliberalism* flattens the complexity of the Caribbean's current moment.[4] Rather, in the Caribbean we see an amalgam of neocolonialism, postcolonial elite domination, *and* neoliberalism, which have undermined the conditions of possibility for any kind of social democracy—far less the democratic-socialist experiments of a generation ago. We are thus left with antiworker states seduced and secured by client politics and a lurking ruthless authoritarianism. That is our political moment in the Caribbean and the terrain of struggle of this book, *Beyond Coloniality: Citizenship and Freedom in the Caribbean Intellectual Tradition*.

> Between 1979 and 1983, there was an extraordinary idealism and enthusiastic boldness of commitment right through the region. Those four years did something to ignite and activate people in all kinds of fields. But the tragedy that [the Grenada] Revolution took such a fall, it traumatized the left—and we have not yet quite recovered the meaning of that event.
>
> George Lamming interviewed by Paul Buhle (1987)[5]

It is by now well acknowledged that political regimes in the Anglophone Caribbean have what Paget Henry has wryly termed "high legitimacy deficits."[6] Practically every political theorist in the Anglophone Caribbean has used the language of crisis to describe the sociopolitical condition of the contemporary Caribbean state, from Brian Meeks's "hegemonic dissolution," to Holger Henke's diagnosis of a "severe moral and ethical crisis," Anthony Bogues's Caribbean "postcolony," Obika Gray's "predation politics," and Selwyn Ryan's worry over the sustainability of democratic governance.[7] This contemporary moment of crisis has been attributed to a series of events in the last four decades of which the 1983 end of the Grenada revolution stands as a significant landmark. The Grenada revolution was principally a movement by the people of that island for self-determination beyond the confines of neocolonialism. It was also the most critical stand made by a regional leftist movement against empire in the postindependence era, and activists from all over the region lent their support toward its survival. Grenada also engendered a form of internationalism seldom seen in the postindependence Anglophone Caribbean, with activists from the American Indian Movement (AIM) and the Palestine Liberation Organization (PLO) visiting, sharing their experiences, and declaring their solidarity with the movement.[8] The end of the Grenada revolution not only scattered the Caribbean Left across the region and throughout the Caribbean diaspora but, as Lamming notes, traumatized the Left and fatally undermined its ability to advance any revolutionary overthrow of the neocolonial state in the postindependence Caribbean. The collapse of Grenada, coming after the murder of Walter Rodney and the electoral defeat of Michael Manley in 1980, was followed by a decade of structural adjustment imposed by the International Monetary Fund (IMF) and World Bank and ended with the collapse of authoritarian governments in eastern Europe, soon to be followed by the disintegration of the Soviet Union. Staggering from structural adjustment to neoliberal globalization in the decade that followed, with a Left transformed or vanished and technocratic governments in place that would have been denounced as apologists for local and global apartheid two decades previously, the legitimacy crisis of the Caribbean state is not hard to perceive.[9] This has been the context of our struggle in the region over the last generation.

This account of the experience of the preceding forty years, in which Grenada represents the great moment of decline from a radical Caribbean striving for freedom, is a popular one, but with definite limits.[10] Since the end of the

Grenada revolution, we have seen a collapse of efforts to capture the state and deploy it as the means to effect radical social change in the Caribbean. However, we have seen a flowering and deepening of claims to a postcolonial citizenship barely imaginable in the heady days of socialist experimentation. This suggests that rather than a tale of incomprehensible decline, we should instead be alert to the changing contours of the demands surrounding postcolonial citizenship in the last generation and their implications for an analysis of the Caribbean's present and potential futures.

The challenge, as with all engagements with the social world, is complex. I agree with the many members of the Caribbean intelligentsia who suggest that the Caribbean is enmeshed in crisis and echo the bewilderment felt by so many over the seeming absence of political will from nonstate actors to transform the region and the incredible diminution of and lethargy within the Left. How could one not argue the case that global neoliberalism since the beginning of the 1980s has severely damaged not just regional economies but imaginations, the very dreams of transformation articulated in the past? Is it possible not to wilt before the searing argument that the steady march of Western consumerist individualism in the Caribbean has made past inspired programs of self-sufficiency as familiar today as artifacts of a forgotten millennia-old civilization? Yet the constant language of doubt misses transformations as acute in their possibility for new futures as the previous litany of setbacks engenders despair.

Principal among these has been the outpouring of an incredible array of multidisciplinary, genre-defying activism and work by (and on behalf of) Caribbean women, their lives, and Caribbean gender relations.[11] The dazzling talent of Caribbean women writers was evident before the 1980s, but the presence of many new writers from 1980 onward would transform the Caribbean literary landscape utterly and fundamentally.[12] In the arena of social and political thought, Caribbean feminisms have not only made signal contributions to every pressing field of inquiry—including political economy, citizenship, historiography, the law, race and ethnic studies, and labor history—but their contributions have been the key to unmasking the ruses of postcolonial citizenship.[13] Caribbean feminisms thus constitute the single most decisive change to the intellectual culture of the region over the last generation. But they have left an even more acute, indelible mark on law, language, and lived experience, in a manner that has revised the conditions of possibility through which Caribbean people conceive of their belonging and citizenship within their nation-states.

The meaning of Grenada, then, may well be otherwise than has been repeatedly articulated. Two outstanding recent studies of its revolution have—in their focus on the memory and meaning of the event—gone beyond the previous scholarship on it and posed challenging questions about how we perceive its aftermath. Shalini Puri's contention in *The Grenada Revolution in the Caribbean*

Present is that past scholarship on the revolution, as illuminating as it has been, does not "address the *subjective* heart of things," which her study, tracing the contemporary memory of the revolution, seeks to uncover.[14] Puri notes that the fall of the revolution "paralyzed" the regional Left, but her study can be seen as working actively against that tale of angst and sorrow, partly by revealing the sheer resonances of Grenada in the life and thought of the region over the last thirty years. Puri frames her work as a "meditation on memory," with the belief that the "best hopes for resolution and reconciliation in Grenada lie not in the TRC (Truth and Reconciliation Commission) or other state-led efforts but rather in everyday and artistic practices."[15] Uncovering tales of how people live with "deep *dis*agreements" holds the promise not just of comprehending the weight of Grenada's revolution, but a pathway to how Caribbean society might deal with difference in a number of spheres of existence.[16] David Scott's *Omens of Adversity* also recognizes the Grenada revolution as a "watershed event," one that has been almost talismanic for a generation in the Caribbean.[17] Scott's interest is less in the memory of the event in the region than in "the temporality of the aftermaths of political catastrophe, the temporal disjunctures involved in living *on* in the wake of past political time, amid the ruins, specifically, of postsocialist and postcolonial futures past."[18] Scott accomplishes a difficult double—he both provides persuasive reconstructions of the events leading to the October 1983 catastrophic end of the revolution and the sham trial in its aftermath and takes the revolution's history as the ground for a wider meditation on themes from political action to transnational justice. Both texts will doubtless elicit controversy, but the value of Puri's and Scott's contributions is that they have given Grenada a certain *rest* in our imagination.[19] Rather than the turmoil and grief that Lamming speaks of in the above epigraph, Grenada becomes not a moment that marks the fatal diminution and end of the Anglophone Caribbean Left but a signal event in our ongoing attempt to craft a Caribbean future beyond our neocolonial present.

The focus of *Beyond Coloniality* on questions of citizenship and freedom puts it in conversation with a number of texts published in the region over the last generation, work both on citizenship and its exclusions and on the Caribbean intellectual tradition.[20] It is my view that in the current generation, we are seeing a series of social movements, individual actors, and pressure groups striving for a revised articulation of the contours of postcolonial citizenship.[21] We might well see Anglophone Caribbean radical social and political thought in the era after the collapse of the Grenada revolution as occupying two broadly conceived and certainly overlapping traditions of thought. On one hand, a number of Caribbean thinkers have advanced a conceptual terminology—including the terms *clientelism, false decolonization*, and *hegemonic dissolution*—that has been highly influential for those interested in comprehending the character of the Caribbean postcolonial state. Another set of theorists, located within both regional and transnational circles and emergent in the last two decades, has been more consciously concerned with theorizing citizenship and its denials within the Caribbean state and has not only expanded previous understandings of the character of the colonial and postcolonial state but also posed searching questions about the limits of human freedom under coloniality. Neither of these trends is hermetically sealed off from the other, and *Beyond Coloniality* represents an effort to deliberately think of them in concert. The theoretical grounding of *Beyond Coloniality* lies within the radical Caribbean intellectual tradition that is its basis of study, which raises the question of what constitutes Caribbean theory.

The Search for a Caribbean Method

In a 2004 interview with Anthony Bogues, George Lamming was asked the question, what "is the oxygen of the Caribbean intellectual tradition?" His immediate reply was "history and politics. . . . These are the generative elements of our tradition."[22] This perspective from one of the region's most celebrated fiction authors is less strange when one recalls the nature of so much of Lamming's work—dense novels in which the weight of history shadows the text, partly the consequence of growing up in Barbados, which during the period of direct colonial rule was one of the most class-stratified societies in the Anglophone Caribbean. Lamming represents one of the most intriguing bridges of what Paget Henry terms the historicist and poeticist traditions of Caribbean thought, seen most clearly in Lamming's lectures and essays since the mid-twentieth century.[23] His lifework, like that of so many of the giants of the Caribbean intellectual tradition—for example (and I deliberately limit myself to five representatives here), Erna Brodber (novelist/sociologist), Kamau Brathwaite (poet/historian), Aimé Césaire (poet/political theorist), Edouard Glissant (novelist/cultural theorist), and Alejo Carpentier (novelist/cultural historian)—explodes the boundaries of established disciplines in the Western academy. He is also the figure that the Caribbean has constantly turned to at its moments of crisis and despair to craft a message that could begin the work of healing the community after immense loss—as seen in his eulogies for Walter Rodney, Maurice Bishop and his colleagues, and C. L. R. James.[24]

Lamming also embodies a particular *style* that animates the best work in the Caribbean intellectual tradition.[25] Take, for example, the following passage from a 1938 speech by C. L. R. James: "The idea that anyone who supports Britain in a war would be supporting democracy is either criminal hypocrisy or equally criminal stupidity. The British Empire is the greatest instrument of tyranny and oppression known to History, and its overthrow would be a great step forward in human progress. Side by side with the struggle for colonial independence must go the struggle for socialism. . . . Either socialism, with material progress, peace, and fraternal relations between peoples, or empire-increasing racial hatred and imperialist wars."[26]

The resonance of James's words and the truths they contain were as evident in summer 2016 on the release of the British government's official report on their imperialist assault on the Iraqi people as they were on the eve of World War II.[27] But the style I refer to is not just the charismatic power and truth of James's words. It is a radical anticolonial praxis that has been so central to the formation of Caribbean thought, succinctly described by Mimi Sheller as the "distinctively Caribbean confluence of two theoretical traditions: a class-centered tradition of anticapitalist political theory and praxis and an aesthetic centered tradition of anticolonial cultural theory and praxis."[28] It is this theoretical anchor that has emboldened Caribbean radicals who in speaking truth *about* power have engendered a fabulous intellectual tradition of global renown today.

Over the last generation in the Anglophone Caribbean, the work of charting the intellectual history of the region and its social, political, and cultural thought has been the labor of a Caribbean intelligentsia in many scholarly fields. The developed nature of the scholarship in Caribbean literary studies and Caribbean history is such that not only are there a number of superlative monographs within each, but major texts considering the field as a field in its own right have been published. None of these is more impressive than *The Routledge Companion to Anglophone Caribbean Literature*, with sixty-five contributions and a discussion of authors, texts, and critical fields that will make it a standard work for some time to come.[29] Caribbean social and political thought as a distinctive terrain of academic inquiry has had a more gradual development for a number of reasons—the primary commitment of the figures who can be perceived to be its chief theorists to radical social change rather than the creation of scholarly manuscripts, its expression in the manifesto and the speech rather than the scholarly tome, and the profound (and uncompleted) epistemological decolonization necessary in order to have this work recognized as worthy of critical study and engagement. Caribbean theorists' profoundly multidisciplinary and metatheoretical approach to expressing ideas also belies the scholarly distinctions of the Western academy, producing work that defies any easy categorization and requiring an intellectual inventiveness, often absent both in the region and beyond its shores for a true appreciation of its value.

I would suggest that at least three broad trends exist within this wide, overlapping field of Caribbean thought, which straddles intellectual history and social, cultural, and political thought. The first constitutes nonfiction work by Caribbean thinkers who seek to discern what I will term here a Caribbean method. This set of texts, which has come to constitute a tradition in its own right, contains works familiar to the intelligentsia of the region—C. L. R. James's *The Black Jacobins* (1938) and *Beyond a Boundary* (1963), Fernando Ortiz's *Cuban Counterpoint* (1940), Eric Williams's *Capitalism and Slavery* (1944), Aimé Césaire's *Notebook of a Return to My Native Land* (1947), Frantz Fanon's *Black Skin,*

White Masks (1952), George Lamming's *The Pleasures of Exile* (1960), Elsa Goveia's, *Slave Society in the British Leeward Islands at the End of the Eighteenth Century* (1965), George Beckford's *Persistent Poverty* (1972), Kamau Brathwaite's *The Development of Creole Society in Jamaica, 1770–1820* (1971), Edouard Glissant's *Caribbean Discourse* (1981), the uncollected Caribbean writings of Sylvia Wynter from 1968 to 1984, and Jacqui Alexander's *Pedagogies of Crossing* (2005).[30] The second tendency is constituted by a number of important texts on individual figures and social movements, and a few ambitious texts have tried to account for that tradition in its entirety, a daunting task. Elsa Goveia's *A Study on the Historiography of the British West Indies to the End of the Nineteenth Century* (1956) was a remarkable study of the colonial historiography of the region and the earliest text of its kind in the Anglophone Caribbean.[31] A decisive early contribution to the field of ideas in the entire region came from Gordon Lewis, whose *Main Currents in Caribbean Thought* (1983) was perhaps the first to chart the social and political thought of the region, unencumbered by the linguistic divides that complicate scholarship on it. This was followed by Denis Benn's *Ideology and Political Development: The Growth and Development of Political Ideas in the Caribbean, 1774–1983* (1987) and Silvio Torres-Saillant's *An Intellectual History of the Caribbean* (2006), ambitious texts with an interest in discerning key debates across the thought of the region.[32] The interest in Caribbean thinkers has resulted in a vast secondary literature: a plethora of studies of figures like Frantz Fanon, C. L. R. James, José Martí, and Aimé Césaire, to name just a few; the Caribbean Reasonings Series from Ian Randle Publishers in Jamaica; and within the last decade, new work on understudied figures like Claudia Jones and Sylvia Wynter.[33]

The last trend I wish to consider comprises work that seeks through a sustained meditation with the Caribbean intellectual tradition to apply Caribbean thought as a critical praxis through which a new Caribbean future might be achieved. An early, and too often overlooked work, Patrick Taylor's *The Narrative of Liberation*, combined Caribbean social and political thought with a study of its literature and the popular, pioneering a style of criticism that would become more popular in the field over a decade later.[34] The turn of the millennium saw the publication of two highly influential texts, David Scott's *Refashioning Futures: Criticism after Postcoloniality* (1999) and Paget Henry's *Caliban's Reason: Introducing Afro-Caribbean Philosophy* (2000).[35] In the former, the stakes are the demand of postcolonial criticism in the present, while the latter engages in an art of recovery of a buried philosophical tradition and advances the argument that Caribbean thought might best make an explicit turn to philosophy in its quest for epistemological decolonization. It is the spirit of this tradition of scholarship that *Beyond Coloniality* identifies with most closely, in which the critical appraisal of Caribbean thought becomes a pathway toward the region's freedom.

The story we tell of a tradition of thought and the texts we mobilize are always conjunctural. Indeed, all new disciplinary moments, as Stuart Hall reminds us, are born out of specific conjunctures—the sociohistorical moments that allow for their genesis, the emergent problems that seem irreconcilable with current intellectual paradigms, and the political moments that sunder allegiances and force us to think our world anew.[36] Over the last fifteen years, my work on the Caribbean has been concerned with two broad overlapping interests. The first is animated by a worry over the influence of neocolonialism, neoliberalism, and the subsequent transformations in citizenship, identities, sovereignty, and development in the Caribbean.[37] The second is driven by a profound appreciation of the Caribbean intellectual tradition, which has consistently articulated different ways of imagining the region, far beyond the vision of its governing elites. At the beginning of this decade, I commenced a serious consideration of the intellectual history of the political thought and cultural thought of the region, the latter work with my colleague Yanique Hume.[38] In doing so, I was influenced by my location as a lecturer in cultural studies at the preeminent university in the Anglophone Caribbean, the University of the West Indies, and guided by an interest in proffering a way of considering the Caribbean intellectual tradition and presenting it to another generation of scholars, students, and a larger Caribbean intelligentsia. This work resulted in four volumes of collected readings on Caribbean thought: *Caribbean Political Thought: The Colonial State to Caribbean Internationalisms* (2013) and *Caribbean Political Thought: Theories of the Post-Colonial State* (2013), and in partnership with Yanique Hume *Caribbean Cultural Thought: From Plantation to Diaspora* (2013) and *Caribbean Popular Culture: Power, Politics and Performance* (2016), which attempt to sketch the necessarily provisional contours of a Caribbean tradition of political and cultural thought.[39] What emerges from these works is not just the wealth of the contributions made by Caribbean figures to global thought over the last two centuries but also the ways in which a distinctive Caribbean experience unsettles the assumptions of Western canonical disciplines as well as the periodization of fields like postcolonial studies and cultural studies. To the key words of contemporary cultural studies—*hegemony, discourse, articulation, governmentality*—Caribbean cultural thought presents the *plantation, creolization, transculturation, erotic marronage*, and *tidalectics* and proffers searching questions to complacent theories of Western modernity and cultural diasporas.[40] The never simple matter of categorizing the "postcolonial" raises myriad questions in the region. The different colonizing powers had the effect of turning regions under their political control in the Caribbean into what we might term a "governable singularity," and the very diverse histories of territories in the region means that the postcolonial experience, while sharing traces, is fundamentally different, as we would expect since flag independence came to Haiti in 1804, the Dominican Republic in 1865, and Cuba in 1902, with the Anglophone Caribbean a relative latecomer in the 1960s.[41] In *Beyond Coloniality*, the theory I utilize is Caribbean and borrowed from thinkers throughout the region. However, when I turn to a description of the distinctive features of the Caribbean polity, I refer to and draw on examples derived from the Anglophone Caribbean state. This is hardly due to an interest in reinforcing the linguistic divides that haunt scholarship on the region but rather because of the insurmountable difficulties in reasonably addressing the complexity of the political moment in countries as diverse as Haiti, the Dominican Republic, Cuba, and Guadeloupe (to take just four)—all with different histories of colonialism and contested sovereignty.

Beyond Coloniality is a long meditation on Caribbean thought and attempts to effect a challenging alliance. It discusses a social and political moment complex in its territorial specificity and not easily generalized across the region, while engaging radical Caribbean thought as the means to comprehend the coloniality of our present and to imagine a turn to an embattled future beyond coloniality. In *Beyond Coloniality* a range of Caribbean theorists whose work is of inestimable value in understanding our present are closely considered, among these, Jacqui Alexander, Kamau Brathwaite, Aimé Césaire, Frantz Fanon, Paget Henry, Percy Hintzen, Claudia Jones, George Lamming, Shalini Puri, Gordon Rohlehr, and David Scott. However, it is primarily a meditation on the work of two towering figures in the Caribbean intellectual tradition, C. L. R. James and Sylvia Wynter. The thought of James and Wynter is both mobilized in critique of the coloniality of the contemporary Caribbean and as an intimation toward a future beyond our present condition. The technique employed here, particularly in the chapters on James and Wynter, is in part what Gary Wilder has called "intellectual history as critical theory," in which the studied reflection on illuminating primary (and in some cases unpublished) documents, along with widely known texts, is considered with a constant reflective eye toward our present concerns and conjunctural moment.[42] The extraordinary range and commitment evident in the writings of both James and Wynter have left few of the conundrums of contemporary life untouched. It is through their writing that we see the best presentation of a method capable of providing both a profound critique of the contemporary Caribbean and the contours of a—necessarily provisional and unsettled—future beyond coloniality.

My choice of James and Wynter may evoke the query, Why pair these two thinkers over others? What adventures would a coupling of Wilson Harris and Frantz Fanon, in which the labyrinth of the imagination struggling to move beyond colonialism and toward an alternate future, from decidedly different directions, give me? Or alternatively, why not Edouard Glissant and Kamau Brathwaite, whose sympathy for intercultural understanding as the constituent element of the Caribbean experience, twinned with a thoroughgoing rejection for cultural imperialism, shelters so much of the ethics Caribbean thought has presented to the world?[43] Might not the contrasting lives of the Trinidadians Claudia Jones and Lloyd Best cause us to ponder the tradition of the independent radical public intellectual in the region and its diaspora, independent of institutional structures of power? Or would consideration of the triumvirate of George Beckford, Norman Girvan, and C. Y. Thomas, the most innovative political economists of their time, reveal the possibility of sovereign futures beyond the wreckage of our economies? And does not the profoundly secular orientation of both James's and Wynter's work pose a special challenge in the Caribbean, where religion and spirituality play such a dominant role in the constructions of identities and the articulation of forms of belonging and citizenship for its residents?

The labor of recognizing what *Beyond Coloniality* attempts to accomplish— to engage with a living tradition of Caribbean thought as a prolegomenon to what Caribbean life might be, as a "free community of valid persons"—is given expression in, but is also *beyond*, this book and already the work of a radical intelligentsia and the lived experience of Caribbean people who refuse to live within the limitations of a colonial citizenship.[44] It is worth recalling Cedric Robinson's comments on the nature of the community that sheltered the work of the renegade black intelligentsia. Robinson reminds us, "We must keep in mind that their brilliance was also derivative. The true genius was in the midst of the people of whom they wrote. There the struggle was more than words or ideas but life itself."[45] James and Wynter would support Robinson's observations here, as their contributions to a theory of the Caribbean popular remains one of their signal contributions to Caribbean letters and a key site of convergence of their intellectual interests.[46] The claim of this text is then that the scope, provenance, and political urgency of the work of C. L. R. James and Sylvia Wynter (and the radical Caribbean intellectual tradition that lies behind it) help us clarify the questions of the contribution Caribbean thought can make to Caribbean self-determination beyond coloniality.[47] This book is guided both by the radical Caribbean intellectual tradition and *also* by the anticolonial thought of a global black radical tradition, one of the most compelling theoretical resources for comprehending the nature of global coloniality today. In the remainder of this opening chapter, I wish to take two moments in the work of James and Wynter, both as an initial exploration of their thought applied to the questions posed by this text and as an example of the method deployed in *Beyond Coloniality*.

C. L. R. James and Postindependence Caribbean Politics

In August 1960, C. L. R. James delivered a series of six lectures on modern politics at the Trinidad Public Library. By then, James was barely two years back in the Caribbean, and rumors of the split between him and the premier, Eric Williams, were rife, which probably partly accounted for the large crowds that came to hear him speak.[48] The drama some of the crowd may have come to hear did not take place until after the lectures. James's lectures, originally published by the People's National Movement (PNM) Publishing Company the same year, under the title *Modern Politics*, were suppressed by Williams, their distribution banned in Trinidad and Tobago with the books placed in a warehouse under guard. Aldon Lynn Nielsen captures well the ironies of this episode in James's life: "When Williams eventually relented and allowed the books a reprieve, it was so that the whole lot could be taken out of Trinidad by a New York book dealer. Thus C. L. R. James, who had been deported from the United States largely on the evidence of his published books, saw his books deported for political reasons from Trinidad and circulated by a sort of literary commodities futures trader in the United States."[49]

What remains more remarkable about this episode is how Williams's determination to suppress James's thought squares with what James actually said in these lectures.[50] *Modern Politics* is styled as a series of lectures on the history of political thought, and James presents a compelling reading of the Western tradition from the ancient Greeks to modern times. From the preface to its powerful conclusion, James is concerned with the political choices faced by Caribbean people at the moment of independence and the consequences of a decision that might "ruin our lives for at least a generation."[51] The choice that James wishes his audience to make is a deliberate decision to engage with Marxism as the route to true self-determination and freedom for not only their society but humankind, and it is James's characteristic charismatic appeal in making his case that likely heightened Williams's concerns.[52] However, even in his last lecture, where Western popular art figures prominently, and the last section of that lecture titled "The Ascent of Man to Complete Humanity," Caribbean politics and the Caribbean popular are noticeably absent in the lectures.[53] The one brief gesture to events in contemporary Trinidad and Tobago comes in his fifth lecture and appears to be an unscripted comment apart from the genealogy of political ideas he was trying to map. Cautioning against any sense of nationalist euphoria over battles for self-government or the returning of the US base at Chaguaramas, James said: "When the British go and the Americans go and the British flag comes down and the West Indian flag goes up and all face one another—it is then you are going to see real politics. That is not to say that what has happened up to now is not real. It is very real, but it is preliminary. When all that is achieved, then the fundamental forces inside this country, as in every country, will begin to show themselves."[54]

The present work takes as part of its thesis that James's multiple writings on the Caribbean in the late 1950s and 1960s constitute landmark texts in the development of political thought in the Anglophone Caribbean and anticipate many of the themes that would later be more fully developed by numerous social and political theorists in the region. James's writings from those decades came at a critical time in Caribbean history, during the ill-fated federal experiment that was followed by the advent of full self-government in some of the territories within the region.[55] In his text *Party Politics in the West Indies*, his longest exposition on politics in the Caribbean of that time, his chief concern is arguably with the politics of citizenship in the postcolonial Anglophone Caribbean. This interest, I would contend, resulted in a strategic shift from a Marxist or Pan-Africanist perspective as his guiding principal theoretical agenda toward one whose primary concern was with the coloniality of citizenship and the peculiar racialized class formations of Caribbean society.[56] James's achievements here were also shadowed by a failure to introduce a more radical narrative about the possibilities of the Caribbean than his (at times vaguely defined) democratic-socialist, anti-imperialist platform. This dilemma—the political form of a sovereign state in the Caribbean—is not limited to James's struggle in the 1960s Caribbean but is one that still bedevils radical Caribbean social and political thought and is exacerbated in contemporary times by the crisis presented by neoliberalism and the disillusionment of the political Left.[57]

In contrast to the many posts he held at US universities from the late 1960s through the 1970s, James never held a teaching appointment at the University of the West Indies, but his lectures at the university in 1960–1961 attracted younger scholars like Norman Girvan and Lloyd Best to his work and became a crucial event in the formation of the transnational community he would forge over the next two decades. This community included a study group on Marxism run by James for West Indian students in London, whose participants included Walton Look-Lai, Orlando Patterson, Richard Small, Joan French, Raymond Watts, Stanley French, and Walter Rodney.[58] According to David Austin, Norman Girvan introduced Robert Hill to C. L. R. James in London, a significant introduction as Robert Hill would become a founding member of the C. L. R. James Study Circle and the Caribbean Conference Committee, both based in Montreal.[59] The Caribbean Conference Committee in Montreal was arguably the "most active site of exile Anglophone Caribbean *political* activity" in the late 1960s and early 1970s, and the leading personalities within it played key roles in the intraregional radicalism of this period.[60] James's lectures throughout the region itself in the early 1960s also coincided with an event that would become critical to the gestation of the political Left in the Anglophone Caribbean—the establishment of the Faculty of Social Sciences at the University of the West Indies–Mona campus in 1962. The full extent of his influence on the first generation of postindependence Anglophone Caribbean social and political theorists has, however, perhaps not been adequately understood. The work of Lloyd Best and Archie Singham, two of the most important theorists of the nature of the Caribbean political in the first decade of Anglophone Caribbean independence, was considerably influenced by James.[61] This is a fact of no little note, as Lloyd Best is widely recognized as one of the most important public intellectuals in the Caribbean of the last forty years, cofounder of the New World Group, and a leading theorist of the plantation society model of development.[62] Archie Singham was one of the founding members of the Department of Government at the University of the West Indies–Mona; he provided much of the stability to be found there in its first decade and made a decisive contribution to its intellectual direction. His book *The Hero and the Crowd in a Colonial Polity*, published almost simultaneously with Best's essay "Independent Thought and Caribbean Freedom," was the first study of its kind written by a professionally trained political scientist in the Anglophone Caribbean context, and the theory of the Caribbean political system Singham develops from his study of Grenada merits further examination.[63]

The Hero and the Crowd in a Colonial Polity emerged out of the 1962 constitutional crisis in Grenada, a crisis that Singham believed was not attributable to "isolated phenomena but is inherent in the colonial situation."[64] Singham's speculations about the nature of the colonial condition in the Caribbean turn on considerations about dependency and subordination in the Caribbean polity and the size of Caribbean territories. Dependency is evidenced in "the economy, the polity, and the value system" and in "scale and demographic features," while the colony as a "subordinate system" is kept in its place by force but, over time, does not need metropolitan power to "maintain system integration."[65] The reasons for this seemingly overly structuralist account of colonial power become clear when Singham turns to a discussion of the charismatic leader in the British West Indies and what he terms personal government. A decisive feature of charismatic leaders is their "ability to politicize and mobilize the mass, not merely to propagandize them."[66] However, for Singham, the illiteracy of the masses in the post-1930s period made the seductions of "demagoguery and propagandizing the mass" difficult for leaders to resist, leading to a hero-crowd relationship between leader and masses, soon to be institutionalized as ruler and ruled.[67] Singham, in this formulation, places the burden on the lack of education of the masses rather than the authoritarianism of the trade union movement, but he also points to the understandings of legitimacy and realities of exploitation that were a crucial part of colonialism, which the mainly middle-class elite leadership that emerged after the 1930s rebellions had a limited interest in countering. The persistence of personal government is, however, seen as a direct relic of colonialism and the small size of the British West Indian territories.[68] A shift from personal government to "party and institutional government" may seem salutary, but this presents its own array of problems in the form of "cuckoo politics," or mimicry, in which the obsession is with the "forms of parliamentary government, not the content," leading to a bureaucratic routinization of the Westminster model of government.[69] A Caribbean federal arrangement could "lessen the reliance on personal government" but faces two powerful challenges. The construction of elite-mass relationships in the different territories has been predicated on intimate relationships peculiarly local, idiosyncratic, and likely highly resistant to being subsumed into a federal model.[70] The economic and bureaucratic elites' newfound control of the state opens too many opportunities for self-aggrandizement for them to sacrifice their political power in the name of regional integration. At the "mass level," there is a substantial, genuine commonality that exists (though not devoid of differences) but without the leadership or social movement that might move federation from the status of an idea to that of an immediate necessity.

Singham's work, in its attempt to theorize the Caribbean polity within the framework of its own rationalities, has been highly influential not just for scholars interested in the comparative study of Caribbean politics but as a landmark work in Caribbean political culture.[71] Here, the influence of James's ideas in developing a study of Caribbean politics can be seen further. Not only did James sound an important dissenting voice to the existing liberal optimism at the birth of independence but in his essays on the calypsonian the Mighty Sparrow, the cricketer Garfield Sobers, and his semiautobiographical classic *Beyond a Boundary*, he would speak about the relationship between the politics of culture and the culture of politics in a manner not previously heralded in Anglophone Caribbean letters.[72] This relationship between culture and politics has always influenced Caribbean theorists of the political, but only within the last two decades in the collections *Caribbean Charisma* (2001) and *Modern Political Culture in the Caribbean* (2003) has a more detailed series of attempts been made to theorize this relationship.[73] A consideration of the work of James and Singham shows, however, that a twinning of ideas about the cultural and the political was present in postcolonial Caribbean political thought from its inception and that no theory of the Caribbean polity worthy of its name can fail to address the conundrums this presents.

Sylvia Wynter and Tradition and Modernity in the Caribbean

In January 1971, the most illustrious global conference of Commonwealth literature, the Association for Commonwealth Literature and Language Studies (ACLALS), held its meeting for the first time in the Caribbean at the University of the West Indies–Mona campus. The ACLALS was a critical event in Anglophone Caribbean criticism and an integral part of a series of events that made the UWI Mona campus of the late 1960s into early 1970s a charged, unsettled, and enormously productive intellectual space.[74] The previous decade had seen the emergence of the New World Group, black power, the occupation of the Creative Arts Centre, Walter Rodney's mesmerizing impact (curtailed after less than a year), and the birth of the journals *Abeng* and *Savacou*.[75] Since its inaugural edition, the year prior to the conference, *Savacou* under the editorship of Kamau Brathwaite had begun the labor of sketching the contours of a Caribbean literary and aesthetic tradition of criticism. ACLALS was the international literary conference at which the tensions surrounding this newly emergent Caribbean criticism would explode and become posed as a number of irreconcilable polar opposites—the responsibility of the Caribbean intellectual versus the disinterested writer, represented by Kamau Brathwaite and Vidia Naipaul; the allegiance of literary criticism with the folk versus a Leavisite criticism, represented by Sylvia Wynter and Kenneth Ramchand.

Sylvia Wynter's paper "Novel and History, Plot and Plantation" is one of the most sophisticated renditions of the stark intellectual disagreements that haunted this conference. In one of her most compelling early contributions to Caribbean thought, Sylvia Wynter established a methodology for thinking about the novel and resistance in the Caribbean. The novel's rise, for Wynter, is intimately tied to the birth of Caribbean plantation society; indeed, they "are twin children of the same parents."[76] The centrality of the Caribbean in the story of the rise of the West and the advent of modernity indicates that "[Caribbean] societies were both cause and effect of the emergence of the market economy; an emergence which marked a change of such world historical magnitude, that we are all, without exception still *'enchanted', imprisoned, deformed and schizophrenic* in its bewitched reality."[77] Caribbean history and its contemporary legacy is itself an elaborately crafted fiction, a myth formulated and perpetuated by those in power, James Joyce's nightmare from which he hopes to wake, manifesting in the Caribbean as a somnambulism from which we can only escape through radical acts of subversion of the status quo.[78] For Wynter, as Martin Carter was not afraid to know, all are involved, all are consumed.[79]

In her positing of the plantation versus the plot, Wynter's arguments are consistently dependent on a discourse of tradition and modernity, which lies beneath her main argument about the radical alterity of the plantation and plot in Caribbean society.[80] This discussion of tradition and modernity takes place amid a series of readings of literary texts from the Caribbean and Africa and an interrogation of the infamous Jamaican Morant Bay rebellion of 1865. Wynter travels all over the Africana world in search of novels to make her plantation/plot argument, which slides away from this strict dichotomy when she comes to Chinua Achebe's *Things Fall Apart* and James Ngugi's *Weep Not Child* and becomes more a meditation on the status of communities forced to undergo sudden, wrenching change, due to what Aníbal Quijano calls the "coloniality of power."[81] The question of a black peasant culture, holding on steadfastly outside a predatory coloniality and Western influence and crafting livable forms of community, that is implicit in Wynter's essay is also a recurring theme in African American and diasporic texts like Zora Neale Hurston's *Their Eyes Were Watching God*, Gloria Naylor's *Mama Day*, and Paule Marshall's *Praisesong for the Widow*. "Novel and History, Plot and Plantation" marks an important inaugural moment in theorizing Caribbean literature, as we see that a central motif of it has been the tension between tradition and modernity—the dissolution of one form of community by change, the impact of new modern formations, and anxieties over whether indeed the community will survive—and this theme arguably runs through many of the great Caribbean novels. To Wynter's discussion of *New Day* and *A House for Mr. Biswas*, we may well add George Lamming's *In the Castle of My Skin* and Merle Hodge's *Crick Crack, Monkey*.

The plantation was not merely an economic unit but a system that upheld and reproduced a particular "version of history."[82] The plot is an "indigenous, autochthonous system," first developed on the land given by planters to enslaved Africans, so they could feed themselves. It is primarily concerned with use-value rather than exchange-value, and so the plot—and by extension, tradition—is precapitalist.[83] While the plantation was "the superstructure of civilization . . . the plot was the roots of culture,"[84] or, as Michel-Rolph Trouillot puts it, "it was time to create culture knowingly or unknowingly."[85] The plot, and folk culture generally, offers us "a point outside the system where the *traditional* values can give us a focus of criticism against the impossible reality in which we are enmeshed."[86] Nothing we have done so far in the Caribbean has truly faced up to the enormous challenge that awaits us, as "a change in the super-structure of the plantation, a new Constitution, *even Independence*, were changes which left the basic system untouched; and which only prolonged the inevitable and inbuilt confrontation between the plantation and the plot . . . between those who justify and defend the system; and those who challenge it."[87]

These traditional values are seen by Wynter as somewhat easily separable from existing coloniality, a difficult argument to make considering Wynter's emphasis on the plantation's interpellation of all of our lives in the Caribbean. Wynter's schema is not completely reliant, however, on a dichotomy in which plantation/plot represent civilization/culture or coloniality/traditional values. Rather, she would declare: "For if the history of Caribbean society is that of a dual relation between plantation and plot, the two poles which originate in a single historical process, the ambivalence between the two has been and is the distinguishing characteristic of the Caribbean response. This ambivalence is at once the root cause of our alienation; and the possibility of our salvation."[88]

The potential result of reconciling this rift between plantation and plot is then nothing less than the end of living in a state of colonial abduction in the Caribbean.

The question of modernity is, as Jean and John Comaroff succinctly put it, "profoundly ideological and profoundly historical."[89] Given how in vogue discussions of "alternative modernities" or "tradition and modernity" are today, the query arises: why mobilize these terms at all in a work seeking to provide a theory of the coloniality of citizenship and freedom beyond it in the contemporary Caribbean? Does the discourse of tradition/modernity trap us unendingly in the fictions of a "North Atlantic universal" that is heuristically unedifying for a consideration of Caribbean life and thought?[90] Are the embattled meanings the modern evokes rich enough in their theoretical innovations and pitfalls that we should avoid dispensing with discussions of the modern entirely?

The question of modernity has been addressed with considerable discernment by Caribbean scholars over the last generation, but the claim that a consideration of the Caribbean experience makes necessary a radical revision to the hegemonic Western tale of the modern goes back at least to C. L. R. James.[91] In his 1938 text *A History of Negro Revolt*, James argued that the enslaved persons of San Domingo "were closer to a modern proletariat than any group of workers in existence at that time."[92] James's comments in this text were a mere prelude to his more extensive history of the San Domingo revolution, *The Black Jacobins*, published in the same year, in which he would further portray the former slaves as a revolutionary force in the world politics of the age and link the rise of capitalism to the British abolition of slavery.[93] He was thus among the first to firmly locate plantation slavery as a modern process, in a move heretical to both the complacent evolutionary anthropology of the early twentieth century and to Marxism-Leninism. In his 1966 essay "The Caribbean as a Socio-Cultural Area," Sidney Mintz, one of the Caribbean's most renowned anthropologists, would distinguish the Caribbean experience of colonization from those experienced in the rest of the world as follows:

> The Caribbean colonies . . . were, in fact, the oldest "industrial" colonies of the West outside Europe, manned almost entirely with introduced populations, and fitted to European needs with peculiar intensity and pervasiveness. It is extremely important to note that in the Caribbean region, the plantation system was a capitalistic form of development, a fact partly concealed by its dependence on slavery; that its organization was highly industrial, though this is difficult to discern because of its basis in agriculture; that the notion of "citizenship" generally did not form part of the imperial intent of the colonizers; and that *with or without political independence*, the formation of any cultural integrity always lagged behind the perpetuation of traditional bipolar social and economic structures, usually established relatively early in the period of settlement of each territory.[94]

Mintz's argument about the Caribbean modern suggests that European accounts of its birth are ahistorical and only work by denying that "those aspects of modern western society regarded as most depersonalizing and 'anti-human'— the view of persons as things and as numbers, interchangeable, expendable, and faceless—have a very lengthy history in the Caribbean area."[95] For Mintz, a claim to modernity is premised less on industrial innovation than on a recognition and ability to adjust to rapid social change, and an appreciation of—rather than an incredulity and hostility toward—cultural difference.[96] His claim that the

Caribbean is the site of a "precocious modernity" is a determined act to show the Caribbean's historic relevance in the emergence of the modern world system, and there is much to concur with here, despite its limits. His fellow anthropologist Michel-Rolph Trouillot would take a different approach to this question. For Trouillot, "modernity disguises and misconstrues the many Others that it creates."[97] Trouillot's commitment here is not the claim that the Caribbean was modern before Europe but rather overturning the edifices of fictions that sustain modernity and all other North Atlantic universals.

It is often attested that "the idea of modernity rests on rupture" or, differently, a "discontinuity of time: a break with tradition."[98] The historical context of New World colonization after the late fifteenth century disrupts narratives that suggest a straightforward break with a settled tradition is constitutive of modernity, as the realities of genocide and slavery have been foundational to the experience of the Western hemisphere. Further, every single one of the cherished symbols of the march of "progress," "rationality," "freedom," and "modernity" in the West— the Renaissance, the American and French Revolutions, and the Industrial Revolution—are impossible to imagine without their darker side, namely, the systematic theft of the land and lives of millions and the labor of colonial populations. As Walter Mignolo puts it, "there is no modernity without coloniality, because coloniality is constitutive of modernity."[99] Or as David Goldberg notes, the modern state is a racial state.[100] That the elision of the stories of conquest, genocide, slavery, colonization, and racism from the commonly told narrative of modernity continues to support a triumphal tale of Western reason is scarcely in doubt can be best seen in the elision of the importance of the Haitian revolution to world history.[101] However, here, I am primarily interested in the conceptual labor the tradition/modernity dichotomy is asked to do in the contemporary Caribbean.

It seems at times that the claim that African diaspora populations constitute a modern population tread on, when they do not explicitly articulate, a vindicationist argument.[102] The claim here is far from inhabiting a space we might call "tradition," with all its resonances within a hegemonic Western discourse as static and unhistorical, Caribbean and African societies in the New World are constitutively modern. Classically vindicationist arguments contain multiple flaws—their bourgeois love of civilization and historical-redemptive limits. While contemporary discourses on Caribbean and black modernity do not quite fall into these traps, they often implicitly reproduce the dichotomy of tradition/ modernity, with consequences they would otherwise disavow. As Victoria Collis-Buthelezi points out, "it is telling that often in our desire to articulate what the Caribbean is and who Caribbean people are, we seem unable to escape the double-bind of (European) modernity and (African) tradition (read unmodern)."[103] Melanie Newton has noted how this story of the Caribbean modern writes indigenous communities out of Caribbean history—"iterations of a

Caribbean 'modernity' based on the plantation and aboriginal absence set up the Caribbean in disturbing and inaccurate ways, as a place apart from the rest of the Americas, as well as from other parts of the global South."[104] It is worth recalling Stephan Palmié's suggestion in *Wizards and Scientists* that Western modernity is a "tradition in its own right" and that what is termed Afro-Cuban tradition "emerged from a larger 'Atlantic' process of (structured) modernization."[105] It is also useful to remember the Latin roots of the word *tradition*—which can mean either "to hand down/on" or "to betray."[106] The dominance of the first definition in popular understandings of tradition should be clear; the possibilities of sub-version through the latter meaning is one I will argue has consistently sustained a radical Caribbean intelligentsia.

In a series of critical essays, David Scott has developed a number of insights into how we might reposition our thinking about tradition within African dia-sporic modernity in the Americas.[107] Drawing on the insights of Talal Asad, Mi-chael Walzer, and Alasdair MacIntyre, Scott dispenses with the Enlightenment binary of tradition/modernity and notes that for these thinkers "the concept of a 'tradition' is essentially a discursive (as opposed to a sociological) concept."[108] Scott's concern in part is that tradition be understood to "presuppose an active relation in which the present *calls upon* the past," enabling a Foucauldian history of the present that allows it to stand less for "nostalgia than memory, and memory more as a source and sustenance of *vision*."[109] Tradition thus becomes conceived as "a differentiated field of discourse whose unity, such as it is, resides not in an-thropologically authenticated traces, but in its being constructed around a dis-tinctive group of tropes or figures, which together perform quite specific kinds of rhetorical labor."[110] The three types of labor performed by tradition are "to secure connections among a past, a present, and a future," "securing what we might call a distinctive community of adherents," and to "link narratives of the past to nar-ratives of identity."[111] The benefit of this consideration of the meaning of tradition for populations of African descent in the Americas is that it "seek[s] . . . to describe the tradition of discourse in which they participate, the local network of power and knowledge in which they are employed, and the kinds of identities they serve to fashion."[112] It is this kind of consideration of discourses of tradition and mo-dernity that I apply to my analysis of the contemporary Caribbean in this work. Thinking about discourses of tradition/modernity in the Caribbean not only al-lows us to dissect the geography of colonial reason and its categories of high/low culture and little/great traditions but, crucially, gives us a critical perspective on the formation and reproduction of *political* identities and, thus, the intersections of the cultural with the political. Tradition and modernity continue to be mo-bilized in a profoundly politically manner, as Jacqui Alexander has recently re-minded us, often to serve the interests of the reproduction of coloniality in the Caribbean.[113] One of the central concerns of this work is to consider the means by which discourses of culture predicated on tropes of tradition and modernity (often misused in the public sphere in a manner that belies the distinctions between modernity, modernism, and modernization) can further inscribe colonialism or, at least, secure its legacies from any sustained attack. Against the theoretical fictions of Western epistemology, *Beyond Coloniality* calls on the radical Caribbean intellectual tradition, a living tradition of great purpose and value even as some of its members become ancestors each year, as a pathway toward creating new forms of life in the region beyond neocolonial citizenship.[114]

Beyond Coloniality is divided into two parts. The first, titled "The Coloniality of the Present" and comprised of chapters 2 and 3, considers the contemporary Caribbean scene. By coloniality, I refer here to a particular form of power with its genesis in the colonial relation, which now defines "culture, labor, intersubjective relations, and knowledge production well beyond the strict limits of colonial administrations."[115] In chapter 2, I theorize the coloniality of citizenship in the contemporary Anglophone Caribbean, which I consider to be a complex amalgam of elite domination, neoliberalism, and the legacy of colonial authoritarianism, a tripartite system that continues to frustrate and deny the aspirations of many Caribbean people. My argument is that that the coloniality of citizenship lies at the heart of the postcolonial state and secures its rule. The aim of this chapter is to continue the long process of uncovering what Kamau Brathwaite has called the "inner plantation" and Paget Henry the "othering practices" of Caliban's reason through an extended meditation on the state of the contemporary Anglophone Caribbean.[116]

Chapter 3 makes a Caribbean contribution to the now significant body of work often grouped under the title "critical race theory." This chapter interrogates the paradox of theories of creolization, créolité, and creoleness, which, while based on the unarguable cultural mixing that has created Caribbean cultures and identities, have been unable to resolve the contradictions posed by existing coloniality in the region and have been shown to be often perfectly compatible with elite domination. Creoleness is in many ways *the* Anglophone Caribbean's theory of multiculturalism. It advances a discourse of cultural citizenship that does little to resolve the tense relationships between some ethnic communities in the Caribbean, particularly notable in the consistent battles over the cultural constitution of the public sphere in Trinidad and Tobago and Guyana, between communities of African and Indian descent. Questions I address in the chapter include the following: In what ways might the idea of creolization continue to reinscribe antiblack racism in the Caribbean? Are theorists who utilize creole models not sufficiently aware of the historical complicity of ideas that valorize cultural mixing with racist discourses? The reading I propose here, which involves critical discussions of the work of Kamau Brathwaite and the créolistes of Martinique, seeks to unsettle the manner in which creoleness can become a space of theoretical "safety," away from supposedly essentialized identities, while leaving the thorny problems of racism and the perpetuation of a particular creole bourgeois subjectivity intact as the paradigmatic figure of the human in the Caribbean. My argument thus poses the following questions: What are the stakes of highlighting the racialized production of social marginality, class oppression, and the plight of colonial condemnation, in the contemporary Caribbean? How do we account for the persistence of racial states in the Caribbean? Are models of cultural mixing often guilty of theorizing race, while *forgetting* about existing racism in the Caribbean?

Part II, titled "The Caribbean Beyond," consists of chapters on C. L. R. James and Sylvia Wynter and considers the thought of these two theorists toward a vision of Caribbean freedom beyond the coloniality of our present moment. The term *beyond* has a curious history in many landmark Caribbean texts. It finds its way in like a thief in the night past authorial intention and the desired titles of work. C. L. R. James's *Beyond a Boundary*, once called by Hazel Carby "one of the most outstanding works of cultural studies ever produced," was originally titled by its publishers, Stanley Paul, "Cricket Crusaders," itself a shift from James's working title "Who Only Cricket Know."[117] It was under the influence of George Lamming that the title became *Beyond a Boundary*, itself still forsaking intention, as Lamming says he was clear that the definite article *the* should have been used rather than the indefinite *a*.[118] Simone Schwarz-Bart's landmark novel *Pluie et vent sur Télumée Miracle* in translation became *The Bridge of Beyond*—far from the more literal translation "Rain and wind on miracle-woman Télumée."[119] In Sylvia Wynter, we see the use of the beyond in a more conscious form—as a speculation on the possibility of the human after "man" in African diasporic letters, and an urgent awareness of the need to move beyond global neoliberalism for the sake of the survival of human life on this planet. The beyond, I will argue in what follows, is key to understanding the thought of C. L. R. James and Sylvia Wynter and their imaging of a future for the Caribbean.

C. L. R. James is the subject of my fourth chapter, and the moments in James's extensive and brilliant career I wish to focus on stretch from the late 1950s to his death in 1989. In the early 1960s, James wrote a number of books—*Modern Politics, Party Politics in the West Indies*, and, perhaps his best-known work of that time, *Beyond a Boundary*—which contain extensive considerations on the transition from colonial rule and its forms of subjection and the role of culture in politics. Haunting these texts is the question of what he called the "new society," a category created by James to describe the transformations he was then witnessing in both metropolitan society and the rapidly decolonizing third world. James constantly seeks recourse in a discourse of tradition/modernity in his description of the new society, and well beyond the modernist conceits of many descriptions of the "new," he manages to fashion a highly nuanced perspective on the relationship between tradition and modernity in the Caribbean. On the cusp of the 1960s, we see James, struggling toward formulating the ethics of an anticolonial desire.[120] It is my contention that this anticolonial desire is seen in his quest to imagine a new Caribbean at the moment of its Anglophone territories' independence and in his struggles to reimagine the place of women in the new society.

Chapter 4 is divided into two parts. I commence with a reading of James's understandings of tradition/modernity in the Caribbean, as articulated in a number of his essays and speeches published in the 1950s and 1960s. The connection between this section and the second one is James's *Beyond a Boundary*, and I take up the comment by James in this text that the British public school code, transplanted to the colonies, affected Caribbean people "not only in social attitudes but in our most intimate personal lives, in fact there more than anywhere else" as a gateway toward discussing the fascinating questions around gender and sexuality that arise in his work. This consideration of James on gender is done through a reading of his work from *Beyond a Boundary* to the last decade of his life, which produced his article "Three Black Women Writers" (on Toni Morrison, Alice Walker, and Ntozake Shange) and his stunning unpublished essay "My Experiences with Women and Sex." The second section of this chapter is thus a reading of James on the new society and gender relations. Here I wish to use James's discussion of cricket culture and his subsequent declarations of the inseparable linkage between human freedom and women's liberation as a point of departure to consider the coloniality of gender relations in the Caribbean. My claim here is that part of James's creativity as an original thinker after he left the United States in 1953 was his ability to integrate a complex array of different forces into his vision of the new society. It was this that led him to become one of the most decisively important Marxist cultural critics and theorists of third world liberation of the twentieth century.

The subject of my fifth chapter is the Jamaican theorist, novelist, and playwright Sylvia Wynter. Sylvia Wynter's work is now receiving greater critical attention by Africana scholars interested in the question of the intersections between tradition, coloniality, and modernity. My reading of her work is based on a major unpublished manuscript that she wrote in the 1970s for the Institute of the Black World, titled "Black Metamorphosis: New Natives in a New World." This incredible work, which Wynter describes on its opening page as "the cultural metamorphosis by which the multi-tribal African became the *native* of that *area of experience* that we call the New World" is, I would argue, the most important unpublished philosophical work by an Anglophone Caribbean intellectual.[121] The search by Wynter here is not for black origins or authenticity but cultural self-determination, a hemispheric phenomenon, which demands a metamorphosis of consciousness, culture, and being. "Black Metamorphosis" serves as a crucial link between Wynter's earlier Caribbean-focused essays and literary work and her post-1984 work on the genesis and legacy of Western humanism. I focus on "Black Metamorphosis" in order to further clarify her call for and vision of a *beyond* to coloniality and the epistemic daring of her demand for the human *after* Western man. The analysis of Sylvia Wynter's work in this chapter places her within a tradition of radical Caribbean humanism, also seen in the work of Aimé Césaire and Frantz Fanon, and discusses her distinctive rereading of the birth and legacy of colonial modernity. The question of culture is, for Wynter, decisive in any call for a transformative postcolonial citizenship. Her quest to craft a place for culture in discourses of human freedom beyond the pitfalls of a cultural nationalism not sufficiently attuned to cultural difference, while simultaneously beyond what she herself has termed a "fraudulent multiculturalism," is also discussed. The scope of her vision here encompasses the Americas, with a special consideration of the Caribbean's responsibility to enchant new human forms of life in a neocolonial world. In my conclusion, I track the terrain of what I term a "Caribbean sympathy," or the route to the self-determination we all long for in the region, through the debates on Caribbean regionalism and diaspora, guided by the Caribbean intellectual tradition.

Beyond Coloniality is a work on neocolonial citizenship, coloniality and freedom and the conundrums and despair of contemporary Caribbean existence. It is also about the epistemological uprising that must occur to effect human freedom beyond colonialism. I devote entire chapters to the work of C. L. R. James and Sylvia Wynter because I believe that the future of the Caribbean radical tradition may well lie somewhere between James, the anticolonial Marxist intellectual, always attuned to the paradoxes of his location within the West, and Wynter, the radical humanist, whose vision for human freedom beyond coloniality may well be the most profound and creative of any Caribbean thinker. The thought of C. L. R. James and Sylvia Wynter is behind the critique of the contemporary Caribbean fashioned in each chapter, and so this is in many ways a work on their thought, while simultaneously a meditation on the Anglophone Caribbean after fifty years of independence and postcolonial bourgeois domination. This meditation is centrally concerned with resuscitating the Caribbean radical tradition's critique of elite domination within the contemporary Caribbean. The Caribbean elites, in the post-Grenada era, seem to have forgotten that there is a Caribbean radical tradition. It, however, has not forgotten about them. Or, as James put it in his contribution to the *New World Quarterly*'s Guyana independence issue:

Colonialism versus independence
Slavery versus freedom
That is still the issue.[122]

Notes

1. The Bandung conference, or Afro-Asian conference, was a meeting of states from Asia and Africa that were in their first decade of independence or about to emerge from colonialism. It took place in Bandung, Indonesia, from April 18 to 24, 1955. The Tricontinental Conference of Solidarity of the Peoples of Africa, Asia, and Latin America, convened in January 1966 in Havana, Cuba, superseded Bandung in its importance for the anticolonial world in its gathering of activists from throughout the non-Western world and commitment to an independent, radical anticolonial socialism.

2. Ato Sekyi-Otu, *Fanon's Dialectic of Experience* (Cambridge, MA: Harvard University Press, 1996), 20–21.

3. Sekyi-Otu, *Fanon's Dialectic*, 240.

4. From the 1960s, the Anglophone Caribbean had its own profound critique of economic dependency in the form of the New World group of economists and social scientists. For a retrospective on this movement, see Brian Meeks and Norman Girvan, eds., *The Thought of New World: The Quest for Decolonisation* (Kingston: Ian Randle, 2010). Considering its impact, neoliberalism is strangely undertheorized in the Anglophone Caribbean; however, see Hilbourne Watson, "Caribbean Options under Global Neoliberalism," in *The Caribbean: New Dynamics in Trade and Political Economy*, ed. Anthony T. Bryan (New Brunswick, NJ: Transaction Books, 1995), 165–206; Holger Henke and Don Marshall, "The Legitimacy of Neo-Liberal Trade Regimes in the Caribbean: Issues of 'Race', Class and Gender," in *Living at the Issues in Caribbean Sovereignty and Development*, ed. Cynthia Barrow-Giles and Don Marshall (Kingston: Ian Randle, 2003), 118–64.

5. Paul Buhle, "C. L. R. James: West Indian. George Lamming interviewed," in *C. L. R. James's Caribbean*, ed. Paget Henry and Paul Buhle (Durham, NC: Duke University Press, 1992), 33.

6. Paget Henry, *Caliban's Reason: Introducing Afro-Caribbean Philosophy* (London: Routledge, 2000), 219.

7. Brian Meeks, *Radical Caribbean: From Black Power to Abu Bakr* (Kingston: University of the West Indies Press, 1993); Holger Henke, "Ariel's Ethos: On the Moral Economy of Caribbean Existence," *Cultural Critique* 56 (2004): 33; Anthony Bogues, "Politics, Nation and Postcolony: Caribbean Inflections," *Small Axe* 11 (2002): 1–30; Obika Gray, "Predation Politics and the Political Impasse in Jamaica," *Small Axe* 13 (March 2003): 72–94; Selwyn Ryan, "Democratic Governance in the Anglophone Caribbean: Threats to Sustainability," in *New Caribbean Thought: A Reader*, ed. Brian Meeks and Folke Lindahl (Kingston: University of the West Indies Press, 2001), 73–103.

8. I would like to thank Chris Searle, himself one of the British radicals who worked for the revolutionary government, for this insight. For Searle's work on Grenada, see Chris Searle, *Words Unchained: Language and Revolution in Grenada* (London: Zed, 1984).

9. I borrow the phrase "apologists for local and global apartheid" from Sidney Lemelle; see Sidney J. Lemelle, "The Politics of Cultural Existence: Pan-Africanism, Historical Materialism and Afrocentricity," *Race and Class* 35, no. 1 (1993): 108.

10. For two renderings of the standard tale, see Brian Meeks, "On the Bump of a Revival," in Meeks and Lindahl, *New Caribbean Thought*, viii–xx; Aaron Kamugisha, "The Coloniality of Citizenship in the Contemporary Anglophone Caribbean," *Race and Class* 49, no. 2 (2007): 20–40.

11. One wonders if it is still too early for an intellectual history of the means by which this transformation took place in the region. Critical signposts here might include the publication of the Women in the Caribbean Project papers, the journal *Savacou*'s 1977 special issue on Caribbean women, the founding of CAFRA (Caribbean Association for Feminist Research and Action) in 1985, and the publication of Carole Boyce Davies and Elaine Savory Fido, eds., *Out of the Kumbla: Caribbean Women and Literature* (Trenton, NJ: Africa World Press, 1990). On the connections between the radical Left and the emergence of autonomous feminist organizations in the region, see David Scott, "Counting Women's Caring Work: An Interview with Andaiye," *Small Axe* 15 (2004): 123–217.

12. I return to this in chapter 4.

13. Tracing the key writers and texts is a task far beyond a footnote, and so instead I will list some of the most important edited volumes that have emerged over this time, which is one of the best ways of tracing the development of Caribbean feminisms. Patricia Mohammed and Catherine Shepherd, eds., *Gender in Caribbean Development* (Kingston, Jamaica: University of the West Indies School of Continuing Studies, 1988); Verene Shepherd, Bridget Brereton, and Barbara Bailey, eds., *Engendering History: Caribbean Women in Historical Perspective* (London: Palgrave Macmillan, 1995); Kamala Kempadoo, ed., *Sun, Sex and Gold: Tourism and Sex Work in the Caribbean* (Lanham, MD: Rowman & Littlefield Publishers, 1999); Patricia Mohammed, ed., *Gendered Realities: Essays in Caribbean Feminist Thought* (Kingston, Jamaica: University of the West Indies Press, 2002); Eudine Barriteau, ed., *Confronting Power, Theorizing Gender: Interdisciplinary Perspectives in the Caribbean* (Kingston, Jamaica: University of the West Indies Press, 2003); Rhoda Reddock, ed., *Interrogating Caribbean Masculinities: Theoretical and Empirical Perspectives* (Kingston, Jamaica: University of the West Indies Press, 2004); Barbara Bailey and Elsa Leo-Rhynie, eds., *Gender in the Twenty-first Century Caribbean: Perspectives, Visions and Possibilities* (Kingston, Jamaica: Ian Randle Publishers, 2004); Gabrielle Hosein and Lisa Outar, eds., *Indo-Caribbean Feminist Thought: Genealogies, Theories, Enactments* (London: Palgrave Macmillan, 2016).

14. Shalini Puri, *The Grenada Revolution in the Caribbean Present: Operation Urgent Memory* (New York: Palgrave MacMillan, 2014), 6, original emphasis.

15. Puri, *Grenada Revolution*, 23.

16. Puri, *Grenada Revolution*, 24, original emphasis.

17. David Scott, *Omens of Adversity: Tragedy, Time, Memory, Justice* (Durham, NC: Duke University Press, 2014), 21.

18. Scott, *Omens of Adversity*, 2.

19. See here Don Robotham's review of both texts, "Two Views on Grenada," *Social and Economic Studies* 65, no. 1 (2016): 189–99, with responses from Puri and Scott.

20. The work here is considerable and is the subject of chapter 2 of this manuscript. For the best single monograph that considers these questions of citizenship and exclusion from a historical-sociological pan-Caribbean perspective, see Mimi Sheller, *Citizenship from Below: Erotic Agency and Caribbean Freedom* (Durham, NC: Duke University Press, 2012).

21. While one may note wryly that with scholarly advance, we know so much more about the region now than we did thirty years ago, though we are no further toward—and in fact, in active retreat from—the self-determination spoken of so haltingly at independence; part of the labor of scholarship is to give us more conscious control over the social and political decisions we make through patient argument and the presentation of evidence.

22. Anthony Bogues, "The Aesthetics of Decolonisation—Anthony Bogues and George Lamming in Conversation," in *The George Lamming Reader: The Aesthetics of Decolonisation*, ed. Anthony Bogues (Kingston: Ian Randle, 2011), 198.

23. Henry, *Caliban's Reason*. For Lamming's many essays, see Bogues, *George Lamming Reader*; and earlier, Andaiye and Richard Drayton, eds., *Conversations: George Lamming, Essays, Addresses and Interviews 1953–1990* (London: Karia House, 1992).

24. See here "On the Murder of Rodney," in Bogues, *George Lamming Reader*, 81–84; "C. L. R. James, Evangelist," in Bogues, *George Lamming Reader*, 95–100; on Grenada, see "The Tragedy of a Whole Region," in Andaiye and Drayton, *Conversations*, 237–43.

25. See David Scott, "The Sovereignty of the Imagination: An Interview with George Lamming," *Small Axe* 12 (September 2002): 120–21, 164. Here I am thinking with Lamming and David Scott but considering the meaning of the individual writer's style in the context of an intellectual tradition.

26. C. L. R. James, "Twilight of the British Empire," summary of speech at Irving Plaza, New York City, November 30, 1938. I am indebted to Christian Høgsbjerg for providing me with a copy of the summary of this address. For the quoted passage, see Christian Høgsbjerg, *C. L. R. James in Imperial Britain* (Durham, NC: Duke University Press, 2014), 199.

27. See Guardian Staff, "Chilcot Report: Key Points from the Iraq Inquiry," *Guardian* (UK), July 6, 2016, https://www.theguardian.com/uk-news/2016/jul/06/iraq-inquiry-key-points-from-the-chilcot-report.

28. Mimi Sheller, "Towards a Caribbean Cultural Political Economy," *New West Indian Guide* 80, nos. 1 and 2 (2006): 91.

29. Michael A. Bucknor and Alison Donnell, eds., *The Routledge Companion to Anglophone Caribbean Literature* (London: Routledge, 2011). On Caribbean historiography, see Barry Higman, *Writing West Indian Histories* (London: Macmillan, 1999).

30. It should be unnecessary to point out that this list is hardly exhaustive. Here I am concerned with highlighting just a few of the nonfiction texts—roughly a dozen—by Caribbean authors that have become *framing texts* through which we consider the Caribbean experience.

31. The cultural and intellectual riches of Haiti, independent since 1804, and Cuba (with the University of Havana founded in 1728) make this survey of writing the intellectual history of the Caribbean an unfortunately limited and provisional one, which this writer acknowledges. The main problem here is not merely the translation of texts, but their circulation, and the recognition of Caribbean intellectual history and Caribbean social and political thought as distinctive fields of inquiry, without which the illuminating studies that are undoubtedly to be found in Haiti and the Hispanophone Caribbean will not easily be recognized for their contribution to Caribbean intellectual life.

32. Gordon Lewis, *Main Currents in Caribbean Thought: The Historical Evolution of Caribbean Society in Its Ideological Aspects, 1492–1900* (Baltimore: John Hopkins University Press, 1983); Dennis Benn, *The Growth and Development of Political Ideas in the Caribbean, 1774–1983* (Kingston: Institute of Social and Economic Research, University of the West Indies, 1987); Silvio Torres-Saillant, *An Intellectual History of the Caribbean* (New York: Palgrave Macmillan, 2006). Benn's book would be later updated and published under the title *The Caribbean: An Intellectual History, 1774–2003* (Kingston: Ian Randle, 2004). Also see the discussion of Torres-Saillant's book in *Small Axe* 26 (2008).

33. The secondary work on figures like Fanon, C. L. R. James, José Martí, and Aimé Césaire is too large to profitably summarize here. On Claudia Jones, see Carole Boyce Davies,

Left of Marx: The Political Life of Black Communist Claudia Jones (Durham, NC: Duke University Press, 2008). On Wynter, see my discussion of scholarship on her in "'That Area of Experience That We Term the New World': Introducing Sylvia Wynter's 'Black Metamorphosis,'" *Small Axe* 49 (March 2016): 37–46. The Caribbean Reasonings series has published texts on the thought of Sylvia Wynter, Stuart Hall, George Padmore, Gordon K. Lewis, Rupert Lewis, M. G. Smith, George Lamming, the New World Group, and Richard Hart, the product of a series of memorable conferences mainly held at the University of the West Indies–Mona campus in the first two decades of the twenty-first century.

34. Patrick Taylor, *The Narrative of Liberation: Perspectives on Afro-Caribbean Literature, Popular Culture, and Politics* (Ithaca, NY: Cornell University Press, 1989).

35. David Scott, *Refashioning Futures: Criticism after Postcoloniality* (Princeton, NJ: Princeton University Press, 1999); Paget Henry, *Caliban's Reason*.

36. Stuart Hall, "Cultural Studies and Its Theoretical Legacies," in *Stuart Hall: Critical Dialogues in Cultural Studies*, ed. David Morley and Kuan-Hsing Chen (London: Routledge, 1996), 262–75.

37. See here the special issue of the journal *Race and Class*, "Caribbean Trajectories: 200 Years On," edited by myself and Alissa Trotz and timed to commemorate the two hundredth anniversary of the abolition of the British slave trade.

38. I have also spent the last decade (2006–present with a one-year interruption in 2007–8) living in the Caribbean, which has indelibly shaped the concerns I raise in this work.

39. Aaron Kamugisha, ed., *Caribbean Political Thought: The Colonial State to Caribbean Internationalisms* (Kingston: Ian Randle, 2013); Aaron Kamugisha, ed., *Caribbean Political Thought: Theories of the Post-Colonial State* (Kingston: Ian Randle, 2013); Yanique Hume and Aaron Kamugisha, eds., *Caribbean Cultural Thought: From Plantation to Diaspora* (Kingston: Ian Randle, 2013); *Caribbean Popular Culture: Power, Politics and Performance* (Kingston: Ian Randle, 2016). Nigel Bolland's *The Birth of Caribbean Civilization* was an earlier, and salutary attempt to reproduce key texts in the Caribbean intellectual tradition, though he puzzlingly groups his thinkers by region (Anglophone, Francophone and Hispanophone Caribbean) rather than by theme. O. Nigel Bolland, *The Birth of Caribbean Civilization: A Century of Ideas about Culture and Identity, Nation and Society* (Kingston, Jamaica: Ian Randle Publishers, 2004).

40. See here Aaron Kamugisha, "On the Idea of a Caribbean Cultural Studies," special issue on Caribbean studies, *Small Axe* 41 (2013): 43–57; Yanique Hume and Aaron Kamugisha, "Caribbean Cultural Thought in the Pursuit of Freedom," in Hume and Kamugisha, *Caribbean Cultural Thought*, xiii–xxiv.

41. For the phrase "governable singularity," see Louis Chude-Sokei, "The Incomprehensible Rain of Stars: Black Modernism, Black Diaspora," dissertation submitted to UCLA, 1995, UMI Dissertation Services No. 9601378.

42. Gary Wilder, *Freedom Time: Negritude, Decolonization, and the Future of the World* (Durham, NC: Duke University Press, 2015), 12–13.

43. Brathwaite and Glissant have explored their common stance in at least one dialogue; see Kamau Brathwaite and Edouard Glissant, "A Dialogue: *Nation Language* and *Poetics of Creolization*," in *Presencia criolla en el Caribe y América Latina/Creole Presence in the Caribbean and Latin America*, ed. Ineke Phaf (Madrid: Iberoamericana, 1996), reprinted in Hume and Kamugisha, *Caribbean Cultural Thought*, 290–300.

44. The phrase "free community of valid persons" is Martin Carter's. See Martin Carter, "A Free Community of Valid Persons," *Kyk-Over-Al* 44 (May 1993): 30–32.

45. Cedric Robinson, *Black Marxism: The Making of the Black Radical Tradition* (Chapel Hill: University of North Carolina Press, 2000), 184. It is worth recalling here that one of the three figures that Robinson examines in depth in *Black Marxism* is C. L. R. James.

46. See chapter 5 below, and also Kamugisha, "Idea of a Caribbean Cultural Studies"; Hume and Kamugisha, *Caribbean Popular Culture*.

47. Despite the vast range of their work, James and Wynter will not take me toward Caribbean political economy, though their work is not without insights here. See C. L. R. James, Grace Lee Boggs, and Raya Dunayevskaya, *State Capitalism and World Revolution* (Chicago: Charles Kerr, 2013 [originally published 1950]); Sylvia Wynter, "Is Development a Purely Empirical Concept or Also Teleological: A Perspective from 'We the Underdeveloped,'" in *Prospects for Recovery and Sustainable Development in Africa*, ed. Aguibou Yansane (Westport, CT: Greenwood, 1996), 299–316; Paget Henry, "C. L. R. James and the Caribbean Economic Tradition," in Henry, *C. L. R. James's Caribbean*, 145–73; Paget Henry, "C. L. R. James, Walter Rodney and the Rebuilding of Caribbean Socialism," in *Journeys in Caribbean Thought: The Paget Henry Reader*, ed. Jane Gordon, Lewis Gordon, Aaron Kamugisha, and Neil Roberts (Lanham, MD: Rowman and Littlefield, 2016), 199–223.

48. At the beginning of his fifth lecture, James estimated that there were between five and six hundred people at each of the previous lectures. C. L. R. James, *Modern Politics* (Detroit: Bewick, 1973), 94.

49. Aldon Lynn Nielsen, *C. L. R. James: A Critical Introduction* (Jackson: University Press of Mississippi, 1997), xv. George Lamming, in his address at the C. L. R. James Centenary Conference in St. Augustine, September 2001, disputed claims that James was deported from the United States, stating instead that James left shortly before his inevitable deportation, as being formally deported would have made his future reentry into the United States even more difficult than it later would be. This does not, however, minimize the constant theme of encirclement, incarceration, and abduction central to the lives of black radicals in the twentieth century. See here Carole Boyce Davies, "Deportable Subjects: U.S. Immigration Laws and the Criminalizing of Communism," *South Atlantic Quarterly* 100, no. 4 (2001): 949–66.

50. James's far more powerful, and with direct relevance to Trinidad and Tobago, *Party Politics in the West Indies* was published two years later in Trinidad. I have not come across any evidence that Williams went to the same lengths to suppress the circulation of this book as he did *Modern Politics*.

51. James, *Modern Politics*, iii.

52. On James's speaking style, see Constance Webb, "C. L. R. James: The Speaker and his Charisma," in *C. L. R. James: His Life and Work*, ed. Paul Buhle (London: Allison and Busby, 1986), 168–76.

53. *Modern Politics* is thus considerably different from the tone James would take six years later (albeit after a failed electoral campaign against Eric Williams) in which he would say the following in a speech in Montreal: "Some of you, I have no doubt, are profoundly aware of the savage ferocity of some of the West Indian rulers today to the populations who have put them in power. In 1966, this is appearing in island after island in the Caribbean. What we have to do is to see the origin of this, its early appearance at the very moment when freedom was won." C. L. R. James, "The Making of the Caribbean Peoples," lecture delivered at the Second Conference on West Indian Affairs held in Montreal, Canada, Summer 1966, reprinted in C. L. R. James, *Spheres of Existence* (London: Allison and Busby, 1980), 184.

54. James, *Modern Politics*, 100. In considering this comment by James, it is worth reflecting on David Scott's reading of Jamaica in 1944 and the "new reorganization" of the political

that emerges with adult suffrage. I would suggest that in this passage, James similarly notes the rupture that will be effected by independence and the new Caribbean postcolonial political sphere that will emerge. See David Scott, "Political Rationalities of the Jamaican Modern," *Small Axe* 14 (2003): 20.

55. Jamaica and Trinidad and Tobago gained their independence in 1962. They were followed by Barbados and Guyana in 1966, Antigua and Barbuda (1981), the Bahamas (1973), Belize (1981), Dominica (1978), Grenada (1974), St. Kitts and Nevis (1983), St. Lucia (1979), and St. Vincent (1979). It should be noted that many of the islands that received independence in the 1970s and early 1980s had associated statehood by the end of the 1960s, with Britain responsible only for their foreign policy and defense. As a result, the central dynamics of what we might call "Caribbean postcolonial politics" were well in place in most islands by the end of the 1960s.

56. This is not an argument that James suddenly ceased to be a Marxist when he returned to the Caribbean nor the easy assertion that he was forced to keep these sides of himself hidden to survive within Eric Williams's People's National Movement (PNM). Rather, it is that the contingencies of the Caribbean situation caused James to adopt different theoretical and mobilizing strategies and also influenced him in thinking his world anew. I return to a longer discussion of James in chapter 4 of this work.

57. For a commentary on the state of the Caribbean Left, see Perry Mars, *Ideology and Change: The Transformation of the Caribbean Left* (Kingston: University of the West Indies Press, 1998).

58. David Austin, "In Search of a National Identity: C. L. R. James and the Promise of the Caribbean," in *You Don't Play with Revolution: The Montreal Lectures of C. L. R. James* (Oakland, CA: AK, 2009), 9. On the London group, see Walter Rodney's reflections in *Walter Rodney Speaks: The Making of an African Intellectual* (Trenton, NJ: Africa World Press, 1990): 28–29.

59. Austin, "In Search of a National Identity," 28–29.

60. Austin, "In Search of a National Identity," 11, original italics.

61. For their own remarks on this influence, see David Scott, "The Vocation of an Intellectual: An Interview with Lloyd Best," *Small Axe* 1 (1997): 119–39; see also A. W. Singham and N. L. Singham, "Cultural Domination and Political Subordination: Notes Towards a Theory of the Caribbean Political System," *Comparative Studies in Society and History* 15, no. 3 (June 1973): 258–88.

62. See the obituary and tribute to Lloyd Best by Cary Fraser, "Lloyd Best: 1934–2007," *Race and Class* 49, no. 2 (2007). This tribute was included in the inner cover page of the journal.

63. Archie Singham, *The Hero and the Crowd in a Colonial Polity* (New Haven, CT: Yale University Press, 1968); Lloyd Best, "Independent Thought and Caribbean Freedom," *New World Quarterly* 3, no. 4 (1967): 13–34.

64. Singham, *Hero and the Crowd*, vii.

65. Singham, *Hero and the Crowd*, 303, 305.

66. Singham, *Hero and the Crowd*, 311.

67. Singham, *Hero and the Crowd*, 311.

68. Singham, *Hero and the Crowd*, 328.

69. Singham, *Hero and the Crowd*, 319. For Singham on "cuckoo politics," see "Three Cases of Constitutionalism and Cuckoo Politics: Ceylon, British Guyana and Grenada," *New World Quarterly* 2, no. 1 (1965): 23–33.

70. Singham, *Hero and the Crowd*, 328–29.

71. The editors of the anthology *Modern Political Culture in the Caribbean* go as far as to suggest that "apart from . . . *The Hero and the Crowd in a Colonial Polity*, one is hard pressed to find a sustained debate about political culture in the Caribbean." Holger Henke and Fred Reno, "Introduction: Politics and Culture in the Caribbean," in *Modern Political Culture in the Caribbean*, ed. Holger Henke and Fred Reno (Kingston: University of the West Indies Press, 2003), xii. This comment can hardly hold for the Anglophone Caribbean, far less the entire region, but it does show the canonical importance attached to this text within Anglophone Caribbean political science circles. While Singham's work has had an important impact on Caribbean political science, it should be noted that in its language and methodology, it is not dissimilar to much of the work in comparative politics of its time.

72. In his lecture at the C. L. R. James Centenary Conference, held at the University of the West Indies at St. Augustine campus in September 2001, Gordon Rohlehr, the foremost scholar of calypso in the region, acknowledged his indebtedness to James and noted that when he was writing his own landmark essay "Sparrow and the Language of Calypso," James's essay on the Mighty Sparrow was the only extant writing on Sparrow that he was aware of. See Gordon Rohlehr, "Sparrow and the Language of Calypso," *Savacou* 2 (1970): 87–99. The relationship of culture to politics in James's thought can be found in his work from the 1930s and in his introduction to *A History of Pan-African Revolt*. Robin Kelley argues that James "claim[s] that revolutionary mass movements take forms that are often cultural and religious rather than explicitly political." Robin D. G. Kelley, "Introduction" to C. L. R. James, *A History of Pan-African Revolt* (Chicago: Charles H. Kerr, 1995), 15.

73. Anton Allahar, ed., *Caribbean Charisma: Reflections on Leadership, Legitimacy and Populist Politics* (Kingston: Ian Randle, 2001); Henke and Reno, *Modern Political Culture in the Caribbean*.

74. The Association for Commonwealth Literature and Language Studies (ACLALS) was held on January 3–9, 1971, at the University of the West Indies in Mona, Jamaica. A sustained discussion of this conference does not yet exist, but for accounts by major participants, see Edward Baugh, "Confessions of a Critic," *Journal of West Indian Literature* 15, nos. 1 and 2 (November 2006): 15–28; and Kamau Brathwaite, *Barabajan Poems* (New York: Savacou North, 1993), 321–25. For analyses of the importance of the conference, see Laurence A. Breiner, *An Introduction to West Indian Poetry* (Cambridge University Press, 1998) and Norval Edwards, "The Foundational Generation: From *The Beacon* to *Savacou*," in *The Routledge Reader in Anglophone Caribbean Literature*, ed. Michael Bucknor and Alison Donnell (New York and London: Routledge), 111–23.

75. The most accessible place to gain an appreciation of the ferment of that time at the University of the West Indies–Mona remains a series of interviews conducted by David Scott in *Small Axe*. See especially "The Vocation of a Caribbean Intellectual: An Interview with Lloyd Best," *Small Axe* 1 (1997): 119–39; "Memories of the Left: An Interview with Richard Hart," *Small Axe* 3 (1998): 65–114; "The Archaeology of Black Memory: An Interview with Robert A. Hill," *Small Axe* 5 (1999): 81–151; "The Dialectic of Defeat: An Interview with Rupert Lewis," *Small Axe* 10 (2001): 85–177. For an examination of that turbulent decade in Jamaica, see Obika Gray, *Radicalism and Social Change in Jamaica, 1960–1972* (Knoxville: University of Tennessee Press, 1997).

76. Sylvia Wynter, "Novel and History, Plot and Plantation," *Savacou* 5 (June 1971): 95.

77. Wynter, "Novel and History," my italics.

78. James Joyce's famous line "History is the nightmare from which I am trying to awake" serves as the epigraph for Derek Walcott's essay "The Muse of History." See Derek Walcott, "The Muse of History," in *Is Massa Day Dead? Black Moods in the Caribbean*, ed. Orde Coombs (New York: Anchor Books, 1974), 1–27.

79. Martin Carter, "You are Involved," in Martin Carter, *Poesias Escogidas/Selected Poems*, ed. David Dabydeen, trans. Salvador Ortiz-Carboneres (Leeds, UK: Peepal Tree, 1999), 91.

80. I return to a more extensive reading of Wynter's work in chapter 5 below.

81. Aníbal Quijano, "Coloniality of Power, Eurocentrism, and Latin America," *Nepantla* 1, no. 3 (2000): 533–80.

82. Wynter, "Novel and History," 96.

83. Wynter, "Novel and History," 97.

84. Wynter, "Novel and History," 100. Wynter makes it clear that her "appreciation and revaluation of the folk is not . . . the heroic folkish mythology of a Hitler."

85. Michel-Rolph Trouillot, "Culture on the Edges: Creolization in the Plantation Context," *Plantation Society in the Americas* 5, no. 1 (Spring 1998): 26.

86. Wynter, "Novel and History," 100, my italics.

87. Wynter, "Novel and History," 102, my italics.

88. Wynter, "Novel and History," 99.

89. Jean and John Comaroff, "Introduction," in Jean and John Comaroff, eds., *Modernity and Its Malcontents: Ritual and Power in Postcolonial Africa* (Chicago: University of Chicago Press, 1993), xi. In my discussion of modernity in this work, I will be considering a series of questions about the nature of modernity that arise out of the colonization of the Americas, transatlantic slavery, and the rise of the West. There is undoubtedly a far different series of questions that would have to be considered if my interests were ideas of the modern in Africa or Asia.

90. The phrase "North Atlantic universals" was coined by Michel-Rolph Trouillot. See his essay "The Otherwise Modern: Caribbean Lessons from the Savage Slot," in *Critically Modern: Alternatives, Alterities, Anthropologies*, ed. Bruce M. Knauft (Bloomington: Indiana University Press, 2002), 220–37.

91. Sidney Mintz, while discussing modernity, capitalism, and the Caribbean experience, would state that this critical discussion "began with C. L. R. James." Sidney W. Mintz, "Enduring Substances, Trying Theories: The Caribbean Region as *Oikoumene*," *Journal of the Royal Anthropological Institute* 2, no. 2 (1996): 299.

92. James, *History of Pan-African Revolt*, 39. James's *A History of Negro Revolt* was republished under the title *A History of Pan-African Revolt* in 1969.

93. C. L. R. James, *The Black Jacobins: Toussaint L'Ouverture and the San Domingo Revolution* (New York: Vintage, 1963), esp. 47–57. In his 1963 appendix to *The Black Jacobins*, titled "From Toussaint L'Ouverture to Fidel Castro," James would again stress the "modern life" of the enslaved Africans; see *Black Jacobins*, 392.

94. Sidney W. Mintz, "The Caribbean as a Socio-Cultural Area," *Journal of World History* 9, no. 4 (1966): 930–31, original italics.

95. Mintz, "Caribbean as a Socio-Cultural Area," 937.

96. Mintz, "Enduring Substances."

97. Trouillot, "Otherwise Modern," 221.

98. Saurabh Dube, "Introduction: Enchantments of Modernity," *South Atlantic Quarterly* 101, no. 4 (2002): 729.

99. Walter D. Mignolo, *The Idea of Latin America* (Malden, MA: Blackwell, 2005), xiii.

100. David Theo Goldberg, "Racial States," in David Goldberg and John Solomos, eds., *A Companion to Racial and Ethnic Studies* (Malden, MA: Blackwell, 2002), 233.

101. As argued by Michel-Rolph Trouillot in *Silencing the Past: Power and the Production of History* (Boston: Beacon Books, 1995) and Sybille Fischer's magisterial work *Modernity Disavowed: Haiti and the Cultures of Slavery in the Age of Revolution* (Durham, NC: Duke University Press, 2004).

102. By "vindicationism," I refer to a form of African diaspora historicism that Wilson Moses defines as constituting a "project of defending black people from the charge that they have made little or no contribution to the history of human progress. Sometimes vindicationism may imply the even more basic struggle to secure recognition of the fact that black people are human at all." See Wilson Moses, *Afrotopia: The Roots of African American Popular History* (Cambridge: Cambridge University Press, 1998), 21. The second part of this definition threatens to encompass the whole of the African diasporic intellectual tradition, but Moses suggests that the vindicationists main concern is with black achievement in the past.

103. Victoria Collis-Buthelezi, "Caribbean Regionalism, South Africa, and Mapping New World Studies," *Small Axe* 46 (2015): 43.

104. Melanie Newton, "Returns to a Native Land: Indigeneity and Decolonization in the Anglophone Caribbean." *Small Axe* 41 (2013): 112.

105. Stephan Palmié, *Wizards and Scientists: Explorations in Afro-Cuban Modernity and Tradition* (Durham, NC: Duke University Press, 2002), 15–16.

106. For this point on the roots of the word *tradition*, see Grant Farred, *What's My Name? Black Vernacular Intellectuals* (Minneapolis: University of Minnesota Press, 2003), 103. Farred goes on to note that "betrayal is founded here upon a recognition of the conflicted (and conflictual) relationship with an antagonistic set of traditions" (105).

107. See principally here David Scott, "That Event, This Memory: Notes on the Anthropology of African Diasporas in the New World," *Diaspora* 1, no. 3 (1991): 261–84, reprinted in Hume and Kamugisha, *Caribbean Cultural Thought*; and David Scott, "'An Obscure Miracle of Connection': Discursive Tradition and Black Diaspora Criticism,"*Small Axe* 1 (1997): 19–38.

108. Scott, *Refashioning Futures*, 124.

109. Scott, *Refashioning Futures*, 115, original italics.

110. Scott, "That Event," 278.

111. Scott, "That Event," 278–79.

112. Scott, "That Event," 280.

113. See especially M. Jacqui Alexander, "Transnationalism, Sexuality and the State: Modernity's Traditions at the Height of Empire," in *Pedagogies of Crossing: Meditations on Feminism, Sexual Politics, Memory, and the Sacred* (Durham, NC: Duke University Press, 2005), 181–254.

114. Each year, one of the great thinkers formative to our understanding of the Caribbean passes on to become an ancestor: Edouard Glissant (2011), Norman Girvan (2014), Stuart Hall (2014), Austin Clarke (2016), Derek Walcott (2017), Wilson Harris (2018).

115. Nelson Maldonado-Torres, "On the Coloniality of Being: Contributions to the Development of a Concept," *Cultural Studies* 21, nos. 2 and 3 (2007): 243.

116. Kamau Brathwaite, "Caribbean Man in Space and Time," *Savacou* 11/12 (1975): 1–11; Henry, *Caliban's Reason*, 279.

117. Hazel V. Carby, "Proletarian or Revolutionary Literature: C. L. R. James and the Politics of the Trinidadian Renaissance," *South Atlantic Quarterly* 87, no. 1 (1988): 51.

118. For Lamming's influence on the publication of *Beyond a Boundary*, see George Lamming, "Letter to C. L. R. James," June 27, 1961, C. L. R. James Archive, University of the West Indies–St. Augustine, Box 3 Folder 76; Robert Anderson, "Letter to C. L. R. James," September 23, 1962, C. L. R. James Archive, Box 3 Folder 76; David Scott, "The Sovereignty of the Imagination: An Interview with George Lamming," *Small Axe* 12 (2002): 110.

119. Simone Schwarz-Bart, *The Bridge of Beyond*, trans. Barbara Bray (Oxford, UK: Heinemann, 1982).

120. Timothy Brennan uses the phrase "properly socialist desire" to describe James's quest at midcentury; my contention is that a different interest emerges in James's work during his Trinidad years. See Timothy Brennan, *At Home in the World: Cosmopolitanism Now* (Cambridge, MA: Harvard University Press, 1997), 208.

121. Sylvia Wynter, "Black Metamorphosis: New Natives in a New World" (unpublished manuscript, Institute of the Black World Papers at the Schomburg Center for Research in Black Culture, New York), 1, my emphasis.

122. C. L. R. James, "Tomorrow and Today: A Vision," in "Guyana Independence Issue," special issue, *New World Quarterly* 2, no. 3 (1966): 88, original italics.

PART I
THE COLONIALITY OF THE PRESENT

2   The Coloniality of Citizenship in the Contemporary Anglophone Caribbean

> But if the designing of the future and the proclamation of ready-made solutions for all time is not our affair, then we realize all the more clearly what we have to accomplish in the present—I am speaking of a *ruthless criticism of everything existing*, ruthless in two senses: The criticism must not be afraid of its own conclusions, nor of conflict with the powers that be.
>
> Karl Marx, "For a Ruthless Criticism of Everything Existing" (1844)[1]

> The question must be squarely faced. What sort of people are these who live in the West Indies and claim their place as citizens and not as subjects of the British Empire?
>
> C. L. R. James, *The Life of Captain Cipriani* (1932)[2]

THE ABOVE QUOTATION from C. L. R. James's earliest political text, *The Life of Captain Cipriani: An Account of British Government in the West Indies,* provides a particularly wry and prescient comment on the question of the subject status of Caribbean people in the era of formal colonialism. *The Life of Captain Cipriani,* written by James while in Trinidad and taken with him to London in February 1932, is a strange text. Part of the curiosity that the book holds is that we find it impossible to read it now without reflecting on his later radicalism, for within less than half a decade of its composition, James would substantially revise his worldview, becoming a leading figure of the Trotskyist movement in Britain and authoring the history of that movement.[3] Reading his biography of Cipriani, one becomes aware that this is the mind of a particularly astute and thoughtful member of the colonial middle classes, but one whose liberal social and political vision does not extend beyond the daring and seditious (for the time) call for self-government within the British Empire.[4] *The Life of Captain Cipriani,* until recently out of print for eighty years, is not, however, merely an artifact of James's early thought.[5] In it we see a first rendition of how James would choose to approach his book-length discussions of the Caribbean, with sections of chapters devoted to considering the peculiar color/class location of specific societal groups, from white colonials to the black majority, a technique later to be repeated in *Party Politics in the West Indies* (1962) and his better known *The Black Jacobins* (1938).[6] An abridged version of *The Life of Captain Cipriani*, under the title "The Case for West Indian Self-Government," was published by the Hogarth Press of Leonard and Virginia Woolf in London in 1933 and proved to be more enduring and influential than the book.[7]

"The Case for West Indian Self-Government" sheds any of the ambiguities about its political mission that the longer book from which it was derived may have given its reader. As an anticolonial text, it is easily superseded by James's later work, and it is tempting to see its value as merely a transitional text in his thought. This, however, would miss its relevance as an article that chronicles the rapidly changing political-historical conditions in Trinidad and the Caribbean. In it, we see James making an argument for the self-governing capacities of Caribbean people from a vindicationist perspective, in which proof of nonwhite people's full humanity rests within coordinates established by European social and historical experience.[8] In "introducing" the West Indian people to a British audience, James relies on highly questionable notions, suffused with colonial understandings, that a national characteristic can be discerned that defines them as a people: "quicker in intellect and spirit than the English, they pay for it by being less continent, less stable, less dependable."[9] In a twist of ideas about tradition/modernity, which habitually presented colonials as a people lost in an unchanging past, James would say that "if their comparative youth as a people saves them from the cramping effects of tradition, a useful handicap to be rid of in the swiftly-changing world of today, yet they lack that valuable basis of education which is not so much taught or studied as breathed in from birth in countries where people have for generation after generation lived settled and orderly lives."[10] Here tradition/modernity is juggled in a manner that gives the colonized clear agency in their pursuit of self-determination, though it is far removed from the argument that James would make of the modernity of the slave plantations in *The Black Jacobins*, which would become a widely influential view on questions of black modernity seventy years later.[11]

Yet "The Case for West Indian Self-Government" contains many keen observations about Trinidadian society that portray well the diminution of human life in a society sutured to a color-caste hierarchy that a century after emancipation it was still loath to relinquish. For James, "in a West Indian colony the surest sign of a man's having arrived is the fact that he keeps company with people lighter in complexion than himself," a sardonic comment with much resonance still two generations after independence.[12] His declaration that Caribbean people must be "free to gain that political wisdom and political experience which come only from the practice of political affairs" was a compelling and unanswerable argument for its time, at least within the strict limits of a view that privileged above all else British constitutional parliamentary democracy.[13]

It is back to *The Life of Captain Cipriani* to which we must turn for the arresting question that James poses in the epigraph above, which comes early in a section of the book titled "The Coloured People."[14] James's rhetorical question challenges official views of the legal status of the colonized and queries whether citizenship should be conceived as only a state-conferred status rather than a means of being political. The claim here is that the self-activity of some of the "coloured" population of the Caribbean showed they rejected a *subject* status, no matter what their *juridical* status might be.[15] Colonized Afro-Caribbean and Indo-Caribbean people had certainly acted politically from the time they arrived in the Caribbean. However, by the time James's text was published, almost a century had elapsed since the emancipation of enslaved persons in the Caribbean and two decades since the end of indentureship, with little substantial improvement in the life chances of the masses. James's text hardly stood alone as an indictment of British colonialism in the Caribbean, as he himself noted a written tradition that stretched back at least to J. J. Thomas and had recently been given a revolutionary fillip by Garveyism.[16] Nonetheless, it did serve as part of a grand rehearsal for the 1930s labor rebellions, which were to inaugurate a new Caribbean.[17]

Discourses of citizenship and movements that claim social and political rights beyond that proffered by a colonial and neocolonial world system have a long history in the Caribbean. Michael Hanchard's comment that "virtually all discussions and literatures pertaining to people of African descent, ranging from black nationalism to Pan-Africanism, to anti-colonialism and civil rights, are undergirded by premises of and reactions to some notion or practice of modernity" is perhaps even more applicable to discourses of citizenship, which appear throughout the intellectual history of the region.[18] Haiti's revolution, through which, in Dessalines's immortal words, Haitians "avenged America," is now understood to be what it always was: an event of global significance, with a seismic effect on the entire Atlantic world.[19] In the Francophone Caribbean, as Laurent DuBois notes, "during the early 1790s, slave insurgents gave new content to the abstract universality of the language of rights, expanding the scope of political culture as they demanded Republican citizenship and racial equality."[20] The very language of universal rights and freedoms emerged then out of the "challenges posed by colonial insurgents," which would then be re-presented "as a gift from Europe and a justification for expanding imperialism."[21] The complexity of the political terrain of the territories seized by France in the Caribbean is in itself a particularly rich ground for examining the deployment of concepts of citizenship in the Caribbean. Apart from Haiti's struggle and independence, in Martinique and Guadeloupe, the early emancipation wrested by slaves would be reversed with slavery's reinstitution, not finally abolished until 1848. The nature of the French republic meant that this

emancipation granted enslaved men French citizenship, with black women reduced to "'chattels', subordinate to the power of men," an arresting reminder
of the patriarchal limits of even wide-ranging reformulations of citizenship in
the nineteenth century.[22]

In the Anglophone Caribbean, the long century between full emancipation
in 1838 and the labor rebellions of the 1930s was premised on a very different
interpretation of the fitness of colonial subjects to attain full membership in an
imperial community than that of French assimilationist policy. The nineteenth
century witnessed a constant battle by the planter class to limit the right to full
participation in the political affairs of the colony by the majority black population through a number of strategies—limits on the franchise, control of labor
(facilitated through restrictive emigration and occasionally liberal immigration
policies), and exploitation of the price of land.[23] Caribbean populations were
thus caught between the Scylla of the colonial elites and the Charybdis of the
Colonial Office, and it is a testimony to the reactionary conceit of the former
that the latter was preferred as a place to petition for expanded rights within
the colony. In the metropole, Britain's most prominent philosopher of the nineteenth century, John Stuart Mill, would state in *On Liberty*, that "despotism is a
legitimate mode of government in dealing with barbarians, provided the end be
their improvement."[24] There is a not indiscernible line connecting Mill and the
Colonial Office's paternalistic "self-government when fit for it," and Caribbean
social historians have catalogued what Cecilia Green calls the "submerged human costs of the colonial regime" of this long century.[25] Amid the multiple and
difficult-to-categorize discourses of belonging and citizenship enmeshed in the
social history of these many, and different, countries, two strands can be discerned with direct relevance for this book. The first, as illustrated in the work of
Melanie Newton on free people of color in Barbados, shows the lack of any contradiction in the world of many elite blacks between a quest to ameliorate racial
injustice while maintaining a steadfast commitment to "claiming full citizenship
in the British imperial nation."[26] Indeed, for Newton, "Afro-Barbadians of the
early post-emancipation era sought to reimagine Britishness as an expansive and
inclusive basis for claims to citizenship and equality within the empire."[27] The
second, present throughout the Americas, is best described as a form of transnational citizenship, in which "rights and allegiances that cut across national
boundaries" are mobilized against empire.[28]

The story of the social transformation of the Anglophone Caribbean in less
than a generation has been repeated many times and is now an indelible part
of the historical consciousness of the people of the region.[29] In it, the aftermath
of the 1930s labor rebellions lead to the formation of modern trade unions and
political parties, universal adult suffrage, and local self-rule, followed by national

independence. In the section that follows, I want to track the retelling of this story by political sociologist Percy Hintzen and transnational feminist theorist Jacqui Alexander. It is my view that in their attention to the mechanisms through which elite domination has consolidated in the region, Alexander and Hintzen have fashioned particularly discerning critiques of the contemporary Anglophone Caribbean neocolonial state and produced compelling discussions of our contemporary predicament.

Hintzen and Alexander on Contemporary Elite Domination

In the last two decades, the work of the political sociologist Percy Hintzen has provided one of the most comprehensive retellings of the nature of nationalism, elite domination, and the postcolonial state in the Anglophone Caribbean. Hintzen's central concerns are expressed in two questions: "Why are relations of domination and conditions of economic exploitation that are little different, and sometimes more severe, than those suffered under colonialism understood and interpreted differently in the postcolonial era? What explains the universal predisposition of those who engaged in and supported anticolonial struggles to accept the conditions of postcolonial repression and exploitation?"[30] Hintzen's work is an attempt to understand why Caribbean nationalist discourse not only was not a "narrative of liberation" but also resulted in "even more egregious forms of domination, super-exploitation, and dependency."[31] This reading of the postcolonial Caribbean suggests it cannot be understood without an appreciation of the interplay between cultural and political frames of reference, identity, and legitimacy constructs.

The recounting of preindependence Anglophone Caribbean nationalism is crucial in any attempt to formulate a history of the present, for the class ideologies established in this period, the bases of their legitimacy constructs, and the forms of regimentation introduced at that time still haunt the Caribbean today. Here, a distinction should be noted between anticolonial thought and struggle— a sentiment present in the masses and the radicalized intelligentsia—and Afro-creole nationalism, the mobilizing ideology of the Caribbean middle classes. Afro-creole nationalism is here seen as a convoluted mixture of early-century Garveyism and black consciousness, Fabian socialism, twentieth-century trade unionism, and recognition of the shifting relationship between the colonizing power of Britain and the new superpower, the United States—all filtering into the ideology of the black middle classes.[32] The middle-class participation in the nationalist movement, complicated and influenced by a variety of sources as it was, was also, in large part, a response to colonialism's inability to maintain power and fully accommodate the material and self-governing demands of this class. The critique of colonialism by the middle class was a contestation over whites' right to rule, and its nationalist claim in the Caribbean became that "the colonial condition of inequality and white superiority was artificial and imposed. Once removed, a 'natural state' of equality would assert itself." Anticolonial nationalism, a broad-based sentiment encompassing large parts of the population, must thus be distinguished from Afro-creole nationalism, the ideology of the middle classes. By Hintzen's reckoning, "anticolonial nationalism was, first and foremost, an expression of the general will for equality. This expression was transformed by petit bourgeois ideology into demands for sovereignty and development."[33] The poverty of creole nationalism is that it "left intact the racial order underpinning colonialism while providing the ideological basis for national 'coherence'. It left unchallenged notions of a 'natural' racial hierarchy."[34]

Colonial and postcolonial bureaucratic formations are of considerable import here, as the wresting of control of these away from the colonizer in the immediate preindependence period opened up pathways for postindependence regime consolidation. The transfer of this bureaucratic structure, with little interrogation of its underlying premises, allowed the Caribbean state to gain control over revenue-generating activities, the surpluses of which were now under its direction and grew with postcolonial state expansion.[35] State bureaucracies (and potential state largesse) also expanded further with the new responsibility for defense and foreign affairs, which allowed governing elites "violent coercive retaliation against those challenging their authority and legitimacy . . . [and] direct access to international resources necessary for regime survival," respectively.[36] The middle classes' basis of power in unions and political parties after the 1930s rebellions and the social and cultural capital they possessed facilitated their ascendancy to the head of the nationalist movements. In Hintzen's reading, "by the time adult suffrage was introduced . . . the lower class was firmly organized into political and labour bureaucracies dominated by middle-class leadership. Where they were not, Britain showed extreme reluctance to move the constitutional process along to full independence."[37] The Anglophone Caribbean postcolonial state was, in part, a gift of the British to the Caribbean middle classes, who were seen as possessing the social and cultural capital and a commitment to Western capitalism that made them fit to rule.

The collapse of the West Indies Federation resulted in the advent of independence in the 1960s for a number of the territories within the Anglophone Caribbean and the arrival of associated statehood for others.[38] The moment of independence was simultaneously a moment of recolonization, as "all the leaders who came to power during the sixties did so while announcing their commitment to a moderate ideological position and to a pro-capitalist program of development for their respective countries."[39] Further, the United States' post–World War II dominance resulted in the annulment of the possibility of any authentic decolonization within Anglophone Caribbean states. The postcolonial elite demand for "sovereignty and development," allied to an "industrialization by invitation" developmental strategy, led to discourses of modernization taking center stage in debates about the future of the Caribbean state. Nationalism demanded the local utilization of surpluses previously appropriated by metropolitan imperialism. Its leaders' disinterest in linking colonial abjection to capitalism meant that development programs predicated on capitalist modernization could gain hegemony without a contest. The decline of the radical movements of the late 1960s and 1970s, which contested this postindependence neocolonial condition, and the rise of an even more predatory neoliberal globalization has meant that the postcolonial elite's dream of equality of nation-states and its liberal ideal of the equality of citizens within Caribbean nation-states looks more like a nightmare than anything else: "Once the condition of equality becomes asserted in the postcolonial context, everything associated with postcolonial inequality is rendered irrelevant and subject to different interpretations, irrespective of the objective conditions. What once was exploitation becomes sacrifice. What was domination becomes functional organization. What was privilege becomes reward. What was discrimination becomes strategic allocation. These transformations are explained by the logic of equality embedded in the meaning of nationalism. Presuppositions of postcolonial equality become the force driving predispositions toward the acceptance of conditions of extreme inequality."[40]

The concepts of "the modern" and of modernization were fused in a calculus that regarded a Euro-American "modern" and modernization as the only future for the region. Quite simply, "to be 'modern' was to be 'equal.'"[41] In the terms of a Caribbean elite that sought to define itself on the standards of a global bourgeois class, this meant adopting the consumption patterns of the West and acquiring its cultural capital.[42] That the consumption patterns of the middle classes of the Anglophone Caribbean are incompatible with the economies of the Caribbean is a point that has been made incessantly by Caribbean scholars like George Beckford and Rex Nettleford. Today, to critique the desire for those tastes from a cultural nationalist position quickly risks being fruitless, as "such tastes are no longer understood as 'foreign', 'white' or 'colonial'. They are the 'styles' and 'tastes' of development, and *modernity's prerequisites for equality*."[43]

What, then, does this mean for attempts to theorize the Anglophone Caribbean postcolonial state? To trace the rise of the Afro-creole elites, as Hintzen does, is to pose serious questions about the nature of democracy and citizenship in polities still structured in dominance. It reveals again the deep limitations of the "cultural citizenship" offered (often hesitantly) to the postcolonial masses by the middle-class elites, a citizenship often bereft of the revolutionary potential of anticolonial nationalism after it has gone through the organizational rationalities of the middle class. Like all of the most pervasive systems of power, which operate through rendering their guises invisible, "creole culture serves to hide a racialized division of labor and a racialized allocation of power and privilege."[44] Race, color, and culture and the bifurcations they cause in class formations in the postcolony suggest that the Caribbean postcolonial state is a racial state as much as it is simultaneously a state that expresses its political-economic interests based on a global elite's hegemonic norms and values.[45]

For Hintzen, creole nationalism, as outlined earlier, is the cultural ideology that legitimates middle-class domination in the Anglophone Caribbean. Claims to belonging and citizenship in the Caribbean state turn on arguments about creolization.[46] "To be 'Caribbean' is to be 'creolized' and within this space are accommodated all who, at any one time, constitute a (semi)-permanent core of Caribbean society."[47] Creole identity, far from being a harmonious space of mixed identities, is one thoroughly and unashamedly colonial: "Creole discourse has been the bonding agent of Caribbean society. It has functioned in the interest of the powerful, whether represented by a colonialist or nationalist elite. It is the . . . glue that bonds the different, competing, and otherwise mutually exclusive interests contained within Caribbean society. It paved the way for accommodation of racialized discourses of difference upon which rested the legitimacy of colonial power and exploitation."[48]

The colonial provenances of "creoleness" are not only to be found in the power relations it reinscribes but in the centrality of European and African culture to its frame of reference. Thus: "The combination of racial and cultural hybridity determines location in between the extremes. For the European, this pertains to the degree of cultural and racial pollution. It implies a descent from civilization. For the African, creolization implies ascent made possible by the acquisition of European cultural forms and by racial miscegenation whose extensiveness is signified by color. This, in essence, is the meaning of creolization. It is a process that stands at the center of constructs of Caribbean identity."[49]

Here we see again the limitations of the criticism of colonialism fashioned by the Caribbean nationalist elites. At times, Africa occupied a significant space in their thoughts, but this was invariably "associated with the freedom and transcendence denied the colonized" rather than a repudiation of its image as a "space for exploitation and for the exercise of paternalism."[50] The reproduction of domination on to those now considered to *be* black—namely, the poor, or in Jamaican parlance "the sufferers," who are the newly condemned of the Caribbean—could thus be facilitated without contradiction by the postcolonial Afro-creole elites.

Jacqui Alexander's analysis of the Caribbean postcolonial state has been no less compelling than Hintzen's, and in its framing of gender and sexuality as constituent elements of any discussion of the state, it has announced new pathways for Caribbean social and political thought. Alexander's central concern is with the *revision* of citizenship to exclude those who practice a sexuality that differs from the heteronormative impulses of the state.[51] In Alexander's reading, the colonial state, predicated on an ideology of white supremacy, "made ownership of property, wealth, whiteness, and masculinity the primary conditions of citizenship."[52] The advent of universal adult suffrage "severed the colonial links among ownership of property, colonial respectability, manliness and rights of political representation," an uncontestably significant achievement. The advent of postcolonial rule would reinscribe some of the most obscurantist aspects of colonial ideas about citizenship, in its flight to secure rule under a new authority—black, heterosexual, middle-class Caribbean men. The new Caribbean nations were created in concert with fictions so damaging in Western states—the nation as masculine, the nation as heterosexual.[53] When the crises of the postcolonial state would be fully exposed in the structural adjustment crises of the 1980s and in the aftermath of the 1970s experiments in Caribbean radicalism, Caribbean state managers would develop an acute interest in proffering to their populations and securing for themselves some ground of legitimation. Given that the region is "perhaps more thoroughly dominated by transnational capital than any other region of the Third World" and with little end to this neocolonial reality in sight, the intense turn to the control and disciplining of bodies by the state might have been expected.[54] This has created a condition that could lead Alexander to state, in the first line of her most famous essay, "I am an outlaw in my country of birth: a national; but not a citizen."[55]

Heteropatriarchy is reinvented in order to sustain Afro-creole patriarchy's control of the postcolonial state and to facilitate neocolonial rule.[56] Discourses of tradition and modernity would be mobilized "as shifting ideological authorizations," flexible enough to assert a new form of postcolonial hegemonic authority over Caribbean bodies.[57] The new, postindependence legislation that explicitly criminalizes homosexual sex in many Caribbean jurisdictions not only makes the "psyche of homosexuality . . . the psyche of criminality" but confirms that citizenship "continues to be premised within heterosexuality and principally within heteromasculinity."[58] The Caribbean middle classes "mobilized consensus for nation building, moulded psychic expectations about citizenship," all in the attempt to prove to late British colonial rule that "self-government when fit for it" had finally been achieved.[59] In a devastating critique of black masculinity and its claims to legitimation in the postcolony, Alexander writes:

> Black nationalist masculinity needed to demonstrate that it was now capable of ruling, which is to say, it needed to demonstrate moral rectitude, particularly on questions of paternity . . . It . . . required distancing itself from, while simultaneously attempting to control, Black working-class femininity that ostensibly harboured a profligate sexuality: the "Jezebel" and the whore who was

not completely socialized into housewifery, but whose labour would be mobilized to help consolidate popular nationalism. Of significance is the fact that Black nationalist masculinity could aspire toward imperial masculinity and, if loyal enough, complicitous enough, could be knighted although it could never be enthroned. It could never become king.[60]

The counterpoint to this subjection of working-class women by the colonial state would be a practice of "erotic autonomy," the very definition of what a decolonized authentic citizenship for Caribbean women might be—but fraught with dangers for the neocolonial elites: "Erotic autonomy signals danger to the heterosexual family and to the nation. And because loyalty to the nation as citizen is perennially colonized within reproduction and heterosexuality, erotic autonomy brings with it the potential of undoing the nation entirely, a possible charge of irresponsible citizenship, or no responsibility at all. Given the putative impulse of this eroticism to corrupt, it signals danger to respectability—not only to respectable black middle-class families, but most significantly to black middle-class womanhood."[61]

It is through such an amalgam of heteropatriarchal will to power, neocolonial respectability, and religious-sponsored homophobia that heteronormativity was inscribed and continues to be inscribed in the Caribbean state. One might surmise that Caribbean patriarchy needs homosexuality. If it did not exist (which Caribbean state managers sometimes claim), then it would have to be invented.[62] It is through such guileless means that a "marginal underground of noncitizens" has been perpetuated across two generations of postindependence rule in the Caribbean.[63]

Both Hintzen and Alexander lay the blame for the Caribbean's contemporary despair at the feet of Caribbean state managers, the group Walter Rodney termed the "comprador bourgeoisie" of the region, content to proffer Caribbean resources and lives for the consumption of metropolitan populations and to perpetuate neocolonial rule.[64] This class has been responsible for a series of historical compromises that have so attenuated any possibility of Caribbean freedom in the post-independence era—the elite whose conservatism stalled the potential of a radical nationalist movement under the People's National Movement (PNM) in 1950s Trinidad; the middle classes who removed their capital and fled Jamaica, hobbling Michael Manley's democratic socialism of the late 1970s; the hostility to socialism and black consciousness of the entire class spanning the region. Caribbean statecraft is presented by Alexander and Hintzen as mere middle-class domination, whether its ruses take the form of clientelism or naked authoritarianism. This suggests that it is worth taking a closer examination of the Caribbean middle classes, their historical genesis and consolidation in the state, and the criticism that has been levied against them since the end of direct British rule.

The Caribbean Middle Classes

> I do not know any social class which lives so completely without ideas of any kind. They live entirely on the material plane.
>
> C. L. R. James, *Party Politics in the West Indies* [65]

> Each generation must, out of relative obscurity, discover its mission, fulfil it, or betray it.
>
> Frantz Fanon, *The Wretched of the Earth* (1961) [66]

In 1961, a hemisphere apart, two Caribbean intellectuals made powerful statements about the historical conjuncture their communities inhabited, statements filled with a desperate urgency for the future of the anticolonial revolution to which they had devoted their lives. These were indeed heady times. A year previously, seventeen African countries had gained their independence, while the Caribbean had been shaken by Cuba's revolution of 1959. Despite the collapse of the West Indies Federation, independence for the Anglophone Caribbean was on the horizon, with Jamaica and Trinidad and Tobago gaining theirs in 1962, followed by Guyana and Barbados in 1966 and associated state status for much of the rest of the Anglophone Caribbean in 1967. Yet, simultaneously, the tragedy of neocolonialism was never far from the surface. The Republic of the Congo's first prime minister, Patrice Lumumba, had been deposed and murdered in a coup stage-managed by Western imperialism, while the nature of the demise of the West Indies Federation and the temper of its elites left no reason to believe that the quality of the Anglophone Caribbean's independence would be much else but neocolonial.

That C. L. R. James and Frantz Fanon are the exemplary political thinkers of the Caribbean's 20th century is scarcely in doubt. In their texts *Party Politics in the West Indies* and *The Wretched of the Earth*, they both advanced a critique of the new elites who were then poised to guide third world countries to independence, a critique that remains unsurpassed in its prescience about the persistence of colonial arrangements in the postindependence state. Fanon's well-known critique of the then newly emerging national elites reaches its zenith in his warning about what he terms "the pitfalls of national consciousness," in chapter 3 of *The Wretched of the Earth*, but his conclusions about the limitations and corruption of this class begin in his celebrated first chapter on violence. "Spoilt children of yesterday's colonialism and of today's national governments," these "wily intellectuals" emerge to organize the tremendous upheavals against colonialism from below.[67] For Fanon, unlike the bourgeoisie of Europe, they are not a true bourgeoisie but a "little greedy caste," in a quest for "its historic mission: that of intermediary" between metropolitan power and the postcolonial masses.[68] Beyond their parasitic irrelevance, the national middle classes are to blame for the absence of a truly purposeful national consciousness, the fruits of their "intellectual laziness . . . spiritual penury, and . . . [their] profoundly cosmopolitan mould" of existence.[69] Imitation here weds bourgeois ideology to coloniality's dehumanization: "Bourgeois ideology . . . which is the proclamation of an essential equality between men, manages to appear logical in its own eyes by inviting the sub-men to become human, and to take as their prototype Western humanity as incarnated in the Western bourgeoisie."[70]

C. L. R. James, writing against the encroaching lethargy and betrayals of the People's National Movement (PNM) of Trinidad on the cusp of independence, in concert with Fanon stresses the intermediary position of the middle classes, a people with status but "no knowledge or experience of the productive forces of the country."[71] James's lament concerned the role of this class as a facilitator of colonial governmentality and its lack of a historical imagination, ideas of their own, or indeed *anything* beyond a desire for acceptance by the ruling elites. Perhaps the one perspective the middle classes maintain—crystallizing into something close to an ideology, which James would suggest members of this class possess—is an "unshakeable principle that they are in status, education, morals and manners, separate and distinct from the masses of the people." James's analysis of the new elites closed with the ominous observation: "The ordinary people of the West Indies . . . do not want to substitute new masters for old. They want no masters at all . . . history will take its course, only too often a bloody one."[72] Over thirty years into a global neoliberal project that has seen appalling levels of material impoverishment for citizens of the global south and soaring rates of violence in these societies, James's warning appears more farsighted than he could have imagined.

These texts by Fanon and James constitute the most searching critiques of the new postcolonial elites by Caribbean intellectuals writing at the moment of Anglophone Caribbean independence. They represent a wider critical work by African diaspora intellectuals on class formation, beyond the reduction of people of African descent in the Americas to an undifferentiated governable singularity by colonialism. The work of African diaspora sociologists, pioneered by W. E. B. Du Bois in the late nineteenth century, constantly faced the problem of racist caricatures and distortions of Africana communities' lives, which Du Bois well described as the treatment of black people as the problem rather than a people with problems.[73] By the mid-twentieth century, the African American sociologist E. Franklin Frazier's classic monograph *Black Bourgeoisie* (1957) sounded a warning about the conspicuous consumption of this class and its genuflection to Euro-American tastes, styles, and ideals. In Greg Thomas's summary of this text, "this 'lumpen-bourgeoisie' is characterized not only by racial subordination and socio-economic dependence, but also by systematic political collaboration, a deep-seated inferiority complex, a compensatory set of self-righteous mythologies, and a profound self-hatred exceeded only by an intense loathing of the black masses on top of flagrant, idolatrous imitation of whites, or an abject conformity to white Western ideals. In short, a comprehensive material and subjective investment in the domestic and global status quo is in evidence."[74]

In an intricate dissection of E. Franklin Frazier's career, Greg Thomas has shown that despite his undoubtedly progressive denunciation of this elite, Frazier remains a "sociologist of integration," who perceived that the future of African Americans lay not in "self-determination" but "mass assimilation led by an elite which should be as genteel as culturally possible."[75] In a related fashion, we may see the critique of that class advanced in Nathan Hare's work *The Black Anglo-Saxons*.[76] *The Black Anglo-Saxons*, a devastating indictment of the black elites, was influenced enough by Frazier for Oliver Cox to refer to them in his critical introduction as part of the same school of thought.[77] Hare's work functions less as the structured historical-sociological study that Frazier's work is and more as a lampooning of the tastes and values of this elite, with sardonically titled chapters ranging from "The Dignitaries: Eunuch Leaders" to "The Mimics," from "The Supercitizens" to "The Cosmopolitans." In his critique of this work from the Left, Oliver Cox takes Frazier and Hare as his targets and reaches the conclusion that their work is beset with methodological problems, resulting in flawed analyses of this class, particularly in their descriptions of black institutions and their reading of the black upper class as fundamentally rootless. These errors can be partly attributed to an overplaying of the authors' ideological investments, but Cox's worry about this work extends deeper than this, as he claims that Frazier, in *Black Bourgeoisie*, "hardly confronted even tangentially a real power structure."[78] In this reading, the focus by Frazier on the foibles of the black upper class comes at the price of a criticism of white supremacy in capitalist America.

In the Anglophone Caribbean, intellectual labor on the question of black middle-class formation, whether as sociological study or radical critique, lies enmeshed within the arguments about social stratification, pluralism, and creolization debated by Caribbean theorists since the 1950s. Historians of the Anglophone Caribbean have noted that the defining features of the black middle class in the postemancipation era were occupational status (particularly a job without manual labor), a functional level of literacy, and an investment in European cultural styles, behaviors, and attributes; however, these signs of middle class status were indelibly influenced by a complex series of social prohibitions and exclusions premised on race and color.[79] Black middle-class respectability was thus secured by literacy and professional success and a conservative view on social change, with educational accomplishments being the most highly prized single attribute distinguishing the middle class from the poor and the peasantry. Profoundly reformist in its social and political outlook and certain that the possession of European tastes and values would lead to their ascension to the ranks of the fully human, those middle classes of the nineteenth century seem to fit well Fanon's and James's descriptions of them a century later. Yet this same class produced a number of prominent figures who advocated race pride in a vindicationist spirit, including J. J. Thomas of Trinidad and Robert Love of Jamaica, who stand as major figures in the genesis of a tradition of anticolonial thought and political theorizing in the Anglophone Caribbean. Here, even at the height of the colonial era, the difficulty involved in flattening the complexity of this class becomes clear for, as Belinda Edmondson has shown, from the nineteenth century they were never reduced to being solely an imitative rendition of British culture.[80]

The development of sustained intellectual labor on the question of the Caribbean social in the Anglophone Caribbean in the 1950s twinned questions of class with race, which led to a particularly theoretically inventive era in Caribbean social thought. The theories of this era are known to Caribbeanists under the nomenclature of the plantation school, pluralism, and creolization. Lloyd Braithwaite's pioneering 1953 study, *Social Stratification in Trinidad*, with its elucidation of social and racial hierarchies, including those of color, shade, and kinship, showed well how an ethnically diverse society remained captive to systems of domination established under slave society and economy.[81] In his ethnographic approach to middle-class tastes and assumptions, Braithwaite illustrates how the heraldry of whiteness permeates social and economic relations from the intricate assessment of potential marriage partners to the prospects of a career in color-coded fields of employment. The intermediary middle class in this colonial arrangement is not reactionary in any easy manner for Braithwaite; rather, he describes a "tendency to radicalism" along with one toward "compulsive conformity" within them.[82] Writing twenty years later, and in the development of a theory meant to serve as a forceful counterpoint to the social stratification and plural society models, Kamau Brathwaite would adopt a not completely divorced tack, referring to the middle classes as the "most finished product of unfinished creolization," obsessively concerned with a mimicry with little subversive potential and an apt description of the ascriptive value of whiteness in their lives.[83]

The postindependence critique of the middle class arguably reached its zenith in the outpouring of leftist activism in the region in the late 1960s and 1970s.[84] Here the Caribbean state became figured, to gloss Marx's famous lines, as merely a management committee for the affairs of a local bourgeoisie and international capitalist interests. A highly significant but generally unheralded article by Walter Rodney is one of the best examples of the thought of this period.[85] Rodney commences with the observation that most Anglophone Caribbean states have now achieved constitutional independence, tying this historical development to the dramatic collapse of European empire in the thirty years after World War II. The limited character of that independence is a central part of Rodney's considerations, and in it he stresses the importance of distinguishing colonialism from neocolonialism as "the patterns of politics continue to change after the initial transfer of power to a local ruling class."[86] The consolidation of a new form of rule in the postcolonial Caribbean represents the continued march of Western imperialism, but the emergence of new forms of politics requires the use and clarification of the term *neocolonialism*. For Rodney, "neo-colonial politics are those that derive from the consolidation of the petty bourgeoisie as a class around the state."[87] The appearance of this class over and over again across various Caribbean territories and in regimes that claim political orientations that should be radically different—from liberal-democratic, democratic-socialist, to authoritarian states—led Rodney to declare that "to speak of petty bourgeois dictatorship in the English-speaking Caribbean is no play with words."[88] Rodney's vision for a different Caribbean rested on a Pan-African socialism, the ultimate aim of which was a dismantling of the structures of power of colonial dominance and its ideological corollaries. For Rodney, "expropriating bourgeois knowledge" should be the purpose of radical intellectuals located in the academy, as "the major and first responsibility of the intellectual is to struggle over ideas."[89] Neo-colonialism was his historical moment, and the questions he raised about it were never confined to an assertive critique but sought the deeper meaning behind the fictions engendered by colonialism, their reproduction so seamlessly in the postcolonial state, and the quest for a different future. The historical conjuncture is crucial as "neo-colonial man is asking a different set of questions than the old colonial man."[90] The momentous contemporary importance of the third world is that its people "are now at the heart of the human condition."[91]

Rodney wrote before the full advent of neoliberalism, charted by many as emerging along a US-British axis with the electoral triumphs of Margaret Thatcher in 1979 and Ronald Reagan in 1980. A generation later, with the collapse of state socialist alternatives throughout the world and the harsh conditionalities of structural adjustment, a different accent emerged in debates about the role of the middle classes in Caribbean society by members of the Caribbean Left. Two articles, by Don Robotham and Rupert Lewis, prominent former members of the Worker's Party of Jamaica, make this shift from the analyses of the 1960s and 70s clear.[92]

Robotham's essay "Blackening the Nation" follows the P. J. Patterson administration's attempt in Jamaica to create a black capitalist class rather than the standard Caribbean postindependent arrangement of black political power and leadership in the cultural sphere and minority (largely white) economic dominance. For Robotham, the "black bourgeoisie has the potential, but only the potential, in the course of its attempt to gain and consolidate power to implement reforms of critical benefit to the majority of the people."[93] There is more than a suggestion here that capitalism is the only game in town, and the sole question for the state becomes merely how well one can "walk the tightrope" between satisfying a populace's demands and the acquisitive accumulative imperatives of capitalism.[94] Rupert Lewis's "Reconsidering the Role of the Middle Class in Caribbean Politics" travels a different, though not completely dissimilar, terrain. Lewis starts by suggesting that "social-democratic and Leninist ideas [in the region] . . . have run their ideological course." The past criticism of the middle classes (James is specifically mentioned) needs updating in order to account for the significant class mobility we have seen in the last generation and to comprehend the constitution of this middle class, which is drawn far more from entrepreneurial groups than the civil service and the professions. Lewis thus eschews the tendency by the Caribbean Left to dismiss the middle classes, stating that the study of Caribbean politics teaches us that after "any wave of social upheaval, mass protest or revolutionary transition new forces from the middle strata arise to implement and direct alternative policies in the process of institutionalizing change."[95] His hope rests in the creation of a new entrepreneurial class, which will be constitutively different in its vision and social outlook than the predatory minority colonial elites of the last few centuries.[96] This privileging of entrepreneurship within a developmental vision for the Caribbean state sits uneasily with the previous hard-won gains of generations of trade unionism. It also remains difficult to reconcile with the clear signs that the contemporary heralding of entrepreneurship in the Caribbean emerges from public- and private-sector interests who actively seek a devolution of the state's responsibility for its citizens.

Yet, simultaneous to these changing perspectives on the middle class by the region's political theorists, another pathway was being forged through the discipline of anthropology that sought to consider and explain class stratification in the Caribbean. This track relied more on manifestations of social difference in the realm of popular culture and more consciously thematized questions of gender and power in the public sphere. Peter Wilson's essay "Reputation and Respectability: A Suggestion for Caribbean Ethnology" and subsequent book *Crab Antics* is the most influential work in this field and an essential work in what is now termed masculinity studies in the Caribbean.[97] Wilson's thesis that the crucial organizational tension in Caribbean society is the dichotomy between reputation and respectability, spheres inhabited by men and women respectively, has been subjected to searching commentary by a generation of Caribbean scholars.[98] Perhaps the greatest weakness of Wilson's approach is exposed by Jean Besson's critique, which claims that Wilson's thesis is painfully unaware of the "unequal and exploitative gender relations" that structure his case study. For Besson, Wilson forgets that women compete for status too and thus have their own forms of "reputation," and his schema suggests that "Afro-Caribbean women are . . . bearers and perpetuators of the Eurocentric colonial value system."[99] Despite this, Wilson's dichotomy and the conundrum it seeks to articulate have remained an important touchstone in Caribbean cultural criticism, in work as diverse as

Shalini Puri's thoughts toward a new Caribbean cultural studies to David Murray's ethnography of homosexuality in Barbados.[100] For Puri (following Daniel Miller), the emphasis in studies of Caribbean culture on carnival versus Christmas is symptomatic of a privileging of reputation over respectability and is the Caribbean version of the "fetishization of resistance and transgression in cultural studies."[101] David Murray's ethnography shows the complex ways in which performances and disavowals of same-sex relationships are captive to the mesmerizing power of respectability, which often bedevils his informants' attempts to achieve true erotic autonomy and freedom.

The respectability portion of the reputation/respectability divide in the Caribbean is thus premised on a very different version of respectability than that which is classically understood to secure middle-class hegemony in Western societies since the nineteenth century.[102] Its raison d'être is to secure middle-class rule, but it has a different relationship to discourses of middle-classness because it is suffused with coloniality. This Peter Wilson understood well and outlined in his "A Polemic by Way of Conclusion," the final chapter of *Crab Antics*. For Wilson, "respectability is the moral force behind the coercive power of colonialism and neo-colonialism."[103] The tragedy of the new West Indian middle classes at independence is the dawning realization within them that the values they have sought and their "straining ambivalently toward respectability" have been for naught, as these values are built on a series of pleasures and prohibitions created in a foreign land. Their hegemony can only remain weak, and in a quest to solidify it, the lure of colonial authoritarianism is likely to be too great to disavow. Wilson acknowledges that despite his call for a Caribbeanization of the social values now claimed by respectability, some "new legitimation of authority" will hardly be uniformly progressive.

Two decades after independence, Diane Austin would show the transformations caused by the search for new forms of legitimation when she observed that the Jamaican middle class elite "has shifted its ideological emphasis from color to education, from birth to socialization, from 'manners' to social competence [while] retaining . . . their privileged class position"—a discerning and generalizable insight on middle-class hegemony in the contemporary Anglophone Caribbean.[104] The denouement of all this is our current moment, an era described by some as one of hegemonic dissolution, in which new forms of domination are being actively reproduced on Caribbean populations by new elites.[105]

Bringing together the threads of the different discourses I have been charting about the Caribbean middle classes, I wish to propose the following. Given its modern location within the West and despite the peculiarities of intensely small geographical size and multicultural communities sutured together by coloniality, the expansion and rise to power of a postindependence Caribbean upper middle class should not be of any great surprise; nor does it require an elaborate explanation.

Rather, it is closely allied to a global historical event that has been in process since the late 1960s, which Neil Lazarus has termed "a *consolidation* of the historical patterns of bourgeois class domination."[106] Meanwhile, middle-class social conservatism in the form of its obsession with respectability becomes what Lindon Barrett once described as a "crush of racial, gendered, domestic, and commercial prohibitions and imperatives."[107] This amalgam of genuflection to Western capital *and* its social order has produced a specifically Caribbean brand of social and economic conservatism, wedded to coloniality, and a will to power over the only beings that it can subject—those reduced to second-class citizenship within the state.

The Contemporary Scene

> Elections where your stomach hurts endlessly. An economy of frustration. The cave where your dependency becomes bloated.
>
> Edouard Glissant, *Caribbean Discourse*[108]

The complaint and unbearable disillusionment that Glissant reveals above is best apprehended through a consideration of the following stark realities about our Caribbean moment:

Guyana has reportedly the highest suicide rate in the world.[109]

In Jamaica at the paupers' supermarkets, bread is sold by the slice for those who cannot afford to buy an entire loaf.[110]

The average *official* unemployment rate in Grenada from 2013 to 2015 was over 30 percent.[111]

In September 2014 Barbados, in the midst of its worst postindependence recession, introduced tuition fees for its citizens at the University of the West Indies, with a corresponding 35 percent decline in the number of undergraduates on campus within eighteen months.[112]

The rates of sexual assault in three Caribbean countries rank them in the top ten countries in that category in the world.[113]

The seven countries with the top rates of emigration of educated workers to Organization for Economic Co-operation and Development countries are all from the Caribbean.[114]

The Caribbean has been assessed as being the most food-import-dependent region in the world.[115]

Every Anglophone Caribbean country with the exception of Trinidad and Tobago is in a formal structural adjustment program with the International Monetary Fund or following the precise dictates they would have to if they were in one.

With all of these chilling tales, it is not even necessary to refer to the feature of contemporary Caribbean life best known in the region and afar—its status as the region with the highest murder rate in the world, a consequence of its links to the international trade in narcotics, which has shown a relentless capacity to devour the lives of two generations of young people in the postindependence Caribbean. Some Caribbean state managers have a ready reply to this: one controversial head of Jamaica's Crime Management Unit, when questioned about his tactics of policing that have led to several charges of extrajudicial killings, responded by repeatedly calling his methods "the final solution" to the crime problem in Jamaica—unaware of or unconcerned with the historical resonances of that term.[116] It is all, as Fanon once remarked, an infernal cycle.[117]

The flowering of such sturdy hardships in the Anglophone Caribbean, a region with a tradition of liberal democracy in its postindependence history, may legitimately cause some surprise. Why liberal democracy, even if it is little more than a guise for middle-class elite domination? Why has the Anglophone Caribbean not devolved into a more formal state authoritarianism, of which there are copious examples within the region and beyond? Here, the intimacy of the Caribbean polity must be examined, as both fundamental to domination in the present and, paradoxically, to fashioning resistance. The extraordinarily close relationship between governed and government in some of the smallest independent states in the world cannot be emphasized enough, as it affects strategies of political mobilization, bases of authority, and the techniques of domination used to manufacture consent and legitimacy. Unlike other regimes in the West, the Caribbean state cannot ignore the vote of significant parts of its populations. Hence, in its more ugly manifestations, it resorts to rigging elections (Guyana under Forbes Burnham), buying the vote through ridiculously open forms of patronage (Antigua under the Vere and Lester Bird administrations), or creating such an atmosphere of violence, patronage, and intimidation in areas popularly known as "garrison communities" that votes are assured (Jamaica in the 1970s through 1990s under both major parties).[118] In times in which the necessity of regime survival is less directly under threat, elections can descend into a cult of personality and a tasteless consumerism financed by white elites, while nationalist slogans are chanted from political platforms (Barbados's elections of the twenty-first century). It is not often necessary to resort to assassination as a technique of power to control recalcitrant leftists, though occasionally it is utilized, most notably in the murder of Walter Rodney by agents of the Burnham regime in Guyana. The small size of the populations and the ease of isolating or co-opting individual radicals mean that power can be sure of itself without allying with practices that might damage its international human rights record. In small societies, compulsory unemployment within the entire country can be often engineered for radicals by the ruling elites, rumors engendered, and personal lives destroyed, leaving many with the choice that the Trinidadian installation artist Chris Cozier once referred to as "Migrate or Medal/Meddle."[119] Arthur Lewis's reflections on the end of the West Indies Federation are still relevant today: "In a small island of 50,000 or 100,000 people, dominated by a single political party, it is very difficult to prevent political abuse. Everybody depends on the government for something, however small, so most are reluctant to offend it. The civil servants live in fear; the police avoid unpleasantness; the trade unions are tied to the party; the newspaper depends on government advertisements; and so on. This is true even if the political leaders are absolutely honest. In cases where they are also corrupt . . . the situation becomes intolerable."[120]

Jamaican political theorist Carl Stone has shown that this state of affairs inevitably leads to a form of rule best termed "client politics."[121] Carlene Edie in her contribution to the debate on the postindependence Jamaican state notes that "clientelism prevents authoritarianism by dispersing resources; democracy, as a result, survives by default."[122] Jamaica's postindependence social and political crisis has been more intense and protracted than any other Anglophone Caribbean state with the exception of Guyana and has transfixed the region and its diaspora. This crisis has stimulated the production of the most discerning body of social and political theory on any state in the Anglophone Caribbean. In coining the phrase "hegemonic dissolution," Brian Meeks sought to explain a specific moment that emerged within the Jamaican state in the 1990s, at that point reeling from over a decade of structural adjustment and neoliberal globalization, which had considerably attenuated the state's ability to provide social services for the majority of its population. When this was allied to the fact that the middle classes (and, by extension, middle-class values) are seen as irredeemably corrupt, visionless, and elitist, new sources of authority and empowerment are sought after by the poor and working classes. These may range from popular music to the trafficking of narcotics. All of this becomes a critical part of a complex social environment, features of which include mounting crime rates and a sense of despair among a significant portion of the population. Meeks's explanation, "hegemonic dissolution," described a scenario in which the "old hegemonic alliance is unable to rule in the accustomed way, but equally, alternative and competitive modes of hegemony from below are unable to decisively place their stamp on the new and fluid situation."[123] Obika Gray's analysis of contemporary Jamaican politics suggests that it might be more fruitful to see state power there as a type of "predatory rule" by the elites on the poor, rather than the client-state relationship previously theorized by a number of Caribbean political scientists.[124] Gray's analysis consistently deploys the language of "citizenship," suggesting that key to its limits and denial are elite "anxieties [over] moral citizenship" and posing the question of "what consequences follow from permitting the Jamaican people culturally significant forms of social power yet denying them politically relevant forms of citizenship."[125] Jamaica's crises are both unique to the deadly polarization of the country's political sphere, its 1970s experiment with democratic socialism, and the colonial production of a society of such inequality that within a couple years of independence in 1962 it was assessed as the country with the greatest income inequality in the world.[126] To further apprehend the nature of postcolonial citizenship in the Anglophone Caribbean, let us consider two features of contemporary Caribbean life—the nature of the tourist industry and the gendered nature of the Caribbean state—that persist across the region and help us to understand the coloniality of contemporary Caribbean citizenship.[127]

Tourism

In the last couple of decades, with the decline of a number of movements that took a radical perspective on Caribbean development (notably in Jamaica, Guyana, and Grenada), the general theme has been a development strategy that posits itself as nonideological, as simply a professional and technocratic response to changing global and local configurations.[128] Such a concept of development in countries exploited for their wealth has resulted in the power of this exploitative potential being transferred to governments and the upper middle class, who have perpetuated a legacy of underdevelopment. This can best be seen in the rise of the tourist industry, which demands caricatures of the Caribbean similar to those of the colonial project.[129] My reflections about tourism are not identical with its association, in some radical quarters, with slavery or a purely unmediated form of colonialism, arguments that have been made many times in the past. What I wish to think about are the ways in which tourism configures Caribbean people's citizenship in the postindependence Caribbean, thus allowing for a more thoroughgoing critique of it as an enterprise.

One feature of the purest versions of the "tourism economy" is that far more people enter the islands as visitors annually than there are citizens in the countries.[130] This seemingly innocuous observation, a figure subjected to little analysis within the Caribbean and, indeed, trumpeted by tourism managers, is noteworthy as it problematizes understandings of who constitutes the citizen within the tourist economy. The dependence of the tourist economy on visitors means that production within the island is geared with them in mind. This production may take the form of food (often imported at a profit by the elites who control the distributive sector), entertainment, cultural performances, and a whole variety of goods and services both legal and illegal. Landscapes are rigorously reconfigured to present a vision that the tourist might enjoy, a process that may mean the production of a fictionalized history, the enclosure of desirable spaces along the shoreline, and the rehabilitation of capital cities and towns to more closely approximate models to be found in the urban North Atlantic. Local projects as apparently straightforward as the replacement of a statue or the introduction of Breathalyzer tests must first be thought of in terms of tourists' tastes and their effect on the tourism industry and scuttled if, on reflection, deemed inappropriate.[131] Movements for black economic enfranchisement or any radical redress of structural socioeconomic inequalities must pass the same scrutiny.[132] That the typical visitor is a white Westerner means that, again, the West consumes the Caribbean by means not noticeably distinguishable from the colonial period.[133]

What is perhaps even more disturbing is what all these seemingly unconnected events mean for the status of the tourist. Tourists occupy a space we might term "extraterritorial citizens." Their desires are analyzed before they arrive, indeed, before the thought of even visiting the country has entered their minds. Their time spent in the country is carefully orchestrated in such a way that a country is not just created as mythical (as in the advertisements that draw them to it) but is materially constructed to suit their desires with a tremendous amount of epistemic (and occasionally physical) violence done to its permanent residents. After their departure, efforts are continually made to make them return. If this same effort was made to assess the needs and aspirations of Caribbean citizens, the Caribbean might, as the old cliché goes, actually be a better place to live. As it is, despite state managers' frequent efforts to deny or silence popular dissent, Caribbean *citizens* often feel "like an *alien* in we own land."[134]

Caribbean state managers' complicity in reproducing these understandings can further be seen in their desire to use educational programs to mold servile populations, suited to the tourists' tastes. There is no better example than the comment made by Jean Holder, a former long-serving secretary-general of the Caribbean Tourism Organization, that some employees in the tourism sector in the Caribbean are unable "to distinguish between service and servitude."[135] Or, as one state-sponsored advertisement in Dominica put it, "SMILE. You are a walking tourist attraction."[136] This phrase—"a walking tourist attraction"—is especially poignant because of its (unconscious?) association with the sex tourism industry. Sexual services are not a marginal part of the tourist industry in the Caribbean but a constitutive element of it, and sex tourism provides one of the best examples of the intersecting coloniality of race, class, gender, and sexuality in contemporary Caribbean life.[137] This particular form of sexual desire is premised, in part, on a "desire for an extraordinarily high degree of control over the management of self and others as sexual, racialised and engendered beings."[138] It is impossible to imagine Caribbean tourism without the sex industry, as can be seen in the nativist and colonial tropes used in its advertising campaigns. As Kamala Kempadoo puts it, "that sex industries today depend upon the eroticization of the ethnic and cultural Other suggests we are witnessing a contemporary form of exoticism which sustains post-colonial and post-cold war relations of power and dominance."[139] The irony, as Jacqui Alexander has noted, is that Caribbean state managers can pass legislation "against certain sexualities while relying upon women's sexualized bodies and a political economy of desire in private capital accumulation."[140] The bodies and dignity of Caribbean people are offered up again for the "good" of the nation and the enjoyment of citizens from metropolitan locations.

Gender and the State

Gender is a crucial factor in any critique of the coloniality of citizenship. It is here that one finds some of the most pervasive and crude denials of citizenship in the Caribbean state and apprehending the rationales for these denials moves us closer to explaining the crises of citizenship within the contemporary Caribbean state. The complexities involved in analyzing the gendered nature of Caribbean citizenship are immense. Like women throughout the world, Caribbean women's citizenship is constrained by gendered violence, poor access to reproductive health rights, lower wages for comparable work, higher rates of unemployment, and the burden of a disproportionate amount of caregiving work. The legacy of structural adjustment has been the destruction of the capacity of the state to provide social services and, hence, a corresponding increase in the burden of caregiving work performed by women and, simultaneously, a crisis of legitimacy in the ranks of state managers. Thus, tracing contemporary coloniality forces an interrogation of the masculinist dimensions of creole nationalism.

The critique of patriarchy and gender inequalities in the Caribbean is complicated not only by colonialism but also by the seemingly progressive actions of some Caribbean leaders in their mobilization of women as part of the nationalist struggle.[141] Despite the obvious political rationales for these stances—the need to mobilize women as an important constituency of voters for electoral victory— significant gains were made in the areas of education and labor force participation at this time.[142] It is hard not to come to the conclusion that many of these leaders had a genuinely felt but, ultimately, highly paternalistic view of women's rights. Thus, when women make new demands on the state in the postindependence era, this is deemed illegitimate due, in part, to the erroneous perception that women's movements did not exist before independence and, more centrally, because the problem of the coloniality of gender formations in the Caribbean was never adequately addressed at that time. The problem becomes the hostility of the Caribbean state to further demands placed on it by women's groups, with previous progressive affiliations forgotten and their mobilization perceived as a recent development "contaminated" by contact with Western feminisms. Women's issues are, in short, expected to take a back seat to more important matters of state. In a situation in which a popular discourse of "male marginalization" has been advanced to explain male underachievement in the educational system, any advance made by women is seen to be at the expense of men. Men are the paradigmatic citizens, and their "right to leadership, household headship and the resources of the state are taken for granted."[143] Women do not deserve any achievements they may wrest from societies in which men are today still overwhelmingly represented in parliaments, private business, state institutions, and the courts.

These issues are perhaps seen most starkly in the relationship of women to the law. Reflecting on the status of women in Commonwealth Caribbean jurisprudence, Tracy Robinson states the following:

> In the early stages of the creation of independent Caribbean nation states, there were manifestly classes of citizenship rights for men and women. Women were cast as the dependents of men—put in constitutional language, they obtained rights to participate in civil society *through* men. That has changed and, in all but a few Caribbean countries, "equal treatment regardless of sex" and gender-neutral language have become the mode of constitutional discourse. Even so, men continue to be the paradigm of a citizen . . . *second-class citizenship* describes not only the hierarchy between men and women but also the hierarchy of roles for women: in one case, women are *second* to men as citizens, and in the other, citizenship is perceived as *secondary* for women.[144]

The Caribbean state repeatedly reinscribes the patriarchal understanding of the public/private domain, which has been tirelessly critiqued by Caribbean feminists. Given the state's disinterest in gender justice, it can claim that the fundamental rights and freedoms provided by Caribbean constitutions do not protect against gender discrimination; nor should they do so as, according to a Jamaican attorney general, this is not a matter of the "utmost importance."[145] The fusion of globally authorized and inscribed patriarchy, postcolonial masculine anxieties, bad faith, and the legacy of the colonial law can thus result in the abridgement of the sexual citizenship of Caribbean citizens, for Robinson, "the use of state power to re-authorize heteropatriarchy, retrench sexual freedom, and outlaw sexual dissidence."[146] One should not be surprised, then, that in the Jamaican parliament in 2003, one legislator could suggest that schoolgirls under sixteen undergo virginity testing, while another opined that women with more than two children outside marriage should be sterilized.[147] This is nothing more than the specter of colonialism's abduction of Caribbean women's bodies, which just will not lie down and be still.

What can we make of these tales, this "acute paralysis of will and sheer vacancy of imagination, the rampant corruption and vicious authoritarianism, the instrumental self-interest and showy self-congratulation" that have become symptomatic of our postcolonial present?[148] How can we apprehend these middle-class state manager performances of rule, rife with colonial anxieties that continue to reverberate into the second decade of the twenty-first century? Fanon and James, two of the Caribbean's greatest thinkers, could speak so clearly about them because their revolutionary commitment was unmistakable and the world they imagined had two unequivocal options: neocolonialism or a sovereign social-ist postcolonial society. The contemporary predicament is in part the debris of middle-class formation in emerging liberal democracies—a middle-classness constructed as a normative genre of the human, in the form of Western bourgeois heterosexual man. Since that overrepresentation of the human as Western man is largely devoid of revolutionary critique in the contemporary Caribbean public sphere, its power grows, until it assumes a state of being we cannot *not* want. It is here that the weight of David Scott's discerning comment that "thinking through the deadend present we live in requires less a story of what we have been excluded from than a story of our desire for *that* inclusion."[149] Fanon's warning here deserves repetition:

> The settler's world is a hostile world, which spurns the native, but at the same time is a world of which he is envious. We have seen that the native never ceases to dream of putting himself in the place of the settler—not of becoming the settler but of substituting himself for the settler. This hostile world, pon-derous and aggressive because it fends off the colonized masses with all the harshness it is capable of, represents not merely a hell from which the swiftest flight possible is desirable, but also a *paradise* close at hand which is *guarded by terrible watchdogs.*[150]

Terrible watchdogs. Postcolonial elites seduced by the allure of Western bourgeois citizenship, bereft of the knowledge of the psychological price of neo-colonial incorporation. It must quite simply be said: Caribbean state managers have no discernible project of Caribbean development that is not anchored to the reproduction of Western capitalist man. That this moment is untenable and has resulted in (to use Frederic Jameson's phrase) "grisly and ironic reversals" of the possibilities of an authentic Caribbean self-determination spoken of so halt-ingly at independence is now clear.[151] The betrayals of the comprador elite and their education into the dependency of client politics of the working classes of the Caribbean all point to the inability to surmount a deeper malaise, expressed by Sylvia Wynter as follows: "This issue is that of the genre of the human, the issue whose target of abolition is the ongoing collective production of our pres-ent ethnoclass mode of being human, Man: above all, its overrepresentation of its well-being as that of the human species as a whole, rather than as it is veridically: that of the Western and westernized (or conversely) global middle classes."[152]

Absurdity in Past and Present

> Fierceness and bleakness of vision are characteristic of the 1970s. Our poets at home have become furiously driven men . . . which is a direct response to the quality of chaos which exist in the contemporary Caribbean.
>
> Gordon Rohlehr, "Articulating a Caribbean Aesthetic"[153]

Absurdity is a tough word to use to describe the paradoxes of citizenship in the contemporary Caribbean. It immediately brings to mind V. S. Naipaul's dehumanizing contempt of a generation ago and, on first blush, seems to be the ultimate reinscription of coloniality—a reproduction of tropes that have for so long presented Caribbean people as deficient, backward, and incapable of the considered reflection that could lead to genuine transformations of their societies.[154] But what if absurdity was instead a reflective position, a momentary sigh, before a cry of ethical revolt against the present?[155]

This use of absurdity can find a longer genealogy in writers far removed from Naipaul's neocolonial intentions. In her essay "The American Negro and the Image of the Absurd," Esther Jackson anticipates Lewis Gordon's black existentialism in her consideration of the category of the "absurd" in modern literature and its relationship to black suffering in the United States.[156] For Jackson, "the modern arts . . . have dramatized the fact that an ever larger segment of humanity seems to share the kind of existence which has been the lot of the Negro for some three centuries or more . . . his alienation from the larger community, his isolation within abstract walls, his loss of freedom, and his legacy of despair."[157] The trope of humanity's existence as absurd is hardly new, but Jackson argues that its *modern* articulation cannot be deliberated without pondering the nature of black suffering or—as W. E. B. Du Bois articulated the central question facing blacks—how it feels to be a problem.[158] Jackson states: "But the fundamental absurdity of his condition—like that of modern man in general—may be traced to an even more critical ideological encounter: to the tension arising from the collision between the ethic of power and the idea of moral law. It is this moral crisis—the culmination of a long historical struggle—which engages the mind of our epoch; its implications extend far beyond the projected solution of the Negro's immediate problem to the question of human survival on this planet."[159]

The condition of the condemned of the earth is not theirs alone to endure, as the future of humanity will depend on what answers their creative self-activity gives to the world. Black radicals from Dessalines to the contemporary movement have understood this only too well. Indeed, the black radicals of a century ago would have known exactly what to do. Gathered in Madison Square Garden, New York City, in August 1920, they produced a document, "The Declaration of the Rights of the Negro Peoples of the World," which became the greatest collective manifesto produced by the Garvey movement. Produced when the Universal Negro Improvement Association was at the height of its powers, it stands as a definitive document of its time that set forth the anger felt by people of African descent at their relegation to second-class citizenship in the Americas. Listen to some of their demands, which resonate so clearly for our time: "We believe that any law or practice that tends to deprive any African of his land or the privileges of free *citizenship* within his country is unjust and immoral, and no native should respect any such law or practice"; "We believe in the self-determination of all peoples"; "We believe that any limited liberty which deprives one of the complete rights and prerogatives of full *citizenship* is but a modified form of slavery."[160]

Yet it is a dream to suggest that past radicalism can be so easily resuscitated or to posit an unbroken line from its past to our present. The task of confronting our contemporary neocolonial condition requires considering the ways in which consumerism, spiraling unemployment, and violence have substantially subverted processes of class solidarity toward a different future.[161] Not just exploitation and greed demand analysis here, but lethargy and the vanishing of alternatives. The Caribbean question becomes how much have radical dreams become attenuated over the accumulated betrayals of two postcolonial generations.

The disenchantment and worry over the Caribbean's future expressed by its leading radical economists is a further reminder of the critical conjuncture the region now faces. In his paper "Existential Threats in the Caribbean," Norman Girvan noted the transition in the Caribbean from "agro-exporting economies to tourism-driven economies and emigration-driven economies."[162] For him, neoliberal globalization has "resulted in a *progressive loss of policy autonomy* of Caricom governments," giving little reason to deny that its effect is recolonization in practice.[163] Girvan's chartering of the impact of neoliberal globalization on the Caribbean—rising indebtedness, economic marginalization, fiscal colonialism, economic predation and vulnerability, IMF trusteeship, energy dependence, and food dependence—leads him to state that "insular independence has become largely shambolic and economic sovereignty an illusion."[164] The "existential threats" that give Girvan's paper its title are "a constellation of economic, social and environmental pressures that threaten the viability of our societies as functional entities in any meaningful sense."[165] His conclusion would appear apocalyptic, if he was not one of the finest political economists of his generation in the Anglophone Caribbean: "I don't think it would be an exaggeration to say that under a business as usual scenario, the Caribbean *as we know it* will have ceased to exist by the middle of the present century."[166] His fellow economist, Jamaican Michael Witter's, assessment is a gloomy echo. For Witter, "it is possible to become a consuming appendage of North America financed by remittances, drug transshipment, loans, tourism services, and offshore financial services, with the attendant implications for Caribbean culture and society."[167]

A turn to one of the leading theorists of Caribbean cultural politics in the postindependence era illustrates well the implications of the postcolonial malaise of our present moment and the conundrums of cultural citizenship that seem emblematic of the Caribbean state. Gordon Rohlehr's 1970 essay "History as Absurdity," styled as a literary critic's reply to the writings of Eric Williams, was an astute and brave response to Williams at one of the most challenging times for a university-based public intellectual in the postindependence Anglophone

Caribbean.[168] In Williams, we see the historian turned politician who, when he casts his eye back to history, treats it as the venue for political propaganda, a "polemicist of no mean order" whose "obsessive factuality . . . drains *Black experience* of its humanity."[169] Williams's work bears a striking resemblance to Naipaul, as both appear "paralyzed by the nightmare of West Indian history" and so mesmerized by the abductive power of coloniality that no pathway toward self-determination can be countenanced.[170] We are left then with a litany of woes and tragedies, which, in the absence of a commitment to a theory of radical social change, devolve into the perspective that Caribbean societies are marred by their incomprehensible, incongruous nature. The politician-historian Williams, in his "need to prove mastery returns him and his rebellion to absurdity."[171] Williams's writings on history illustrate his belief that Caribbean history is absurd, the withering response by Rohlehr is that Williams himself "contributed so richly to the perpetuation of such absurdity."[172] Rohlehr's rejoinder to Williams is as simple as it is poignant: "it is not the decline of the West Indies that should engage our sentiment, but rather their endurance as a perennially fertile hunting ground for everyone except the people who live there."[173]

A quarter century later, Rohlehr would return to the theme of the culture of Williams but with some acute developments on his earlier work, predicated on the evidence of the last decade of Williams's rule (1970–1981) and his legacy sixteen years after his death.[174] Williams is still figured, over the course of his twenty-five-year sojourn as Trinidad and Tobago's premier and then prime minister, as inaugurating and perpetuating "a theatre of the postcolonial Absurd," but now the lens of criticism is not his published historical work but emanates from the calypsonians who have responded to his rule as supportive advocates and his harshest critics.[175] Rohlehr's focus on the *political culture* of Williams illustrates that the many conundrums of postindependence rule in the Anglophone Caribbean afflict its most prosperous and powerful state, and the only one at the current moment not enmeshed in a declared or implicit structural adjustment program with an international financial agency. The temper of Williams's language in his public addresses, his flair for the "linguistic register of the street," represents an exploitation of the captivating expressive possibilities of nation languages.[176] His use of it was disconcerting to those on the receiving ends of his denunciations that caused them real social and material harm in small societies and was merely the public face of the state terror that ultimately secured the regime.[177] Williams, the model for Lloyd Best's term "doctor politics," was convinced that the educated middle-class professionals alone had the right to rule the newly emergent Caribbean states.[178] As Rohlehr notes, "such a powerful derogation of grass-roots militancy as irrelevant to the new age strangled the popular will to a self-empowerment crucial to the practice of independence."[179] Client politics in Trinidad and Tobago, awash with oil wealth in the 1970s, would take on forms of patronage and encourage conspicuous consumption unparalleled elsewhere in the region and would naturally take an ethnic turn, in which the relative weight ascribed to African and Indian culture by the state would be debated tenaciously through the 1990s.[180] In Rohlehr's reading, culture under Williams "became a manipulable lever in an elaborate machinery of patronage on the part of the controlling elite and clientelism on the part of the common folk."[181] Or, to put it more comprehensively, "the political manipulation of culture by the PNM has inscribed in the national mind the notion that cultural production has, like everything else, become part of the patron-client syndrome. Every creed and race has learned to demand of the regime in office its 'piece of the action,' and to view every other creed and race as a rival in the competition for space and spoils, where it is more important to clarify one's difference than to identify those substantial areas of similarity and shared attitudes."[182]

Rohlehr's shifting interpretation of Williams can be read as a move from a critical interpretation of an encroaching neocolonial dominance within a decade of independence to an assessment of the means by which postcolonial statecraft enacts power through its manipulation of cultural citizenship. The Caribbean has moved from activism to recognize the validity of the "little tradition" of its masses, long denied by colonial rule and its local white and brown elites in the late colonial order, to a state patronage that insists it can serve as an authentic judge of taste and value. Caribbean popular and expressive cultures, long the scene of antagonistic relationships between state and subjects, would now become reconciled under the mantle of postcolonial governmentality.

Rohlehr's scrupulous readings of Williams, among the finest work on Caribbean political culture, remind us of what Stefano Harney, in his assessment of Trinidad, terms the "relationship between neo-colonial rhetoric and internal class oppression."[183] From the vantage point of denials of citizenship in the postindependence Caribbean, the tragic absurdity of the Caribbean postcolony becomes clear. It is not history that is absurd; it is the *contemporary* that is absurd. History may haunt, but the *contemporary* is what hurts.

Notes

1. Karl Marx, "For a Ruthless Criticism of Everything Existing," in *The Marx-Engels Reader*, ed. Robert C. Tucker (London: W. W. Norton, 1978), 14, original italics.

2. C. L. R. James, *The Life of Captain Cipriani: An Account of British Government in the West Indies* (Nelson, UK: Coulton, 1932), 10.

3. C. L. R. James, *World Revolution 1917–1936: The Rise and Fall of the Communist International* (Atlantic Highlands, NJ: Humanities Press International, 1993). Originally published in 1937.

4. James would later recount his views at the time as follows: "My hitherto vague ideas of freedom crystalized around a political conviction: we should be free to govern ourselves. I said nothing to anyone. After all, I was working for the Government. When I told my brother some of my ideas his only comment was: 'You will end up in gaol.'" C. L. R. James, *Beyond a Boundary* (Durham, NC: Duke University Press, 1994), 115. The transition between this James and the figure who would become one of the leading Marxists and Pan-Africanists of the twentieth century has been marvelously recounted by Christian Høgsbjerg in his account of James's six-year stay in Britain and need not detain us here. See Christian Høgsbjerg, *C. L. R. James in Imperial Britain* (Durham, NC: Duke University Press, 2014).

5. *The Life of Captain Cipriani* was republished in the Duke University Press series The C. L. R. James Archives in 2014.

6. See Walton Look-Lai, "C. L. R. James and Trinidadian Nationalism," in *C. L. R. James's Caribbean*, ed. Paul Buhle and Paget Henry (Durham, NC: Duke University Press, 1992), 174–209, for this observation.

7. This pamphlet was republished twice in 1967 and collected in two major collections of James's work, Anna Grimshaw, ed., *The C. L. R. James Reader* (Oxford: Blackwell Publishers, 1992) and *The Future in the Present: Selected Writings* (London: Allison and Busby, 1977). For details on the 1967 republications, see Grimshaw, *C. L. R. James Reader*, 428.

8. On "vindicationism," see Wilson Moses, *Afrotopia: The Roots of African American Popular History* (Cambridge: Cambridge University Press, 1998), 21.

9. C. L. R. James, "The Case for West Indian Self-Government," in Grimshaw, *C. L. R. James Reader*, 50. Traces of these ideas never escaped James, as an unnoticed lecture at the University of the West Indies three decades later shows. See James, "West Indian Personality," *Caribbean Quarterly* 35, no. 4 (1989): 11–13. This lecture was delivered in the Michaelmas term of the 1959–60 academic year.

10. James, "Case for West Indian Self-Government," 50

11. For James's influence on this debate, see my article "C. L. R. James's *The Black Jacobins* and the Making of the Modern Atlantic World," in *10 Books That Shaped the British Empire: Creating an Imperial Commons*, ed. Antoinette Burton and Isabel Hofmeyr (Durham, NC: Duke University Press, 2014), 190–215. In chapter 4, I will return to the similarity between James's argument here and his many rehearsals of the vexed question of tradition/modernity in his writings on the Caribbean in the 1950s and 1960s.

12. James, "Case for West Indian Self-Government," 51.

13. James, "Case for West Indian Self-Government," 62.

14. This quote is to be found in *The Life of Captain Cipriani* but not in the abridged "The Case for West Indian Self-Government."

15. See also here Mimi Sheller, *Citizenship from Below: Erotic Agency and Caribbean Freedom* (Durham, NC: Duke University Press, 2012), 89.

16. On J. J. Thomas, see his text *Froudacity: West Indian Fables by James Anthony Froude* (London: New Beacon, 1969), originally published in 1889.

17. James kept a careful eye on events in the Caribbean during his six years in the United Kingdom between 1932 and 1938, though the focus of his activism on questions of world revolution and African liberation meant that the Caribbean was not his area of concentrated concern. See here Christian Høgsbjerg, "'A Thorn in the Side of Great Britain': C. L. R. James and the Caribbean Labour Rebellions of the 1930s," *Small Axe* 35 (2011): 24–42.

18. Michael Hanchard, "Afro-Modernity: Temporality, Politics, and the African Diaspora," *Public Culture* 11, no. 1 (1999): 245.

19. Jean-Jacques Dessalines, "Liberty or Death, Proclamation," in *Caribbean Political Thought: The Colonial State to Caribbean Internationalisms*, ed. Aaron Kamugisha (Kingston: Ian Randle, 2013), 21–23, originally published in 1804; Sibylle Fischer, *Modernity Disavowed: Haiti and the Cultures of Slavery in the Age of Revolution* (Durham, NC: Duke University Press, 2004).

20. Laurent DuBois, *A Colony of Citizens: Revolution and Slave Emancipation in the French Caribbean, 1787–1804* (Chapel Hill: University of North Carolina Press, 2004), 2.

21. DuBois, *Colony of Citizens*, 4.

22. Myriam Cottias, "Gender and Republican Citizenship in the French West Indies, 1848–1945," *Slavery and Abolition* 26, no. 2 (2005): 233. On the question of gender in the aftermath of Haitian independence, see Mimi Sheller, "Sword-Bearing Citizens," in *Citizenship from Below*, 142–65.

23. Kevin A. Yelvington, Jean-Pierre Sainton, Michel Hector, and Jean Casimir, "Caribbean Social Structure in the nineteenth Century," in *UNESCO General History of the Caribbean Vol. IV: The Long Nineteenth Century; Nineteenth Century Transformations*, ed. K. O. Laurence (Paris: UNESCo, 2011), 283–333.

24. John Stuart Mill, *On Liberty* (Indianapolis: Hackett, 1978).

25. Cecilia Green, "Disciplining Boys: Labor, Gender, Generation and the Penal System in Barbados, 1880–1930," *Journal of the History of Childhood and Youth* 3, no. 3 (2010): 366–90. The scholarship of the social history of this period is considerable; however, see particularly Michele Johnson and Brian Moore, *Neither Led nor Driven: Contesting British Cultural Imperialism in Jamaica, 1865–1920* (Kingston: University of the West Indies Press, 2004); Bridget Brereton and Kevin A. Yelvington, eds., *The Colonial Caribbean in Transition: Essays on Postemancipation Social and Cultural History* (Kingston: University of the West Indies Press, 1999); Diana Paton, *No Bond but the Law: Punishment, Race and Gender in Jamaican State Formation, 1780–1870* (Durham, NC: Duke University Press, 2004); Melanie Newton, *The Children of Africa in the Colonies: Free People of Color in Barbados in the Age of Emancipation* (Baton Rouge: State University of Louisiana Press, 2008); Brian Moore, *Cultural Power, Resistance and Pluralism: Colonial Guyana 1838–1900* (Kingston: University of the West Indies Press, 1995).

26. Newton, *Children of Africa in the Colonies*, 204.

27. Newton, *Children of Africa in the Colonies*, 221.

28. David Luis-Brown, *Waves of Decolonization: Discourses of Race and Hemispheric Citizenship in Cuba, Mexico, and the United States* (Durham, NC: Duke University Press, 2008), 22.

29. For the most comprehensive account of this period, see O. Nigel Bolland, *The Politics of Labour in the British Caribbean: The Social Origins of Authoritarianism and Democracy in the Labour Movement* (Kingston: Ian Randle, 2001). For the changing face of life in the Caribbean in the last half of the twentieth century, see Bonham C. Richardson and Joseph L. Scarpaci, "The Quality of Life in the Twentieth Century Caribbean," in *General History of the Caribbean Volume V: The Caribbean in the Twentieth Century*, ed. Bridget Brereton (Paris: UNESCO and London: Macmillan, 2004), 627–66.

30. Percy Hintzen, "Rethinking Democracy in the Postnationalist State," in *New Caribbean Thought*, e Brian .Meeks and Folke Lindahl (Kingston: University of the West Indies Press, 2001), 105.

31. Percy Hintzen, "Reproducing Domination: Identity and Legitimacy Constructs in the West Indies," *Social Identities* 3, no. 1 (1997): 48.

32. See especially Percy Hintzen, "Afro-Creole Nationalism as Elite Domination: The English-Speaking West Indies," in *Foreign Policy and the Black (Inter)National Interest*, ed. Charles P. Henry (New York: State University of New York Press, 2000), 185–215.

33. Hintzen, "Rethinking Democracy," 105, 121.

34. Percy Hintzen, "Creoleness and Nationalism in Guyanese Anticolonialism and Post-colonial Formation," *Small Axe* 15 (2004): 113.

35. Percy Hintzen, "Democracy and Middle-Class Domination in the Anglophone Caribbean," in *Democracy in the Caribbean: Myths and Realities*, ed. Carlene J. Edie (Westport, CT: Praeger, 1994), 13. Hintzen cites Max Weber's well-known observation that "once it is established, bureaucracy is among the social structures which are the hardest to destroy," with clear resonances for the Caribbean's contemporary predicament.

36. Hintzen, "Democracy and Middle-Class Domination," 14.

37. Hintzen, "Democracy and Middle-Class Domination," 17.

38. Jamaica (1962), Trinidad (1962), Barbados (1966), and Guyana (1966) achieved their independence in this decade, while associated state status, which meant local self-government with Britain retaining control of foreign affairs and defense for the territory, came to Antigua, Dominica, Grenada, and St. Lucia in 1967. Full independence came to most of these territories in the 1970s and early 1980s: Antigua (1981), the Bahamas (1973), Belize (1981), Dominica (1978), Grenada (1974), St. Kitts and Nevis (1983), St. Lucia (1979), and St. Vincent (1979).

39. Hintzen, "Afro-Creole Nationalism," 200.

40. Hintzen, "Afro-Creole Nationalism," 106.

41. Hintzen, "Reproducing Domination," 63.

42. Hintzen, "Reproducing Domination," 70.

43. Hintzen, "Reproducing Domination," 70, my italics.

44. Percy Hintzen, "The Caribbean: Race and Creole Ethnicity," in *A Companion to Racial and Ethnic Studies*, ed. David Theo Goldberg and John Solomos (Oxford: Blackwell, 2002), 493.

45. On the racial state, see David Theo Goldberg, "Racial States" in Goldberg and Solomos, *Companion to Racial and Ethnic Studies*. This global elite is hegemonically white but far from solely so, as it is perfectly willing to admit members who possess European cultural capital and a neoliberal capitalist ethos or what Walter Rodney, among others, once called the comprador elite of the third world.

46. I return to the question of creolization in chapter 3.

47. Percy Hintzen, "Race and Creole Ethnicity in the Caribbean," in *Questioning Creole: Creolisation Discourses in Caribbean Culture*, ed. Verene A. Shepherd and Glen L. Richards (Kingston: Ian Randle, 2002), 92.

48. Hintzen, "Caribbean: Race and Creole Ethnicity," 477.

49. Hintzen, "Caribbean: Race and Creole Ethnicity," 478.

50. Hintzen, "Reproducing Domination," 55.

51. Jacqui Alexander, "Not Just (Any)Body Can Be a Citizen: The Politics of Law, Sexuality and Postcoloniality in Trinidad and Tobago and the Bahamas," *Feminist Review* 48 (1994): 6.

52. Jacqui Alexander, *Pedagogies of Crossing: Meditations on Feminism, Sexual Politics, Memory, and the Sacred* (Durham, NC: Duke University Press, 2005), 29.

53. Alexander, *Pedagogies of Crossing*, 46–47, 50.

54. Alexander, *Pedagogies of Crossing*, 58.

55. Alexander, "Not Just (Any)Body," 5.

56. Alexander, *Pedagogies of Crossing*, 23–24.

57. Alexander, *Pedagogies of Crossing*, 193, 220.

58. Alexander, "Not Just (Any)Body," 7, 10.

59. Alexander, "Not Just (Any)Body," 13. The phrase "self-government when fit for it" was the condescending term used by the British to justify their delay in granting full self-government to its Caribbean colonies. See James, "Case for West Indian Self-Government," 62.

60. Alexander, "Not Just (Any)Body," 13.

61. Alexander, "Not Just (Any)Body," 22–23.

62. These lines deliberately pun Hortense Spillers's well-known opening paragraph in "Mama's Baby, Papa's Maybe: An American Grammar Book," *Diacritics* 17, no. 2 (1987): 65.

63. Jacqui Alexander, *Pedagogies of Crossing*, 25.

64. Alexander's use of the term "state managers" is insightful, as it dispenses with the tendency to blame politicians alone for the region's condition but rather incorporates a wider field of players including senior public servants, private-sector managers, and leading figures in civil society institutions. It is often the case that these state managers are often even more socially conservative and neoliberal than the politicians, as they have no constituency to answer to and, hence, embody an even greater contemptuousness toward their fellow citizens.

65. C. L. R. James, *Party Politics in the West Indies* (San Juan, Trinidad and Tobago: Vedic Enterprises, 1962), 133.

66. Frantz Fanon, *The Wretched of the Earth*, trans. Constance Farrington (London: Penguin Books, 1990), 166.

67. Fanon, *Wretched of the Earth*.

68. Fanon, *Wretched of the Earth*, 141, 122.

69. Fanon, *Wretched of the Earth*, 119.

70. Fanon, *Wretched of the Earth*, 131.

71. James, *Party Politics*, 131.

72. James, *Party Politics*, 139.

73. See here W. E. B. DuBois's landmark essay "The Study of Negro Problems," *Annals of the American Academy of Political and Social Science* 11 (January 1898): 1–23. Thanks to Lewis Gordon for alerting me to the existence of this essay; see Gordon, "Du Bois' Humanistic Philosophy of Human Science," *Annals of the American Academy of Political and Social Science* 568 (March 2000): 265–80.

74. Greg Thomas, "Sexual Imitation and the Lumpen-Bourgeoisie: Race and Class as Erotic Conflict in E. Franklin Frazier," in *The Sexual Demon of Colonial Power: Pan-African Embodiment and Erotic Schemes of Empire* (Bloomington: Indiana University Press, 2006), 58.

75. Thomas, "Sexual Imitation," 74.

76. Nathan Hare, *The Black Anglo-Saxons* (New York: Marzani and Munsell, 1965).

77. Oliver Cox, "Introduction," in Hare, *Black Anglo-Saxons*, 1–14.

78. Cox, "Introduction," 13.

79. Patrick Bryan, "The Black Middle Class in Nineteenth Century Jamaica," in *Caribbean Freedom: Economy and Society from Emancipation to the Present*, ed. Hilary Beckles and Verene Shepherd (Kingston: Ian Randle, 1993), 284–95; Bridget Brereton, "The Development of an Identity: The Black Middle Class of Trinidad in the Later Nineteenth Century," in Beckles and Shepherd, *Caribbean Freedom*, 274–83.

80. Belinda Edmondson, *Caribbean Middlebrow: Leisure Culture and the Middle Class* (Ithaca, NY: Cornell University Press, 2009).

81. Lloyd Braithwaite, *Social Stratification in Trinidad* (Kingston: Institute of Social and Economic Research, University of the West Indies, Mona Campus, 1975). Originally published in *Social and Economic Studies* 2, nos. 2 and 3 (1953).

82. Braithwaite, *Social Stratification*, 107. For a fascinating perspective on these dynamics within Trinidad's carnival, see Barbara Powrie, "The Changing Attitude of the Colored Middle Class Towards Carnival," *Caribbean Quarterly* 4, nos. 3 and 4 (March/June 1956): 224–32.

83. Edward Kamau Brathwaite, *The Development of Creole Society in Jamaica 1770–1820* (Oxford: Oxford University Press, 1971), 311.

84. See here George Lamming's address "The Honourable Member," a sardonic "social portrait" of a Caribbean cabinet minister. George Lamming, "The Honourable Member," in *The George Lamming Reader: The Aesthetics of Decolonization*, ed. Anthony Bogues (Kingston: Ian Randle, 2011), 101–9.

85. Walter Rodney, "Contemporary Political Trends in the English Speaking Caribbean," *The Black Scholar* (September 1975): 15–21.

86. Rodney, "Contemporary Political Trends," 15. In this essay, Rodney shows a significant debt to Frantz Fanon, or more specifically, the analysis of the colonial transitioning to independent third world state as developed by Fanon in *The Wretched of the Earth*.

87. Rodney, "Contemporary Political Trends," 15.

88. Rodney, "Contemporary Political Trends," 18.

89. Walter Rodney, *Walter Rodney Speaks: The Making of an African Intellectual* (Trenton, NJ: Africa World Press, 1990), 113.

90. Rodney, *Walter Rodney Speaks*, 69.

91. "The Black Scholar Interviews Walter Rodney," *The Black Scholar* 6, no. 3 (1975): 43.

92. Don Robotham, "Blackening the Jamaican Nation: The Travails of a Black Bourgeoisie in a Globalized World," *Identities* 7, no. 1 (March 2000): 1–37; Rupert Lewis, "Reconsidering the Role of the Middle Class in Caribbean Politics," in Meeks and Lindahl, *New Caribbean Thought*, 127–43.

93. Robotham, "Blackening the Jamaican Nation," 3.

94. Robotham, "Blackening the Jamaican Nation," 8.

95. Lewis, "Reconsidering the Role," 140.

96. See Lewis's comments on entrepreneurial activity on pages 133, 135, 139.

97. Peter Wilson, "Reputation and Respectability: A Suggestion for Caribbean Ethnology," *Man* 4, no. 1 (1969): 70–84; Peter Wilson, *Crab Antics: The Social Anthropology of English-Speaking Negro Societies of the Caribbean* (New Haven, CT: Yale University Press, 1973). See also here Rhoda E. Reddock, ed., *Interrogating Caribbean Masculinities: Theoretical and Empirical Analyses* (Mona, Jamaica: University of the West Indies Press, 2004).

98. See the discussion in Daniel Miller, *Modernity: An Ethnographic Approach, Dualism and Mass Consumption in Trinidad* (Oxford: Berg, 1994).

99. Jean Besson, "Reputation and Respectability Reconsidered: A New Perspective on Afro-Caribbean Peasant Women," in *Women and Change in the Caribbean: A Pan-Caribbean Perspective*, ed. Janet Momsen (Bloomington: Indiana University Press, 1993), 19. See here Wilson, *Crab Antics*, 234.

100. Shalini Puri, "Beyond Resistance: Notes Towards a New Caribbean Cultural Studies," *Small Axe* 14 (2003): 23–38; David Murray, *Flaming Souls: Homosexuality, Homophobia and Social Change in Barbados* (Toronto: University of Toronto Press, 2012).

101. Puri, "Beyond Resistance," 24.

102. See here George Mosse's introduction "Nationalism and Respectability" to his work *Nationalism and Sexuality: Respectability and Abnormal Sexuality in Modern Europe* (New York: Howard Fertig, 1985).

103. Wilson, *Crab Antics*, 233.

104. Diane J. Austin, "Culture and Ideology in the English-Speaking Caribbean: A View from Jamaica," *American Ethnologist* 10, no. 2 (May 1983): 236.

105. See here Brian Meeks, "The Political Moment in Jamaica: The Dimensions of Hegemonic Dissolution," in *Radical Caribbean: From Black Power to Abu Bakr* (Mona, Jamaica: University of the West Indies Press, 1993), 124–43; Hintzen, "Afro-Creole Nationalism"; Aaron Kamugisha, "The Coloniality of Citizenship in the Contemporary Anglophone Caribbean," *Race and Class* 49, no. 2 (2007): 20–40.

106. Neil Lazarus, *Nationalism and Cultural Practice in the Postcolonial World* (Cambridge: Cambridge University Press, 1999), 19, original emphasis.

107. Lindon Barrett, "Black Men in the Mix: Badboys, Heroes, Sequins, and Denis Rodman," *Callaloo* 20, no. 1 (1997): 125.

108. Edouard Glissant, *Caribbean Discourse: Selected Essays*, trans. Michael Dash (Charlottesville: University Press of Virginia, 1989), 9.

109. Farahnaz Mohammed, "Guyana: Mental Illness, Witchcraft and the Highest Suicide Rate in the World," *Guardian* (UK), June 3, 2015, http://www.theguardian.com/global-development-professionals-network/2015/jun/03/guyana-mental-illness-witchcraft-and-the-highest-suicide-rate-in-the-world.

110. Kimmo Matthews, "Bread Sold by the Slice," *Jamaica Observer*, October 7, 2013, http://www.jamaicaobserver.com/news/Bread-sold-by-the-slice-_15053101.

111. See Rose Bhagwan, "Unemployment Rate Decreasing," NOW Grenada, April 22, 2016, http://nowgrenada.com/2016/04/unemployment-rate-decreasing/.

112. Yvette Best, "Roll Tumbles," *Daily Nation* (Barbados), August 27, 2014, 3A; Heather Lynn-Evanson, "Not All Gloom," *Daily Nation* (Barbados), August 29, 2015, 3.

113. United Nations Office on Drugs and Crime and the World Bank, *Crime, Violence and Development: Trends, Costs and Policy Options in the Caribbean* (March 2007).

114. Alissa Trotz and Beverley Mullings, "Transnational Migration, the State, and Development: Reflecting on the 'Diaspora Option,'" *Small Axe* 41 (2013): 163.

115. Tony Weis, "Small Farming and Radical Imaginations in the Caribbean Today," *Race and Class* 49, no. 2 (2007): 112.

116. Bernard Headley, "Man on a Mission: Deconstructing Jamaica's Controversial Crime Management Head," *Social and Economic Studies* 51, no. 1 (2002): 188. The logical conclusion to this pattern of state-sponsored violence would be the May 2010 Tivoli Gardens massacre by the Jamaican security forces, which remains unsuitably investigated to this day, despite Jamaican activist Lloyd D'Aguilar's brave efforts to secure justice for its victims.

117. Frantz Fanon, *Black Skin, White Masks* (New York: Grove, 1967), 116.

118. By other regimes in the West, I refer here to the United States and the debacle of the 2000 election, particularly the result in the state of Florida, where there is little doubt that systematic disenfranchisement took place directed especially toward black voters. See "Black Election 2000," *The Black Scholar* 31, no. 2 (Summer 2001).

119. The title of a 1998 exhibition by Trinidadian artist Chris Cozier: the "medal" refers to the acknowledgment given routinely to citizens deemed to have given good service to the nation and often comes in the form of knighthoods, "crowns of merit," and other such colonial titles.

120. Arthur Lewis, "The Agony of the Eight," in Kamugisha, *Caribbean Political Thought*, 352. Originally published by the Barbados Advocate Company, 1965.

121. Carl Stone, "Clientelism, Power and Democracy," in *Democracy and Clientelism in Jamaica* (New Brunswick, NJ: Transaction Books, 1980), 91–110.

122. Carlene Edie, *Democracy by Default: Dependency and Clientelism in Jamaica* (Boulder, CO: Lynne Rienner, 1990), 7.

123. Meeks, "Political Moment in Jamaica," 134.

124. Obika Gray, "Predation Politics and the Political Impasse in Jamaica," *Small Axe* 13 (2003): 72–94.

125. Gray, "Predation Politics," 74.

126. David Lowenthal, *West Indian Societies* (Oxford: Oxford University Press, 1972), 298.

127. These are necessarily, brief, polemical vignettes—as the terrain covered here fills volumes and has been the lifework of many scholars.

128. See Clive Thomas, *The Poor and the Powerless: Economic Policy and Change in the Caribbean* (New York: Monthly Review Press, 1988); Tennyson Joseph, "'Old Expectations, New Philosophies': Adjusting State-Society Relations in the Post-Colonial Anglophone Caribbean," *Journal of Eastern Caribbean Studies* 22, no. 4 (1997): 31–67; Percy Hintzen, "Structural Adjustment and the New International Middle Class," *Transition* (Guyana), February 24, 1995, 52–74.

129. The rise of tourism is linked to the fact that Caribbean countries, beset by a legacy of underdevelopment that necessitates the importation of a large amount of food and manufactured goods, have consistently needed large flows of foreign exchange to stabilize their economies. As Polly Patullo points out, "for two decades tourism has distinguished itself as the *only* steady growth sector for the region." Polly Patullo, *Last Resorts: The Cost of Tourism in the Caribbean* (Kingston: Ian Randle, 1996), 12.

130. The purest versions of the tourism economy in the Caribbean can be found in Antigua, the Bahamas, Barbados, St. Kitts, St. Lucia, and Grenada, and most other Anglophone Caribbean islands are trying desperately to emulate the patterns these islands have established. Tourism in Jamaica is more specific to particular locations within the island. Trinidadian tourism is mainly linked to carnival, resulting in a somewhat different set of circumstances to what I discuss above.

131. In Barbados from the late 1990s and into the twenty-first century, heated debate revolved around the government's decision to remove a statue of Horatio Nelson from the central square in the capital. While much of the debate was between the white elite and conservative blacks versus local Pan-Africanists, one of the arguments that gathered most force and was frequently repeated in the newspapers was that British tourists (the largest tourist market) liked the statue, which should be reason enough to retain it. Indeed, there were reports in British newspapers (notably, the *Guardian*) about the controversy, and travel agents reported that British tourists had asked if they were not welcome in Barbados any more. As of 2018, the statue remained in place. Similarly, in Barbados in 2003, comments were made in the press that the proposed introduction of Breathalyzer tests might harm the tourism industry; the test has subsequently not yet been introduced.

132. Hilary Beckles notes this in his book *Corporate Power in Barbados: The Mutual Affair* (Bridgetown, Barbados: Lighthouse, 1989).

133. Mimi Sheller, *Consuming the Caribbean: From Arawaks to Zombies* (London: Routledge, 2003).

134. "Like an Alien in We Own Land" was a popular St. Lucia calypso in the 1990s; see Patullo, *Last Resorts*.

135. Patullo, *Last Resorts*, 63.

136. Patullo, *Last Resorts*, 62.

137. Amid a now substantial literature, see Kamala Kempadoo, ed., *Sun, Sex and Gold: Tourism and Sex Work in the Caribbean* (Lanham, MD: Rowman and Littlefield, 1999).

138. Julia O'Connell Davidson and Jacqueline Sanchez Taylor, "Fantasy Islands: Exploring the Demand for Sex Tourism," in Kempadoo, *Sun, Sex and Gold*, 37.

139. As quoted in Davidson and Taylor, "Fantasy Islands," 37. A discussion of sex work in the Caribbean raises the far more intricate question of the extent of agency that sex workers have in their work and lives, and I would certainly disavow any analysis that sees them as merely the helpless prey of Western imperialism. Nonetheless, this does not diminish the fundamental *coloniality* of the desires that create a market for their services in the tourism industry.

140. Alexander, "Not Just (Any)Body," 19.

141. Patricia Mohammed, "Midnight's Children and the Legacy of Nationalism," *Small Axe* 2 (1997): 19–37. See also A. Lynn Bolles, "Michael Manley in the Vanguard Towards Gender Equality," *Caribbean Quarterly* 48, no. 1 (March 2002): 45–56.

142. It should be recalled here that this was part of a global movement toward greater democratization of the state, which benefitted both women *and* men, in the form of universal adult suffrage and the social democratic policy decisions that transformed the class configuration of many Caribbean countries. One should also distinguish between the decidedly different politics of democratic-socialist versus neoliberal regimes.

143. Tonya Haynes, "Sylvia Wynter's Theory of the Human and the Crisis School of Caribbean Heteromasculinity Studies," *Small Axe* 49 (2016): 106.

144. Tracy Robinson, "Fictions of Citizenship, Bodies without Sex: The Production and Effacement of Gender in the Law," *Small Axe* 7 (March 2000): 25, original italics.

145. Tracy Robinson, "Beyond the Bill of Rights: Constituting Caribbean Women as Citizens," in *Confronting Power, Theorizing Gender: Interdisciplinary Perspectives in the Caribbean*, ed. Eudine Barriteau (Kingston: University of the West Indies Press, 2003), 240.

146. Tracy Robinson, "Authorized Sex: Same Sex Sexuality and Law in the Caribbean," in *Sexuality, Social Exclusion and Human Rights*, ed. Christine Barrow, Marjan de Bruin and Robert Carr (Kingston: Ian Randle, 2009), 3.

147. Robert Best, "Controlling Sex Results," *Daily Nation* (Barbados), August 5, 2003; Deborah Thomas, "Public Bodies: Virginity Testing, Redemption Songs and Racial Respect in Jamaica," *Journal of Latin American Anthropology* 11, no. 1 (2006): 1–31.

148. David Scott, *Conscripts of Modernity: The Tragedy of Colonial Enlightenment* (Durham, NC: Duke University Press, 2004), 2.

149. Stuart Hall, "Interview with David Scott," *Bomb* 90 (2005): 59, original italics.

150. Fanon, *Wretched of the Earth*, 41.

151. I am thinking here of this remarkable passage from Frederic Jameson: "History is what hurts, it is what refuses desire and sets inexorable limits to individual as well as collective praxis, which its "ruses" turn into grisly and ironic reversals of their overt intention." Frederic Jameson, *The Political Unconscious*, quoted in Saidiya V. Hartman, *Scenes of Subjection: Terror, Slavery and Self-Making in Nineteenth-Century America* (New York: Oxford University Press, 1997), 49.

152. Sylvia Wynter, "Unsettling the Coloniality of Being/Power/Truth/Freedom: Towards the Human, after Man, Its Overrepresentation—an Argument," *CR: The New Centennial Review* 3, no. 3 (Fall 2003): 313.

153. Gordon Rohlehr, "Articulating a Caribbean Aesthetic: The Revolution in Self-Perception," in *My Strangled City and Other Essays* (Port of Spain, Trinidad and Tobago: Longman, 1992), 15.

154. V. S. Naipaul, *The Middle Passage* (Harmondsworth, UK: Penguin, 1969).

155. Nelson Maldonado-Torres, *Against War: Views from the Underside of Modernity* (Durham, NC: Duke University Press, 2008.

156. Esther Merle Jackson, "The American Negro and the Image of the Absurd," *Phylon* 23, no. 4 (1962): 359–71; Lewis R. Gordon, *Existentia Africana: Understanding Africana Existential Thought* (London: Routledge, 2000); Lewis R. Gordon, ed., *Existence in Black: An Anthology of Black Existential Philosophy* (London: Routledge, 1997).

157. Jackson, "American Negro," 359.

158. Du Bois, "Study of the Negro Problems."

159. Jackson, "American Negro," 360.

160. "Declaration of Rights of the Negro Peoples of the World," in *The Philosophy and Opinions of Marcus Garvey, or Africa for the Africans, Vol. 1 and 2*, ed. Amy Jacques Garvey (Dover, MA: Majority, 1986), 135–43, my emphasis.

161. Paget Henry, "Globalization and the Deformation of the Antiguan Working Class," paper presented at the University of the West Indies, Antigua and Barbuda Country Conference, November 13–15, 2003, http://www.open.uwi.edu/sites/default/files/bnccde/antigua/conference/papers/henry.html.

162. Norman Girvan, "Existential Threats in the Caribbean: Democratising Politics, Regionalising Governance," C. L. R. James Memorial Lecture, May 11, 2011, Oil Workers Trade Union, Cipriani College of Labour and Cooperative Studies, Valsayn, Trinidad and Tobago, p. 15.

163. Girvan, "Existential Threats in the Caribbean," 16, original italics.

164. Girvan, "Existential Threats in the Caribbean," 21. See pp. 16–21 for Girvan's elaboration on each of these effects of neoliberal globalization.

165. Girvan, "Existential Threats in the Caribbean," 25. Girvan specifically cites the question of climate change, which threatens a number of small island development states with actual extinction.

166. Girvan, "Existential Threats in the Caribbean," 24.

167. Michael Witter quoted in Tony Weis, "Agrarian Reform and Breadbasket Dependency in the Caribbean: Confronting Illusions of Inevitability," *Labour, Capital and Society* 36, no. 2 (November 2003): 174–99.

168. Gordon Rohlehr, "History as Absurdity," in *My Strangled City*, 17–51. At the time of Rohlehr's essay, Eric Williams was prime minister of Trinidad and Tobago. See especially here Gordon Rohlehr, "The Dilemma of the West Indian Academic in 1970" in *Power: The Black Power Revolution 1970, a Retrospective*, ed. Selwyn Ryan and Taimoon Stewart (St. Augustine, Trinidad and Tobago: Institute of Social and Economic Research, 1995), 381–402.

169. Rohlehr, "History as Absurdity," 18–19, 27, 30, my italics. I return to the question of black experience in chapter 5.

170. Rohlehr, "History as Absurdity," 32. For Rohlehr on this connection between Naipaul and Williams, see also pp. 31, 36–37, 46–48.

171. Rohlehr, "History as Absurdity," 33

172. Gordon Rohlehr, "History as Absurdity," in *Is Massa Day Dead?* ed. Orde Coombs (New York: Anchor Books, 1974), 69–108. For a contemporary critique of Williams's historiography, see Elsa Goveia, "New Shibboleths for Old," *New Beacon Reviews* 1 (1968): 48–54; and Wilson Harris, "History, Fable and Myth in the Caribbean and Guianas," in *Selected Essays of Wilson Harris: The Unfinished Genesis of the Imagination*, ed. Andrew Bundy (New York: Routledge, 1999), 152–66. Wilson Harris, in his shrewd analysis of the epistemological linkages between the historiography of anticolonial and imperial historians, declares that "such a dead-end of history in which 19th century imperialist and 20th century anti-imperialist come into agreement is material for a *theatre of the absurd*" (my italics).

173. Rohlehr, "History as Absurdity," 32.

174. Gordon Rohlehr, "The Culture of Williams: Context, Performance, Legacy," *Callaloo* 20, no. 4 (Fall 1997): 849–88.

175. Rohlehr, "Culture of Williams," 850. This critical turn is due in no small measure to Rohlehr's development during this time into the leading calypso critic in the postcolonial Caribbean.

176. Rohlehr, "Culture of Williams," 857. On the term "nation language," see Kamau Brathwaite, *History of the Voice: The Development of Nation Language in Anglophone Caribbean Poetry* (London: New Beacon Books, 1984).

177. Rohlehr, "Dilemma of the West Indian Academic," 393.

178. Rohlehr, "Culture of Williams," 866. On Lloyd Best's "doctor politics," see "West Indian Society 150 years after Abolishment: A Re-examination of Some Classical Theories," in *Out of Slavery: Abolishment and After*, ed. Jack Hayward (London: Frank Cass, 1985), 132–58.

179. Rohlehr, "Culture of Williams," 866.

180. Selwyn Ryan, *The Jihandi and the Cross: The Clash of Cultures in Post-Creole Trinidad and Tobago* (St. Augustine, Trinidad and Tobago: Institute of Social and Economic Studies, 1999).

181. Rohlehr, "Culture of Williams," 868.

182. Rohlehr, "Culture of Williams," 876

183. Stefano Harney, *Nationalism and Identity: Culture and the Imagination in a Caribbean Diaspora* (Kingston: University of the West Indies Press, 1996), 171.

3   Creole Discourse and Racism in the Caribbean

West Indian society is a veritable laboratory of racialism. We virtually invented racialism.

Walter Rodney, *The Groundings with My Brothers* (1969)[1]

Black people did not invent the legend of color, but only Black people can destroy it, Blacks being the only people who do not need it.

James Baldwin, *The Evidence of Things Not Seen* (1985)[2]

FASHIONED BY A modernity predicated on a coloniality that it was the first to experience in its ruthless totality, the Caribbean state has always been a racial state. The curiosity that the phrase "racial state" might create due to the culturalist turn of Caribbean scholarship in the last two decades is worth addressing via an elaboration of the uses of that term by one of its leading theoreticians. For David Goldberg, the "modern state, in short, is nothing less than a racial state."[3] While Goldberg argues that "there is no singular totalized phenomenon we can name the racial state; more precisely, there are racial states and racist states," his position on the pervasiveness of the racial state is clear:

> It must be insisted relatedly that the racial state is racial not *merely* or reductively because of the racial composition of its personnel or the racial implications of its policies—though clearly both play a part. States are racial more deeply because of the structural position they occupy in producing and reproducing, constituting and effecting racially shaped spaces and places, groups and events, life worlds and possibilities, accesses and restrictions, inclusions and exclusions, conceptions and modes of representation. They are *racial* in short, in virtue of their modes of population definition, determination, and structuration. And they are racist to the extent such definition, determination, and structuration operate to exclude or privilege in or on racial terms, and in so far as they circulate in and reproduce a world whose meanings and effects are racist. This is a world we might provocatively identify as a *racist world order.*[4]

The racial state has tremendous consequences for the nature of citizenship in the postcolonial state. In the postemancipation Anglophone Caribbean, as in other sites of colonial rule, a paternalistic "racial historicism" would be the main ideology used to consistently defer full citizenship rights to subjects of the British Empire.[5] In contemporary times, it is impossible to deny that the preponderance of the absurdities of postcolonial citizenship I have outlined in the last chapter show that Caribbean societies are still subject to a racial rule that is both material and epistemological. That this often frustrates and denies the lived reality of many Caribbean people should not be surprising, for as Goldberg points out, "racial rule by definition serves the interests of those conceived as white."[6]

That these understandings have been apparent to generations of thinkers and activists in the black radical tradition should be obvious. I began this chapter with two epigraphs that bear further scrutiny, as they exemplify well the argument of this chapter, perhaps not apparent to its end. Walter Rodney's depiction of the Caribbean as a "laboratory of racism" is an arresting phrase, apprehending so well the small size of Caribbean societies, the almost complete nature of their geographic colonization by European powers, and the experimentation that took place within them to create one of the most unjust forms of human oppression ever known—chattel slavery. Not only were slaves exported from the Caribbean elsewhere after an initial period of forced subjugation on the plantations but laws and techniques of control circulated outwards too, in a reversal of the way in which, in contemporary times, Western scientific procedures travel from European and American laboratories to the third world.[7] Modern racism is, for Rodney, a gift of the Caribbean to the world, though a present the majority of its inhabitants would doubtlessly not have wanted to confer on it.

James Baldwin provides a related and compelling meaning. *The Evidence of Things Not Seen* was Baldwin's last book, which he struggled to get published, before it finally appeared in print two years before his death. It is not difficult to see why despite his great accomplishments as a writer, Baldwin found it hard to secure a publisher. As his biographer James Campbell states, in it "the compact, epistolatory, intimately lyrical manner of the 1950s and early 1960s had deserted him for good, as a singer's voice will coarsen or a painter's style congeal."[8] In this wooden, sometimes nearly incoherent text, Baldwin is battling for fitness and form, nowhere near the fierce polemicist he was in the 1950s and '60s. His comment on the legacy of color and black people's relationship to it is, however, worthy of further consideration. Black people are the conscripts of one of modernity's greatest legacies, "race," of which they have been more savagely dehumanized than any other group of people.[9] This does not necessarily mean that they have an ethical requirement greater than any other group of humans to discredit it, but as they can never benefit from it, it may well be that only they can lead to its ultimate repudiation.

These comments by Rodney and Baldwin are arguably the product of a different times' engagement with race.[10] But their firm intent to highlight marginality and the existential plight of blackness and to theorize race *without forgetting about racism* is what I hope to keep in mind in this consideration of creole discourse, cultural theory, and existing racism in the postindependence Anglophone Caribbean. Approaches to questions of identity in the independent Caribbean took on a different meaning than in other parts of the newly emerging third world. The issue of "roots" and "origins" as one of the primary means to affirm cultural identity became complicated, since it is difficult to locate a Caribbean "origin" for the regions' people, with the genocide suffered by many of the indigenous people of the region and the transplanting of persons from all over the Old World to the Caribbean. Responses to this dilemma vary, with Kamau Brathwaite seeing one integral part of the Caribbean experience as being "its sense of rootlessness, of not belonging to the landscape; dissociation, in fact, of art from act of living." The problem for Caribbean intellectuals and artists for Brathwaite thus becomes the absence of a "sense of 'wholeness'."[11]

While this debate on roots has continued, with some like Antonio Benitez-Rojo taking a postmodern approach to refute the search for roots, debates about Anglophone Caribbean culture within the last thirty years have arguably centered on the concept of creolization and the unarguable mix of cultures that took place during the colonial period, creating a new, distinctively Caribbean culture.[12] Creolization, for a number of writers, represented a theoretical advance over previous understandings of Caribbean societies, which stressed their "plural" or "stratified" nature.[13] Both what we might term the "social stratification" and the "creolization" schools of thought have an intimate connection to debates about the anthropology of the African diaspora in the Western Hemisphere. As Kevin Yelvington has shown, the paradigmatic debate in this field has always been the contention between Melville J. Herskovitz and E. Franklin Frazier on the extent of African influence in the constitution of New World African-descent communities.[14] However, Yelvington also notes that a more thorough intellectual history of the African diasporic experience establishes the foundational role of scholars like W. E. B. Du Bois, St. Clair Drake, Zora Neale Hurston, Katherine Dunham, Jean Price-Mars, Arturo A. Schomburg, and Anténor Firmin as not only pioneers of this anthropological tradition but scholars a generation ahead of their time in their reflections on racialization, transnationalism, citizenship, and colonialism.[15] The Caribbean's location as a site that could not fit into the "savage slot" assigned to non-Western societies by Western anthropology, a region peculiarly modern but possessing a majority nonwhite population and thus "non-Western," meant that it has always been a location of interest for theories about cultural continuity and change in the Americas.[16]

Kamau Brathwaite's *The Development of Creole Society in Jamaica, 1770–1820* is widely acknowledged to have coined and deployed the term *creolization* as a theory of Caribbean culture, a concept he later developed in his text

Contradictory Omens: Cultural Diversity and Integration in the Caribbean.[17] I will return to Brathwaite's formulation of creolization shortly, but it is worth reflecting briefly on the sheer intransigence of a term that defies any easy definition. Those who have tried to track the term *creole* have uncovered evidence that it may be of Spanish, Portuguese, or African origin, and so it may not even have its "origins" in the New World.[18] Perhaps the most identifiable source of agreement among Caribbeanists who utilize the term *creole* may be "the importance of nativity within the concept," as *creole* suggests for most a local or native provenance within the Caribbean, as opposed to an extraregional or very recently arrived presence.[19] The question posed by Carolyn Allen—"How feasible is dialogue in the abstract when the concrete term itself is so unstable?"—is an apt warning to all those who would wish to secure too hasty a meaning of the concept of creolization or too quickly attribute an ideological position to its use. It is similarly worth noting that from its inception creolization was used both by radical cultural nationalists to stress the Africanity of Caribbean culture and by cultural conservatives who wished to suggest that Caribbean culture had arrived at a harmonious creolization of its constitutive elements. Power does not demand, nor need, a unified coherent idea of "race" or "culture" to justify oppression—though as Sylvia Wynter has noted, "to be effective, systems of power must be discursively legitimated."[20] Nor should we expect theories of culture like creolization that, as I will demonstrate, are often *premised* on the idea of race to show some specific ideological coherence.

A counterdiscourse to postindependence elite representations of a harmoniously creolized society can be seen in a scholarly tradition that emphasized the nature of the discursive space occupied by Africa within creolization and was articulated in the early 1970s by Elsa Goveia, Rex Nettleford, and Sylvia Wynter. In her essay "The Social Framework," Goveia acknowledged the sole integrating factor within West Indian society as "the acceptance of the inferiority of Negroes to whites." Wynter targeted the concept of creolization directly as a "fraudulent multiculturalism," and Nettleford acknowledged that "the mixture (of European and African cultures) has produced a Creole culture in which European and African elements persist and predominate in fairly standard combinations and relationships with things European gaining ascriptive status while things African were correspondingly devalued, including African racial traits."[21] All of these interventions point not just to the tensions inherent in conservative, nationalist, and radical discourses on culture but to something else, too often unremarked within contemporary debates about creolization and culture—namely, actually existing racism in the Caribbean.[22]

Most contemporary studies of race in the Caribbean have been silent on the question of the contribution of critical race theory to our understandings of the conceptual category of race.[23] It is my position that discourses of creole, while ostensibly discourses about culture and society, are also very prominently discourses of race, raising the thorny question of the potential complicity of discourses of creoleness with the idea of race.[24] Reading creolization with the recent work on critical race theory in mind need not quite equate discourses of creoleness with racism; rather, it attempts to show the ways in which creole theorists may well be complicit with racial understandings they might otherwise disavow. Thinking of the "creole project" in the light of recent critical race theory also has the potential to further problematize its conceptual limitations and delineate how it has been mobilized as a paradigm of both conservative antiblack cultural nationalism and revolutionary anticolonial nationalism. The aim of this chapter is to reflect on the wider arguments made by creole cultural theorists and thus attempt to apprehend the nature of creolization as a discourse on Caribbean culture. I will draw on recent articulations of the ambiguities of the creole project from Kathleen Balutansky and Marie-Agnes Sourieau's *Caribbean Creolization*, Verene Shepherd and Glen Richards's *Questioning Creole: Discourses in Caribbean Culture*, and the work of the Martinican créolistes. I also utilize principally the work of Frantz Fanon, Percy Hintzen, Aisha Khan, and Lewis Gordon to consider the following questions: In what ways might the idea of creolization continue to reinscribe racism in the Caribbean? How can creole discourse, predicated on an understanding of the legitimacy of the category of "race," contribute to dismantling racism, especially when we consider that nationalism is often in its essence a discourse of race and Caribbean creole nationalism has been perfectly compatible with elite domination?[25] Are theorists involved who utilize creole models unwittingly prey to the "complicity of culture" with racist discourses, as examined by Robert Young in *Colonial Desire*?[26] In what manner does creolization replicate fashionable understandings of "mixed-race" identities as seen in the work of Naomi Zack and as has been criticized by Lewis Gordon?[27]

This reading of creolization has similarities to Ann Stoler's challenge to racial historians and critical race theorists in her essay "Racial Histories and Their Regimes of Truth."[28] In this essay, Stoler mounts a bold challenge to contemporary work on race, highlighted in her question "are these anti-racist histories so much a part and product of racial discourse that they are, despite intention, subject to its regimes of truth?"[29] The debate about the dilemmas and pitfalls of using the category of race to theorize racism and point to alternative forms of black subjectivity has a long history, with one of its most famous interventions coming in the questions put by Jean-Paul Sartre and Frantz Fanon to *négritude*.[30] Stoler's methodology is explicitly Foucauldian, which she uses to signal her lack of interest in the quest for an "origin" of race or racism and to clarify what she believes are the erroneous uses of the term *discourse* in current scholarship. The following definition of racial discourse is offered: "a discourse is racial not because it displays shared political interests but rather because it delineates a field and set of conditions in which it becomes impossible to talk about sexuality, class membership, morality, and childbearing without talking about race."[31] Postcolonial critiques that stress the fluidity of racial categories may not be as insightful or counterhegemonic as they seem, as one of the features of racial discourse is that it "combines notions of fixity and fluidity in ways that are basic to its dynamic."[32] Stoler addresses the guileful nature of racial discourse and its use by different political agendas in the following comment: "For if Foucault is right that one of the defining features of racism is its 'polyvalent mobility,' that it may vacillate and be embraced by those opposed to and beleaguered by the state at one moment and become an integral part of the technologies of state rule at another, then the fact that racial discourses contain and coexist with a range of political agendas is not a contradiction but a fundamental historical feature of their *non-linear, spiraling* political genealogies."[33]

It should be apparent that Stoler's understanding of "racial discourse" is fundamentally relevant to contemporary Caribbean societies, and indeed it is difficult to imagine any New World societies whose contemporary social and political contexts are not predicated on racialized discourses. Turning to creolization with Stoler's arguments in mind, we might examine the following comment by Brinda Mehta and Paget Henry from the editorial introduction to a special issue of the *C. L. R. James Journal* with different eyes: "Common to all of the papers is the difficult tension between processes of hybridization and creolization on the one hand, and the persistence of strong attachments to purist conceptions of race and ethnicity on the other."[34]

My suggestion is that this dichotomy of hybridization/creolization versus pure conceptions of race/ethnicity can only appear true if it is believed that concepts of hybridity and creolization are devoid of a deep, ongoing entanglement with understandings of race. In part, my concern here is the work that creolization as a cultural and social theory is asked to perform within discourses of Caribbean nation building. What deeper interrogation of racist culture in the Caribbean may its use obscure, particularly when that use is celebratory or is too easily suggested to be an advance on prior notions of race and culture? In what ways may it represent a retreat from the candor of the analysis of Caribbean racism proffered in the past by revolutionary scholars like Walter Rodney?

Kamau Brathwaite and Creolization

> the idea is to try to see the fragments/whole . . .
>
> Kamau Brathwaite, *Contradictory Omens* (1974)[35]

Creolization is often presented as a theory with hemispheric resonance, providing a theoretical model for explaining every form of cultural mixing that has taken place in the New World; and now that the term has been globalized in what Mimi Sheller has called a "theoretical piracy on the high seas," the whole world appears seduced by the term.[36] Given the multiple and contradictory uses to which the term has been applied, it is worthwhile to return to its generally accepted first systematic elaboration as a term denoting a cultural theory in the Anglophone Caribbean, since this articulation is still one of the most complex and thoroughgoing applications of it as theory.[37] Kamau Brathwaite's *The Development of Creole Society in Jamaica, 1770–1820* is widely recognized as an inaugural moment in discussions of creolization as a cultural theory in the Caribbean.[38] I would suggest that its value today is further enhanced by the fact that Brathwaite's theory of creolization anticipates many of the contradictions that continue to bedevil the term and its use. Brathwaite defines creolization as "a cultural process that took place within a creole society—that is, within a tropical colonial plantation polity based on slavery" and further as "a cultural action—material, psychological and spiritual—based upon the stimulus/response of individuals within the society to their environment and—as white/black, culturally discrete groups—to each other."[39] No one description can adequately summarize Brathwaite's theory of creolization, and an examination of two of his 1970s texts, *Contradictory Omens* and "Caribbean Man in Space and Time," adds important additional complexities to this initial definition. Brathwaite's expressed ideas about creolization are always somewhat unfinished and speculative in nature, in keeping with his understanding that it results not in a "finished type" but is "a process, resulting in subtle and multiform orientations from or *twoards* ancestral originals."[40] Creolization "rounds the sharp edges off the dichotomy" of an original clash of African and European cultures, which resulted in a friction that "was cruel, but . . . also creative."[41]

The complexity of the different processes that Brathwaite tries to harness under the term creolization is well seen in his full-length treatment of the concept, *Contradictory Omens: Cultural Diversity and Integration in the Caribbean*. New terms are introduced, including intercreolization, selective creolization, lateral creolization, and incomplete creolization, while creolization is further elaborated to be "a specialized version of the two widely accepted terms acculturation and interculturation, the former referring . . . to the process of absorption of one culture by another; the later to a more reciprocal activity, a process of intermixture and enrichment."[42] Brathwaite contests Sylvia Wynter's claim that creolization amounts to assimilation while indigenization signifies resistance by signaling the extent to which his understanding of creolization (and Caribbean culture) is "both imitation (acculturation) and native creation ('indigenization')."[43] Creolization as a cultural concept simply does *not* exist outside the categories of force, theft, subversion, and abduction in both its conservative and liberatory potentials. Nor, despite its lived reality, is it truly hegemonic—it has become "the tentative cultural norm of the society," but "this norm, because of the complex historical factors involved in making it . . . is not whole or hard . . . but cracked, fragmented, ambivalent, not certain of itself."[44] As a process it is a "slow, uncertain but organic progress (from imitation/initiation to invention) evolving into ac/act/accent, style and *possibility*."[45] There are certainly a number of theoretical dilemmas posed by Brathwaite's terminology here; however, I will concentrate on four aspects of his contribution to discourses of creolization—the idea of racial mixture and creolization, the space the colored middle classes occupy within creolization, the East Indian population of the Caribbean, and the vision of creolization.

While discussing the genesis of creolization in eighteenth-century plantation society, Brathwaite makes the following comment: "But it was in the intimate area of sexual relationships that the greatest damage was done to white creole apartheid policy and where the most *significant*—and *lasting*—inter-cultural creolization took place."[46] If creolization is truly a theory of "cultural mixing" and not "racial mixing" what are we to make of this sentence?[47] The mixed class produced here apparently "acted as a bridge, a kind of social cement," which facilitates the further development and transformation of creole culture.[48] Brathwaite is hardly unaware of the color hierarchy of colonial society, the "mimic men" it produced, and the relationship between class and color divisions in the colonial Caribbean—a region where one can have "a white *or* black mulatto."[49] He could thus describe the "educated middle classes" as the "most finished product of unfinished creolization," an apt description of the ascriptive value of whiteness in their lives.[50] This genre of creolization Brathwaite would disavow, as it produces a mimicry with little subversive potential. In short, the "finished" appearance of the middle classes is deceptive, and is produced by the coloniality of the society, a coloniality that limits its ability to reach "finished creolization."

The questions raised by the gendered nature of Brathwaite's argument deserve further exploration. Creolization emerges here as a theory of the (re)production of society. Brathwaite's comment that "it was in the intimate area of sexual relationships that the greatest damage was done to white creole apartheid policy and where the most significant—and lasting—inter-cultural creolization took place" has been justly criticized by Nigel Bolland, who notes that these "relationships" were rooted in the sexual exploitation of the bodies of enslaved or putatively "free" black women.[51] A contemporary Caribbean example also shows the difficulties that these formulations of cultural mixing pose for women. In the case of Trinidad and Tobago, the research of Rhoda Reddock has shown that in the process of douglarization, Indo-Caribbean women are consistently seen as "race traitors" by Indo-Caribbean men for having interracial intimate relationships.[52] The control of women's sexuality is certainly a common thread of patriarchy, but in racially stratified societies the double standards and violence that Indo-Caribbean women sometimes face for engaging in these relationships should raise questions about both creolization and gender *and* the gendered nature of theories of creolization.

The problem of difference in Anglophone Caribbean theories of creolization is often best seen in the uncertain relationship that Indo-Caribbean people have to notions of creolization. Brathwaite's original articulation of creolization was based on a study of Jamaican society, and his uncertain comments about East Indians show his struggle to incorporate cultural difference beyond the European-African divide.[53] In *Contradictory Omens*, he returns to this problematic in a passage that seeks to think through ideas of cultural difference in the contemporary Caribbean: "The wholeness of the society therefore . . . now depends not only upon our original 'mulatto' capability . . . but on the response of the 'new' groups to this, and this to them. It will depend too on the kind of influence their ancestral cultures can and wish to exert; on their response to this influence; and their response, too, to the existing submerged mother of the creole system, Africa.[54]

The figuring of Africa in the Caribbean here is similar to Antonio Benitez-Rojo's formulation in his theory of the repeating island: "formal models come mainly from African cultures, which is not to exclude Asian, Indoamerican and European presences. But if the structure of the myth is African, its theme is unquestionably Caribbean."[55] Nevertheless, Brathwaite's model still positions Indo-Caribbeans as relative newcomers to the Caribbean. Aisha Khan thus can legitimately aver that "because his theory's historical context is slavery, Brathwaite's creole society rests on a black/white axis, where the message of loss is still resonant, and where nonblacks/nonwhites, although acknowledged, remain interlopers."[56]

Much mischief has been made of "African primacy" in the Caribbean by certain postcolonial governments, and it bears stating that Brathwaite, despite the difficulties inherent in his cultural theory, has no patience with those forms of vulgar cultural nationalism.[57] Nor does Brathwaite ever reduce creolization to an assimilative ethos largely at ease with the hegemonic sociocultural status quo. Brathwaite wants the "little tradition" of the Afro-creole masses to gain legitimacy and in turn become a "great tradition"—not to replace one hegemonic narrative with another but to "support the development of a new parochial wholeness, a difficult but possible creole authenticity."[58] The central problem here is that "because of its history . . . Afro-Caribbean culture has remained largely invisible within the region, and the representatives of this culture, though in a majority throughout most of the area, are treated (and *behave*) like a minority."[59] This is not an issue of what today is dismissed as "identity politics." In his ruminations on democracy, representation, and minority rights, all under the framework of a still ongoing attempt to think about creole culture, Brathwaite states that "we are faced . . . with a problem in *political philosophy*."[60] Here again, the cultural and the political in Caribbean thought are inseparable from each other. Brathwaite's creolizing vision causes him to lament that "we remain part creole, part coloni-al, seeking many-ancestoried conclusions."[61] This statement is, in part, an apt consideration of the lack of value placed in Caribbean society on autochthonous Caribbean culture, of the inability to think about the Caribbean through the framework of its own rationalities, and is an intervention very much of its time, the 1970s.[62] This formulation of creole versus colonial, however, while expressing Brathwaite's yearning for a different society, suggests that creole is *not* colonial and minimizes the *coloniality* of creole formulations.[63]

Creole, Créolité, Critique?

The difficulties involved in theorizing creolization in the midst of coloniality are far more pronounced in the position on creoleness advocated by the Martinican créolistes, Patrick Chamoiseau, Raphaël Confiant, and Jean Bernabé. Authors of the infamous "Éloge de la créolité" (In praise of Creoleness), they consider themselves to be at the vanguard of a renascent cultural project in the French Caribbean that specifically privileges "creole" as the defining linguistic and cul-tural reality of the Antilles.[64] Créolité as a concept has been influential far beyond Martinique, and its framing of creole culture has had a global influence on dis-cussions of creoleness.[65] Debates on créolité have also been extraordinarily con-troversial and have led to several criticisms of the movement and to a number of book-length collections of essays, both critical and celebratory.[66] My aim here is not to provide a detailed tracing of these controversies but to briefly discuss them and a selection of the créolistes' work in order to highlight the problems posed by theories of creolization, its relationship to elite domination, and the problem of race and racism in the Caribbean.[67]

As I mentioned previously, the major theoretical statement by the créolistes is the "Éloge de la créolité," published in 1989 by Jean Bernabé, Patrick Chamoi-seau, and Raphaël Confiant.[68] In this daring essay, a manifesto for a creole cul-ture is presented through a reading of the terrain of Antillean intellectual history and cultural memory. Creoleness is defined as "the interactional or transactional aggregate of Caribbean, European, African, Asian, and Levantine cultural ele-ments, united on the same soil by the yoke of history."[69] As a concept, it is dis-tinct from "Americanness" or "Caribbeanness." Americanness describes cultures in the New World that, because of historical circumstances, exist in "splendid isolation" from other cultures within them.[70] Here the créolistes cite "the native redskins" of North America, "the Boni and Saramak blacks of Guyana," the nineteenth-century Italian immigrants to Argentina, and "the Hindus ... of Trini-dad" as examples of Americanization.[71] Caribbeanness is a "geopolitical concept" and is "the only process of Americanization of Europeans, Africans, and Asians in the Caribbean archipelago."[72] This formulation is followed by an acknowledg-ment that there existed "in certain islands ... more than mere Americanization, a phenomenon of Creolization (and therefore Creoleness)."[73] The phenomenon of cultural mixing and interaction appears to be, for the créolistes, more pronounced in the Creolephone/Francophone Caribbean than in its Anglophone or Hispanophone counterparts. The créolistes thus conclude that

> the word "Caribbean" says nothing of the human situation of Martinicans, Guadeloupeans, or Haitians. As Creoles, we are as close, if not closer, anthropologically speaking, to the people of the Seychelles, of Mauricius, or the Réunion, than we are to the Puerto Ricans or the Cubans . . . We the Caribbean Creoles, enjoy, therefore, a double solidarity:
> - *a Caribbean solidarity (geopolitical) with all the peoples of our Archipelago regardless of our cultural differences—our Caribbeanness; and*
> - *a Creole solidarity with all African, Mascarin, Asian, and Polynesian peoples who share the same anthropological affinities as we do—our Creoleness.*[74]

There is a lot that can be unpacked here regarding the créolistes' reading of Caribbean history, privileging of the anthropological as a guarantee of cultural authority, and belief in the ability of language to create intimacy between distant populations. Two issues appear of critical importance here and in the rest of the "Éloge": the central role of language in discourses of créolité and the contradictory affirmations and disavowals of universalism. For the créolistes, "Creoleness is not monolingual. . . . Its field is language. Its appetite: all the languages of the world."[75] Yet creoleness's appetite for language seems strangely attenuated in the Anglophone and Hispanophone Caribbean compared to the apparently more resonantly Francophone/Creolephone world. Though "Creoleness is an annihilation of false universality, of monolingualism, and of purity," its relationship to the universal is more complex than that.[76] While "Creole literature will have nothing to do with the Universal," it is clear that "the world is evolving into a state of Creoleness."[77] The key here is understanding the relationship of creoleness to diversity in the world today; as "our primary diversity will be part of an integrating process of world diversity, recognized and accepted as permanent, our Creoleness will have to recover itself, structure itself, and preserve itself, while changing and absorbing. *It will have to survive in Diversity.*"[78]

It is difficult not to be sympathetic to the dilemma faced by the créolistes in a Martinique that seventy years after departmentalization and a generation after decentralization continues to show a steady recolonization by French and Eurozone capital. It is similarly hard to deny that négritude, subjected to rigorous and legitimate critique, simply does not have the critical counterhegemonic force it once possessed in the 1940s. Négritude's institutionalization by Aimé Césaire, with little corresponding change in patterns of cultural and economic recolonization, is also hardly likely to appease cultural activists convinced that a permanent loss of their cultural traditions may take place in the near future.[79]

Nevertheless, créolité itself has elicited considerable controversy, and it is worth considering the array of arguments that have been mobilized in criticism of the créolistes.[80] Many acknowledge the brilliance of the novels of Chamoiseau and Confiant, and there is also little doubt that their assertive attempts to valorize the legitimacy of creole culture since the 1970s have been met with some appreciation by their critics.[81] However, a number of questions have been raised about "the stakes of créolité."[82] Maryse Condé acknowledges the talent of the créolistes but criticizes their lack of innovation outside the realm of language and particularly their conservatism with respect to sexuality. For Condé, sexuality in the work of the créolistes is forever configured through a relentlessly male gaze, and female characters' roles are reduced to the "stereotypical or negative."[83] Even the "sumptuous invention of a language" we see in the créolistes does not truly add anything new, as their polemical arguments merely distort and polarize the terms of a very complicated argument about language, the postcolonial writer, and notions of cultural authority.[84] Créolité "presumes to impose law and order" and is, among theories of cultural mixing, "alone in reducing the overall expression of creoleness to the creole language," the sign of a "terrorizing" turn to authenticity that Condé would disavow. The créolistes, then, "have not yet extricated themselves from . . . the binary opposition of colonizer and colonized."[85] In his critique, cultural critic A. James Arnold targets the masculinist culture of the créolité movement and its marginalization of women writers, a view shared by Richard and Sally Price, as well as by Condé.[86] The minimal role ascribed to women in the créolistes interpretation of Martinican social history and their privileging of the male figure of the *conteur* is for Arnold not only ahistorical but symptomatic of a heteronormative, masculine gaze still wedded to colonial gender categories. The contrast with Francophone Caribbean women writers is noteworthy, as they avoid the seduction of a "grand theory" in their work—the theory is the literature itself—and they do not fetishize the creole language in the manner of the créolistes. These musings on the cultural politics of the créolistes leads Arnold to declare that his "hypothesis is that in the minds of the créolistes cultural production is a masculine activity."[87]

In one of the most comprehensive appraisals of the créolistes to date, the anthropologists Richard and Sally Price have provided a devastating interrogation of the historical bases of the créolistes claims about creole culture. The créolistes stand accused of inventing Old World homogeneity in order to facilitate their theories of New World diversity. The selectivity of who counts as "creole" means that Indo-Trinidadians adapted without creolizing, as apparently did maroons. Price and Price argue that "by understating the tremendous diversity of African cultures and languages represented in any early Caribbean colony . . . the créolistes obscure the ways in which these maroon communities were, in fact, the most thoroughly (and earliest fully) 'creolized' of *all* New World Communities."[88]

The arguments of the créolistes show little knowledge of the considerable debates about and work on creolization in the other linguistic spheres of the region, not completely surprising when one considers the linguistic nationalism of their claims, which perceives Antilleans as having more in common with the inhabitants of Réunion, Mauritius, or Seychelles than Puerto Ricans or Cubans.[89] There is a real question about the place of diaspora—whether a Caribbean diaspora or an African diaspora—in the thought of the créolistes, with their resolute emphasis on local invention divorced from larger diasporic trends, causalities, and relationships.[90] Nor can the créolistes even hold the status of "cultural rebels" without contest. Rather, for the Prices, they "fit comfortably within . . . [a] historical moment" in Martinique that is "profoundly assimilationist in spirit" and gives space to particular cultural productions that can be read less as honouring the past than validating a "museumified Martinique."[91]

A turn to the words of the créolistes themselves, in two lengthy interviews and an essay by Ernest Pépin and Raphaël Confiant, sadly does not diminish the force of these criticisms but rather illuminates even more the tension between the créolistes vision of creoleness and their rather narrow view of the world. Of particular interest here is the lengthy interview done by Lucien Taylor in the journal *Transition*, given the fitting title "Créolité Bites."[92] One of the most noteworthy points in this interview comes when Lucien Taylor presses the créolistes on their understanding of creolization and demolishes the anthropological bases of the créolistes argument by showing how "invented" their idea of what constitutes a creole society is when one considers the potential for making similar comments about African societies.[93] The créolistes response to this critique is notable for the understanding of modernity and globalization that they mobilize in order to defend their vision of creoleness. In a remarkably uncritical celebration of globalization, the créolistes suggest that the new world order "operates without armies, gulags, or dungeons"—apparently unaware of the global prison-industrial complex or Euro-American military rule of the world—and although referring to Western technological imperialism as a "furtive domination," propose that "we absorb them in the name of modernity, liberty, and progress."[94] In a comment that flirts with the rhetoric of neoliberal globalization, Chamoiseau says it is "easier to be Antillean or Breton or black in a world that is linked up than it was in the old shackles of nation-states" and that "all the Americas are places of creolization—as, increasingly, are all the big Western megapoles."[95] One wonders how many times political economists and activists will have to note that in today's globalized global economy capital is mobile but labor is not, the gap between rich and poor on a worldwide basis is wider than ever before, and more people live in a state of misery than at any other time in human history. Chamoiseau also further inflates the term creolization to encompass anything or everyone in the Americas, giving rise to the questions, if everything is in a state of creolization, why is there a need for the Francophone-creole linguistic vanguardism that the créolistes so obviously promote, and what work can such a global theory perform in explaining local culture?[96] With charming condescension, Chamoiseau declares African literature to be "a little sorry for itself nowadays," apparently because it "is having problems coming to terms with the immense mutations of the world and the tremendous phenomena of creolization."[97] One wonders how this headstrong desire to make Africa occupy the space of a static, unchanging, monolithic, culturally bereft tradition escapes the charge that it constitutes antiblack racism.[98] It is fascinating to observe how dependent the créolistes' formulations are on an uncritical formulation of tradition and modernity, with a cast occupying identical discursive spaces as those under formal colonialism. The modern world is the capitalist West, a potential colonizing force but one whose material bases of oppression need not be considered seriously, for as Chamoiseau puts it, "the battle against oppression and domination has moved into the realm of the *imaginary* . . . The risk in today's world is of *homogenization*."[99]

Despite the forthrightness of the créolistes' claims to marginality and their immodest positioning of themselves at the vanguard of cultural freedom against metropolitan cultural domination, a strange conservatism presents itself when the issue of political "independence" for the Francophone Caribbean departments is raised. Independence would be "suicidal," as departmental status has rendered Martinicans "irresponsible," and a "period of apprenticeship" would be needed, as Confiant has said in another interview, "an indeterminately long transition period."[100] Great care must be taken—otherwise, "we would sink into a state of misery, like other Caribbean nations"; in fact "without some . . . intermediary period, we'd end up like black African countries that won independence in the 1960s. They weren't ready for it, and now they are plunged into chaos."[101] The sum of all fears would be the following scenario: "if we were granted independence overnight, we'd become like Congo or Chad . . . or Haiti. It would be catastrophic."[102] Given their emphasis on linguistic sovereignty, it is fascinating that the language of neocolonialism is an unknown tongue to the créolistes. They can then defend their novels against charges of sexism and homophobia on the grounds that their critics are attempting to impose Western gender norms on them, ignoring the colonial basis of the very homophobia and sexism they articulate.[103] Creole culture is apparently *not* colonial and in need of reassessment. Creolization demands contact with Europe and North America for the créolistes, both in its formative (the emergence of creole from plantation society) and in its contemporary (creole culture in the age of globalization) manifestations, but with little critique of the racial contract that is being signed for their version of multiculturalism.[104]

There is something deeply ironic about the sociocultural theories of the créolistes, theories that are too often grim reminders of the omnipresence of race and color in Caribbean life and cultural theory. In elucidating his idea of chabinité (a mixed-race theory if there ever was one!), Raphaël Confiant tries to enlist Malcolm X as an illustrious example of his theory![105] One wonders what Confiant would make of Malcolm X's comment that "I was among the millions of Negroes who were insane enough to feel that it was some kind of status symbol to be light-complexioned. . . . But, still later, I learned to hate every drop of that white rapist's blood that is in me."[106] Or closer to the Creolephone/Francophone Caribbean, Condé's comment that "there is nothing West Indian society hates more than facing the reality of colour prejudice which reminds it of the days of slavery, of the time when to be black was a curse and to possess a fair skin was regarded as a blessing."[107] According to Confiant, "our present . . . isn't tragic like Rwanda's or Haiti's—no one is dying of hunger in Martinique. Nor is our situation pathetic or dramatic. It is rather comic and absurd."[108] The comment is an even more appropriate description of the theory he has helped to construct than of Martinique. His theoretical abstractions away from the realities of racism, class oppression, and human suffering and the continual means by which créolité shifts from being a theory of cultural mixing to racial mixture and back again are symptomatic of the problems of créolité as a cultural theory.

Creole, Douglarization, and Caribbean (Post)Colonial Desire

I have earlier stated that discourses of creole, while discourses of culture, are also very evidently discourses of race. The idea behind this statement comes in part from Robert Young's *Colonial Desire: Hybridity in Theory, Culture and Race*.[109] *Colonial Desire*'s contribution to postcolonial theory was its illustration of the way in which understandings of culture and race (mediated through language) are premised on sex and desire, an extension of a line of argument classically developed in Fanon's *Black Skin, White Masks*. In a passage linking these concepts, Young notes, "The historical links between language and sex were, however, fundamental. Both produced what were regarded as 'hybrid' forms (creole, pidgin and miscegenated children), which were seen to embody threatening forms of perversion and degeneration and became the basis for endless metaphoric extension in the racial discourse of social commentary."[110]

The idea of "mixed race" is linked to the notion of "hybridity," and Young again notes the difficulty of establishing any precise definition of this term.[111] In a discussion of black British cultural politics' use of a term as ambiguous and loaded with racialized and colonialist understandings as "hybridity," Young makes the following observation: "The identification here of hybridity with carnivalization and creolization as a means towards a critical contestation of a dominant culture suggests that the threat of degeneration and decay incipient upon a 'raceless chaos' has been not yet . . . fully redeployed and reinflected. Hybridization as creolization involves fusion, the creation of a new form, which can then be set against the old form, of which it is partly made up. Hybridization as 'raceless chaos' by contrast, produces no stable new form but . . . a radical heterogeneity, discontinuity, the permanent revolution of forms."[112]

I interpret Young's passage as an acute warning of the dangers of the terms *hybridization* and *creolization*, which can become divorced from their potential for progressive change and instead merely reinscribe past relationships of domination and false racial categories. Despite Stuart Hall's apparent scorn for Young's questioning of contemporary cultural theory's return to notions of hybridity, in which he refers to "the inexplicably simplistic charge in Robert Young's *Colonial Desire* (1995) that the post-colonial critics are 'complicit' with Victorian racial theory *because both sets of writers deploy the same term—hybridity—in their discourse!*" there are questions to be asked about the easy redeployment of as troubled a term as "hybridity."[113] As Aisha Khan has noted, "whether or not creolization is akin to hybridity depends on the political project that the concepts serve; and that theoretical concepts serve certain ends is not nullified by making them increasingly abstract or encompassing."[114] Considering discourses on creole at this point, one might note that debates about creole are usually couched in terms of language and culture, while ignoring the vital question of sexual relations. This circuitous avoidance of sex hides the crucial issue of desire and masks the reasons why mixed-race bodies are often privileged and sought after in the Caribbean.[115] It also masks one's ability to see creoleness as in part a "mixed-race" ideology—and vulnerable to the same critiques.

The work of the Africana philosopher Lewis Gordon bears some scrutiny here. In his essay "Race, Biraciality, and Mixed Race in Theory," Gordon addresses the complex issue of mixed-race relationships in the United States and the possibilities of a critical mixed-race theory.[116] Critical mixed-race theory is considered to be mired in bad faith, as it elides the central question of the status of black humanity in its considerations of mixed-race identity. In contemporary times, many black people are not trying to be white or "pass for being white, but instead to pass for being *mixed*."[117] The irony of this is that black populations in the Americas are "mixed" populations anyway (something that escapes many mixed-race theorists) and, more deeply, illustrates that today "one is more of a human being to the extent to which one is less black."[118] Certain varieties of "antirace" theory, particularly those tied to notions that "mixed-race constructions" deconstruct hegemonic "pure" identities possess their own flaws:

> The antirace people therefore miss the point. Even if they show that race is a social construction, even if they show that races are no more than cultural or social formations, even if they show that races are pseudoscientific fictions, they still need to address the ways in which phenomena understood as racial phenomena are lived. Not all black people know what races are, but they know what hatred of black people is. They read it in the symbols of value and the

objective sites of power and lack thereof in which they are immersed in their waking moments, and even in their dreams.[119]

Gordon's understanding of the lack of value of blackness is (Western) hemispheric in its reach and global when one considers this blackness as the condition of Fanon's condemned of the earth and a consequence of global white supremacy.[120] Theories of creolization, mixed-race identity, and hybridity risk either a facile and ultimately conservative liberalism or risk replicating colonial social and color hierarchies, in which "whites function as normative standpoints of humanity."[121]

The Caribbean's contemporary obsession with mixedness as the epitome of aesthetic beauty has a widely acknowledged long history dating back to slavery. The antiblackness at the center of this is constantly occluded in a region in which the manifestos of nationalism, as Shalini Puri has shown, are proclamations of multicultural desire.[122] This flight from blackness is predicated on an unsavory racism that is acknowledged and known, with studies ranging from Lloyd Braithwaite's influential 1953 study *Social Stratification in Trinidad* to the present day of this phenomena. Yet surprise and consternation is the popular response when practices like skin bleaching are publicized, as if the presence of a social hierarchy predicated on skin color has not been a constituent part of Caribbean social formations for centuries.[123] The recent scholarship of Jemima Pierre on skin bleaching in Ghana and the social and labor market benefits of having light skin points to a too-often unacknowledged truth: that "within the context of global White supremacy, Whiteness/lightness—in terms of its symbolism, corporeal representation, and material benefits—is desired by most, including those who already have membership within racial Whiteness."[124] The young black woman who in protest and resignation at the color-caste complex of employment in mid-twentieth-century Trinidad sighs, "To relieve me of the grief of being a negro," would find common ground with her sistren in both Ghana and Jamaica at the turn of the millennium.[125] It is only by a combination of a historical amnesia about their own societies, coupled with an ignorance—or investment—in the hemispheric and global significance of white supremacy, that Caribbean publics can fête mixed bodies while abhorring dark-skinned blackness.

A discussion of the discourse on a "dougla aesthetic" in Trinidad is necessary here. The term *dougla*, as commonly used in Trinidad and Guyana, denotes a person born as a result of a union between an African and an Indian parent. The term has its origins in Hindu culture, and Rhoda Reddock's research has suggested that *dougla* refers "in the first instance—to 'progeny of inter-varna marriage,' acquiring the connotation of 'bastard,' meaning illegitimate/son of a prostitute, only in a secondary sense."[126] While interracial relationships have certainly been extant between Indians and blacks since indentureship, Reddock notes that "the term 'douglarization' emerged in the 1980s among mainly Indian politicians and cultural leaders."[127] In her book *The Caribbean Postcolonial: Social Equality, Post-Nationalism, and Cultural Hybridity*, Shalini Puri undertakes a complex and nuanced discussion of the ways in which the idea of hybridity has been a constant factor in discourses of Caribbean culture *and* Caribbean nationalism.[128] Early in her text, Puri states that "at the core of my work is the belief that we need to connect a poetics of hybridity to a politics of equality."[129] Puri certainly discerns that hybridity can be both conservative and progressive and an idea that was a "narrative resource of racism" in the past.[130] Hybridity's conception in sin does not invalidate it; rather, it provides a "malleability that . . . should preclude absolutist endorsements or condemnations of the term," which combined with a "conjunctural approach" might allow one to imagine new possibilities while firmly holding in mind past legacies.[131]

One of Puri's primary sites of investigation of Caribbean hybridities is the notion of the dougla in Trinidad. Puri cites a number of texts that she suggests might constitute "a minor history in which the figure of the dougla has served as a means to rethink cultural hybridity in relation to projects of political equality and critiques of racialized national-bourgeoisies."[132] The very "anxieties" surrounding the dougla in racially stratified societies might be translated into a different, more progressive condition, as it may provide a "disruption of the notions of racial purity upon which racial stereotypes depend."[133] A strong caveat is added: "I am emphatically not suggesting a dougla poetics as somehow paradigmatic of postcolonial, West Indian, or even Trinidadian aesthetics . . . rather I am making a conjunctural—and conjuncturally circumscribed—claim about the possibilities of a dougla poetics in Trinidad today."[134] However, note these three passages:

> I have been suggesting that the very anxiety surrounding the figure of the dougla is a measure of its radical possibilities. If creolization as a figure for hybridity has exhausted its radicalism in contemporary Trinidad (leading some to refer ironically to "Afro-Saxon" culture), now serving status quoist class agendas and perhaps racially exclusive ones, and if, as Aisha Khan's work suggests, the fluid hybridity designated "Spanish" is non-threatening in part because it functions as a euphemism for more conflictual identities, then a dougla hybridity might offer some useful alternatives.[135]
>
> I suggest that the figure of the dougla and a dougla poetics could provide a vocabulary for disallowed, delegitimized racial identities; furthermore, they could offer ways—and have offered ways—of reframing the problematic of black-Indian party politics as well as race, gender, and sexual relations.[136]
>
> What distinguishes a dougla hybridity at this conjuncture from liberal multiculturalist tropes of hybridity such as callaloo, "Spanish," and, arguably, Creole, is the ability of the term to place cultural hybridity in relation to

equality, and the potential of a dougla poetics to unmask power and symboli-
cally redraw its lines. A dougla poetics thus offers a vocabulary for a political
identity, not a primarily biological one.[137]

It is not difficult to understand the appeal of a theory that seeks to achieve
some resolution to the persistent "battle for space" between African and Indian
identities in the contemporary Caribbean.[138] There is a sense of complete weari-
ness among many Caribbean commentators on the ethnic competition that continues to bedevil Trinidad and Tobago and Guyana.[139] Trinidad's oil wealth and
the resulting political largesse the state has been able to dispense have meant a
continual deferral of their social crisis, while in Guyana each election brings the
threat of ethnically motivated political violence. However, one can only ponder
how the very embodiment of the dougla is supposed to perform such powerful
antiracist work, without any more searching forms of antiracist activism. The
national imaginary of the Trinidadian nation was constructed around an understanding of Afro-creole culture that left a legacy not merely *discursive* but with
deep material significance, particularly, considering our topic, in the nature of
state patronage in the arena of culture.[140] While I have no brief to make for "creoleness," there is little in Puri's analysis to suggest that a "dougla aesthetics" will
be any more socially transformative.[141] Furthermore, in the race to distinguish a
"dougla poetics" from a "biological" notion of identity, Puri forgets the condition
of "actually existing" douglas; the particular struggles that they face are elided.[142]
Douglas—or rather, an imagining of their potential identities—are presented as
the solution to the dilemmas of postcolonial Trinidad. Puri's reading of the songs
"Lick Down Me Nani" and "Jahaji Bahai," compelling as they are in places, raises
the question of how cultural forms that by her own admission are multiaccented
and ambivalent can be harnessed to as complex a project as dismantling racialized institutional power and popular racism in Trinidad and Tobago and the
wider Caribbean. In a similar vein to Puri, Rosanne Kanhai states that "a Caribbean dougla feminism can provide a model for Caribbean integration as has not
been attempted before."[143] Discourses of creoleness and dougla aesthetics potentially leave both Afro- and Indo-Caribbean communities disempowered—the
former as they are still predicated on a flight from blackness and an inability to
deal with the reality of an antiblack world, the latter as the marginality of their
culture to notions of the Caribbean nation remains unaddressed, and both as
they pay little attention to the formative role of class in constructions of culture.

Nigel Bolland's suggestion that we "distinguish between analytical and ideological usages of the concepts of creolization and creole societies" is echoed in the
work of the anthropologist Aisha Khan, one of whose major concerns centers on
the limitations of creolization as a theory of culture and power.[144] Khan's disquiet
with the use of creolization, based on over two decades of fieldwork in Trinidad,

is best expressed in her article "Journeying to the Center of the Earth: The Caribbean as Master Symbol."[145] Khan distinguishes between two broad uses of creolization—its use as "analytical tool or interpretive category, and . . . as (empirical) description of the workings of culture."[146] As an ethnographer, the disciplinary lens through which she undertakes her investigation of the Caribbean is anthropology, and she believes the role of anthropology is to "understand the different modes in which traditions and their remaking in the Caribbean intersect with various structures and varieties of power. An iconic Caribbean cannot produce . . . description or explanation."[147] The task of her article is thus to provide a critical reflection on "the extent to which 'creole/ization,' as an interpretive category, advances anthropological inquiry, and the extent to which reliance on the concept accomplishes the descriptive and theoretical tasks of ethnography."[148]

Creolization is revealed to be at best progressive when compared with a colonial ethnography obsessed with essences and notions of "pure" cultures but regressive in an attempt to develop a sophisticated understanding of contemporary Caribbean society.[149] It occupies a pivotal place in the history of ideas about African diaspora culture in the New World, but herein lies part of the problem. For Khan, "born out of the tension between themes of cultural retention and loss, the concept of creolization replicates this axis as its discourses shift between celebration and lament."[150] The problem of creolization has always been a problem of ideology, but the challenge this poses in the Americas is in part related to the assumptions about cultural difference still held by some scholars who claim a creole identity. The questions here are "why is New World heterogeneity a given" and (deceptively simply) "when does creolization start? And what, then, has ended?"[151] If something is "creole," what is "not creole"?[152]

Indo-Caribbeans historical marginalization within discourses of creolization is a central part of Khan's concerns, which further demonstrate the difficulties of utilizing creolization as a theory of Caribbean culture. In a response to the créolistes' claim that Indo-Caribbeans adapted to the Caribbean "without really creolizing," Khan states that "the issue of Indo-Trinidadians' assimilation is trapped in a tautology: their incongruity is due to their being unfamiliar; yet this remoteness is what makes them incongruous."[153] The provenances of the creolization debate make it an exercise in futility for Indo-Trinidadians: "By participating in a discourse of creolization, Indo-Trinidadians reinforce their own subordination . . . Although it is the basis on which they, too, struggle, this creolization discourse is a game they cannot win, because they are not players, so to speak, as are their Afro and Euro counterparts—even when the logic of Trinidadian nationalist ideology suggests they can be."[154]

Khan believes that "creolization arguably is dispensable as an organizing principle," but if one accepts the deficiencies of creolization as a cultural theory, questions remain as to what paradigms can be used to theorize the nature of ethnicity, cultural difference, and mixing in the contemporary Anglophone Caribbean. Toward the end of her essay "Journey to the Center of the Earth," Khan starts to map what an alternative way of looking at Caribbean culture might be, with the requisite attention to diversity and class within an epistemology of Caribbean culture. This involves a greater turn to ethnography, which is seen as capable of resisting "such glosses as 'creolization'" but also demands that ideas about culture "undergo theoretical revisions."[155] It also requires far closer attention to the role of class in the production of culture: "Considering cultural change from the standpoint of class membership helps our escape from the creolization-as-culture tautology. If we approach culture as the symbolic (and empirical) attestation of class position, then the creolization concept may in fact prove an invaluable tool. Specific to the Caribbean are the class transformations undergone by subaltern populations— Afro, Indo, Euro—under particular forms of colonial rule. Perhaps what is globally applicable about creolization is not culture (as reified abstraction) *but class and the cultures of particular class positions.*"[156]

This perspective on creolization and the study of culture in the Caribbean might well move debates on creolization from what Khan calls a "relatively safe counterhegemonic position."[157] It has the potential to resurrect Kamau Brathwaite's shrewd comment that "the superordinate European element achieved its hegemony largely by remote control" and link to Hintzen's critique of a global middle classes' norms and values in its focus on the cultures of particular class positions.[158] This attention to class allows us to distinguish between elite creolization (creole nationalism, elite domination) and vernacular creolization—the lived experience of cultural mixing and the negotiation of cultural difference that people routinely have as they go about their daily lives.[159] At stake here is not the petit bourgeois cultural nationalism of the créolistes but an unmasking of the coloniality of cultural citizenship and the means by which it creates and reinscribes new forms of domination over citizens in the contemporary Anglophone Caribbean.

Frantz Fanon and Sylvia Wynter

> The national bourgeoisie . . . which has totally assimilated colonialist thought in its most corrupt form, takes over from the Europeans and establishes in the continent a racial philosophy which is extremely harmful for the future of Africa. By its laziness and will to imitation, it promotes the ingrafting and stiffening of racism which was characteristic of the colonial era. Thus it is by no means astonishing to hear in a country that calls itself African remarks which are neither more nor less than racist, and to observe the existence of paternalist behaviour which gives you the bitter impression that you are in Paris, Brussels or London.
>
> Frantz Fanon, *The Wretched of the Earth* (1961)[160]

The extent of the theoretical labor around the term *creole* that exists in Caribbean scholarship suggests a curious flight from or disinterest in the sociopolitical context of the contemporary Caribbean. One is forced to ask: Does the creole not contain within it neocolonial *formations*, as opposed to simply colonial *legacies*? Can we instead then speak of *creole neocolonialism*, rather than *only* invoke creolization to make suggestive allusions to its creativity and transgression in the contemporary conjuncture? In his criticism of the constant valorization of the creole over the putatively universal in Francophone Caribbean thought, the Guadeloupean philosopher Jacky Dahomay has noted that "there may exist tomorrow independent West Indian political systems, completely creole [*en toute créolité*], in which human beings can be massacred."[161] This has already happened more times than we may care to recount, as the examples of Rafael Trujillo's murder of Haitians in the Parsley Massacre of 1937 or the reign of terror of the Duvaliers in Haiti attest.[162] It is almost as if theorists whose eagerness to apply creolization as a Caribbean theory in the pursuit of the epistemological decolonization of the Western academy are reluctant to acknowledge the similarity of the conditions of white supremacy and neoliberal predation that exist unashamedly in the metropolis *and* in the region.

The work of Frantz Fanon and Sylvia Wynter on race is of immense value here, as it contains the key to dismantling the neocolonial relations of power embodied in contemporary racist practice in the region, which are consistently occluded by discourses of creolization. In September 1956, Frantz Fanon delivered a speech at the First Congress of Negro Writers and Artists in Paris titled "Racism and Culture," which remains one of his most remarkable single addresses and emblematic of a crucial transitionary moment in his views on race and colonialism from his first work *Black Skin, White Masks* to his final book *The Wretched of the Earth*.[163] The transformations in global politics over the preceding decade are worth recalling—the end of World War II and the global revulsion at the consequences of the Nazi holocaust, the 1948 Universal Declaration of Human Rights, the anticolonial movement in Asia and Africa. A year after the congress, Ghana would become the first sub-Saharan African country to gain its independence; three years later in 1960, UN resolution 1514 would declare that "the peoples of the world ardently desire the end of colonialism in all its manifestations," that colonial subjection was an abridgement of human rights and its perpetuation a threat to world peace.[164] Fanon himself was in transition at this time, already clandestinely working with Algeria's resistance movement, the FLN (Front de libération nationale), and would resign from his position as medical director at the Blida-Joinville psychiatric hospital before the end of the year.[165] From its inception, "Racism and Culture" marks that moment of transition in global perspectives on race, colonialism, and empire, inescapable at the time. Changes in the dominant ideology that secures understandings of cultural difference have progressed from societies devoid of culture, to "a hierarchy of cultures," to "cultural relativity."[166] This changing view of culture is twinned with a similar transformation in racism, in which a biological racism has evolved into a cultural racism—"the object of racism is no longer the individual man but a certain form of existing."[167] One may demure here that racism is always cultural, but it is Fanon's insight into the impossibility of separating racism from the culture that gives it shelter and protection that makes this essay remarkable. For Fanon, "racism . . . is only one element of a vaster whole: that of the systematized oppression of a people."[168] Race here is delinked from any relationship to biology, geography, or culture and firmly positioned as the ultimate tool of colonial governmentality—the perfected mechanism through which to manage people in a colonial world. Colonialism's tactics require "a continued agony (rather) than a total disappearance of the pre-existing culture," the manifestation of which in that caricature of autonomy termed indirect rule is "the most utter contempt . . . the most elaborate sadism."[169] Racism immerses a society completely; "racism is never a super-added element discovered by chance in the course of the investigation of the cultural data of a group. The social constellation, the cultural whole, are deeply modified by the existence of racism."[170] The rage and terror of white supremacy creates a moment of colonial abduction: "the oppressor, through the inclusive and frightening character of his authority, manages to impose on the native new ways of seeing, and in particular a pejorative judgment with respect to the original forms of existing."[171] In the realm of human experience, colonial abduction is never total, and the colonized, caught between dread and captivation, acts in a manner that may portend either utter assimilation or revolt—"having judged, condemned, abandoned his cultural forms, his language, his food habits, his sexual behaviour, his way of sitting down, of resting, of laughing, of enjoying himself, the oppressed *flings himself* upon the imposed culture with the desperation of a drowning man."[172] The all-encompassing nature of racism in modern society can only be understood in the starkest of terms: "the racist in a culture with racism is therefore normal. He has achieved a perfect harmony of economic relations and ideology."[173]

The prescience of Fanon's observations on race resound today, overturning the fictions that secure racial rule two generations later. The "utter contempt" and "sadism" of indirect rule is as appropriate a description of neocolonial rule in the postindependence Caribbean as can be found in print, at a time when the region courts foreign capital as the only solution to its economic crises in a manner not seen with such an intensity since Arthur Lewis's strategy (dubbed "industrialization by invitation" by Lloyd Best) of the 1950s. The "certain form of existing" that Fanon considers to be the target of a shifting racism moves in the postindependence condition from the perpetual sign of abjection and nonvalue, dark-skinned blacks to those who embody a non-middle-class mode of being.

Here the epigraph to this section from *The Wretched of the Earth* should also capture our attention. The neocolonial racism that gives Fanon the "bitter impression" that he is in the metropole rather than an ostensibly postcolonial state is a consequence of the nationalist bourgeoisie's "laziness and will to imitation," which perpetuates the racism of the colonial era, giving it an added legitimation in the contemporary moment fifty years after the advent of flag independence.

The thought of the subject of this study, Sylvia Wynter, also provides insights on the relationship between a liberal creole multiculturalism and the persistence of racism in the postindependence Caribbean. In her 1972 critique of Kenneth Ramchand, she would condemn the "liberal posturing, [and] false universalism" of "the ambivalent creole eye."[174] Creole theory represents an "evasion of black reality" and serves as a vehicle for "that fraudulent multiculturalism, which is the greatest barrier to the negation of racism."[175] This position by Wynter is in concert with her dismissal of creolization in favor of indigenization as a theory of cultural change among people of African descent in the New World, first given articulation in her study of the festival of Jonkonnu in Jamaica.[176] A quarter century later, Wynter would return to this theme, in a direct response to the créolistes of Martinique. The difference between négritude and créolité is figured as a distinction between a presumption of "radical alterity" seen in Caribbean writers like George Lamming and Aimé Césaire, versus multiculturalism's preoccupation with an "acultural ethnicity," represented by the créolistes.[177] The tendency of radical alterity in Caribbean literature aims to "recode the code" or dismantle the ideological fictions that imprison blacks within coloniality.[178] The créolité movement, in contrast, in its disdain for and misunderstanding of anticolonial thought, remains trapped within a Western epistemological order: "Hence the paradox that, its existence imagined *in* the very terms of the 'universal' Western culture against which it states its alleged self-contained and autonomous particularity, the Créolité movement (like all other variants of contemporary multiculturalism) must use the properties of that Western same to claim its ostensibly unique particularity."[179]

Césaire's négritude is at least a struggle worth recalling and defending, for it understood the battle against cultural "blanchitude" had to be fought on the grounds of a radical alterity to the Western order, rather than as a mere question of the cultural respect due to different ethnicities.[180] Césaire understood well that the basis of black struggle lay not in a racial essentialism but, as he stated at the first Congress of Negro Writers in 1956, in "a *horizontal solidarity*, that is, a solidarity created for us by the colonial . . . situation imposed upon us from without; and on the other, a vertical solidarity, a *solidarity in time*, due to the fact that we started from an original unity, the unity of African civilization, which has become diversified into a whole series of cultures."[181] Césaire's thought represents a great heresy for Western thought, one that "refused the black's imposed role as conceptual Other to the representation of generic Man," which creole theories, in the first generation of independence and at the end of the millennium, cannot emulate.[182] The Francophone Caribbean's particular dilemma results from the fact that "the Antillean subject had . . . to become reflexively autophobic to its own specific physiognomic being as the condition of its attaining to the middle-class model of desire, of being."[183]

This question of middle-class desire Wynter would return to in an essay devoted to aesthetics. For Wynter, "*the taste* of the middle classes of the 'developed' worlds—and therefore its culture-specific mode of aesthetic gratification and 'preference' and, by extrapolation, its existential experiencing of our present socio-global universe—[is projected] as the general equivalent of human 'taste' and, therefore, its world and class-specific existential experience [is advanced] as the general equivalent of *all* human existence."[184]

Multicultural discourse thus facilitates the reproduction of Western bourgeois man in his Caribbean variant. In the contemporary moment, in the absence of radical movements contesting antiblackness, the reterritorialization agenda of white supremacy gains more power, emboldened by a global frontal assault by racist states on black people's lives.

From Creole, the Inescapable Enigma, to Theorizing Caribbean Racism

> To continue to hang national development upon the hook of a creolized unity is to chase a phantom, to reproduce the racial distinctions that the rhetoric of cultural amalgamation obscures.
>
> Deborah Thomas, *Modern Blackness*[185]

In the contemporary Anglophone Caribbean, we have seen a postindependence shift from color being a key modality through which class is lived to a marginality secured by a class-color disempowerment matrix that, while more clinal than the abrupt ruptures evinced under colonialism, persists nonetheless and cascades on vulnerable groups in a manner that frustrates possibilities for social ascent, far less the revolutionary overthrow of a neocolonial social order. The persistence and consolidation of racism in the Caribbean simply cannot be overturned by multicultural glosses of any form, noted shrewdly in Wilson Harris's reflection, based on personal experience, that "creoleness became a form of self-deceptive division even as it harboured within itself a potential for the renascence of community."[186] Rather than a "miracle begging analysis," two generations after Anglophone Caribbean independence, the valorization of creole forms may well be an ambiguous adventure.[187] The generative organizing principle of Caribbean society is not creolization. Rather, it is, as Goveia reminded us so many years ago, "the acceptance of the inferiority of Negroes to whites," or, antiblack racism.[188]

Creoleness as a discourse retains a fabulous ability to render Afro-Caribbeans, Indo-Caribbeans, and Indigenous Caribbeans as not *quite* true citizens of the nation.[189] Its interest in describing the process of cultural cross-fertilization that created Caribbean culture cannot be honestly denied. Nor can the integrity of some of its most sophisticated proponents desire to create a mechanism for examining Caribbean cultural identity that truly promotes intercultural understanding. However, haunting creoleness still is its association with antiblack racism, elite domination, and its inability to provide a true—and as important, *continuous*—reassessment of the place of "blackness" and Africa in the minds of Caribbean people. It is difficult to escape the charge that creoleness in its multiple forms forgets actually existing racism.

I wish to suggest three approaches to the study and *confrontation* of racism in the Caribbean that I believe would be of greater utility than the culturalist approaches tracked above. Philomena Essed's highly productive category of "everyday racism," an approach to the study of racism focused not on "extreme incidents . . . [but] mundane practices" rejects the popular distinction between racism as "either an individual problem or an institutional problem."[190] The former approach fetishizes the individual while being unaware of the gravity of history; the latter forgets that our lives are not merely governed by institutions. We thus need to search beyond this approach if we wish to fully appreciate the diminution of people's lives caused by racism. In her study, Essed identifies "three strands of everyday racism . . . the *marginalization* of those identified as racially or ethnically different; the *problematization* of other cultures and identities; and symbolic or physical *repression* of (potential) resistance through humiliation or violence."[191] Everyday racism, as Fanon had the foresight to see in his essay "Racism and Culture," is subsequently processual and constantly changing: "Everyday racism is a *process* in which (1) socialized racist notions are integrated in meanings that make practices immediately definable and manageable, (2) practices with racist implications become in themselves familiar and repetitive, and (3) underlying racial and ethnic relations are actualized and reinforced through these routine or familiar practices in everyday situations. Everyday racism is experienced *directly* and *vicariously.*"[192]

A Caribbean context requires an addition to this approach—one that accounts for the pressure and violence caused by internalized racism and the self-hatred it has engendered, what Martin Carter once famously called "the scorn of myself," which has posed one of the most vexed of the legacies of colonialism to undo.[193] Everyday racism's attention to the mundane and the commonplace, in which sites of stubborn privilege can be interrogated and intimate choices subjected to scrutiny, provides an important conceptual lens for illuminating Caribbean people's lived experiences with racism.

Everyday racism alone is not enough, as, despite its most productive intentions, it risks capture by a liberal agenda in which the task of dismantling racism never evolves to a thoroughgoing critique of the structure of neocolonial society. There is an urgent need to address what Paget Henry calls "the changing political economy of Caribbean racism."[194] One of the troubling features of social science scholarship produced in the Anglophone Caribbean over the last generation has been the retreat from the considerable work of the 1970s and 1980s that detailed the means by which color-class privilege wedded to corporate power created vast asymmetries of wealth in the contemporary Caribbean and reproduced racism.[195] The reasons for the flight from this work, particularly in the disciplines of sociology and economics at the University of the West Indies, are multifaceted and include the formation and overwhelming popularity of business schools on all campuses; a timidity with frontal assaults (even from the pages of academic journals) on elite power following the end of radical alternatives to Caribbean neocolonial misrule; the growth of attractive offers to market social-science skills to international development agencies, the private sector, and governments in the region; and a sense of futility, swimming against the tide of neoliberalism.[196] Alissa Trotz and Beverley Mullings have also astutely noted that the structural adjustment and social crises of the 1990s led to a retreat from a concern with challenging minority-entrenched racial rule in the economy and a return to a "courting of foreign capital."[197] There is a corresponding lacuna in our knowledge of the current patterns of corporate ownership at both the national and regional level, the extent of international conglomerate control of the economy, or details about the rise and consolidation of the middle class and the intensification of poverty.[198] A deliberate turn to rehearsing some of the work of a generation past that so insightfully portrayed power and domination in the Caribbean would give us a clearer perspective of how the political economy of race has changed in the region over the last generation and insight into the forces and mechanisms that institute racial rule in the region.

Finally, Sara Abraham's historical-sociological study of multiracial alliances in the postindependence Anglophone Caribbean adds a welcome series of insights on how common purpose can lead to movements for social change across supposed racial divides.[199] Eschewing the academic discussion centered on "ethnic conflict or . . . transnational identity formations," Abraham instead seeks to clarify what multiracialism at its best has meant in the Caribbean— "a very precise project for the labour movement, later the nationalist project and presently the women's movement."[200] The point here is to understand how solidarity gets forged across the suspicion of ethnic difference engendered by coloniality and how it emerges from the formation of new political movements disillusioned with the entrenchment of neocolonial politics in the postindependence state.[201]

Race, as James Baldwin was not afraid to know, is something that black people only can destroy, as they are the one people who do not need it. This comment becomes powerful and a telling indictment of our contemporary predicament if we wrest it away from a class-unspecified connection to *all* people of African descent and consider it as a statement applicable to those living the condition of the condemned of the world today, whether Indigenous, Asian, Palestinian, or of African descent. The Caribbean, the crucible of so many of modernity's greatest crimes and, for Walter Rodney, the laboratory that engendered it all, has for five hundred years not existed outside a racialized world. It may not have a responsibility more than others to change it, but a commitment toward an alternative to the coloniality of the contemporary moment seems the only future worth imagining.

Notes

1. Walter Rodney, *The Groundings with My Brothers* (London: Bogle-L'Ouverture, 1969), 60.

2. James Baldwin, *The Evidence of Things Not Seen* (New York: Holt, Rinehart and Winston, 1985), 99.

3. David Theo Goldberg, "Racial States," in *A Companion to Racial and Ethnic Studies*, ed. David Goldberg and John Solomos (Malden, MA: Blackwell, 2002), 233. This article, the basis for his subsequent book *The Racial State* (Malden, MA: Blackwell, 2002), shows a shift from his earlier work on culture to the state. See Goldberg, *Racist Culture: Philosophy and the Politics of Meaning* (Oxford: Blackwell, 1993), and his reflections on his previous work in "Reflections on 'Modernity, Race, and Morality,'" in *Race: Critical Theories*, ed. Philomena Essed and David Goldberg (Malden, MA: Blackwell, 2002), 422–25.

4. Goldberg, "Racial States," 239, original italics.

5. Goldberg, "Racial States," 239.

6. Goldberg, "Racial States," 243.

7. Barry Gaspar, "With a Rod of Iron: Barbados Slave Laws as a Model for Jamaica, South Carolina, and Antigua, 1661–1697," in *Crossing Boundaries: Comparative History of Black People in Diaspora*, ed. Darlene Clark Hine and Jacqueline McLeod (Bloomington: Indiana University Press, 1999), 343–66.

8. James Campbell, *Talking at the Gates: A Life of James Baldwin* (Berkeley: University of California Press, 2002), 263; see also 266–67.

9. For the term "conscripts of modernity," see David Scott, *Conscripts of Modernity: The Tragedy of Colonial Enlightenment* (Durham, NC: Duke University Press, 2004).

10. My interest in the claims made by Rodney and Baldwin is less in their supportability as statements of fact and more in the ethical insights they bring about the Caribbean and the condition of people of African descent respectively.

11. Kamau Brathwaite, "Timehri," in *Is Massa Day Dead? Black Moods in the Caribbean*, ed. Orne Coombs (New York: Anchor Press, 1974), 29–44.

12. Antonio Benitez-Rojo, "The Polyrhythmic Paradigm: The Caribbean and the Postmodern Era," in *Race, Discourse and the Origin of the Americas: A New World View*, ed. Vera Hyatt and Rex Nettleford (London: Smithsonian Institution Press, 1995), 255–67.

13. Some classic texts that stressed the chasms separating social classes and racialized groups within Caribbean societies include M. G. Smith, *The Plural Society in the British West Indies* (Berkeley: University of California Press, 1965) and Philip Curtin, *Two Jamaicas: The Role of Ideas in a Tropical Colony 1830–65* (New York: Atheneum, 1955).

14. Kevin Yelvington, "The Anthropology of Afro-Latin America and the Caribbean: Diasporic Dimensions," *Annual Review of Anthropology* 30 (2001): 227–60.

15. Yelvington, "Anthropology," 227.

16. For the term *savage slot*, see Michel-Rolph Trouillot, "The Otherwise Modern: Caribbean Lessons from the Savage Slot," in *Critically Modern: Alternatives, Alterities, Anthropologies*, ed. Bruce M. Knauft (Bloomington: Indiana University Press, 2002), 220–37.

17. Kamau Brathwaite's use of creolization as a concept has been among the most thoroughgoing of scholars in the Anglophone Caribbean. The complexity of this body of work, which is an oeuvre present in his fiction, historical writings, and critical essays, means that it can scarcely be dealt with adequately in the confines of this chapter. For his two most famous statements on creolization, see *The Development of Creole Society in Jamaica, 1770–1820* and *Contradictory Omens: Cultural Diversity and Integration in the Caribbean.*

18. Carolyn Allen, "Creole: The Problem of Definition," in *Questioning Creole: Creolisation Discourses in Caribbean Culture*, ed. Verene Shepherd and Glen Richards (Kingston: Ian Randle), 49.

19. Allen, "Creole," 52

20. Sylvia Wynter, "Beyond the Categories of the Master Conception: The Counterdoctrine of the Jamesian Poiesis," in *C. L. R. James's Caribbean*, ed. Paget Henry and Paul Buhle (Durham, NC: Duke University Press, 1992), 65.

21. Elsa Goveia, "The Social Framework," *Savacou* 2 (September 1970): 7–15; Sylvia Wynter, "Creole Criticism—a Critique," *New World Quarterly* 5, no. 4 (1972): 12–37; Rex Nettleford, "The Melody of Europe, the Rhythm of Africa," in *Carifesta Forum: An Anthology of 20 Caribbean Voices*, ed. John Hearne (Kingston: Institute of Jamaica, 1976), 139–54.

22. For a notable exception, see Aisha Khan, "Journey to the Center of the Earth: The Caribbean as Master Symbol," *Cultural Anthropology* 16, no. 3 (2001): 271–302.

23. The work in the field of critical race theory and the broader terrain of critical studies of race is vast. For some key texts within it, see Kimberlé Crenshaw and Neil Gotanda, eds., *Critical Race Theory: The Key Writings That Formed the Movement* (New York: The New Press, 1996); Philomena Essed and David Goldberg, eds., *Race: Critical Theories: Text and Context* (Malden, MA: Wiley-Blackwell, 2001), Goldberg and Solomos, *Companion to Racial and Ethnic Studies.*

24. I will return to this idea at greater length later.

25. Percy Hintzen, "Reproducing Domination: Identity and Legitimacy Constructs in the West Indies," *Social Identities*, 3, no. 1 (1997): 47–75.

26. Robert Young, *Colonial Desire: Hybridity in Theory, Culture and Race* (New York: Routledge, 1995).

27. See Naomi Zack, *Race and Mixed Race* (Philadelphia: Temple University Press, 1993); Lewis Gordon, "Mixed Race in Light of Whiteness and Shadows of Blackness: Naomi Zack on Mixed Race," in *Existentia Africana: Understanding Africana Existential Thought* (New York: Routledge, 2000), 96–117.

28. Ann Stoler, "Racial Histories and Their Regimes of Truth," *Political Power and Social Theory* 11 (1997): 183–206; see also the subsequent discussion of this essay by Virginia R. Dominguez, David Roediger, Loic J. D. Wacquant, and Uday Singh Mehta.

29. Stoler, "Racial Histories," 184.

30. See Frantz Fanon, *Black Skin, White Masks*, trans. Charles Lam Markmann (New York: Grove Press, 1967); Jean-Paul Sartre, "Black Orpheus," *Massachusetts Review* 6 (Autumn/Winter 1964/5): 13–52.

31. Stoler, "Racial Histories," 194.

32. Stoler, "Racial Histories," 198

33. Stoler, "Racial Histories," 191

34. Brinda Mehta and Paget Henry, "From the Editors," in "Indo-Caribbean/Afro-Caribbean Thought," special issue, *C. L. R. James Journal* 9, no. 1 (Winter 2002/3): 2.

35. Edward Kamau Brathwaite, *Contradictory Omens: Cultural Diversity and Integration in the Caribbean* (Mona, Jamaica: Savacou, 1974), 7. This line is repeated slightly differently in "Caribbean Man in Space and Time," where it reads, "our problem is how to study the fragments/whole." "Caribbean Man in Space and Time," *Savacou* 11/12 (1975): 1–11, reprinted in *Caribbean Cultural Thought: From Plantation to Diaspora*, ed. Yanique Hume and Aaron Kamugisha (Kingston, Jamaica: Ian Randle, 2013), 174–84.

36. For the term "theoretical piracy on the high seas," see Mimi Sheller, *Consuming the Caribbean: From Arawaks to Zombies* (London: Routledge, 2003), 188. For two statements that show the expansive use of creolization I suggest above, see David Buisseret, "Introduction," in *Creolization in the Americas*, ed. David Buisseret and Steven G. Reinhardt (College Station: Texas A&M University Press, 2000), 3–17; and Ulf Hannerz, "The World in Creolization," in *Readings in African Popular Culture*, ed. Karin Barber, 12–18 (Bloomington: Indiana University Press, 1997). For one of the most thoroughgoing essays on the concept, see Stephan Palmié, "Creolization and Its Discontents," *Annual Review of Anthropology* 35 (2006): 433–56.

37. It should be noted that creolization as a specific mode of scholarly enquiry first emerged in the field of linguistics, work that is outside the ambit of this study. See Michel-Rolph Trouillot, "Culture on the Edges: Creolization in the Plantation Context," *Plantation Society in the Americas* 5, no. 1 (Spring 1998): 11, for this point.

38. Edward Kamau Brathwaite, *The Development of Creole Society in Jamaica* (Oxford: Oxford University Press, 1971).

39. Brathwaite, *Development of Creole Society*, 306, 296. The link between Brathwaite's work and prior theories of plantation systems in the new world should be noted here; see especially *Plantation Systems of the New World: Papers and Discussion Summaries of the Seminar Held in San Juan, Puerto Rico* (Washington, DC: Pan American Union, 1959), for one of the earliest discussions of New World plantations.

40. Brathwaite, "Caribbean Man," 204, the word *twoards* is one of Brathwaite's signature wordplays; the italics are also his. In *Contradictory Omens*, Brathwaite further emphasizes that creolization is a "process, not a product"; see p. 6.

41. The first quote here is from "Caribbean Man," 204. The second is from *Development of Creole Society*, 307, and also reappears in *Contradictory Omens*, 22.

42. Brathwaite, *Contradictory Omens*, 34, 54, 63, 11.

43. Brathwaite, *Contradictory Omens*, 16. Brathwaite is here contesting Sylvia Wynter's early critique of creolization; see "Creole Criticism," 12–37.

44. Brathwaite, *Contradictory Omens*, 7.

45. Brathwaite, *Contradictory Omens*, 21, original emphasis.

46. Brathwaite, *Development of Creole Society*, 303, my italics. This line is repeated verbatim in *Contradictory Omens*, 19.

47. I ask the reader to for one moment hold the obvious question/comment about the complete implication of notions of "culture" with ideas of "race" and "nation."

48. Brathwaite, *Development of Creole Society*, 305.

49. Brathwaite, "Caribbean Man," 203. On Caribbean "mimic men," see V. S. Naipaul, *The Mimic Men* (London: André Deutsch, 1967).

50. Brathwaite, *Development of Creole Society*, 311.

51. Brathwaite, *Development of Creole Society*, 303; O. Nigel Bolland, "Creolisation and Creole Societies: A Cultural Nationalist View of Caribbean Social History," in Shepherd and Richards, *Questioning Creole*, 35.

52. Rhoda Reddock, "Jahaji Bhai: The Emergence of a Dougla Poetics in Trinidad and Tobago," *Identities* 5, no. 4 (April 1999): 589–90. *Dougla* is the term in the Anglophone Caribbean for children born of relationships between people of African and Indian ancestry.

53. See here Brathwaite's bracketed comment about the "East Indian problem" in *Development of Creole Society*, 310.

54. Brathwaite, *Contradictory Omens*, 6. Earlier in this paragraph, Brathwaite identifies the "'new' groups" as East Indians and Chinese people brought in the period of indentureship.

55. Antonio Benitez-Rojo, "The Repeating Island," *New England Review and Bread Loaf Quarterly* 7, no. 4 (Summer 1985). Translated from the Spanish by James Maraniss.

56. Aisha Khan, "Journey," 281.

57. I am thinking here particularly of ethnic competition in Guyana and Trinidad and Tobago, and specifically the Forbes Burnham regime of Guyana. On Guyana, see Brackette Williams, *Stains on My Name, War in My Veins: Guyana and the Politics of Struggle* (Durham, NC: Duke University Press, 1991); on Trinidad and Tobago, see Selwyn Ryan, *The Jihandi and the Cross: The Clash of Cultures in Post-Creole Trinidad and Tobago* (St. Augustine, Trinidad and Tobago: Sir Arthur Lewis Institute of Social and Economic Studies, The University of the West Indies, 1999); for a comparative study of both countries, see Percy Hintzen, *The Costs of Regime Survival: Racial Mobilization, Elite Domination, and Control of the State in Guyana and Trinidad* (Cambridge: Cambridge University Press, 1989).

58. Brathwaite, *Development of Creole Society*, 311. This quote is from the concluding sentence of this volume.

59. Brathwaite, *Contradictory Omens*, 43, original italics.

60. Brathwaite, *Contradictory Omens*, 52, my italics.

61. Brathwaite, *Contradictory Omens*, 55.

62. I borrow the phrase "framework of its own rationalities" from Valentin Mudimbe's *The Invention of Africa: Gnosis, Philosophy and the Order of Knowledge* (Bloomington: Indiana University Press, 1988), x.

63. Nigel Bolland makes exactly this point when, in critiquing Brathwaite's creole/colonial dichotomy, he states that "colonialism is *constitutive* of Jamaican society, not external to it." Bolland, "Creolisation and Creole Societies," 37, original italics.

64. Jean Bernabé, Patrick Chamoiseau, and Raphael Confiant's "Éloge de la créolité" was originally delivered in 1989; for an English translation, see Jean Bernabé, Patrick Chamoiseau, and Raphael Confiant, "In Praise of Creoleness," trans. Mohamed B. Taleb Khyar, *Callaloo* 13 (1990): 886–909, with its memorable opening line "Neither Europeans, nor Africans, nor Asians, we proclaim ourselves Creoles."

65. See Okwui Enwezor, Carlos Basualdo, Ute Meta Bauer, Susanne Ghez, Sarat Maharaj, Mark Nash, and Octavio Zaya, eds., *Créolité and Creolization: Docmenta11_Platform3*

(Ostfildern-Ruit, Germany: Hatje Cantz, 2003). Though critical of the Martinican créolistes, Percy Hintzen uses the word "créolité" to refer to the valorization of creole forms both in the Anglophone and Francophone Caribbean, showing that for him the dominant understandings of identity in this term travel quite well across linguistic borders. Percy Hintzen, "Race and Creole Ethnicity in the Caribbean," in Shepherd and Richards, *Questioning Creole*, 92–110.

66. See the essays gathered in *Small Axe* 52 (2017) under the title "Eulogizing Creoleness? Rereading *Éloge de la créolité*," also Maryse Condé and Madeleine Cottenet-Hage, eds., *Penser la créolité* (Paris: Karthala, 1995).

67. For a discussion of the different stages in Francophone Caribbean cultural thought, see Richard Burton, "Ki Moun Nou Ye? The Idea of Difference in Contemporary French West Indian Thought," *New West Indian Guide* 67, nos. 1 and 2 (1993): 5–32. In this chapter, I do not discuss the work of Edouard Glissant, a significant influence on the créolistes though he has subsequently distanced himself from their theories. For a discussion of Glissant and the créolistes, see Celia Britton, "Identity and Change in the Work of Edouard Glissant," *Small Axe* 52 (2017): 169–79.

68. Bernabé, Chamoiseau, and Confiant, "In Praise of Creoleness."

69. Bernabé, Chamoiseau, and Confiant, "In Praise of Creoleness," 891.

70. Bernabé, Chamoiseau, and Confiant, "In Praise of Creoleness," 893.

71. Bernabé, Chamoiseau, and Confiant, "In Praise of Creoleness," 893.

72. Bernabé, Chamoiseau, and Confiant, "In Praise of Creoleness," 894.

73. Bernabé, Chamoiseau, and Confiant, "In Praise of Creoleness," 894.

74. Bernabé, Chamoiseau, and Confiant, "In Praise of Creoleness," 894, original italics.

75. Bernabé, Chamoiseau, and Confiant, "In Praise of Creoleness," 901.

76. Bernabé, Chamoiseau, and Confiant, "In Praise of Creoleness," 892.

77. Bernabé, Chamoiseau, and Confiant, "In Praise of Creoleness," 902.

78. Bernabé, Chamoiseau, and Confiant, "In Praise of Creoleness," 903, original italics.

79. See here Bernabé, Chamoiseau, and Confiant, "In Praise of Creoleness," 888–89, for the créolistes' position on négritude. On Césaire, they would say the following: "Césaire, an anti-Creole? Indeed not, but rather an *ante-Creole*."

80. When speaking of the "créolistes" here, I refer primarily to the work of Jean Bernabé, Patrick Chamoiseau, and Raphaël Confiant.

81. On the latter point, as we shall see, this is certainly not a complete endorsement of the tactics or argumentation that the créolistes have used to validate that culture.

82. Ernest Pépin and Raphaël Confiant, "The Stakes of Créolité," in *Caribbean Creolization: Reflections on the Cultural Dynamics of Language, Literature and Identity*, ed. Kathleen Balutansky and Marie-Agnes Sourieau (Gainsville: University of Florida Press, 1998), 96–100.

83. Maryse Condé, "Order, Disorder, Freedom, and the West Indian Writer," *Yale French Studies* 83 (1993): 129.

84. Condé, "Order, Disorder, Freedom," 129; Maryse Condé, "Créolité without the Creole Language," in Balutansky and Sourieau, *Caribbean Creolization*, 105.

85. Condé, "Créolité," 106, 108.

86. A. James Arnold, "The Erotics of Colonialism in Contemporary French West Indian Literary Culture," *Annals of Scholarship* 12, nos. 1 and 2 (1997): 173; see also Richard Price and Sally Price, "Shadowboxing in the Mangrove." *Cultural Anthropology* 12, no. 1 (1997): 16–20.

87. Arnold, "Erotics of Colonialism," 181.

88. Price and Price, "Shadowboxing," 9.

89. Price and Price, "Shadowboxing," 11.

90. Hal Wylie, "Metellus, Diasporism and Créolité," in Condé and Cottenet-Hage, *Penser la créolité*, 251–62.

91. Price and Price, "Shadowboxing," 13, 15.

92. Lucien Taylor, "Créolité Bites," *Transition* 74 (1997): 124–61.

93. Taylor, "Créolité Bites," 136–37.

94. Taylor, "Créolité Bites," 140.

95. Taylor, "Créolité Bites," 137, 142.

96. See also here Aisha Khan, "Journey."

97. Aisha Khan, "Journey," 142. This again makes interviewer Lucien Taylor's point, asked in a very pointed question on page 136, about whether the créolistes believe that intra-African "creolization" takes place. Chamoiseau answered in the affirmative. It is clear from his later response that he does not think so or holds on to a view of a singular African culture, which means that whatever intercultural dialogues exist there are of little importance.

98. Victoria Collis-Buthelezi captures this tendency in Caribbean thought well with the following observation: "ultimately, in knowing itself as multiracial, creolized, and syncretic, the Caribbean has learned Africa as its opposite." "Caribbean Regionalism, South Africa, and Mapping New World Studies," *Small Axe* 46 (2015): 45.

99. Taylor, "Créolité Bites", 140, my italics.

100. Taylor, "Créolité Bites", 158, 160; and Lucien Taylor, "Mediating Martinique: The "Paradoxical Trajectory" of Raphael Confiant," in *Cultural Producers in Perilous States: Editing Events, Documenting Change*, ed. George E. Marcus (Chicago: University of Chicago Press, 1997), 326.

101. Taylor, "Créolité Bites," 160.

102. Taylor, "Créolité Bites," 158, 160.

103. See Taylor, "Créolité Bites," 149, 154, for Chamoiseau's dismissal of these types of critiques of his work, and Arnold, "Erotics of Colonialism."

104. I refer here to Charles Mills, *The Racial Contract* (Ithaca, NY: Cornell University Press, 1999).

105. *Chabinité* defies easy translation, so let us rely on Confiant's description of the term: "Chamoiseau always says that the *chabin* epitomizes Créolité. It's very difficult to explain what a *chabin* is. Perhaps the most important point to realize is that it's not a racial category . . . *chabins* are an accident of history, apparently something to do with the chromosomes of some of the early white settlers and the Africans. In the *chabin*, you see both elements, white and black. We have light skin and clear eyes—often they're green—but we have an African physiognomy. We're clear with nègre features. Our hair is often light or red, but it's always kinky. So when you look at a *chabin*, you immediately see the two races, each setting the other off in relief." Taylor, "Mediating Martinique," 282. Confiant describes Malcolm X as a *chabin* on page 284 of this interview.

106. Malcolm X, *The Autobiography of Malcolm X*, quoted in Gordon, *Existentia Africana*, 96.

107. Condé, "Order, Disorder, Freedom," 132.

108. As quoted in Price and Price, "Shadowboxing," 16.

109. Robert Young, *Colonial Desire: Hybridity in Theory, Culture and Race* (New York: Routledge, 1995).

110. Young, *Colonial Desire*, 5.

111. To quote Young: "There is no single, or correct, concept of hybridity: it changes as it repeats, but it also repeats as it changes." Young, *Colonial Desire*, 27.

112. Young, *Colonial Desire*, 25.

113. See Stuart Hall, "When Was 'The Post-Colonial'? Thinking at the Limit," in *The Post-Colonial Question: Common Skies, Divided Horizons*, ed. Iain Chambers and Lidia Curti (London: Routledge, 1996), 259, original italics. See also Stuart Hall, "Créolité and the Process of Creolization," in Enwezor et al., *Créolité and Creolization*, 30.

114. Aisha Khan, "Sacred Subversions? Syncretic Creoles, the Indo-Caribbean, and 'Culture's In-Between,'" *Radical History Review* 89 (Spring 2004): 168.

115. Though not always. As Patricia Mohammed notes, ideas of Indian "purity" and the privileging of these forms in some parts of the Indo-Trinidadian community result in the word "creole" being seen as an insult rather than a compliment. Patricia Mohammed, "The 'Creolisation' of Indian Women in Trinidad," in Shepherd and Richards, *Questioning Creole*, 130–47.

116. Lewis Gordon, "Race, Biraciality, and Mixed Race—in Theory," in *Her Majesty's Other Children: Sketches of Racism from a Neocolonial Age* (Lanham, MD: Rowman & Littlefield, 1997), 51–71. Gordon is referring here to the work of Naomi Zack; see her *Race and Mixed Race*.

117. Gordon, "Race, Biraciality," 59.

118. Gordon, "Race, Biraciality," 61.

119. Gordon, "Race, Biraciality," 61.

120. Two other examples here would be the Dalits of India and the Aboriginals of Australia. See here Gordon's discussion of how "blackness transcends North America—and even Africa" in his exploration of the nature of antiblack racism, *Bad Faith and Antiblack Racism* (Atlantic Highlands, NJ: Humanities Press, 1995), 2.

121. Gordon, "Race, Biraciality," 65.

122. Shalini Puri, *The Caribbean Postcolonial: Social Equality, Post-Nationalism, and Cultural Hybridity* (New York: Palgrave, 2004).

123. On skin bleaching in the Anglophone Caribbean, specifically Jamaica, see Winnifred Brown-Glaude, "The Fact of Blackness? The Bleached Body in Contemporary Jamaica," *Small Axe* 11, no. 3 (2007): 34–51; Donna Hope, "From *Browning* to *Cake Soap*: Popular Debates on Skin Bleaching in the Jamaican Dancehall," *Journal of Pan-African Studies* 4, no. 4 (June 2011): 165–94.

124. Jemima Pierre, *The Predicament of Blackness: Postcolonial Ghana and the Politics of Race* (Chicago: University of Chicago Press, 2013), 113.

125. Lloyd Braithwaite, *Social Stratification in Trinidad* (Kingston: Institute of Social and Economic Research, University of the West Indies, Mona Campus, 1975, originally published 1953), 118; Brown-Glaude, "The Fact of Blackness?"

126. Rhoda Reddock, "'Douglarisation' and the Politics of Gender Relations in Contemporary Trinidad and Tobago: A Preliminary Exploration," *Contemporary Issues in Social Science: A Caribbean Perspective* 1 (1994): 101. However, in the late 1980s, Aisha Khan's elderly interlocutors told her that *dougla* originally meant a mixture of Indo with any non-Indo, including whites, and seemingly over time it became reduced to solely Indo-Afro. Thanks to Aisha Khan for this information, conveyed in a personal correspondence in December 2016.

127. Reddock, "'Douglarisation,'" 107.

128. Puri, *Caribbean Postcolonial*.

129. Puri, *Caribbean Postcolonial*, 1.

130. Puri, *Caribbean Postcolonial*, 4. Puri specifically cites Robert Young's *Colonial Desire* here, on the past connections between hybridity and Victorian racism.

131. Puri, *Caribbean Postcolonial*, 3, 5.

132. Puri, *Caribbean Postcolonial*, 216.

133. Puri, *Caribbean Postcolonial*, 192.

134. Puri, *Caribbean Postcolonial*, 218.

135. Puri, *Caribbean Postcolonial*, 220.

136. Puri, *Caribbean Postcolonial*, 220.

137. Puri, *Caribbean Postcolonial*, 221.

138. On "the battle for space", see Rex Nettleford, "The Battle for Space," in *Inward Stretch, Outward Reach: A Voice from the Caribbean* (Basingstoke, UK: Macmillan, 1993), 80–90.

139. See especially here Selwyn Ryan, *Deadlock: Ethnicity and Electoral Competition in Trinidad and Tobago 1995–2002* (St. Augustine, Trinidad and Tobago: Sir Arthur Lewis Institute of Social and Economic Studies, University of the West Indies, 2003); and for Guyana, see "Guyana: The Present against the Past," special issue, *Small Axe* 15 (March 2004).

140. For a discussion of this, see Selwyn Ryan, *The Jihandi and the Cross: The Clash of Cultures in Post-Creole Trinidad and Tobago*.

141. Puri is aware of this and wavers between an interest in making this point herself, and a belief that a dougla aesthetic might be transformative; see, for example, Puri, *Caribbean Postcolonial*, 221.

142. The idea that any articulation of dougla as poetics or identity can escape notions of biological mixing suffers from the same difficulties that creolization faces, as discussed in this chapter.

143. As cited in Brinda Mehta, "Addressing Marginality Through the 'Coolie/Doulga' Stereotype in CLR James's *Minty Alley*," *C. L. R. James Journal* 9, no. 1 (2002/3): 57.

144. O. Nigel Bolland, "Reconsidering Creolization and Creole Societies," *Shibboleths: Journal of Comparative Theory* 1, no. 1 (2006): 1–14.

145. Khan, "Journey."

146. Khan, "Journey," 280.

147. Khan, "Journey," 274.

148. Khan, "Journey," 272.

149. Khan, "Journey," 294.

150. Khan, "Journey," 279.

151. Khan, "Journey," 278.

152. Khan, "Journey," 283. Here Khan gives the example of the Swahili Coast, the same example given by Lucien Taylor in his conversation with the créolistes, to illustrate the New World specificity of the term *creolization*. Khan argues that part of the reason that the Swahili Coast is not described as "creolized" is "that there is no concomitant retention/loss premise in this part of the world."

153. Khan, "Journey," 289.

154. Khan, "Journey," 292.

155. Khan, "Journey," 294, 293.

156. Khan, "Journey," 292, my italics.

157. Khan, "Journey," 272.

158. Brathwaite, *Contradictory Omens*, 62; Percy Hintzen, "Structural Adjustment and the New International Middle Class," *Transition* (Guyana), February 24, 1995, 52–74.

159. I would like to thank Rinaldo Walcott for making this distinction for me.

160. Frantz Fanon, *The Wretched of the Earth* (London: Penguin Books, 1990), 130.

161. As cited in Richard Burton, "Ki Moun Nou Ye? The Idea of Difference in Contemporary French West Indian Thought," *New West Indian Guide* 67, nos. 1 and 2 (1993): 27.

162. See Ernesto Sagás, "The Development of *Antihaitianismo* into a Dominant Ideology During the Trujillo Era," in *Ethnicity, Race and Nationality in the Caribbean*, ed. Juan Manuel Carrión (San Juan, Puerto Rico: Institute of Caribbean Studies, 1997), 96–121; and Michel-Rolph Trouillot, "State against Nation," in *Haiti: State Against Nation: The Origins and Legacy of Duvalierism* (Monthly Review Press, 1989), 163–85.

163. Frantz Fanon, "Racism and Culture," in *Towards the African Revolution: Political Essays*, trans. Haakon Chevalier (New York: Grove Press, 1967), 31–44. For a discussion of this period in Fanon's life, see David Macey, *Frantz Fanon: A Life* (London: Granta Books, 2000), 278–91.

164. United Nations 1514 (XV), "Declaration on the granting of independence to colonial countries and peoples," 947th plenary meeting, December 14, 1960.

165. Frantz Fanon, "Letter to the Resident Minister," in *Towards the African Revolution*, 52–54.

166. Fanon, "Racism and Culture," 31.

167. Fanon, "Racism and Culture," 32.

168. Fanon, "Racism and Culture," 33.

169. Fanon, "Racism and Culture," 34.

170. Fanon, "Racism and Culture," 36

171. Fanon, "Racism and Culture," 38

172. Fanon, "Racism and Culture," 39, original italics.

173. Fanon, "Racism and Culture," 40.

174. Wynter, "Creole Criticism," 12.

175. Wynter, "Creole Criticism," 23.

176. I return to a discussion of this in chapter 5 of this study. See also Sylvia Wynter, "Jonkonnu in Jamaica," *Jamaica Journal* 4, no. 2 (June 1970): 34–48.

177. Sylvia Wynter, "'A Different Kind of Creature': Caribbean Literature, the Cyclops Factor, and the Second Poetics of the Propter Nos," *Annals of Scholarship* 12, nos. 1 and 2 (1997): 153, 155.

178. Wynter, "'Different Kind of Creature,'" 160.

179. Wynter, "'Different Kind of Creature,'" 157–58, original italics. Wynter will also make the point that the irony of the créolistes position is that "Caribbean creoles are stigmatized as a fact of their *alterity* status, not as signifiers of *ethnicity*"; see Wynter, "'Different Kind of Creature,'" 168, original italics.

180. Wynter, "'Different Kind of Creature,'" 159.

181. Aimé Césaire, "Culture and Colonisation," *Présence Africaine* 8–10 (1956), reprinted in Hume and Kamugisha, *Caribbean Cultural Thought*, 30.

182. Sylvia Wynter, "Beyond the Word of Man: Glissant and the New Discourse of the Antilles," *World Literature in Review* 63, no. 4 (1989): 647n15. In this footnote, Wynter notes her "strong disagreement" with Glissant's idea of *mestizaje*, which she critiques in terms similar to her later discussion of the créolistes.

183. Wynter, "Beyond the Word," 642.

184. Sylvia Wynter, "Rethinking 'Aesthetics': Notes Towards a Deciphering Practice," in *Ex-iles:*
> Essays on Caribbean Cinema, ed. Mbye B. Cham (Trenton, NJ: Africa World Press, 1992), 249, original italics.

185. Deborah Thomas, *Modern Blackness: Nationalism, Globalization and the Politics of Culture in Jamaica* (Durham, NC: Duke University Press, 2004), 269.

186. Wilson Harris, "Creoleness: The Crossroads of a Civilization?" in *Selected Essays of Wilson Harris: The Unfinished Genesis of the Imagination*, ed. A. J. M. Bundy (London: Routledge, 1999), 238.

187. Trouillot, "Culture on the Edges," 8. I am also here alluding to Cheikh Hamidou Kane's *Ambiguous Adventure* (London: Heinemann, 1972).

188. Elsa Goveia, "The Social Framework," *Savacou* 2 (September 1970): 7–15, reprinted in Hume and Kamugisha, *Caribbean Cultural Thought*. This hardly claims that the *only* form of existing racism in the Caribbean is antiblack racism premised on African diaspora experience. It is, however, to suggest that similar to Caribbean slave society and economy, antiblack racism is the *generative* event of the Caribbean experience.

189. On the absence of indigenous people from the narrative of creolization, see Shona Jackson, *Creole Indigeneity: Between Myth and Nation in the Caribbean* (Minneapolis: University of Minnesota Press, 2012).

190. Philomena Essed, "Everyday Racism," in Goldberg and Solomos, *Companion*, 204, 205.

191. Essed, "Everyday Racism," 207, original italics.

192. Essed, "Everyday Racism," 208, original italics.

193. Martin Carter, "I Come from the Nigger Yard," in *Poems of Succession* (London: New Beacon Books, 1977), 38–40.

194. Paget Henry, *Caliban' Reason: Introducing Afro-Caribbean Philosophy* (London: Routledge, 2000), 219.

195. Hilary Beckles, *Corporate Power in Barbados, the Mutual Affair: Economic Injustice in a Political Democracy* (Bridgetown, Barbados: Lighthouse, 1989); Stanley Reid, "An Introductory Approach to the Concentration of Power in the Jamaican Corporate Economy and Notes on Its Origin," in *Essays on Power and Change in Jamaica*, ed. Carl Stone and Aggrey Brown (Kingston: Jamaica Publishing House, 1982), 15–44; Selwyn Ryan and Lou Ann Barclay, *Sharks and Sardines: Blacks in Business in Trinidad and Tobago* (St. Augustine, Trinidad and Tobago: Institute of Social and Economic Research, 1992). There is, of course, a larger history of this interrogation of the roots of Caribbean wealth and income inequality, which this work stands on, and I refer here specifically to the scholars who developed the plantation school model and the New World Group from the 1960s. For some of the critical works here, see George Beckford, *Persistent Poverty: Underdevelopment in Plantation Economies of the Third World* (New York: Oxford University Press, 1972); Lloyd Best and Kari Polanyi Levitt, *Essays on the Theory of Plantation Economy: A Historical and Institutional Approach to Caribbean Economic Development* (Kingston: University of the West Indies Press, 2009); Norman Girvan, *Corporate Imperialism: Conflict and Expropriation* (New York: Monthly Review Press, 1976); Norman Girvan, "Aspects of the Political Economy of Race in the Caribbean and the Americas: A Preliminary Interpretation," Institute of Social and Economic Research, University of the West Indies, Mona Campus, working paper no. 7, 1975.

196. See here the contrasting explanations for this phenomenon by Paget Henry and Don Marshall. Paget Henry, "Caribbean Sociology, Africa and the African Diaspora," in *The African Diaspora and the Disciplines*, ed. Tejumola Olaniyan and James H. Sweet (Bloomington: Indiana University Press, 2010), 145–60; Don Marshall, "Academic Travails and a Crisis-of-Mission of UWI Social Sciences: From History and Critique to Anti-Politics," in *Higher Education in the Caribbean: Past, Present and Future Directions*, ed. Glenford Howe

(Kingston: University of the West Indies Press, 2000), 59–84. Also, note Norman Girvan, "New World and Its Critics," in *The Thought of New World: The Quest for Decolonisation*, ed. Brian Meeks and Norman Girvan (Kingston: Ian Randle, 2010), 3–29.

197. Alissa Trotz and Beverley Mullings, "Transnational Migration, the State, and Development: Reflecting on the 'Diaspora Option,'" *Small Axe* 41 (2013): 160.

198. I should note, though, that the work of feminist theorists of the ravages imposed by structural adjustment in the region provides an important intersectional analysis of race, gender, and political economy. For one powerful example here, see Faye V. Harrison, "The Gendered Politics and Violence of Structural Adjustment: A View from Jamaica," in *Situated Lives: Gender and Culture in Everyday Life*, ed. Louise Lamphere, Helena Ragone, and Patricia Zavella (New York: Routledge, 1997), 451–68.

199. Sara Abraham, *Labour and the Multiracial Project in the Caribbean: Its History and Its Promise* (Lanham, MD: Lexington Books, 2007); Sara Abraham, "Multiracialism as More Than the Sum of Ethnicities," *Race and Class* 49, no. 2 (2007): 91–100.

200. Abraham, "Multiracialism," 92.

201. See here Eusi Kwayana, *The Bauxite Strike and the Old Politics* (n.p.: On Our Own Authority, 2014, originally published 1972).

PART II
THE CARIBBEAN BEYOND

4 A Jamesian Poiesis?

C. L. R. James's New Society and Caribbean Freedom

> Given the pluri-consciousness of the Jamesian identity—a Negro yet British,
> a colonial native yet culturally part of the public school code, attached to the
> cause of the proletariat yet a member of the middle class, a Marxian yet a
> Puritan, an intellectual who plays cricket, of African descent yet Western, a
> Trotskyist and Pan-Africanist, a Marxist yet a supporter of black studies, a
> West Indian majority black yet an American minority black—it was evident
> that the Negro Question, and the figure of Matthew Bondsman that lurked
> behind it, could not be solved by an either/or—that is, by either race or class,
> proletariat or bondman labor, or *damnes de la terre*, Pan-African nationalism
> or labor internationalism. The quest for a frame to contain them all came to
> constitute the Jamesian poiesis.
>
> Sylvia Wynter, "Beyond the Categories of the Master Conception: The
> Counterdoctrine of the Jamesian Poiesis" (1992)[1]

James's Legacy

The wonder of the lifework of C. L. R. James, which continues to captivate a
worldwide intelligentsia a generation after his death, is for his Caribbean admirers not just the brilliance of his contribution to global thought but the decisive nature of his influence on every major political and aesthetic movement
in the region from the 1920s to his death in Brixton in 1989. James was one of
the quintessential figures of the twentieth-century black world, an insightful
Pan-Africanist and Marxist theoretician of great subtlety and charisma, and in
his six decades of radical activity attracted an immense range of revolutionary comrades, fellow travelers, and admirers. The awe engendered by the range
of his work has produced in his critics the most unlikely of conclusions. Thus,
Paul Buhle, the historian of American radicalism, could choose to subtitle his
biography of James "The Artist as a Revolutionary," while Frank Birbalsingh,
the literary critic, in an essay on the literary achievement of James, would declare his
history of the Haitian revolution, *The Black Jacobins*, to be a "superlative literary achievement" and "probably the finest piece of non-fiction writing to come

out of the English-speaking Caribbean."[2] George Lamming, in an echo of Sylvia Wynter's epigraph above, would say the following: "What James reinforced in me . . . was the interconnectedness of all enquiry . . . and it is in this sense that I think of him as the supreme example of an intellectual, a man whose life is the life of the mind, whose oxygen was ideas."[3] Yet this deserved praise, while capturing the influence and appeal of James's work, raises the question of whether a central impulse can be interpreted from it. Is there some culmination of James's political ideas that one might discern from his work? And how might it be possible to fashion our Caribbean present with and through his lifework's example?

The quarter of a century since James's death in London has witnessed over fifteen volumes of studies of his life and work, including biographies, edited collections, critical appraisals, and reminisces. A scholarly journal named in his honor, the *C. L. R. James Journal*, is the official journal of the Caribbean Philosophical Association, while Duke University Press has started a series called the C. L. R. James Archive, intended to republish all his work and likely to contain at least twenty volumes. It is the debates *within* this secondary literature that I wish to pay some attention to, as they are a sign of the times, worthy of a study of their own. The generational ruptures between activists who knew James and worked with him, scholars who met James during the formative years of their intellectual careers and were part of the first wave of scholarship on him, and younger scholars with no personal connection to James but attracted to his work have produced some fascinating exchanges at the periodic conferences on James's work over the last two decades.

What has often been at stake in these debates is what constitutes the key contribution of James, often characterized in the following manner—James the radical activist versus James the cultural critic—and first noted by Selwyn Cudjoe in his critical review of *The C. L. R. James Reader* as early as 1992.[4] Nor is Cudjoe the only critic who has observed these competing trends in the scholarship on James. John McClendon, in his own searching examination of James's *Notes on Dialectics*, states it is a "historical falsification . . . [to read] James as not associated in ideological terms with Marxism-Leninism," while Neil Larsen has made the assertion that James's work, properly interpreted, represents a critical interpretation of twentieth-century Western culture that has been too easily appropriated by a North Atlantic cultural studies he would have disavowed.[5] More recently, Christian Høgsbjerg in the best study of James's first sojourn in Britain, has questioned the construction of a cultural James, an assessment shared by Matthew Quest.[6] There is much to concur with in these declarations that failing to interpret James as a fundamentally *political* figure is a misrepresentation of his lifework. I am particularly sympathetic to the assertions made by Høgsbjerg and Quest in this regard, given the nature of the misreadings of James's legacy in print, a fine recent example of which comes in the work of Walter Mignolo. Mignolo mobilizes

Sylvia Wynter's reading of James in order to claim that "James has been read, particularly in the United States, as primarily a Marxist thinker due to his *Notes on Dialectics* (1948) and his *State Capitalism and World Revolution* (1950)—even though his allegiance to Marxism is only partial."[7] This comment is stunning on many levels. It ignores the fact that James *was* a Marxist intellectual and saw his *primary* intellectual contributions as being made to Marxist theory, which even a cursory knowledge of his work reveals. Further, to suggest that the two cited texts are the primary ways in which James is known and interpreted in the United States ignores the fact that *neither* have seen publication by a major US press and that *Notes on Dialectics* has been out of print for decades. Mignolo goes on to suggest that "Wynter removes James from Marxists' co-option"—James is apparently abducted by practitioners of the very theory he helped fashion—and further suggests in a footnote that Antonio Gramsci and C. L. R. James share a similar fate here, figures whose antagonism with Marxism is apparently poorly understood.[8] James and Gramsci, self-declared Marxists and communists respectively, are here transformed into figures beyond their lived experiences and body of work.

A different set of questions is posed by David Scott's influential *Conscripts of Modernity: The Tragedy of Colonial Enlightenment.*[9] Of the recent James scholarship, Scott's book is in many ways closest in intent to my own interests here—a desire to use James to think concretely about the contemporary moment in the postcolonial world—though our interpretations of him differ markedly. Scott wishes to write against the exhaustion of progressive political projects in the postcolonial world and the "acute paralysis of will and sheer vacancy of imagination, the rampant corruption and vicious authoritarianism, the instrumental self-interest and showy self-congratulation" that pervades our present.[10] He argues that rather than the dominant tale of overcoming colonialism, which has been couched in a narrative of anticolonial romance, our times demand a different emplotment: tragedy. James's classic history of the Haitian revolution, *The Black Jacobins: Toussaint L'Ouverture and the San Domingo Revolution*, is mobilized here as between the first and second edition, Scott detects a shift in registers from anticolonial romance to tragedy, which he believes to be part of a more general change in James's work in the 1950s and '60s. James's reflections on tragedy are best seen in his revisions to the second edition of *The Black Jacobins*, specifically the seven paragraphs inserted at the beginning of the last chapter, and are worthy of serious consideration in this moment as "tragedy has a more respectful attitude to the contingencies of the past in the present, to the uncanny ways in which its remains come back to usurp our hopes and subvert our ambitions, it demands from us more patience for paradox and more openness to chance than the narrative of anticolonial Romanticism does, confident in its striving and satisfied in its own sufficiency."[11] A sense of the tragic does not condemn us to despair but should give us a more "critical story of our postcolonial time."[12]

A consideration of James's writing in this period shows this sense of the tragic; however, to me this sense is often grafted onto a cautiously liberatory narrative that does not quite correspond to either the romantic anticolonialism that Scott signals as the dominant trend of the time or his own reading of James's use of the tragic. Instead, in James we get a clear awareness that one of the potential futures of the Caribbean nation may be neocolonialism, yet the acknowledgment of this real possibility is couched within a cautious tale of hope and excitement at the possibilities of the new West Indian nation. This cautious hope is clearly there in James's defiant introduction to his critique of the Trinidadian nation at the moment of independence, *Party Politics in the West Indies*, as well as in his semiautobiographical masterpiece, *Beyond a Boundary*, and several essays of this period.[13] James's writings on the United States and the Caribbean in the 1950s similarly contrast these locales with a Europe that is dour and mired in tragedy, compared to the optimistic individualism of the United States and the new forms of existence that are the gift of the Caribbean to the world. While I share Scott's concern over our present, I pause at the almost totalizing nature of the exhaustion he suggests captivates the postcolonial world—a pessimism that James, always on the lookout for the new social movement, would never share.[14]

In this chapter, I use the occasion of James's 1958 return to the Caribbean and the troubled years he spent there as the central part of my consideration of James's appreciation of the new societies being fashioned at the moment of Anglophone Caribbean independence, principally through a reading of a number of his essays and speeches published in the 1950s and 1960s.[15] I then extend the argument about the "new society" in James's work onward to the last two decades of his life, in which his encounter with feminists sharpened a question that had existed in his thought since the 1950s—the new society and the transformation in gender relations it required. I make the argument that James's firm linkage of human freedom to the liberation of women, while a fragmentary topic that appears and disappears across his texts, is deeply poignant and, as of yet, a generally unacknowledged part of his legacy.

C. L. R. James, the New Society, and Caribbean Modernity

In an interview conducted in 1980–81, C. L. R. James responded to a question about what had been his greatest contribution to human knowledge. His response, perhaps his most succinct comment on his life's work in his last decade, was instructive: "My contributions have been, number one, to clarify and extend the heritage of Marx and Lenin. And number two, to explain and *expand* the idea of what constitutes the *new* society."[16] In this chapter, I am somewhat more interested in exploring James's second proposal about his contributions, though this is hardly to suggest that his propositions are opposed—in fact they are quite dependent on each other.

Here, James's phrasing of his response is important and worth closer examination. He states that his second contribution has been "to explain and *expand* the idea of what constitutes the *new* society." James frequently spoke in superlatives and referred to a number of writers as the best writer he had ever read or the "most astonishing" person he had encountered. Yet his phrase the "new society," or, alternatively, the concept of the "new" in society, particularly captivated him and is a term to be found frequently in his writings from the 1950s onward—best seen in his appendix to the second edition of *The Black Jacobins*, in which he declared, "To be welcomed into the comity of nations a new nation must bring something new. Otherwise it is a mere administrative convenience or necessity. The West Indians have brought something new."[17]

At the risk of sounding pedantic, a detour to thinking more closely about the question of the new is in order here. One of the questions that ideas of the new always raise is what constitutes the old, or how and why is this break with the old taking place. The new suggests a daring rupture with the old, but this hardly guarantees that the terms within which this break are couched are progressive, as its gesture is primarily concerned with "the articulation of a new discursive practice in the zone of representation."[18] Attempts to mobilize the idea of the new, like Alain Locke's "new negro" and Stuart Hall's "new ethnicities," are often vulnerable to critiques that call for a more careful periodization of their claims about the new forms of life they suggest are in the process of emerging.[19] In the case of Locke, legitimate questions have been raised by generations of scholars about the conservatism that clearly shows its face in his definition of the "new negro" and its association with the general elision of black radicalism from the popularly told story of the Harlem Renaissance.[20] Stuart Hall, while not prey to the kind of conservatism that haunts Locke's work, suggests at points that the "new ethnicities" that he sees as emerging are the "*effect* of a theoretical encounter between black cultural politics and the discourses of a Eurocentric, largely white, critical cultural theory."[21] Though Hall is quite clear that in theorizing the new he is not advocating a "substitution of one kind of politics for another" or suggesting that the struggle over old identities has disappeared, he seems to make the complexity of black representations and identities in British society dependent on theoretical formulations within the academy.[22] Stuart Hall's reflections on the new, then, strike me less as an adequate demarcation of the space occupied by old and new identities but more (productively) a series of speculations on how we might think our identities (a)new.

Discourses of the new, in the daring of their challenge to the old, often in some form or other are dependent on discourses of tradition and modernity, and James's work is no different in this regard. In the period of his life I wish to discuss, after he left the United States in 1953, and especially in his writings on the Caribbean in the 1960s, the idea of the new constantly appears, not merely as a rhetorical device, but as an important part of his theorizing about the moment inhabited by both Caribbean and world society. The first clues to James's use of the new come in *American Civilization*, in which the new is used to advance a series of claims about the radical differences between New World and Old World cultures and civilizations. James's central consideration in this text has been described by its editors, Anna Grimshaw and Keith Hart, as "no less than the conditions of survival of modern civilization."[23] Rehearsing the trajectory that this text takes in doing this and situating it within James's lifework would be an unwarranted distraction here.[24] It is important, however, to be aware that *American Civilization*, while a work quite apart from James's Marxist group, the Johnson-Forrest Tendency, and their activities during his time in the United States, can be read as in concert with that tendency's ultimate goals. In his description of the work of Johnson-Forrest on his seventieth birthday, James said, "We brought forward a new conception, not of Russia, but of modern society as a whole."[25] This alternate vision of modern society resulted in a turn by James toward thinking harder about the United States, emergent from World War II as one of the world's two superpowers, as a distinctive civilization in its own right. The difference between the United States and Europe James considered to be linked fundamentally to the idea of tragedy, but in quite a contrasting manner to the presentation of his ideas by David Scott. As James explained in a 1961 letter:

> I do not know that not to have a sense of the tragic is a lack, a fatal weakness. What is this sense of the tragic? It is, in my opinion, a sense of the inability of man in society to overcome the evil which seems inseparable from social and political organization. To have a sense of the tragic, is to be aware of this and to judge humanity by the degree to which man is able to struggle against this overriding doom; to establish moral and psychological domination over the feeling of impotence and futility which it would otherwise impose. The American people of today most certainly have not got this sense of the tragic in the manner that it has pervaded, and still pervades, European literature.[26]

Europe, for James, is dour and mired in tragedy, while the fundamental feature of American civilization is its optimism, in which the struggle for happiness is paramount over all other concerns. The fundamental break between the new and the old, however, goes beyond the Europe-America divide. As early as 1930, in an essay smuggled into Learie Constantine's *Cricket and I*, James would compare the English batsman Patsy Hendren and Constantine as follows: "Where Hendren husbands his energy, Constantine expands his with a reckless, a positively regal, prodigality. It is Europe and the Americas over again—the old world and the new."[27] The contrast between Europe and the Caribbean is thus similarly acute, and James's essay "A New View of West Indian History" also contains an important repudiation of absurdity and its corollary, tragedy. In his critique of Jean-Paul Sartre and T. S. Eliot, James claims that in the Caribbean "we have not yet reached the stage where we are sick of existence and doubtful of the future."[28] While the characters in Orlando Patterson's *The Children of Sisyphus* may be "nasty, mean, stupid, filthy . . . they are not absurd."[29] In the contemporary Caribbean (James is writing in 1965), "we have a lot of sorrow to pass through and maybe at the end of 15 or 20 years we will know what it is to have an absolutely hopeless view of the world. But we have not got it today. We have a lot of things that are quite wrong but that we have not got."[30]

In his 1963 appendix to the second edition of the historical study *The Black Jacobins*, titled "From Toussaint L'Ouverture to Fidel Castro," James would make a number of claims about the modernity of the Caribbean experience that are keys toward comprehending his interpretation of the Anglophone Caribbean experience. For James, "West Indians first became aware of themselves as a people in the Haitian Revolution."[31] A reflection on this statement leads one to consider the impact of the revolution on perceptions of the possibility of black freedom in the Atlantic world, agency against the tide of history, and the sociohistorical features that have fashioned contemporary Caribbean existence. James's appendix is his most concentrated piece of writing on the potential and limits of Caribbean freedom. Caribbean history is, for James, defined by two central features—"the sugar plantation and Negro slavery"—and the entire article is a sustained meditation on the response to those forms of modern colonial power. His study of the Haitian revolution led James to understand enslaved Africans as living a modern existence in a colonial world, and he was among the first to firmly locate plantation slavery as a modern process, in a move heretical to both the complacent evolutionary anthropology of the early twentieth century and to Marxism-Leninism. In *The Black Jacobins*, he writes, "Working and living together in gangs of hundreds on the huge sugar-factories which covered the North Plain, they were closer to a modern proletariat than any group of workers in existence at the time, and the rising was, therefore, a thoroughly prepared and organised mass movement."[32] In this appendix, he would highlight other features of enslaved life in the Caribbean: the highly detailed, mechanized process of sugar production; the dependence of the colonial economy on transnational flows of basic goods, principally food and clothing.[33] These insights by James have been noted by scholars interested in making an argument about the profound modernity of the Caribbean and transatlantic black experience since slavery and, indeed, its primacy in debates about the modern. In the concluding chapter of Paul Gilroy's *The Black Atlantic*, he argues that "the concentrated intensity of the slave experience is something that marked out blacks as the first truly modern people, handling in the nineteenth century dilemmas and difficulties which would only become the substance of everyday life in Europe a century later."[34] As we have seen, Sidney Mintz has constantly highlighted the Caribbean's status as the site of a "precocious modernity," anticipating by generations developments in Europe, and also has suggested that C. L. R. James was the first to illustrate the centrality of the black experience in the formation of the Atlantic world.[35] Given Haiti's seismic impact on the history of the Western hemisphere, an influence that in James's own words would "make history which would alter the fate of millions of men and shift the economic currents of three continents," the Black Jacobins *create* the modern Atlantic world.[36]

The puzzle of what constituted the new and the struggle over a Caribbean modernity would become clear in James's writings on society within the Anglophone Caribbean. At the time of his return in 1958, he had not seen his home in twenty-six years. James's return to the Caribbean is thus intimately linked to his relationship with Eric Williams, which has unfortunately overshadowed perspectives on the meaning of those years in his life. The relationship between James and Williams was the most famously acrimonious of two leading Caribbean scholars, stretching sixty years and filled with debt and counterdebt, betrayals and disavowals. The terrain here was not merely scholarship but the question of postcolonial politics and the future of the Caribbean.[37]

We may well start with a sketch of this sixty-year relationship. It is well established that James first met Williams when he served as his tutor at Queen's Royal College, the secondary school both attended in Port of Spain.[38] Both departed Trinidad in 1932 for Britain, James to create a career for himself as a writer, Williams for Oxford University. During James's six years in Britain, they were in constant contact, and Eric Williams helped James research *The Black Jacobins* in Paris, while James directly inspired Williams's doctoral study, later to become *Capitalism and Slavery*, before they left for the United States around the same time, just before the outbreak of World War II. James's sojourn in the United States lasted fifteen years before he departed, in the face of his inevitable deportation, in 1953. Williams left a couple of years later for Trinidad, where he launched the nationalist party the People's National Movement (PNM) and within a year became the chief minister of the colony. James, invited to come down to Trinidad from London to attend the launch of the Federal Parliament in 1958, stayed to work with the PNM as the editor of the party newspaper, the *Nation*, and as secretary of the West Indies Federal Labour Party.[39] By July 1960, he had resigned from the PNM amid growing differences with Williams and left Trinidad shortly before independence came in 1962, with Williams as prime minister. On James's return to cover cricket test matches in 1965, Williams placed him briefly under house arrest, after which James formed the Workers and Farmers Party, which contested and was ignominiously defeated in the 1966 general election. James left Trinidad shortly after this campaign, not to return to Trinidad again until 1980, when he visited for a few months as the guest of the Oilfield Workers Trade Union, before returning to England for the rest of his life.

While most treatments of the relationship between James and Williams have focused on their split in the early 1960s, the best place to look for an examination of the intellectual *and* political differences between the two men might be James's review of Williams's first book, *The Negro in the Caribbean*.[40] James published this review under the pseudonym W. F. Carlton, and in it he rehearses in a quite prescient manner the break he will have with Williams two decades later. Not only does James flatly assert that "Williams is no Marxist," but also he claims that "the future demands more than Williams has. It needs a conscious theory. He is a sincere nationalist and a sincere democrat, but after so sure a grasp of historical development as he shows in this history of four centuries, he displays an extreme naiveté in his forecasts of the future."[41] Williams's text is a "little triumph"; his "immediate demands—federation, national independence, political democracy—are admirable, but he commits a grave error in thinking, as he obviously does, that these will end or even seriously improve West Indian mass poverty and decay."[42] James's return to Trinidad in 1958 is best understood as somewhere between the act of a reluctant conscript to a nationalist enterprise that he knew would never accommodate his politics and an indication of his sincere interest and excitement at the possibilities that could emerge in the formation of a new Caribbean nation. In a letter to George Padmore on March 17, 1958, the day after he received his official invitation to attend the inauguration ceremonies of the West Indian Federal Parliament, James wrote: "I have been badly wanting to go home for some years now. I intend to stay for a while and I intend also to take part in the undoubted crisis which the Federation faces. My view is that nothing can save them but independence with a constitution to be decided by a constitutional assembly and not handed down either by the Colonial Office or a Federal Parliament."[43] However, in his semiautobiographical *Beyond a Boundary*, he wrote: "Once in a blue moon, i.e. once in a lifetime, a writer is handed on a plate a gift from heaven. I was handed mine in 1958."[44] The irony here is that without Williams's endorsement, James, who had left Trinidad twenty-six years previously, could hardly have established his reputation again so quickly or had such a decisive influence on the nationalist movement in Trinidad and the discussions around independence throughout the Anglophone Caribbean as he had. It is another of the cycles of debt to each other, forgotten amid the bitterness of the 1960s.

James's battles with Williams, while critical to understanding his return to the Caribbean, obscure the real legacy of James's stay in the region. I would suggest that this legacy can be found in the ideas that he expressed about the nature of Caribbean society and its people on the cusp of independence.

New Society, New Caribbean

> We stand on the threshold of a tremendous exploration of art in a democracy.
>
> C. L. R. James, "Introduction" to *Caribbean Plays*[45]

In the chapter titled "New Society, New People" of his coauthored 1958 text *Facing Reality*, published the year of his return to the Caribbean, James presents evidence from workers councils, the women's movement, anticolonial struggles, and the arts in a series of observations that are part speculative and part diagnostic about the changes in world society he sees unfolding. The "new nations" are presented as evidence that "vast millions of . . . people are new human beings, ready for the new society," which they have fought for in their anticolonial struggles and is now inevitable.[46] During the 1950s and 1960s, James began to articulate his vision of a West Indian identity and modernity more explicitly, and there are a number of striking features present in his thought at this time. James's consistent reference to the people of the Caribbean as a "new people," a people "unique in the modern world," occupying a "new nation" (the emphasis on new *nation* rather than its plural is important here, as James was making an argument about the necessity of federation), and whose writers were involved in producing a "new view of West Indian history," gives several important philosophical insights into James's view of Caribbean culture at the moment of its Anglophone territories' independence.[47] Coming forth from every page is the sense of excitement that James felt at this time, that the Caribbean would produce something new on the world stage: "the instinctive feelings and readiness of the West Indian populations for adventurous creation in all fields is proved among other proofs by the literature these territories produce."[48]

James's description of a distinctive Caribbean modernity continually rested on a strategy that brought together ideas of tradition/modernity, old/new, and Western/non-Western into one programmatic statement. To give an example:

> The Caribbean territories have a universal significance far beyond their size and social weight. They seem to be a slice of Western civilization put under a microscope for the scientific investigation of the fundamental predicates and perspectives of that civilization itself. Owing to the expatriate character of the whole Caribbean all of the *old* problems seem posed *anew* in terms which are easily grasped, *new* in that they are not dominated as in the older countries by long established growths and accretions; urgent in that the Caribbean problems demand some settlement if not solution; comprehensive and *very modern* in that politics, economics and sociology are one indivisible unit.[49]

Here, the problem of the new society that James's post-1950 work was largely intent on clarifying is positioned in a delicate relationship to Caribbean realities. The Caribbean is part of the West, but the absence of long-held traditions in it means it possesses a very different, intensely modern space within the West. Writing in the epilogue to the 1969 reissue of *A History of Negro Revolt*, James would say of the Caribbean, "Whereas the economy continues to be a colonialist economy . . . the population is a modern population, a population of the twentieth century, learned in the languages and techniques of Western civilization, and highly developed because of the smallness of the islands and the close relations between areas technically known as urban and rural."[50] I will return to the issue of language shortly. What deserves emphasis here is how the Caribbean nation is for James without the slightest trace of a contradiction "a completely *colonial* colony and a completely *modern* population."[51]

James's article on the artist in the Caribbean similarly juggles the potential dichotomies raised above.[52] This article is largely about the problem of the artist in the Caribbean, an acute issue as a "supreme artist exercises an influence on the national consciousness which is incalculable." James notes early on that the practice of art in the Caribbean is based on the use of forms "borrowed from other civilizations." This, however, he sees as a problem that the white settler countries like Australia, New Zealand, and Canada also share—they all have "shallow origins," which prevents the full expression of artistic talent. Shallow origins are not insurmountable; nor is small size, as the Greek city-states have shown. However, "the great artist is the product of a long and deeply rooted national tradition. . . . He appears at a moment of transition in the national life with results which the whole civilized world can recognize as having significance for it."[53] The key phrase here may well be "moment of transition in the national life," which allows James to locate both the cricketer Garfield Sobers and the calypsonian the Mighty Sparrow as artists, emergent at the moment of Anglophone Caribbean independence, formed by the old but heralding the new. Sobers was thus "born into a tradition, into a medium which though transported was so well established that it has created a Caribbean tradition of its own . . . There are no limits to what Sobers can achieve."[54] Sparrow's signal importance is that the "creative national tradition" that he presents to the Caribbean people is not an adjunct to a tradition borrowed from abroad, even if that tradition has been "refashioned by a healer's hand" into something more daring, powerful, and liberatory than could previously have been imagined.[55] Sparrow is the first "genuinely West Indian artist" as he is an exemplary practitioner of a very specifically West Indian cultural form and is heralded by the masses, who "give him all the encouragement that an artist needs."[56] More than a supreme artist, "he is a living proof that there is a West Indian nation."[57]

The problems posed by James's perspective on "tradition" and "origins" in the Caribbean include his reproduction of the trope of the absent indigenous in the Caribbean, in which native people are assumed to have all disappeared following European colonization, and the minimalization of African influences on Caribbean culture.[58] The latter can be seen most starkly in his comments about language and Caribbean society and culture. In a number of speeches in the 1960s, James assumed a complete loss of African languages in the Caribbean and gives undue weight to the mastery of European languages by Caribbean populations.[59] James was consistently revising his attitude toward language, but his appreciation of emergent Caribbean writers of the 1960s seemed mainly to turn on writers like Earl Lovelace and Michael Anthony, who wrote in standard English but with creole inflections in their pages.[60] Following this reasoning, he could thus state that "[Nicholas] Guillen has caught the accent of West Indian speech without taking *refuge* in dialect."[61] In a 1982 interview with Chris Searle, the transitions in his mind on this question would be evident: "I don't think that the language can be transformed. The English language has a certain basis to it which is the result of many centuries of development. What I think is most astonishing is the *use* that people in Africa and the Caribbean, particularly in Africa, have made of this foreign language. We had to adapt it to our own requirements and this gives it the revolutionary range and peculiar depth which colonial English did not have."[62] James did not argue for the "nation language" position later articulated by Kamau Brathwaite; nor is English a "foreign anguish" for James as it is for Marlene NourbeSe Philip.[63] Yet the tradition of ruptures, discontinuities, and abductions for new revolutionary possibilities that he deduces in the responses to the old colonial language is a salutary, though incomplete, response to the dilemmas posed by coloniality and language in the Caribbean.

The language of revolution does not allow James to escape the charge that precolonial Africa's role in the formation of the Caribbean is underplayed in his work. In a response to the racist charge that Africans brought nothing of worth to the New World, James twice noted that they "brought themselves."[64] This observation is not enough, and Paget Henry's reading of James as primarily concerned with what he saw as a modern Africa rather than premodern Africa is well worth noting.[65] James's historicism is a key feature of his thought to be aware of here, as his reluctance to engage further with Africa's role in the making of the Caribbean cannot be attributed just to a residual Eurocentrism within him or the times in which he lived. For James, "we of the Caribbean are a people more than any other people constructed by history."[66] This construction means that his impetus was always toward social movements or key moments in Western history that could be retrieved for their relevance today. The constant comparisons of the ancient Greek city-states to the Caribbean made by James were not made *primarily* to wonder at the "glory" of Greece or to acknowledge Greek politics and philosophy as a vital artifact of Western thought, though James clearly thought Greece should be seen in this light.[67] Rather, they were made to insist that the small size of Caribbean states should not be an impediment to their abilities to achieve great things in the future.[68] James wishes to use a narrowly conceived Western timeline against itself in order to fashion radical possibilities for the future.

The tropes of civilization, progress, and modernization that emerge from these texts contain much of dubious merit and are even more curious emerging from one of the region's leading Marxists. In the same decade that James spoke glowingly about the Caribbean's futures but with a noticeable caution—or perhaps put better, an absence of any discussion of a socialist solution to the Caribbean's problems—he would continue to write articles that attempted to rejuvenate Marxism for an international audience.[69] James, so certain in his reckoning that the experience of the plantation made Caribbean people a modern people long before the masses of Europe and determined in his struggle to clarify the relationship between tradition and modernity for the region at the moment of independence, was at times in the 1960s strangely unsure about whether the Caribbean was part of the "West." In his essay on the Mighty Sparrow, he would state, "We are Western, yet have to separate what is ours from what is Western, a very difficult task."[70] Is this a finely deduced observation, about the Caribbean's location within but simultaneously outside the West, which adequately summarizes James's position?[71] At times, in reading James's work, we are not sure; nor does James seem to be. *Beyond a Boundary* may well be seen as James's grand attempt to resolve that problem, simultaneously reconciling and posing questions about art, politics, and the capacities of Caribbean people on the new field of play called national independence.

Cricket and the Nation

It is now almost thirty years since Hazel Carby described *Beyond a Boundary* as "one of the most outstanding works of cultural studies ever produced," and the questions that it raises still seem inexhaustible, evinced by the continual critical commentary on this work.[72] The specific conjuncture that led to the writing of *Beyond a Boundary* is worth some contemplation, as it has the potential to resolve some of the queries surrounding the question with which I began this chapter, the debate often lamentably structured around an artificial divide between James as a political figure versus James as a cultural critic. In the arresting section of *Beyond a Boundary* titled "What Do Men Live By," the impetus that would eventually result in that text is addressed by James as follows:

> In 1938 a lecture tour took me to the United States and I stayed there fifteen years. The war came. It did not bring soviets and proletarian power. Instead the bureaucratic-totalitarian monster grew stronger and spread. As early as 1941 I had begun to question the premises of Trotskyism. It took nearly a decade of incessant labour and collaboration to break with it and reorganize my Marxist ideas to cope with the post-war world. That was a matter of doctrine, of history, of economics and politics. These pursuits I shared with collaborators, rivals, enemies and our public. We covered the ground thoroughly.
>
> In my private mind, however, I was increasingly aware of large areas of human existence that my history and my politics did not seem to cover. What did men live by? What did they want? What did history show that they had wanted? Had they wanted then what they wanted now? The men I had known, what had they wanted? What exactly was art and what exactly culture?[73]

Here James is clear that his turn to "culture" was approached from the perspective of a revolutionary Marxist intent on reorganizing his worldview within a *Marxist* perspective. His writing and explorations in his decades of intellectual labor after leaving the United States represent not a withering away of Marxist intention but the expansion of a worldview, always secured by Marxism, toward what Wynter terms a "Jamesian poeisis." Here James's originally stated crisis-of-Marxism conundrum/conjuncture transforms into new questions about Caribbean self-determination and freedom.

Beyond a Boundary follows a pattern similar to James's work on the Caribbean since *The Life of Captain Cipriani*, in which biographical sketches of key individuals are used to advance reflections on the wider society. The figure of the cricketing hero, masculinity and the Caribbean nation, and the relationship of the captain to his team are all themes given significant consideration, reflecting James's love of the game of cricket and his belief that it had tremendous social consequences in the emerging Caribbean nation. Cricket also gifted James with a figure that he thought ranked with the most important Caribbean citizens of his time, the West Indian batsman Frank Mortimer Worrell. Worrell, the first black man to gain a regular appointment as captain of the West Indies team, is widely acknowledged as the most important West Indian cricket captain of the twentieth century. He is the West Indian cricket captain that James showed the greatest interest in, and James himself was pivotal to Worrell's appointment, via his agitation on his behalf in the *Nation* (Trinidad), against the racist practice by the West Indies Cricket Board of Control of only hiring white captains for major tours by the West Indies team.[74] James's descriptions of Worrell are, however, worth recounting not merely for the regularly told tale of his successful campaign but because of the discourses of tradition, masculinity, and the "West Indian personality" that can be found within them.

In his contribution to the book *Cricket: The Great Captains*, James commences his argument with the strange assertion that "the essence of Frank Worrell's captaincy is not West Indian."[75] Worrell's legacy is that he is part of a hierarchy of captains of the game and, in James's estimation, one of the three pivotal captains of the twentieth century.[76] The captain as a leader "does not only depend on fine players. He makes the best of them and he makes players who are high class players into men who play above themselves."[77] As a molder of men and fashioner of masculinity, the captain occupies a preeminent place in his team's performance, in large part due to his ability to turn individuals into a team with a common purpose.[78] Worrell's historical importance is not that he captained one of the finest cricket teams of the twentieth century. In a couple of sentences that might have come straight from *Facing Reality*, James said: "It is not too much to say that in the world at large, today and in recent years, we have seen a massive instinctual rejection by people everywhere of the kind of systematized social organization which began with the organization of the economy by J. M. Keynes. This I know is somewhat difficult to accept in regard to a game like cricket, but I cannot think of it otherwise and that is the significance of Frank Worrell as a cricket captain."[79]

The captaincy of Worrell is not merely an expression of the creative self-activity of West Indian men but part of the "new society" being ushered in around the world. His efforts are part not just of the new that the Caribbean brings to cricket but the Caribbean's rethinking of Western modernity. James recounts a conversation that he had with Worrell, in which Worrell states he adopted the following approach to discussions on cricket with team members: "If something was wrong I told them what was right and left it to them."[80] James's reflection on this comment bears further scrutiny: "These words will always ring in my ears. They are something new, not only in West Indies cricket but in West Indies life. West Indians can often tell you what is wrong and some even what will make it right, but they don't leave it to you. Worrell did. It is the ultimate expression of a most finished personality, who knows his business, theory and practice, and knows modern men."[81]

Worrell, for James, "made West Indians and the world aware of what West Indians were capable of when their talents had full play. That is Worrell's gift to the West Indian personality."[82] Yet this invites the question: why the special emphasis on the captain of the team? No writer of James's stature would have been unaware of the class prejudices that were a central part of English cricket life in the midcentury, the animosity between amateurs and professionals, and the attempt at times to preserve the captaincy as the sole domain of Oxbridge players.[83] And what effect might Worrell's social status as a black middle-class man mean for his ability to lead the West Indies team?[84] The energy James threw into his campaign to make Worrell the West Indies cricket captain and his praise of Worrell's progressive leadership abilities do not square with Worrell's own autobiography, which particularly in its description of Caribbean social relations shows not a trace of radicalism.[85]

James himself suggested that some of Worrell's attributes were directly related to his class position, particularly noting in this regard that "he was always clam and unruffled even in times of crisis."[86] Missing here is any perspective on how this might have resulted in a sense of awe that might have becalmed mercurial players like Roy Gilchrist, who is reported to have claimed that while on the 1957 tour of England "Worrell was his father."[87] James's scattered reflections on cricket, tradition, and the West Indian middle classes suggest a perspective on West Indian cricket quite divorced from his revolutionary understandings of the free creative activity of the masses. For James,

> the middle classes in the West Indies have been brought up within a mental and moral framework which is best represented by those three men—Grace, Thomas Arnold . . . and Thomas Hughes . . . But that must come to an end. The West Indies have reached where they are because certain of them have had the opportunity to absorb to a large degree, and to adapt to their own uses, a certain definite tradition. But they have to bring something of their own now to the life that they have to live, and I believe in the cricket that they have been playing over the last two or three years they have found something of their own.[88]

In a related comment in a later article, tracing the same sources of influences, James noted that "juniors grow up and have to make their own independent way. In cricket, the West Indies have evolved a style of their own, even if in independence as a whole they have yet to do so,"[89] which leads James to observe that "we are inheritors, not creators, but we are keeping alive a great *tradition*, and doing so in the only way that is ever done, by adding something of our own, remaking it *anew*."[90] In this puzzling formulation, tradition is passed down here from the English to the West Indian middle classes, who seem to possess no alternative resources to draw on than those bequeathed to them by English culture. To focus just on this, though, is to miss the main thrust of James's point. The West Indian middle classes were creative in their time (in cricket and their anticolonial alliances, however evanescent, with the working classes) but dangerous now in their decline (the immediate preindependence moment).[91] They are, despite exemplary exceptions like Worrell, unable to remake tradition anew.

Arguably, the most revealing single part of *Beyond a Boundary* for any consideration of the themes I have discussed comes at its conclusion. James titles this "Epilogue and Apotheosis," and the *Oxford English Dictionary*'s definition of *apotheosis*—"the highest point in the development of something"—is well seen in these four pages. *Beyond a Boundary* was finished by October 1960, and it is likely that the only reason we now have this epilogue that covers the 1960–61 West Indies tour of Australia is because of the difficulty that James had in securing a publisher.[92] This tour was already significant as a result of the successful campaign waged by James to overturn the racist policy of appointing only white captains to lead the West Indies team, which resulted in Frank Worrell's nomination as captain. But James himself suggests that he was driven to write this epilogue when it became clear that the West Indies team's tour to Australia "had added a new dimension to cricket history."[93] His description of Garfield Sobers's batting and of the final farewell for the West Indies team following the series deserves particularly close attention:

> The first innings of Sobers at Brisbane was the most beautiful batting I have ever seen. Never was such ease and certainty of stroke, such early seeing of the ball and such late, leisured play, such command by a batsman not only of the bowling but of himself. He seemed to be expressing a personal vision. I had thought of him as having too much bowling to do, but after that innings I knew that such batting can come only at moments, and until they come the unfortunate artist has the disruptive task of adjusting himself to what he can do in relation to what he knows is possible. This is a sphere beyond the unfailing self-mastery of a Bradman or a Hutton . . .
>
> Yet my greatest moment was the speech making after the last Test. Sir Donald Bradman was remarkably reminiscent of a chairman at a party celebration meeting. Only in the intervals of the return to a habitual self while he was being applauded did you catch a glimpse of the relentless scorer of

centuries and the watchful, tireless captain. Benaud was fluent, with carefully chosen phrases, full of affection and respect for Frank Worrell and the West Indians (and not forgetting his own team); definitely a man of feeling, not ashamed or wary of it, but a man seeing the whole of his world and steadily. But Frank Worrell, speaking last, was crowned with the olive. Beauty is indeed in the eye of the beholder. I saw all the West Indian ease, humour and easy adaptation to environment. It was after our conversations and I could see his precise and uncompromising evaluations, those it seems are now second nature. But they were draped with that diplomatic graciousness which has apparently so impressed the Australian Prime Minister. If I say he won the prize it is because the crowd gave it to him. They laughed and cheered him continuously. He expanded my conception of West Indian personality. Nor was I alone. I caught a glimpse of what brought a quarter of a million inhabitants of Melbourne into the streets to tell the West Indian cricketers good-bye, a gesture spontaneous and in cricket without precedent, one people speaking to another. Clearing their way with bat and ball, West Indians at that moment had made a public entry into the comity of nations. Thomas Arnold, Thomas Hughes and the Old Master himself would have recognized Frank Worrell as their boy.[94]

James's language here is unsurpassed. His description of Sobers batting is not just reminiscent of Solon's description of the Greek athletes but goes beyond it in its desire for Sobers's performance on the field to be translated into a vision of the Caribbean nation beyond the boundary.[95] The great batsman's command comes not through a tireless mastery of the bowling, which James suggests was the contribution of Bradman, but through the confident knowledge that the field of play is his to control, leading to a demand that his artistic intelligence create something new.

This is not James's only description of Sobers, now widely lauded as the greatest all-round cricketer of all time and a national hero of Barbados.[96] In his 1969 essay "Garfield Sobers," James sets out to counter the notion that Sobers was a "natural cricketer," one endowed with physical gifts that largely explain his prowess on the field.[97] Rejecting this, James declares that he has "always, except for one single occasion . . . [seen him] as the fine fruit of a great tradition."[98] This leads James to stress the "orthodoxy" of Sobers's batting and the "classical character" of his captaincy and claim a genealogy of West Indian batting that stretches back to the planter-merchant class of the early twentieth century. Caribbean masculinity in the nationalist era—Sobers's time—is here presented as strangely dependent on a colonial, minority elite, one that has "a history of its own, going deep, too deep for the present area of discourse."[99] For James, Sobers emerges "not as a fortuitous combination of atoms which by chance have coalesced into a superb public performer . . . [but the] living embodiment of centuries of a tortured history."[100] Similarly, the Guyanese East Indian batsmen Rohan Kanhai and the audaciousness of his play represented not just a new style of West Indian batsmanship. Rather, in him, no longer does the Indo-Caribbean citizen have to prove his right to belong to the Caribbean nation but can creatively extend a newly rising Caribbean tradition.[101] Both Kanhai and Sobers thus "embody some essence of that crowded vagueness which passes for the history of the West Indies."[102]

Returning to the epilogue, we learn that James's "greatest moment" of the tour came not on the field of play. In his descriptions of Bradman, Benaud, and Worrell at the awards presentation ceremony, James sketches his vision of the transitional moments between different cricketing personalities, of different ages, in a mere paragraph. Bradman's personality, tempered by the 1930s in which he was at his zenith as a cricketer, could only play the part of a party chairman with limited success, as behind it was always a steely, watchful masculinity. Richie Benaud, Worrell's counterpart and the current Australian captain, was far more at ease, and in a striking phrase James describes him as "definitely a man of feeling, not ashamed or wary of it." However, Worrell's speech was the highlight of the postmatch ceremony. The "beauty" James described was not merely Worrell's charm or the ease and clarity of his speech but the means by which an indisputably West Indian sensibility could be crafted into a disposition capable of reaching out to a world community, as an equal, on its own terms. The magnetism of Worrell, which James says left him after a couple of hours of conversation "as tired as if I had been put through a wringer," wedded to a productivity of performance in the field and in his assessment of the game, is part of the newness that the West Indian brings to the mix of global identities.[103] Command and mastery of the (masculine) self is as essential as physical prowess on the field of play.[104] This is the expansion of his conception of the West Indian personality that James said Worrell gave him and, indeed, that James gives us—an elegant juggling of tradition and modernity and a constant critical reflection on the old that haunts the new. At a time in which Australia had a whites-only immigration policy and the cricketer and writer J. H. Fingleton could write condescendingly to James at the end of the series about the West Indies team—"The manners of them were admirable and a credit to their race"—the ticker-tape parade by a quarter million residents of Melbourne was an astonishing event.[105] At this moment, "West Indians . . . made a public entry into the comity of nations," and such was the nature of their entry—returning to the golden age of cricket and (re) making tradition anew—that James ends *Beyond a Boundary* with the declaration that "Thomas Arnold, Thomas Hughes and the Old Master himself would have recognized Frank Worrell as their boy."[106]

Our consideration of these final lines should be influenced by the reworkings that James did of them in three articles all written within a year of the publication of *Beyond a Boundary*. In his article "Cricket in West Indian Culture," James repeats his understanding that the West Indies entrance into the "comity of nations" was "done under the aegis of the men . . . [of] the public school trad-ition" but adds the following lines: "But juniors grow up and have to make their own independent way. In cricket, the West Indies have evolved a style of their own, even if in independence as a whole they have yet to do so."[107] The departure of the West Indies team from their 1963 tour of England is seen as having "un-doubtedly registered the West Indies as a national personality in the British con-sciousness."[108] It would be an error to conclude that the West Indian personality is dependent on the recognition of the British or Australian publics of the value of West Indian cricket; in fact, the real breakthrough is that "the West Indians had accepted, recognized themselves, and once you do that, other people always welcome you."[109]

It is not difficult to discern the weight given to discourses of tradition and modernity throughout all of James's thought on Anglophone Caribbean society and culture at the cusp of independence. Every aspect of a newly assertive na-tional culture—whether literature, sports, calypso, theater, or the fine arts—that caught his gaze became part of a series of reflections on what he would call "the old world and the new."[110] *Beyond a Boundary*, penned under the working title "Who Only Cricket Know," provides us with one of James's most poignant dis-cussions of the question of tradition in the Anglophone Caribbean:

> What do they know of cricket who only cricket know? West Indians crowd-ing to Tests bring with them the whole past history and future hopes of the islands. English people, for example, have a conception of themselves breathed from birth. Drake and the mighty Nelson, Shakespeare, Waterloo, the Charge of the Light Brigade, the few who did so much for so many, the success of par-liamentary democracy, those and such as those constitute a national tradition. Underdeveloped countries have to go back centuries to rebuild one. We of the West Indies have none at all, none that we know of. To such people the three W's, Ram and Val wrecking the English batting, help to fill a huge gap in their consciousness and in their needs.[111]

Reflecting on this passage after fifty years of independence, one can't help but be struck by the weight of English tradition on the Anglophone Caribbean, a burden that produced so much anguish for Caribbean people, thrown into an even sharper relief by a sojourn in England. James's discussions of tradition/mo-dernity are full of paradoxes. At times he privileges a middle-class authority that in his political lifework he relentlessly disavowed. There is also a yearning for the popular coupled with a disconcerting uncertainty that the very *modern* Carib-bean (one of his theoretical innovations) has any past/tradition to speak of at all. The Caribbean popular at its finest emerges with the birth of national indepen-dence but cannot escape an ambivalent relationship with centuries of tradition forged in a different land.

Cricket, like many sports passionately consumed by men, also occupies a strangely ambivalent heteronormative space, which James's unconscious "critical darts" help us see more clearly.[112] However, the maleness of cricket remains; men still usher in the new Caribbean nation, and though women have a more complicated interpretive role in the social production of cricket culture than we might expect, they are still, in James's cricketing parlance, marginal to the creation of the West Indian nation.[113] James's insights on the game of cricket are a perspective crucial to the formation of our present Caribbean selves, a scarcely surpassed meditation on coloniality and freedom, on the weight of history on culture. The ironies are considerable here, which we can only fully appreciate after two generations of postindependence Caribbean misrule by the very Caribbean middle-class men that James could not help but salute in his cricketing writings. When we further consider the "fictions of citizenship" that these regimes have meant for Caribbean women, the poor, and the region's LGBT residents, our pause at James's reminisces grows.[114]

The Hearts of Men?

> In an article welcoming the West Indies team of 1957 E.W. Swanton has written in the Daily Telegraph that in the West Indies the cricket ethic has shaped not only the cricketers but social life as a whole. It is an understatement. There is a whole generation of us, and perhaps two generations, who have been formed by it not only in social attitudes *but in our most intimate personal lives, in fact there more than anywhere else.* The social attitudes we could to some degree alter if we wished. *For the inner self the die was cast.* But that is not my theme except incidentally. The coming West Indian novelists will show the clash between the native temperament and environment, and this doctrine from a sterner clime.
>
> C. L. R. James, *Beyond a Boundary*[115]

James was not unaware of the ways in which women are narratively written out of foundational stories of the nation, though he did not address this issue in his cricket writings. His struggle to rethink the premises that resulted in his elision of women's agency and participation in the nation is, I would argue, one of the most compelling parts of his attempt to usher in the new society.

I would like to begin my discussion of this aspect of James's legacy with the epigraph from *Beyond a Boundary* cited above. James's extraordinary comment, ostensibly about the cricket code, is a point at which one might begin a discussion of the fascinating ambivalences around gender and sexuality that arise in his work. The sphere of intimacy is raised by James as the site of the deepest penetration of the public school code, but immediately on acknowledging this, he draws back from its implications, suggesting that West Indian novelists will be the ones to fully explore this terrain. This retreat itself is ironic, for a couple of reasons. First, James's reflections on cricket culture are a critical resource for those interested in exploring the relationship between coloniality, masculinity, and the reproduction of certain forms of gender relations in the Caribbean. These texts reveal not an easily identifiable Caribbean masculinity with an instrumental relationship to sports that simply confirms its prowess but compelling revelations about male homosocial bonding, the complexities and ambivalences of colonial masculinities, and a yearning for a particular productivity of performance by the male body both on the field of play and in the wider Caribbean society.

Second, there is throughout James's texts a *worry* about women and their relationship to the new society he wished to usher into being. A reading of James's critical work on women and gender relations could easily occupy a volume of its own. This examination would include readings of his short story "Triumph," his novel *Minty Alley*, and his series of letters from London in May–August 1932 in which James evinces a great deal of interest in the social environment of his new city and the gender relations that exist within it.[116] His American years, which he referred to as the most creative period in his life, produced his striking letters to Constance Webb and a number of discussions regarding what was referred to in radical organizations as "the woman question," while his celebrated essay on black women writers was published in the 1980s.[117] Late in his life, in a series of articles and interviews, James constantly expressed his disillusionment with his past personal experiences with women, the blame for which he placed squarely at his door. The nature and extent of the ruminations on gender in James's work take on greater importance when we consider how rare reflections of this kind are by black Caribbean men of his generation.[118] It points us not just toward a greater understanding of the coloniality of gender relations in the Caribbean but contains hints for those of us interested in speculating about the place of Caribbean men in Caribbean feminist criticism.[119]

There is another, more compelling reason for considering James's effort to think about women's struggles and gender relations. As I have argued earlier in this book, the most decisive change in the intellectual culture of the region in the last generation has been the outpouring of an incredible array of multidisciplinary scholarship and activism on women, their lives, and Caribbean gender relations.[120] That this work has produced its own backlash is without doubt, and it has disconcertingly revealed the sheer intransigence of sexist culture in the region, wryly expressed by Patricia Mohammed when she notes that "Caribbean patriarchy is not willing to be a taciturn partner in its own deconstruction."[121] A number of questions might well be raised about the now burgeoning body of work on Caribbean masculinities.[122] What is the study of Caribbean masculinity *for*? Is it explicitly guided by feminist ethics, and what futures does it hope to imagine?[123] Beyond discourses about "hegemonic masculinities" with illuminating but somewhat tightly scripted mappings of the "Caribbean male colonization of black female subjectivity," what different perspectives can emerge for examining the interpolation of patriarchy into all of our lives in the Caribbean?[124] What can C. L. R. James and his struggle to theorize the transformations in gender relations he saw over the course of his life tell us about the reception of feminism in the minds of Caribbean men?

Women as a Future

> Great men make history, but only the history that women do the caring work to allow them to make.
>
> Selma James, comment at the C. L. R. James at 100 conference[125]

One of the conundrums of thinking about C. L. R. James on gender is that his early literary work, written in Trinidad in the late 1920s, centers black women's subjectivity and thematizes gendered concerns in a manner that he would not fully return to until the end of his life. Critical interpretations of C. L. R. James from a gendered perspective have focused on his early literary writings rather than his prose, the focus of this essay. In this period, James wrote the short stories "La Divina Pastora" (1927), "La Diablesse" (1928), "Triumph" (1929), "Turner's Prosperity" (1929), "Revolution" (1931), and "The Star That Would Not Shine" (1931) and his only novel, *Minty Alley* (written in 1928 or 1929 but not published until 1936). In these short stories, the influence of social realism on James is unmistakable, and "La Diablesse" and "The Star That Would Not Shine" explicitly take the form of a story related to James or popularly told in his community, to which he added structure and narrative flow. "La Divina Pastora" is perhaps the best example of this, as he states in his autobiographical reflections that this story was related to him by his grandmother, and he "set out to make a literary short story out of it."[126] Of his fiction writings, critical attention has focused on "Triumph," arguably his best short story, and his only novel, *Minty Alley*. Both are set in the barrack yards of Trinidad and, in the pre-1950 Anglo-creole literature of the Caribbean, explore with remarkable candor themes perhaps not unique but generally unheralded up to this time. Poor women are central to the plot rather than marginal to it, and they constantly upstage the male characters with their passion, wit, vitality, and collectivity. In a world of colonial exploitation, barrack-yard women assert their dignity, strategize on how to survive poverty and prejudice, and construct livable, human communities. As Patricia Saunders notes, the ability of these barrack-yard women to find humor, varieties of social living, and fulfillment in a society predicated on institutionalized class, racial, and gendered prejudice is the triumph of the story.[127]

It is not simply that James gives his working-class characters dignity and expressive, complex lives. He also prefigures debates about the conundrums of Afro-Indian solidarity in postindependence Trinidad, and for Brinda Mehta, "the novel's revolutionary and truly innovative merit lies in its ability to spotlight a previously invisible Trinidadian constituency through a literary engagement with Indian-ness by a black author."[128] Moreover, in his autobiographical sketches, he suggests that his literary activities prepared him for his political writings: "With this very clear idea of the importance of the class division between the educated and the uneducated I began to explore politics in 1931 through the activities of Captain Cipriani."[129] Yet in reading these texts, a fascinating contradiction regarding the representations of gender and class becomes apparent. For Hazel Carby, in James's literature "the world of the working class is imagined overwhelmingly through figures of women . . . The class divisions of James's fictional world are gendered: the masses are feminized; the point of view of the intellectual/middle class protagonist is masculine."[130] This is well supported by Faith Smith's reading of *The Black Jacobins*, in which she shows that James's allusions to women in that text are little more than afterthoughts, and they are certainly scripted as marginal to the revolution.[131] However, Carby's comment that "when James abandoned fiction to write about revolutionary politics and revolutionary heroes, he also gave up trying to write about women" is too hasty a conclusion.[132] Rather than a departure from speaking about women toward a Pan-African Marxist revolutionary narrative that while highly gendered had little to say of women, I would suggest that James's texts from the 1930s until the end of his life had much to say about women and the possibility of human liberation through a hesitantly articulated gender politics.

James was never completely unaware of the ways in which women are narratively written out of foundational stories of the nation. A fine example of this can be seen in his 1976 speech "Towards the Seventh: The Pan-African Congress—Past, Present and Future."[133] Like most radicals, James was faced with the problem posed by the sixth Pan-African Congress, which was not only hijacked by postindependence governmental elites in Africa and the Caribbean but, for James, "left *no* particular doctrine behind it."[134] In his statement about the program a seventh Pan-African Congress would need to follow, James called for the end to the deification of the national state in Africa, indicted the new African elites, and insisted that revolutionaries' primary concern must be with the masses. This is a statement as relevant for our time as for a generation ago. Nearing the conclusion of his speech, James turned to a discussion of George Lamming's *Natives of My Person* and its treatment of women to stake a claim for the immediacy and primacy of gender in the liberation struggle to come: "Today, Lamming says, today women represent something, are something, they *are* a future that men must know something about. In other words, what he is saying here is what he has been saying in all his books: that men constitute an elite in relation to women, and women have got a capacity, which men have got to learn."[135]

A capacity which men have got to learn. The African American activist and scholar Geri Augusto has recollected having lunch with James the very day that he finished reading *Natives of My Person*. Augusto says that James asked her opinion on its final page, where Lamming has one of his female characters conclude with the enigmatic line "We are a future they must learn." He then told her that he believed that Lamming was saying that "women are the last revolution."[136] Immediately the multiple meanings of *last* come to mind—*last* as "latest," *last* as "final," *last* as "lingering." These are memorable turns of phrase, the meaning of which can arguably only be understood through a long view of James's appreciation of women's agency in the new society.

However, certainly the romanticism, ambiguities, and occasional paternalism of these formulations by James should also give us pause. In her speech at the C. L. R. James at 100 conference, Selma James said her heart "sank" when she read the last line of Lamming's *Natives of My Person*. For her, women are actually disempowered by Lamming's line, as they must wait for men to understand them, and men take so inordinately long to learn things. James had a complicated relationship to this novel, a point to which I will return. However, my reading of James on gender is not dependent on casting James's comments as uniquely insightful, positioning him as a male feminist or even resolutely profeminist. It is, rather, the contradictions, despair, and worry that animates James's thoughts on women and gender that are the deeply poignant and instructive part of his legacy. In the following, I track some of the concerns he expressed from the mid-1950s onward on this matter in a number of episodic, fragmented, but highly illuminating texts, ranging from *American Civilization* to his unpublished autobiography. I focus on the late, post-1940s James, as it is in the aftermath of World War II and in the midst of his struggles to conceive the new society that we first see James self-consciously trying to theorize the problems posed by gender relations as a central challenge faced by modern societies.

What If C. L. R. James Had Met Claudia Jones in 1948?

> On this, my 37th birthday, I think of my mother. My mother, a machine worker in a garment factory, died when she was the same age as I am today—37 years old. I think I began then to develop an understanding of the sufferings of my people and my class and to look for a way to end them.
>
> Claudia Jones, February 1952[137]

> [My mother] was the centre of my life. I followed literature because of her. When she put a book down I picked it up. She was an unusual woman, who in 1900, at the beginning of the century was reading every book she could put her hands on. She was an educated person in literary matters and in the social world. . . . She had a certain style and elegance which she had learnt, and which she transferred to me.
>
> C. L. R. James, interview with Paul Buhle, 1987[138]

In the late 1940s, within a year of each other, two Trinidadian Marxists living in the United States penned classic texts, both deeply critical of the limitations of the Marxist parties in which they had thrown their hopes for world revolution. These two articles—C. L. R. James's "The Revolutionary Answer to the Negro Problem in the USA" and Claudia Jones's "An End to the Neglect of the Problems of Negro Women!"—remain classics of the black radical tradition but, to my knowledge, have never been read in concert, both for their divergences of opinion and simultaneously for the similarity of their central impulse.[139] James's better known article was his summary position after ten years in the United States on what was then termed the "Negro question," or, alternatively, the place of African Americans in the world revolution he expected would follow the end of World War II. In it, we see an evolution in James's perspective on this question from his earlier position in his 1939 talks with Leon Trotsky in Mexico, at times during which he seemed somewhat more dubious of the possibility of an independent black movement than Trotsky himself.[140] A decade after his Mexico debates, James would sketch a mainstream socialist view of black struggle that insisted on its subordination to organized labor and the Marxist party, before daringly advancing his tendency's position. Not only does black struggle possess a "vitality and validity of its own," but it can "intervene with terrific force upon the general social and political life of the nation."[141] It is a movement that can "exercise a powerful influence upon the revolutionary proletariat," whose members "on the basis of their own experiences, approach the conclusions of Marxism" and, indeed, need not wait on the Marxist party, as they may well act as the ferment of the coming proletarian revolution.[142]

James will further claim that his conclusions are not without precedence. In a masterfully brief survey of major events in US history and blacks' relationship to "revolutionary elements in past revolutionary struggles," James argues that blacks were pivotal in determining the historical progression of events like the Civil War, the Revolutionary War, and populist movements.[143] That this is not a panegyric to past revolutionary glories is clear, as each story ends with an inevitable betrayal, and on blacks "there falls . . . a very terrible repression."[144] The postwar revolutionary movement must realize that the "independent Negro movement . . . must find its way to the proletariat."[145] If this solidarity is not achieved, "the repression of past times . . . will be infinitely . . . more terrible today."[146] In order to understand the black struggle, one must comprehend its culture, an intimacy that reveals that the "hatred of bourgeois society and the readiness to destroy it . . . rests among them to a degree greater than in any other section of the population in the United States."[147]

Claudia Jones's "An End to the Neglect of the Problems of Negro Women!" is no less informed by the urgency of the post–World War II situation in the United States and similarly connects the history of black struggle to contemporary black liberation. Black women's militancy, for Jones, has always played a crucial role in resistance to colonization, racism, and apartheid in the Americas and poses crucial problems for both capitalism and progressive movements. The plight of black women exposes further the hypocrisy of the then emerging Cold War propaganda that lauds the achievements of American women, as "degradation and super-exploitation" are their lot. In the labor market, less pay for equal work and the systematic postwar retrenchment of black women illustrate exploitation by race *and* gender and make black women the potential pivotal agents of change in the social revolution to come.

Considering the political economy of black women's labor and arguing that Aimé Césaire's later formulation that blacks are "doubly proletarianized and alienated" might have to be (pace Fanon) slightly stretched are at the heart of Jones's work.[148] In her critiques of the negative images of black women in the media, the chauvinism of white women, and emphasis on the "special responsibility" of black men in confronting patriarchy, Jones suggests that an anticolonial revolution in social relations is the only route that progressive movements can take in the United States. Colonial knowledge and its hierarchies of social power refuse black women the same social honor and respect accorded to white women, and here Jones's examples range from the "humiliation" of the suffragists, forced to sleep on cots next to black women, to contemporary dances, where black women are neglected while attention is showered on their white and brown counterparts. Moreover, bourgeois ideology understands well that the oppression of black women demands new theories of gendered subordination, designed for *all* women.[149] Black women's struggles can never be a mere adjunct of a wider woman's movement:

> A developing consciousness on the woman question today, therefore, must not fail to recognize that the Negro question in the United States is *prior* to and not equal to, the woman question; that only to the extent that we fight all chauvinistic expressions and actions as regard the Negro people and fight for the full equality of the Negro people, can women as a whole advance their struggle for equal rights. For the progressive women's movement, the Negro woman, who combines in her status the worker, the Negro, and the woman, is the vital link to this heightened political consciousness.[150]

The power of these articles by James and Jones, in their determined refusal to subordinate black struggle to the leading progressive movements of their time, suggests a subterranean commonality of purpose, beyond their obvious differences in emphasis. Nor do the similarities between James and Jones end here. Both were detained on Ellis Island and left the United States against their will—James leaving shortly before what would have been his inevitable deportation in 1953, while Jones was officially deported in 1955. James was among the first to write critically about the Mighty Sparrow and carnival in Trinidad, while Jones was instrumental to the founding of what would become the Notting Hill Carnival. As we see in the epigraphs above, both spoke hauntingly on the influence of their mothers in their formation as radical intellectuals. Both were perceptive critics from the late 1950s of American imperialism in the Caribbean and disavowed the limited character of its Anglophone countries' coming independence. And yet despite their close proximity in New York in the early 1950s and London for around a decade until Jones's untimely death in 1964, there is no record of any collaboration or sustained discussion between them.[151]

The reasons for this are not difficult to discover, as James's Trotskyism and later work as a leading member of the Johnson-Forrest Tendency was anathema to Jones's membership in the Communist Party.[152] One place to begin a contextualization of what James lost from this potential collaboration with Jones are his writings on gender and women's struggles in the 1940s. In a passage in a 1944 letter to Constance Webb, James declared:

> With the increasing opportunities that modern production (and the development of ideas based upon it) gives to women, a new type of woman arises. She is called a career woman. The name is stupid but nevertheless very revealing. A man is never a career man. That is his right and privilege. He can have his career, and the finest fruit of his successful career is wife and children. But the woman is called career woman because her "career" in modern society demands she place herself in a subordinate position or even renounce normal life. The social dice are loaded against her; and the plain fact of the matter is that they are loaded, not only in the economic opportunities, *but in the minds of men*. The men cannot take it. I know my own sex reasonably well. With the best will in the world, a man, a good man, unconsciously demands that a woman submit to him. It is what he wants that matters in the end, not what she wants. Some men are crudely egotistic. Others are not. They believe in equality; but the practice of society dominates them. It must, as long as they do not consciously oppose it.[153]

James's candid assessment of patriarchy refutes any suggestion that the "woman question" could be solved by a vulgarly materialist approach but simultaneously focuses on the middle-class career woman as the locus of his concerns. An explanation of this focus is seen in his 1950 text *American Civilization*, in which James suggests that his decision to focus on this group is due to the intermediate position they hold within society, through which all the ambivalences of women's new freedoms are supposedly most fully crystallized.[154] These women who are the chief beneficiaries of the capitalist system are "the most unhappy . . . the most dissatisfied, the most antagonistic in their relations with men that it is possible to find in history or as far as can be gathered, in other parts of the world."[155] Though the argument has been won over the right of these women to have a career, the "antagonism between theoretical and practical life" continues.[156] While James yields at points in his analysis to the temptations that a highly important but narrow economic determinism might give him—"it is equally obvious that so drastic an overturn in contemporary domestic relations is conditioned upon an equally drastic overturn in economic relations"—he later suggests that "in the modern world the only possible solution of the basic relation between the sexes is that women must become human beings first and women afterwards."[157] Even when the most cursory freedoms seem to have been granted to women via their ability to work outside the home, they bear the weight of the majority of the housework. Even more oppressive than this is that, "except in rare cases, the responsibility for adjustments to differences of personality fall almost automatically upon her."[158] The women's movement is part of a larger struggle for humanity in the present age, as "today . . . equality is not an individual need or the subjective passion of a few intense or rebellious people. *From every point of view it is a social necessity in the modern world.*"[159]

This focus on middle-class women is necessary for James, so he can show the distinctive gendered nature of women's oppression in American capitalist society. Working-class women are given only a cursory treatment, which notes the modern nature of their lives and points out that the same hardships that afflict middle-class women affect them "with tenfold force."[160] In a strange formulation, James adds that working-class women "are less vocal, protest less. History has repeatedly shown that this is not because they feel less but because they see no way out."[161] There is a similar absence of any discussion of race or racialized oppression, leading one to conclude that James's middle-class woman is very likely white.

A thoroughgoing critique of the means by which gendered analysis enters *American Civilization* is complicated by its status as a deliberately provisional document, which James hoped to further revise but which languished after his departure from America. The editors of *American Civilization*, Anna Grimshaw and Keith Hart, have noted that parts of James's analysis of American women, intended for a revised version of *American Civilization*, were incorporated into *Facing Reality*, his evaluation of the 1956 Hungarian revolution.[162] However, the short extract on women from *Facing Reality* reads quite differently from the text of *American Civilization* on the issue of women's relationship to capitalist society.[163] The central paradox of women's lives is that purported equality before the law has only exposed further the restrictions placed on them due to their gendered identities in class society. In his repudiation of the "shams and vulgarity and cruelty of bourgeois mentality," James declared that it is "in the United States, where women are abstractly most free, that there is taking place a colossal struggle for the establishment of *truly human relations between men and women.*"[164] However, in a deft reversal of his previous arguments in *American Civilization*, James notes that "the real battle for new relations between the sexes is being fought above all in the American working class."[165] The tensions in middle-class heterosexual relationships merely signal the problem, one that the middle class is loath to deal with—it can only resort to the dissolution of these unions or greater "antagonism in sex and personal relations."[166] The working classes alone have the potential to transform these relationships into something new and, hence, enable women to "live a complete life."[167] Continuing this line of argument in *Modern*

Politics, his 1960 series of lectures in Trinidad, James would note that "for many centuries women were the most oppressed section of society, and it is common knowledge, common talk, writing among philosophers, that a society was usually to be judged by the position that women occupied in it."[168] Further to this, James suggests that "the beginning of a truly satisfactory relationship in personal lives must begin with a total reorganization of labor relations in every department of life."[169] The solution to the perennial problem of gender injustice, which colonizes both the public and private spaces that women inhabit, is a reorganization of labor in both the public *and* private spheres.[170]

It is impossible not to speculate if the shift we see between *American Civilization* and *Modern Politics* was not as a result of another major influence in James's life, his relationship with Selma James. C. L. R. and Selma first met in New York in 1950, and she has recounted the encouragement he gave to her first publication "A Woman's Place," published in 1952.[171] They later married in England, where Selma James was to become the head of the International Wages for Housework campaign. A profound radical, Selma James debated with James in his later years the value of the unwaged work she had provided to him over the years, in the process of an acrimonious separation.[172] Yet the record from the 1960s does not present straightforward evidence of a growing consciousness and sympathy of James on women's place in the new society. He gave a lecture titled "The Man-Woman Relation" in Montreal in 1967 that was bewildering in its labored attempts to understand the oppression of women and filled with idiosyncratic juxtapositions of Shakespeare, Russia, and the woman question, with little of the sympathy and insights of his musings in the 1940s and 1950s.[173] Similarly, in the final chapter of his draft autobiography, which he declared was the "climax of his political ideas," the question of gender is absent.[174] It suggests a strange ambivalence on this question, essential to acknowledge if we are not to minimize the contradictions that his work arguably never escaped.

The Hearts of Men . . . or Failure

In the 1970s C. L. R. James was similarly preoccupied by the question of gender, and the urgency of these questions seems to have grown at this point in his life. In an interview in the late 1970s by L. Anthony-Welch, James made a number of striking comments about the then newly emergent work of Toni Morrison, Alice Walker, and Ntozake Shange.[175] The value of Morrison's and Walker's work for James is that they are speaking about black women as they exist in the world, without a need to write a "protest" novel about white imperialism's effect on them or produce work that self-reflexively articulates a black aesthetic or, alternatively, reproduces the politics of the (white) women's movement.[176] Here we see the introduction of the category of the "new" again, and James's reading of Morrison and Walker is quite similar to his appreciation of Earl Lovelace, which can be seen in the effusive praise with which he showered both Walker and Lovelace in published reviews of their novels.[177] In response to a question about whether he had written about black women in his prior work, James responded:

> Not particularly, but I have written about black people in general. I have written about black people and have taken society as a whole. But I have been struck, since I came here [the United States] in 1969. It is the first time the entry of the black woman into political and social activity has hit me as never before in my life. Before, they were just a part of the general struggle, and I saw them in Trinidad taking part and doing good work but the way they've come to the front is exciting and nothing is going to take place without them.[178]

James's candor is remarkable, though disconcerting, as one can only wonder about the forms of studied indifference and blindness toward black women's experiences that he and so many of his colleagues shared when he produced some of his most creative work in the middle of the century. Still, his openness to engagement with this new work and the sincerity of his appreciation of it no doubt were the reasons for his close relationship with Walker and Shange in the 1980s, who both visited him in London during this time.[179] One of James's last articles, titled "Three Black Women Writers: Toni Morrison, Alice Walker, Ntozake Shange," celebrates their work not merely for its artistic merits but for the social movement that it embodies. The chief value of these works for James is their ability to open up horizons of possibility in human relations not dreamed of in socialism or in previously articulated visions of African American communities. Resistance to patriarchy and sexual commodification, the ambivalent role of the church in black community formation, and friendships between women are all themes within these texts that James believed announce a new stage of self-awareness within the black community and are part of the new world struggling to be born.

However, I would suggest that it is impossible to understand the significance of James's writings on Morrison, Walker, and Shange without considering parts of his unpublished autobiography. In his interview for the book *Visions of History*, James said, "I know that an autobiography is the best way for me to sum up and to draw some conclusions. It isn't going to be purely what I have already said."[180] According to Anna Grimshaw, James never fully had his heart in the autobiography but labored away nonetheless, producing a number of striking but uneven and overlapping texts.[181] There is one part of this work that James, by his own admission, devoted a considerable amount of time toward—the section titled "My Experiences with Women and Sex." In a 1980 interview, the significance of this chapter is clarified. Not only did James write it early in the process of constructing his autobiography, though it was slated to come toward the end of the work, but he circulated it to a group of his friends for comments.[182] In his answer to a question querying the significance of this chapter, James stated, "Today, in my opinion one of the great events in the world is that women are seeking to find out who and what they are.... That to me is one of the great events that are taking place and I wanted to say what I had to say and make a contribution to that clarification."[183] This suggests that the status of women's liberation as a *social* movement is of primary interest for James, but in his next response, he reverses this perspective with a comment about his personal life. James notes that he has been married three times, and "there were some very satisfactory relations during those marriages but they didn't work out completely as I wished and now during the last ten years I have got to see that wherever they went wrong, the fault was mine."[184] The personal and the political are thus twinned in James's attempt to come to terms with his relationships with women.

A final detour to *Beyond a Boundary* is apt. In his description of the cricketer Wilton St. Hill, James sadly states that on the 1928 tour of England he was "a horrible, a disastrous, an incredible failure, the greatest failure who ever came out of the West Indies."[185] One wonders if these words may not also describe James's essay "My Experiences with Women and Sex." This article is a fifteen-page amalgam of very intimate details about James's awareness of sex and relationships, often couched within some deeply problematic formulations. At points, James blithely and without a trace of criticism describes relationships between men and women in colonial Trinidad that verge on sexual predation and assault. This revelation comes coupled with some striking observations about James's view of and vision for gender relations.[186] The most memorable parts of this article for the considerations I have been following here come in James's discussion of his relationship with his second wife in the United States and deserve to be quoted in full:

> After we had been married together for about a year or perhaps nine months, she told me one day, with a certain passion, "Look here, tell me what you want from me, what you want me to do, what do you think of a wife you can like and what I can give to you. Tell me please but don't leave me in this situation. Tell me something." I could tell her nothing because I had only the vaguest idea of what she was speaking about. It seemed that as a husband, living in the same house, I was most unsatisfactory not sexually nor in my behaviour, I am a well-behaved person, I don't quarrel or shout at people far less shout at my wife, we go out periodically when there is something that we want to see, we have friends, there has always been enough money to carry on the affairs of the household, though at times things were rather sharp but it seems that as a husband, my wife in Trinidad had spotted it, and my first wife in the United States was quite plain about it, my virtues as a husband were entirely negative, but I didn't pay attention to them as human beings sharing a life with me. I had a very active life and dealing with politics, literature and matters of that kind, it was looked upon, not so much by me but for me it was quite natural, by everybody else as a kind of life which was unusual and was worth respect. These women gave it the respect that it seemed such a life demanded but I gave it all that I had in the way of attention and special concern. The plain fact of the matter is as personalities, as individuals sharing a life with me both in Trinidad and the United States, I ignored them completely. It was many years before I discovered that.[187]

Acknowledging this failure would never be enough for James, who then tries to theorize the reasons for his shortcoming. He states that his eyes have been opened to the complexities of his relationships with women by the work of two Caribbean writers, Saint-John Perse and George Lamming, and he cites extensively from Lamming's novel *Natives of My Person*.[188] Some clarifications are in order here on the complicated relationship between James, Lamming, and *Natives of My Person*. Both Paul Buhle and Kent Worcester in their biographies of James state that Lamming used C. L. R. and Selma James's relationship as the basis for his exploration of the wrenching difficulties of relationships between men and women in that novel.[189] In his keynote address at the C. L. R. James at 100 conference in Trinidad in September 2001, Lamming denied this, describing this as one of the errors that have filtered into the historical record since James's death. A misreading perhaps, but in a fabulous twist, it is one that both Selma and C. L. R. James themselves believed and inspired James to reflect further on his relationships with women, another one of the cycles of debt and counterdebt that Bill Schwarz suggests is emblematic of the relationship between James and Lamming.[190] For according to James, "I read the novel without seeing that it referred to me. But, my wife pointed it out to me. She said, there. George has meant you and me."[191] With a passage from Lamming on his mind, which, Selma James had pointed out to him, referred to *their* relationship, James remarked,

> I looked at it and as usual did not talk very much about it to her but I remembered what had happened to my first wife in Trinidad and to the passionate protest of my second wife in the United States—what do you want from me—and that passage written by Lamming built the whole thing up in my mind, showed me that something was wrong and I set myself to discover what it was. The fact remains, I would say, that I had a powerful prejudice against women as women, a prejudice to the extent that I could not give myself completely and allow my affairs etc. to tangle with hers and develop the relationship. I was absolutely unfitted for it. Thackeray, Dickens, even Shakespeare, Aeschylus, they did not educate me on that matter although now that I read Shakespeare, in particular, I can see many hints and references to the essence of a relation. But he didn't make it clear as the French West Indian [Saint-John Perse] and Lamming made it.[192]

James's confusion and despair are evident in the above paragraphs. The heart is truly a lonely hunter. To play counterfactuals and speculate on what James *might* have done raises its own problems.[193] Yet we can only wonder what James would have made of the tremendous Botswanan novelist Bessie Head, dead three years before James in 1986, and her comment in *A Question of Power*: "Men don't really discuss the deep metaphysical profundities with women. Oh, they talk about love . . . but their deepest feelings they reserve for other men."[194] Or ponder if James's sources might have been somewhat different if he had written (or revised) this essay *after* his appreciation of the work of Morrison, Walker, and

Shange, especially considering his long, appreciative quotation from Morrison's *Sula* and his reflections on it.[195]

But as James himself once said of Toussaint L'Ouverture, criticism is not enough.[196] What has the last generation of black feminist thought to proffer to James's sad dilemma? How do we fathom—and explode—the consistent tendency by avowedly radical men to *recoil* at the possibility of feminist social transformation?[197] What then can we say about the hearts of Caribbean men?

The field of inquiry here is vast. I am drawn to one remarkable and justifiably renowned essay, which has been a touchstone for black male academics interested in investigating the contours of a prowomanist or profeminist position.[198] In her essay "Mama's Baby, Papa's Maybe: An American Grammar Book," Hortense Spillers would say the following: "The African-American male has been touched . . . by the *mother, handed* by her in ways that he cannot escape, and in ways that the white American male is allowed to temporize by a fatherly reprieve .. . . The black American male embodies the *only* American community of males which has had the specific occasion to learn *who* the female is within itself . . . It is the heritage of the *mother* that the African-American must regain as an aspect of his own personhood—the power of 'yes' to the 'female' within."[199]

Reflecting on Spillers with James's predicament in mind, one cannot help but be reminded again about the multiple sites of potential convergence in James's life, where an answer to the power of a female voice or a greater sympathy to it might have transformed his despair in his last decade about his past relationships. The tangle of contradictions of the James who spoke so glowingly of his mother's impact on him but could not relate to his wives, who missed collaborating with Claudia Jones and couldn't quite endorse Selma James's Wages for Housework campaign, speaks to the incomprehensibility of it all for him—and questions the reception of and response to the voices of women in the minds of Caribbean men. It remains a conundrum lightly addressed and barely answered.

James's journey here is regrettably unfinished. But what is of greatest interest for my reading of his autobiography is his ready acknowledgment that none of his much-vaunted colonial education and radical experience could prepare him for the complexities of living a truly human existence with a woman. This understanding is carried further in James's comment on black men's ability to form meaningful relationships with their wives. Responding in part to a remembered observation by a group of black women who were all in agreement that this was impossible, James remarked,

> I cannot go along with them that it is black men who are unable to form this relation with the wife. I can't accept that. This matter has wider and deeper connotations than to say that it is my own black people. But, I wouldn't be surprised if ultimately the black man, the slavery of two or three generations and the situation that he finds himself in a world in which things are opening up to him

finds it unable to accept the ideas of western civilization and at the same time, express himself fully and completely to the woman to whom he is married.[200]

Black men cannot internalize the understandings of "western civilization" and live a fully human existence with a woman.[201] Is this merely the confessional writing of an old, tired man or, alternatively, another "explanation" of the perpetuation of patriarchy by black men? Or reading James at his productive limits, is this Sylvia Wynter's "the colonization of desire," coloniality's abduction in the intimate sphere, in what in *Beyond a Boundary* he termed "our most intimate personal lives"?[202] We can practically hear James's sigh when he says, "The social attitudes we could to some degree alter if we wished. For the inner self the die was cast." But his writings on gender, full of inconsistencies, show that his radicalism would not easily accept this defeat.[203] As an attempt to either reconcile his past self-admitted shortcomings or to tentatively propose a theory about the coloniality of gender relations in black communities, "My Experiences with Women and Sex" is a failure. But it is an earnest failure. To use the words James deploys to describe Toussaint L'Ouverture, in him we see "passion not spent but turned inward."[204] The irony that James turned to Saint-John Perse and George Lamming, two male Caribbean writers, and then to African American women writers to understand his relationships with women should not escape us. Only toward the end of his life did James start to become aware that his intellectual journeys involved women at crucial stages—including his grandmother's relating of "La Divina Pastora" to him, his mother's engendering of a love for the literary in him, the powerful Johnson-Forrest theoretical group in which he says he did his most creative work in midcentury America (which consisted of two women, Raya Dunayevskya and Grace Lee Boggs, and James), and his powerful intellectual interlocutors, intimate partners, and wives, Constance Webb and Selma James.[205]

Moreover, James's response to Caribbean women's writing was disappointing. He didn't think much of Merle Hodge's *Crick Crack, Monkey* (1970); like many he missed the signal importance of Paule Marshall's *Brown Girl, Brownstones* (1959), and he seems never to have encountered Simone Schwarz-Bart's *The Bridge of Beyond* (1972).[206] The same year that the grand old man of Caribbean letters was rejoicing in the texts of Shange, Walker, and Morrison in Brixton saw the publication of Erna Brodber's acclaimed *Jane and Louisa Will Soon Come Home* (1980), the papers of the Women in the Caribbean Project, and, in James's native Trinidad, the birth of the Concerned Women for Progress group.[207] A decade later, James would have had the texts of Erna Brodber, Jamaica Kincaid, Dionne Brand, Zee Edgell, Olive Senior, Merle Collins, Michelle Cliff, Lorna Goodison, Marlene NourbeSe Philip, Ramabai Espinet, and Grace Nichols to rely on.[208] In his discussion of the coloniality of men's "intimate lives," James noted, "The coming West Indian novelists will show the clash between the native temperament and environment, and this doctrine from a sterner clime," anticipating so well the critique of coloniality from the future literary tradition—but not the sites where its most daring contestations might emerge.[209] James's unfinished journey never took him back to Caribbean women's experiences. However, James *knew* that women *are* a future. And there is something about the sincerity of James's desire to rethink his past and a determination to move beyond the coloniality of gender relations that still resonates today. And is it not a future that contemporary Caribbean men still have to learn?

Conclusion

A critical reflection on James's struggle to theorize the new society shows us well why Wilson Harris, in a memorable phrase, called him "a great West Indian of complex spirit."[210] This complexity, for Harris, made him a "unique Marxist thinker whose dialectic is attuned . . . to necessity for individual originality as much as it is involved in analyses of historical processes in the life of the people or the body-politic."[211] In *Beyond a Boundary*, James asks the question, "What do men want?" The query of contemporary Jamesian criticism might be, What did *James* want? In *The Black Jacobins* it was the anticolonial African revolution; a decade later in *Notes on Dialectics*, his major work of Marxist theory, it was "free creative activity as necessity." In *Beyond a Boundary*, it is a world where a "more complete human existence" can be fashioned through the ability of all to give their "powers full play."[212] It is this pursuit of human freedom, and not only the Caribbean theme of many of his writings, that secures James as a critical thinker for our Caribbean present.

A return to James's vision at the moment of independence may help us answer the question of his vision of the new society—or, alternatively, what the future was as James saw it.[213] At a time in which many people were leaving the region partly because of anxieties about impending independence and the widely perceived overpopulated and underdeveloped nature of Anglophone Caribbean society, James could say, "Nobody knows what the Caribbean population is capable of. Nobody has even attempted to find out."[214] Any vision of Caribbean futures was inseparable for James from the movement of the masses toward becoming "their own masters" and inseparable from Marxism, that theory of social change that would allow humankind the possibility of an "ascent . . . to complete humanity."[215] The critique of the Caribbean present is necessary, as democracy in the independent Caribbean will be a sham unless it is realized that it is dependent on a transformation of the governing economic relations *and* it is recognized that "the end of democracy is a more complete existence."[216] Despite all of his critiques of the coloniality of the Caribbean, the means by which new elites were beginning to achieve hegemony at the moment of independence, and the first disappointing decade of that so-called independence, James never wavered in his belief that Caribbean people had the ability to continue to make a tremendous impact on world civilization.[217] This can best be seen in two contributions: the first from the special issue of *New World Quarterly* celebrating Guyana's independence, the second his defiant introduction to *Party Politics in the West Indies*:

> My first premise of the West Indian society, in any consideration, is that of all originally colonial peoples West Indians are the most advanced, the most prepared and *the most ready* for achievements and creativity in contemporary civilization more spectacular than any the modern world has seen.[218]
>
> People of the West Indies, you do not know your own power. No one dares to tell you. You are a strange, a unique combination of the greatest driving force in the world today, the underdeveloped formerly colonial coloured peoples; and more than any of them, by education, way of life and language, you are completely a part of Western civilization. Alone of all people in the world you began your historical existence in a highly developed modern industry—the sugar plantation. All those who say or imply that you are in any way backward and therefore cannot in a few years become a modern advanced people are your enemies, satisfied with the positions that they hold and ready to keep you where you are forever. They still bear in their souls the shackles of slavery and the demoralization of colonialism which you, the people, have broken and are ready to cast aside forever. Be of good cheer. *Know that at this stage of world history and your own history there can never be any progress in the West Indies unless it begins with you and grows as you grow.* All that these underdeveloped countries are striving for is at your feet. You have to know what you are, and what you can do. And this nobody can teach you except yourselves, by your own activities and the lessons that you draw from them.[219]

In his post-1950s writings on the Caribbean, this second passage from *Party Politics in the West Indies* may well be James's finest hour. The line "know that at this stage of world history and your own history there can never be any progress in the West Indies unless it begins with you and grows as you grow" can be seen as a development of James's earlier "free creative activity as necessity" and his knowledge that "freedom is creative universality, *not* utility," all essential to his vision of human freedom.[220] There is here more than a hint of the West Indian exceptionalism that some found so insufferable in James and, even more problematic, a further corroboration of Lamming's observation that James thought that the Caribbean had a unique good fortune due to its close ties to European culture, languages, and civilization.[221] Yet what James offers us—a highly nuanced, compelling critique of coloniality, a hope of a different future to come, and a charting of the space that future would have to occupy to create a new Caribbean and world—may well be the very definition of the responsibilities of the radical intellectual. Perhaps the subject of my next chapter, Sylvia Wynter, put it best when she so eloquently said, "James's deconstructive efforts radiate in several directions, simultaneously exploding the theoretical esthetic and metaphorical foundations of the doctrines that sustained Western imperialism. However, James also directed many of these critical darts at earlier formulations of his own thinking, thus subverting their very foundations."[222]

Notes

1. Sylvia Wynter, "Beyond the Categories of the Master Conception: The Counterdoctrine of the Jamesian Poiesis," in *C. L. R. James's Caribbean*, ed. Paget Henry and Paul Buhle (Durham, NC: Duke University Press, 1992), 69.

2. Paul Buhle, *C. L. R. James: The Artist as Revolutionary* (London: Verso, 1989); Frank Birbalsingh, "The Literary Achievement of C. L. R. James," *Journal of Commonwealth Literature* 19, no. 1 (1984): 108–21.

3. David Scott, "The Sovereignty of the Imagination: An Interview with George Lamming," *Small Axe* 12 (September 2002): 164–65.

4. Selwyn Cudjoe, "C. L. R. James Misbound," *Transition* 58 (1992): 124–36.

5. John McClendon, *C. L. R. James's "Notes on Dialectics": Left Hegelianism or Marxism-Leninism?* (Lanham, MD: Lexington, 2005), xxviii; Neil Larsen, "Negativities of the Popular: C. L. R. James and the Limits of 'Cultural Studies,'" in *Rethinking C. L. R. James*, ed. Grant Farred (Cambridge, MA: Blackwell, 1996), 85–102.

6. Christian Høgsbjerg, *C. L. R. James in Imperial Britain* (Durham, NC: Duke University Press, 2014); Matthew Quest, "Review of Christian Høgsbjerg, *C. L. R. James in Imperial Britain*," *Insurgent Notes*, May 2014, http://insurgentnotes.com/2014/05/review-christian-hogsbjerg-c-l-r-james-in-imperial-britain-2014/. There is, however, the question of the response by these authors to work that specifically locates James as one of the most outstanding *Marxist* cultural theorists of the twentieth century, placing him within the company of Georg Lukács, Mikhail Bakhtin, Walter Benjamin, and Raymond Williams. See Neil Lazarus, *Nationalism and Cultural Practice in the Postcolonial World* (Cambridge: Cambridge University Press, 1999), 144.

7. Walter Mignolo, "Sylvia Wynter: What Does It Mean to Be Human," in *Sylvia Wynter: On Being Human as Praxis*, ed. Katherine McKittrick (Durham, NC: Duke University Press, 2014), 112.

8. Mignolo, "Sylvia Wynter," 113, 122n8.

9. David Scott, *Conscripts of Modernity: The Tragedy of Colonial Enlightenment* (Durham, NC: Duke University Press, 2004).

10. Scott, *Conscripts of Modernity*, 2.

11. Scott, *Conscripts of Modernity*, 220.

12. Scott, *Conscripts of Modernity*, 221, 14.

13. Nowhere is Scott's reading of James more difficult to square with James's intentions than in his conscription of *Beyond a Boundary* into his project through James's attention in that text to ancient Greece. I will return to that text at length shortly as *Beyond a Boundary*, a classic text about the birth of a new Caribbean nation striving against neocolonialism, shows the difficulties with Scott's claim that there is a distinctive switch in James's work of this period from a revolutionary anticolonial romance to tragedy.

14. My own concerns about the Caribbean present can be seen in the special issue of the journal *Race and Class* I edited with Alissa Trotz, "Caribbean Trajectories: 200 Years On," *Race and Class* 49, no. 2 (October 2007): 1–130.

15. In this chapter, I focus on James's writings on the Caribbean in the 1950s and 1960s and do not discuss *The Black Jacobins*, which is arguably James's best known and most compelling narrative on the possibilities of Caribbean freedom. I have considered the legacy of *The Black Jacobins* in other work, but to frame it here would distract from my main argument about James's 1960s vision of the Anglophone Caribbean's future. See Aaron Kamugisha,

"C. L. R. James's *The Black Jacobins* and the Making of the Modern Atlantic World," in *Ten Books That Shaped the British Empire: Creating an Imperial Commons*, ed. Antoinette Burton and Isabel Hofmeyr (Durham, NC: Duke University Press, 2014), 190–215.

16. Interview, C. L. R. James with James Early, Ethelbert Miller, Paul Buhle, and Noel Ignatin in *C. L. R. James: His Life and Work*, ed. Paul Buhle (London: Allison and Busby, 1986), 164, my italics.

17. C. L. R. James, "Appendix: From Toussaint L'Ouverture to Fidel Castro," in *The Black Jacobins: L'Ouverture and the San Domingo Revolution* (New York: Vintage, 1963, originally published 1938), 417.

18. Barbara Foley, *Spectres of 1919: Class and Nation in the Making of the New Negro* (Urbana: University of Illinois Press, 2003), 2.

19. Alain Locke, "The New Negro," in *The New Negro*, ed. Alain Locke (New York: Antheum, 1969 [1925]), 3–16; Stuart Hall, "New Ethnicities" in *Stuart Hall: Critical Dialogues in Cultural Studies*, ed. David Morley and Kuan-Hsing Chen (London: Routledge, 1996), 441–49; Stuart Hall, "Old and New Identities, Old and New Ethnicities," in *Culture, Globalization and the World-System: Contemporary Conditions for the Representation of Identity*, ed. Anthony King (Minneapolis: University of Minnesota Press, 1997), 41–68.

20. For a good survey of the literature in this field, see the introduction to Foley, *Spectres of 1919*.

21. Hall, "New Ethnicities," 443, my italics. See also Hall, "Old and New Identities," in which he similarly emphasizes the importance of the "new theoretical discourses" in the emergence of "new ethnicities." For a discussion of this aspect of Hall's work, see Timothy Brennan, "Black Theorists and Left Antagonists," *Minnesota Review* 37 (Fall 1991): 89–113.

22. Hall, "New Ethnicities," 442; "Old and New Identities," 56.

23. Anna Grimshaw and Keith Hart, "*American Civilization*: An Introduction," in *American Civilization* ed. Anna Grimshaw and Keith Hart (Cambridge, MA: Blackwell, 1993), 1.

24. See Grimshaw and Hart, "Introduction," for one attempt.

25. C. L. R. James, "The Old World and the New," in *At the Rendezvous of Victory* (London: Allison and Busby, 1984), 210.

26. C. L. R. James, "Letter to Maxwell Geismar, 11 April 1961," in *The C. L. R. James Reader*, ed. Anna Grimshaw (Oxford: Blackwell, 1992), 278.

27. Learie Constantine, *Cricket and I* (London: Phillip Allan, 1933), 179. James ghost-wrote Constantine's autobiography, in which Constantine quoted James's comparison of himself and Hendren. James would later cite this passage in his seventieth-birthday speech in London; see C. L. R. James, "Old World and the New."

28. C. L. R. James, "A New View of West Indian History," *Caribbean Quarterly* 35, no. 4 (December 1989): 62.

29. James, "A New View," 63.

30. James, "A New View," 64.

31. C. L. R. James, "Appendix: From Toussaint L'Ouverture to Fidel Castro," 391.

32. C. L. R. James, *Black Jacobins*, 86. This line is repeated verbatim in the chapter "San Domingo" in James's text of the same year, *A History of Negro Revolt* (Chicago, IL: Frontline Books, 2004), 9.

33. James, *Black Jacobins*, 392.

34. Paul Gilroy, *The Black Atlantic: Modernity and Double Consciousness* (Cambridge, MA: Harvard University Press, 1993), 221. Gilroy gestures to *The Black Jacobins* and cites at length the key passage on slave life and the modern on pages 251–52.

35. Sidney W. Mintz, "Enduring Substances, Trying Theories: The Caribbean Region as *Oikoumene*," *Journal of the Royal Anthropological Institute* 2, no. 2 (1996): 289–311.

36. James, *Black Jacobins*.

37. For my reading of this relationship, see Kamugisha, "C. L. R. James's *The Black Jacobins*," 197–201. For James's politics in Trinidad, see Walton Look Lai, "C. L. R. James and Trinidadian Nationalism," in Henry and Buhle, *C. L. R. James's Caribbean*, 174–209.

38. James was ten years Williams's senior and returned to Queen's Royal College to teach in his twenties. Ivar Oxaal, *Black Intellectuals Come to Power: The Rise of Creole Nationalism in Trinidad and Tobago* (Cambridge, MA: Schenkman, 1968), 65; Richard Sheridan, "Eric Williams and Capitalism and Slavery: A Biographical and Historiographical Essay," in *British Capitalism and Caribbean Slavery: The Legacy of Eric Williams*, ed. Barbara L. Solow and Stanley L. Engerman (Cambridge: Cambridge University Press, 1987), 317.

39. The correspondence shows that James pressed Williams to invite him to the opening of the Federal Parliament. C. L. R. James, "Letter to Eric Williams," December 10, 1957; Eric Williams, "Letter to C. L. R. James," March 17, 1958, Box 3, Folder 4, C. L. R. James Papers, Columbia University.

40. C. L. R. James, "On *The Negro in the Caribbean* by Eric Williams," in *C. L. R. James on the "Negro Question*," ed. Scott McLemee (Jackson: University Press of Mississippi, 1996), 117–25. This review was originally published in 1942.

41. James, "On *The Negro in the Caribbean*," 118.

42. James, "On *The Negro in the Caribbean*," 125.

43. Letter from C. L. R. James to George Padmore, March 17, 1958, Box 5, Folder 105, C. L. R. James Archive, University of the West Indies, St. Augustine, Trinidad and Tobago.

44. C. L. R. James, *Beyond a Boundary* (Durham, NC: Duke University Press, 1994).

45. C. L. R. James, "Introduction," in *Caribbean Plays*, vol. 2, ed. Errol Hill (St. Augustine, Trinidad and Tobago: Extra Mural Department, University of the West Indies, 1965), vii.

46. C. L. R. James, Grace C. Lee, and Pierre Chaulieu, *Facing Reality* (Detroit: Bewick, 1974, [1958]), 77.

47. C. L. R. James, "West Indian Personality," *Caribbean Quarterly* 35, no. 4 (December 1989): 11–14 (lecture at the University College of the West Indies, 1959/60); "The Making of the Caribbean Peoples," in *Spheres of Existence* (London: Allison and Busby, 1980 [1966]), lecture delivered at the Second Conference on West Indian Affairs, Montreal, Canada, Summer 1966; "The Birth of a Nation," in *Contemporary Caribbean: A Sociological Reader Vol. 1*, ed. Susan Craig (Maracas, Trinidad and Tobago: College Press, 1981); "A New View of West Indian History," *Caribbean Quarterly* 35, no. 4 (December 1989): 49–70; "A National Purpose for Caribbean Peoples," in *At the Rendezvous of Victory* (London: Allison and Busby, 1984 [1964]), 143–58.

48. C. L. R. James, "On Wilson Harris," in *Spheres of Existence* (London: Allison and Busby, 1980 [1964]), 157–72; see also James, "National Purpose," 152.

49. James, "Parties, Politics and Economics in the Caribbean," in *Spheres of Existence*, 154, my italics.

50. C. L. R. James, *A History of Pan-African Revolt* (Washington, DC: Drum and Spear, 1969), 139.

51. C. L. R. James, "Black People and the Black Struggle in the Caribbean, Africa and the United States," quoted in Anna Grimshaw, *The C. L. R. James Archive: A Reader's Guide* (New York: C. L. R. James Institute, 1991), 41, my italics.

52. C. L. R. James, "The Artist in the Caribbean," in *The Future in the Present: Selected Writings* (London: Allison and Busby, 1977), 183–90.

53. James, "Artist in the Caribbean," 185.

54. James, "Artist in the Caribbean," 187; see also James, "Making of the Caribbean Peoples," which concludes with a tribute to Garfield Sobers. James goes on to point out that he believes that even Lamming's talent is more "objectively circumscribed" than Sobers's, while Caribbean painters and musicians are even more so. This observation is worth a thousand words' comment in itself, in terms of what it suggests about the freedom that James thought was embodied in certain art forms as opposed to others. Note also here my later discussion of cricket in this chapter, in which some of these issues, particularly the idea of the artist as cricketer heralding in a new chapter in national life, become hopefully more apparent.

55. The phrase "refashion futures like a healer's hand" is derived from Kamau Brathwaite, "Negus," in *The Arrivants* (London: Oxford University Press, 1973), 222–24.

56. C. L. R. James, "The Mighty Sparrow," in *Future in the Present*, 191.

57. James, "Mighty Sparrow," 191.

58. Melanie Newton, "Returns to a Native Land: Indigeneity and Decolonization in the Anglophone Caribbean," *Small Axe* 41 (2013): 108–22.

59. James, "Making of the Caribbean Peoples," 174; "Birth of a Nation," 28.

60. James, "New View," and his comments on Sam Selvon in "On Federation," in *At the Rendezvous of Victory* (London: Allison and Busby, 1984), 105. Also see the illuminating interview of James done by Chris Searle in October 1982 about language and revolution, in Chris Searle, *Words Unchained: Language and Revolution in Grenada* (London: Zed, 1984): 246–48.

61. James, "Birth of a Nation," 31, my italics.

62. Chris Searle, "Language and the Seizure of Power: An Interview with C. L. R. James," *Race and Class* 50, no. 1 (2008): 79. Also of interest in this interview is James's considerable appreciation of the work of Linton Kwesi Johnson.

63. Marlene NourbeSe Philip, "Discourse on the Logic of Language," in *She Tries Her Tongue, Her Silence Softly Breaks* (Charlottetown, Canada: Ragweed, 1989); Kamau Brathwaite, *History of the Voice: The Development of Nation Language in Anglophone Caribbean Poetry* (London; New Beacon Books, 1984). It is worth remembering Kamau Brathwaite's statement that "it was in language that the slave was perhaps most successfully imprisoned by his master, and it was in his (mis-)use of it that he perhaps most effectively rebelled." Edward Kamau Brathwaite, *The Development of Creole Society in Jamaica* (Oxford: Clarendon, 1971), 237.

64. C. L. R. James, "The Atlantic Slave Trade and Slavery: Some Interpretations of Their Significance in the Development of the United States and the Western World," in *Amistad I*, ed. John Williams and Charles Harris (New York: Vintage Books, 1970): 243; "Making of the Caribbean People," 2, 15.

65. Paget Henry, "C. L. R. James, African and Afro-Caribbean Philosophy," in *Caliban's Reason: An Introduction to Afro-Caribbean Philosophy* (London: Routledge, 2000), 47–67.

66. C. L. R. James, "The West Indian Intellectual," introduction to J. J. Thomas, *Froudacity: West Indian Fables by James Anthony Froude* (London: New Beacon Books, 1969), 46.

67. James did say that "the Greeks were the most politically minded and intellectually and artistically the most creative of all peoples"; see *Beyond a Boundary*, 155–56.

68. For James's attempts to link ancient Greece and the Caribbean, see *Modern Politics* (Detroit: Bewick, 1973 [1960]), 3, 6, 99; "West Indian Personality," 12; "Atlantic Slave Trade," 235; "Tomorrow and Today: A Vision," in "Guyana Independence Issue," special issue, *New World Quarterly* 2, no. 3 (1966): 87.

69. C. L. R. James, "Marxism for the Sixties," *Speak Out*, no. 2 (May 1965) (Detroit: Bulletin of the Facing Reality Publishing Committee), 1–23; "Lenin, Trotsky and the Vanguard Party: A Contemporary View" (Detroit: A Facing Reality Pamphlet, January 1964).

70. James, "Mighty Sparrow," 199.

71. Also see here James's comment in 1984 that "those people who are in western civilization, who have grown up in it, but yet are not completely a part (made to feel and themselves feeling they are outside) have a unique insight into their society." C. L. R. James, "Africans and Afro-Caribbeans: A Personal View," in *Writing Black Britain: 1948–1998* (Manchester: Manchester University Press, 2000), 63.

72. Hazel V. Carby, "Proletarian or Revolutionary Literature: C. L. R. James and the Politics of the Trinidadian Renaissance," *South Atlantic Quarterly* 87, no. 1 (1988): 51.

73. James, *Beyond a Boundary*, 151; see also p. 19, where James refers to a decade-long reorganization of his "view of the world," accomplished between 1940 and 1952.

74. For a classic statement by James on Worrell and the captaincy, see "The Captain for Australia," in *Cricket*, ed. Anna Grimshaw (London: Allison and Busby, 1986), 101–2.

75. C. L. R. James, "Sir Frank Worrell," in *Cricket: The Great Captains, Studies of Eight Great Captains of Cricket History*, ed. John Arlott (Newton Abbot, UK: Sportsmans Book Club, 1972), 135–52.

76. James uses the phrase "hierarchy of captains" in *Cricket*, 98. For James, the other two pivotal captains of twentieth-century cricket are Pelham Warner and Don Bradman.

77. James, "Sir Frank Worrell," 138.

78. James made much of Worrell's insistence that the most important attribute a player possessed was whether or not he was a good team man. I am also alluding here to the essay by James, "A National Purpose for Caribbean Peoples," in *Future in the Present*, 143–58.

79. James, "Sir Frank Worrell", 137.

80. James, *Beyond a Boundary*, 258.

81. James, *Beyond a Boundary*, 258.

82. James, *Cricket*, 167.

83. The opening batsman, Len Hutton became England's first professional captain in 1952.

84. Frank Worrell, *Cricket Punch* (London: Stanley Paul, 1959).

85. Worrell may not have been a radical, but James's claim is that what he *introduced* was radical.

86. James, "Sir Frank Worrell," 142.

87. James, "Gilchrist Before and Gilchrist After," in *Cricket*, 93.

88. James, "The 1963 West Indians," in *Cricket*, 147.

89. James, "Cricket in West Indian Culture", in *Cricket*, 124.

90. James, "Two Cricketing Societies—Glorious Windies and the Defensive English," in *Cricket*, 190, my italics.

91. I borrow here from Wynter's formulations on the Western bourgeoisie, which she describes as follows: "This bourgeois imaginaire social—creative in its time, purely destructive in its decline, dangerous now with the atom split, the social solidarity of humanity and the biosphere we inhabit—has become the primary imperative." See Wynter, "Beyond the Categories," 88. For a discussion of a literary rendition of this preindependence moment, see my essay "The Survivors of the Crossing and the Impossibility of Late Colonial Revolt," the introduction to Austin Clarke, *The Survivors of the Crossing*, 2nd ed. (Leeds: Peepal Tree, 2012, originally published 1964), 7–22.

92. C. L. R. James, "Letter to John Arlott," December 10, 1960, in *Cricket*, 106–7. Also see James's other correspondence during this period on pp. 103–10.

93. James, *Beyond a Boundary*, 257.

94. James, *Beyond a Boundary*, 260–61.

95. While seeing Sobers practicing in the nets on the 1957 West Indies tour of England, James would comment, "I don't remember noticing Sobers, except for his fine physique." See "Garfield Sobers," in Grimshaw, *C. L. R. James Reader*, 387.

96. James himself denied this title of "greatest all-rounder ever," as "unhistorical." See "Garfield Sobers," 383.

97. James, "Garfield Sobers."

98. James, "Garfield Sobers," 379.

99. James, "Garfield Sobers," 384.

100. James, "Garfield Sobers," 389.

101. James, "Kanhai: A Study in Confidence," in *At the Rendezvous of Victory*, 166–71.

102. The full sentence by James reads as follows: "A great West Indian cricketer in his play should embody some essence of that crowded vagueness which passes for the history of the West Indies." See "Kanhai," 166.

103. James's comments here come in *Beyond a Boundary*, 258.

104. It should be clear to the reader here the very heteronormative, masculine nature of the Caribbean subject that James proffers in this work. I would suggest that by the end of his life he was struggling to reassess this, and in the concluding section of this chapter, I indicate some of his breakthroughs and failures in this respect.

105. "Letter from J. H. Fingleton to C. L. R. James," in *Cricket*, 107.

106. James, *Beyond a Boundary*, 261.

107. James, "Cricket in West Indian Culture," 124.

108. James, "The Departure of the West Indians," in *Cricket*, 126.

109. James, "Departure of the West Indians," 127.

110. James, "Old World."

111. James, *Beyond a Boundary*, 233.

112. The phrase "critical darts" is Wynter's; see "Beyond the Categories," 63.

113. Faith Smith has suggested that "women's nonparticipation *as players* in the social world of cricket was of a different order than their participation in constructing its meanings as spectators and theorists. His grandmother and aunts helped James position himself in relation to the players on the field . . . Their running commentary contextualized the game and its players for him, and it was these insights on which he later capitalized in his intellectual production," (original italics). See "Coming Home to the Real Thing: Gender and Intellectual Life in the Anglophone Caribbean" *South Atlantic Quarterly* 93, no. 4 (Fall 1994): 914–15.

114. I borrow the phrase from Tracy Robinson; see "Fictions of Citizenship, Bodies Without Sex: The Production and Effacement of Gender in the Law," *Small Axe* 7 (March 2000): 1–27.

115. James, *Beyond a Boundary*, 41, my italics.

116. These letters have now been collected into a single volume; see C. L. R. James, *Letters from London* (Port of Spain, Trinidad and Tobago: Prospect, 2003). See also Brinda Mehta, "Addressing Marginality Through the 'Coolie/Dougla' Stereotype in CLR James's *Minty Alley*," *C. L. R. James Journal* 9, no. 1 (2002/3): 37–66; Barbara Paul-Emile, "Gender Dynamics in James's *Minty Alley*," in *C. L. R. James: His Intellectual Legacies*, ed. Selwyn R. Cudjoe and

William E. Cain (Amherst: University of Massachusetts Press, 1995), 72–78; and Selwyn R. Cudjoe, "'As Ever, Darling, All My Love, Nello': The Love Letters of C. L. R. James," in Cudjoe and Cain, *His Intellectual Legacies*, 215–43.

117. C. L. R. James, "The Woman Question: An Orientation," a Socialist Workers Party discussion of September 3, 1951, http://www.marxists.org/archive/james-clr/works /1951/09/woman-question.htm. James's review, "Black Ink: On Toni Morrison, Alice Walker, Ntozake Shange," was published in *Cultural Correspondence* (Winter 1983), and later reprinted in Grimshaw, *C. L. R. James Reader*, 411–17.

118. A noteworthy exception would be Kamau Brathwaite's *The Zea Mexican Diary* (Madison: University of Wisconsin Press, 1994), on the death of his wife from cancer, though Brathwaite (b. 1930) is from a different generation than James.

119. I am alluding here to Michael Awkward, "A Black Man's Place in Black Feminist Criticism," in *The Black Feminist Reader*, ed. Tracey Denean Sharpley-Whiting and Joy James (Malden, MA: Blackwell, 2000), 88–108. See also by Awkward, "Black Feminism and the Challenge of Black Heterosexual Male Desire," *Souls* 2, no. 4 (Fall 2000): 32–37.

120. See chapter 1.

121. Patricia Mohammed, "The Future of Feminism in the Caribbean," *Feminist Review* 64 (2000): 117.

122. See especially here Rhoda Reddock, ed., *Interrogating Caribbean Masculinities: Theoretical and Empirical Analyses* (Jamaica, Barbados, and Trinidad and Tobago: University of the West Indies Press, 2004); and Linden Lewis, ed., *The Culture of Gender and Sexuality in the Caribbean* (Gainesville: University Press of Florida, 2003).

123. I am here thinking of Tracy Robinson's comment in her review of M. Jacqui Alexander's *Pedagogies of Crossing*: "there is now an urgent need to speak to and work through what we want to save women *to*, what diverse, partial, unsettled possibilities we can imagine for ourselves and our communities." See Tracy Robinson, "A Loving Freedom: A Caribbean Feminist Ethic," *Small Axe* 24 (2007): 124. Also note Michael Awkward's discerning comment that "perhaps the most difficult task for a black male feminist is striking a workable balance between male self-inquiry/interest and an adequately feminist critique of patriarchy." See Awkward, "Black Man's Place." For a discerning discussion of the pitfalls of one dominant trend in the study of Caribbean masculinity, see Tonya Haynes, "Sylvia Wynter's Theory of the Human and the Crisis School of Caribbean Heteromasculinity Studies," *Small Axe* 49 (2016): 92–112.

124. The phrase "Caribbean male colonization of black female subjectivity" is Wigmore Francis's. See Wigmore Francis, "Nineteenth and Early Twentieth Century Perspectives on Women in the Discourses of Radical Black Caribbean Men," *Small Axe* 13 (March 2003): 139.

125. Selma James made this comment during her lecture on the panel "Reflections on Marxism and the Politics of C. L. R. James" at the conference C. L. R. James at 100: Global Capitalism, Culture and the Politics of World Revolution, September 20–23, 2001. This comment was a deliberate play on James's preface to *The Black Jacobins* in which he said, "Great men make history, but only such history as it is possible for them to make," itself a tip of the hat to Marx's famous line "Men make their own history, but they do not make it as they please; they do not make it under self-selected circumstances, but under circumstances existing already, given and transmitted from the past" in *The Eighteenth Brumaire of Louis Bonaparte*. It was made in recognition of the caring work performed by James's sister, who was the primary caregiver for both of James's parents in their elder years. For James's all-too-brief comment on his sister, see *Beyond a Boundary*, 254.

126. C. L. R. James, "Autobiography, 1932–38," C. L. R. James Archive, University of the West Indies, Saint Augustine Campus, Trinidad and Tobago, 26.

127. Patricia Saunders, *Alienation and Repatriation: Translating Identity in Anglophone Caribbean Literature* (Lanham, MD: Lexington Books, 2008): 36

128. Mehta, "Addressing Marginality," 38.

129. James, "Autobiography, 1932–38," 28.

130. Hazel Carby, *Race Men* (Cambridge, MA: Harvard University Press, 1998), 125.

131. Faith Smith, "Coming Home."

132. Carby, *Race Men.*

133. James, "Towards the Seventh: The Pan-African Congress—Past, Present and Future," in *At the Rendezvous*, 236–50.

134. James, "Towards the Seventh," 245, original italics. For a discussion of James's and Walter Rodney's positions in the debate surrounding the sixth Pan-African Congress, see Rupert Lewis, *Walter Rodney's Intellectual and Political Thought* (Mona, Jamaica: University of the West Indies Press, 1998), 170–79.

135. James, "Towards the Seventh," 250, original italics.

136. Geri Augusto, "A Future We Must Learn," presentation at the C. L. R. James at 100 conference in Trinidad in September 2001, CDs of conference in author's possession. For George Lamming's reflections on this theme in *Natives of My Person*, see "'A Future They Must Learn': An Interview by George Kent," in *Conversations George Lamming: Essays, Addresses and Interviews 1953–1990*, ed. Andaiye and Richard Drayton (London: Karia, 1992), 149–70.

137. Cited in Buzz Johnson, ed., *"I Think of My Mother" Notes on the Life and Times of Claudia Jones* (London: Karia, 1985), 33.

138. Paul Buhle, "The Making of a Literary Life: C. L. R. James Interviewed by Paul Buhle," in Henry and Buhle, *C. L. R. James's Caribbean*, 56. Also see James, *Beyond a Boundary*, 16.

139. C. L. R. James, "The Revolutionary Answer to the Negro Problem in the United States," in Grimshaw, *C. L. R. James Reader* (report delivered to the 13th Convention of the Socialist Workers Party, July 1–5, 1948); Claudia Jones, "An End to the Neglect of the Problems of Negro Women!" in Johnson, *"I Think of My Mother,"* 103–20 (originally published in *Political Affairs*, June 1949).

140. For these conversations, see George Breitman, ed., *Len Trotsky on Black Nationalism and Self-Determination* (New York: Pathfinder, 1978).

141. James, "Revolutionary Answer," 183.

142. James, "Revolutionary Answer," 183, 185.

143. James, "Revolutionary Answer," 185.

144. James, "Revolutionary Answer," 185.

145. James, "Revolutionary Answer," 187.

146. James, "Revolutionary Answer," 187.

147. James, "Revolutionary Answer," 189.

148. René Depestre, "Interview with Aimé Césaire," in Aimé Césaire, *Discourse on Colonialism*, trans. Joan Pinkham (New York: Monthly Review Press, 2000), 94. I allude here to Frantz Fanon's well-known observation that "Marxist analysis should always be slightly stretched every time we have to do with the colonial problem." See *The Wretched of the Earth*, trans. Constance Farrington (London: Penguin, 1990), 31

149. Jones, "End to the Neglect," 113.

150. Jones, "End to the Neglect," 115.

151. Carole Boyce Davies suggests that they might have "lent distant support to the other's positions"; see *Left of Karl Marx: The Political Life of Black Communist Claudia Jones* (Durham, NC: Duke University Press, 2008), 225. Besides their political differences, which I discuss in the succeeding footnote, a fine example of the distance between James and Jones can be seen in the harsh review of his *Party Politics in the West Indies*, published in her periodical, the *West Indian Gazette*. While the review carries no byline except "critic," it seems very likely that it was written by Jones. See Critic, "Review of Party Politics in the West Indies," *West Indian Gazette* (December 1962): 10. For Donald Hinds's affirmation that the review was indeed penned by Jones, see Marika Sherwood, *Claudia Jones: A Life in Exile* (London: Lawrence and Wishart, 1999), 194.

152. James always noted that he was never a communist, having started his radical activity as a Trotskyist in 1930s London. For a vivid portrayal of the sectarianism between the different Marxist groups, see James's description of his experience on Ellis Island in "A Natural but Necessary Conclusion," in *Mariners, Renegades and Castaways: The Story of Herman Melville and the World We Live In* (Hanover, NH: University Press of New England, 2001), 125–67. James's political affiliation as a Trotskyist was sufficient cause for agents of the Communist Party of Great Britain (CPGB) to rebuke Richard Hart's nascent Jamaican communist movement for publishing an article praising James and George Padmore, as Christian Høgsbjerg has shown; see "'A Thorn in the Side of Great Britain': C. L. R. James and the Caribbean Labour Rebellions of the 1930s," *Small Axe* 35 (July 2011): 42. It also affected the reception of *The Black Jacobins* in the United Kingdom; see my article, "C. L. R. James's *The Black Jacobins*."

153. James, "Letters to Constance Webb", in Grimshaw, *C. L. R. James Reader*, 144, 146, all italics original.

154. C. L. R. James, *American Civilization*, ed. Anna Grimshaw and Keith Hart (Cambridge, MA: Blackwell, 1993), 211–25.

155. James, *American Civilization*, 212–13.

156. James, *American Civilization*, 214.

157. James, *American Civilization*, 215, 221.

158. James, *American Civilization*, 214.

159. James, *American Civilization*, 213, original italics.

160. James, *American Civilization*, 220.

161. James, *American Civilization*, 221. This is not only difficult to reconcile with James's Marxism but also as it comes from the creator of the character Maisie in his 1936 novel *Minty Alley*, truly one of the most unforgettable characters in pre–World War II Caribbean literature.

162. Grimshaw and Hart, "Introduction," 17.

163. The section "Women and Equality" amounts to just two pages in the entire 174-page text. See James, Lee, and Chaulieu, *Facing Reality*, 73–75.

164. James, Lee, and Chaulieu, *Facing Reality*, 74, my italics.

165. James, Lee, and Chaulieu, *Facing Reality*, 74.

166. James, Lee, and Chaulieu, *Facing Reality*, 74.

167. James, Lee, and Chaulieu, *Facing Reality*, 75.

168. James, *Modern Politics*, 116. See here Ato Sekyi-Otu, "Women the Measure," in *Fanon's Dialectic of Experience* (Harvard University Press, 1997), 211–35. Sekyi-Otu proposes that "a

propaedeutic to an authentic humanism is to make woman the measure," an argument he suggests Fanon's dialectic gestures toward.

169. James, *Modern Politics*, 120.

170. See also *American Civilization*, 214, 215.

171. In her address at the C. L. R. James at 100 conference, Selma James noted that James had already written the section on women in *American Civilization* when she had her first conversation with him on the topic, and he inspired her to write the pamphlet "A Woman's Place" (1952). It is possible to surmise that from this moment on, much of James's work on women was influenced by Selma James, though she has always been more taciturn in describing her influence on him. Selma James, "A Woman's Place," in Mariarosa Della Costa, *The Power of Women and the Subversion of the Community*, with an introduction by Selma James. (Bristol, UK: Falling Wall, 1972), 55–77.

172. Frank Rosengarten, *Urbane Revolutionary: C. L. R. James and the Struggle for a New Society* (Jackson: University Press of Mississippi, 2008), 93.

173. This lecture was delivered at the same time as those collected by David Austin in *You Don't Play with Revolution: The Montreal Lectures of C. L. R. James* (Oakland: AK, 2009).

174. This section of James's autobiography was written in 1972. James wrote and redrafted a number of parts of his autobiography many times, and the different parts were not written in sequence.

175. L. Anthony-Welch, "Wisdom: An Interview with C. L. R. James," in *Sturdy Black Bridges: Visions of Black Women in Literature*, ed. Roseann P. Bell, Bettye J. Parker, and Beverly Guy-Sheftall (New York: Anchor Books, 1979), 258–62. This interview seems to have been conducted between 1978 and 1979, as James discusses Shange's *For Colored Girls Who Have Considered Suicide: When the Rainbow Is Enuf* (1977) and Morrison's *Songs of Solomon* (1978).

176. Also of interest in this interview is the glowing comment made by James about Sylvia Wynter and his refusal to subscribe to the condemnation of Shange's *For Colored Girls* by some members of the African American intelligentsia.

177. See James, "New View." James remarked that "since the end of WWII [he] had not read a novel superior to this," of *Meridian*, and declared *The Dragon Can't Dance* "a landmark, not in the West-Indian, but in the contemporary novel." See C. L. R. James, "Zenith: Review of *Meridian* by Alice Walker," *Race Today* 14, no. 4 (1982): 140–41; and "Life on the Hill: Review of *The Dragon Can't Dance* by Earl Lovelace," *Race Today* 13 (1980/81): 84. See also Daryl Cumber Dance, "Conversation with C. L. R. James," in *New World Adams* (Leeds, UK: Peepal Tree Books, 1992), 117.

178. L. Anthony-Welch, "Wisdom," 262. Also see James's similar comment in "Old World," 212.

179. Kent Worcester, *C. L. R. James: A Political Biography* (Albany: State University of New York Press, 1995), 205. Shange dedicated her 1991 text *The Love Space Demands* to C. L. R. James and Romare Bearden. See Ntozake Shange, *The Love Space Demands: A Continuing Saga* (New York: St. Martin's, 1991). See also James's talk exclusively on Shange's work, "I'm a Poet," *Race Today* 14, no. 1 (1980/81): 2–6. His appreciation for Alice Walker's work did not stop James from taking a quite critical position on the short stories of Alice Walker. See "Sexual Relations: Review of *You Can't Keep a Good Woman Down*," *Race Today* 14, no. 3 (1982): 111–12.

180. "Interview with C. L. R. James," in *Visions of History by MARHO the Radical Historians Organization*, ed. Henry Abelove, Betsy Blackmar, Peter Dimock, and Johnathan Schneer (Manchester: Manchester University Press, 1983), 265–77. The preamble to the interview states that it is a compilation of two done by Alan Mackenzie (1975) and Paul Gilroy (1982).

181. Grimshaw, *C. L. R. James Archive*, 47. James's autobiography is currently housed in the C. L. R. James Archive at University of the West Indies, St. Augustine, Trinidad.

182. Banyan interview with C. L. R. James, OWTU Guest House, San Fernando, Trinidad and Tobago, September 5, 1980.

183. Banyan interview with C. L. R. James.

184. Banyan interview with C. L. R. James.

185. James, *Beyond a Boundary*, 95.

186. It is difficult to ascertain exactly when James wrote "My Experiences with Women and Sex" and how many times he subsequently revised it. At one point, he states that he is sixty-nine, which indicates it was written in 1970, but George Lamming's *Natives of My Person*, a critical resource in the essay, was published in 1972.

187. James, "My Experiences with Women and Sex," in "Unpublished Autobiography," C. L. R. James Archive.

188. James was hardly the only Caribbean intellectual to claim that crucial insights on the question of gender came to them from Lamming. Note the following comment by Caribbean feminist literary scholar Sandra Pouchet Paquet:

> George Lamming was my first teacher of Caribbean literature. He opened my mind to new avenues of thought; he underscored and updated my very nineteenth-century British understanding of feminism; and he introduced me to Black feminist writing in the US and European thought on sexual politics. My enlightenment as a feminist scholar takes off under his direction. He was very self-aware about his own learning curve, which culminated in his fiction with *Water with Berries* on the one hand, and the magnificent, empowering *Natives of My Person* on the other. I see my work on Lamming as a process of deepening understanding rather than as contradictory. Feminist thought was not a barrier to Lamming, and that was my grounding.

See Sheryl Gifford, "'This Is How I Know Myself': A Conversation with Sandra Pouchet Paquet," Small Axe Salon, May 28, 2012, http://smallaxe.net/wordpress3/interviews/2012/05/28/this-is-how-i-know-myself/#more-102.

189. Worcester, *A Political Biography*, 118; and Paul Buhle, *Artist as Revolutionary*, 128.

190. Bill Schwarz, "C. L. R. James and George Lamming: The Measure of Historical Time," *Small Axe* 14 (2003): 41. It was Lamming who introduced James to his old school friend from Barbados, Frank Worrell. For this and more on their relationship, see David Scott, "The Sovereignty of the Imagination: An Interview with George Lamming," *Small Axe* 12 (September 2002): 134–44.

191. James, "My Experiences with Women and Sex," 8.

192. James, "My Experiences with Women and Sex." James a decade earlier in *Modern Politics* would write the following with clear resonances for the predicament uncovered in his autobiographical musings: "And many young men in the United States are in a serious crisis as to exactly what their attitude should be towards the women to whom they are married" (118).

193. On the problem of historical speculation and the black intelligentsia, see the introduction to Pablo Idahosa, *The Populist Dimension to African Political Thought: Critical Essays in Reconstruction and Retrieval* (Trenton, NJ: Africa World Press, 2004).

194. Bessie Head, *A Question of Power* (Oxford: Heinemann, 1974).

195. I refer here to the memorable passage from *Sula* that reads,

The men who took her to one or another of those places had merged into one large personality; the same language of love, the same entertainments of love, the same cooling of love. Whenever she introduced her private thoughts into their rubbings or goings, they hooded their eyes . . . She had been looking all along for a friend, and it took her a while to discover that a lover was not a comrade and could never be—for a woman. And that no one would ever be that version of herself which she sought to reach out and touch with an ungloved hand. There was only her own mood and whim, and if that was all there was, she decided to turn the naked hand toward it, discover it and let others become as intimate with their own selves as she was.

See Toni Morrison, *Sula* (Knopf, 1976), 120–21.

196. Here I riff off of James's lines "Criticism is not enough. What should Toussaint have done? A hundred and fifty years of history and the scientific study of revolution . . . justify us in pointing to an alternative course." See James, *Black Jacobins*, 282.

197. I am here thinking of the turn of phrase used by one of James's favorite thinkers, V. I. Lenin. See his "Will the Sweep of the Democratic Revolution Be Diminished If the Bourgeoisie Recoils from It?" in *Two Tactics of Social Democracy in the Democratic Revolution* (1905), https://www.marxists.org/archive/lenin/works/1905/tactics/ch12.htm (accessed July 5, 2016).

198. I am thinking particularly here of Michael Awkward, "Black Man's Place"; and Gary L. Lemons, *Womanist Forefathers: Frederick Douglass and W. E. B. Du Bois* (Albany: State University of New York Press, 2009).

199. Hortense Spillers, "Mama's Baby, Papa's Maybe: An American Grammar Book," *Diacritics* 17, no. 2 (1987): 80, original emphasis.

200. James, "My Experiences with Women and Sex."

201. James's strictly heteronormative impulses might give us pause here, but not his *searching* attempt to account for the coloniality of our intimate lives.

202. Sylvia Wynter, "Sambos and Minstrels," *Social Text* 1 (1979): 152; James, *Beyond a Boundary*, 41; Greg Thomas, *The Sexual Demon of Colonial Power: Pan-African Embodiment and Erotic Schemes of Empire* (Bloomington: Indiana University Press, 2007).

203. James, *Beyond a Boundary*, 41. Far more than merely confessional writing, arising from a regret at past mistakes, the sheer volume and sincerity of James's writings on women in the last two decades of his life are indicative of the centrality of gender in his quest for the new society.

204. James, *Black Jacobins*, 418.

205. Frank Rosengarten has also noted the crucial role of women in shaping James's politics in 1930s England; see *Urbane Revolutionary*, 96. Nor is there much acknowledgment by James that the caregiving work of these women made his intellectual work possible.

206. For James's comments on *Crick Crack, Monkey*, see Cumber Dance, "Conversation." This interview was conducted in San Fernando, Trinidad, 1980. It is possible that James's aloofness here may have been a rejoinder to Merle Hodge's review of the republication of *Minty Alley*; see Merle Hodge, "Peeping Tom in the Nigger Yard," *Tapia*, 2 (April 1972): 11–12. On the reception to Paule Marshall's work, among a now voluminous literature, see Simon Gikandi, "Paule Marshall and the Search for the African Diaspora," *New West Indian Guide* 73, nos. 1 and 2 (1999): 83–88. It should be noted here that Sylvia Wynter made the identical mistake. In her interview in *New World Adams*, and in response to the question, "Who are the outstanding names among women in Caribbean literature, particularly Anglo-Caribbean?" she stated "I don't think there are any." Cumber Dance, "Conversation with Sylvia Wynter," 280. Wynter goes on to mention Merle Hodge briefly and to astutely note that

the burden of caring work limits the development of women writers, a limit she perceived as soon coming to an end. Yet like James, she also misses the work of authors like Paule Marshall and Simone Schwartz-Bart. It is a comment that neither James nor Wynter would have repeated a decade later.

207. The Women in the Caribbean Project can be fruitfully seen as the beginnings of systematic feminist research in the Anglophone Caribbean, and it put out seven volumes of its research findings between the late 1970s and early 1980s. In her review of the 1980s feminist movement in Trinidad, Patricia Mohammed hesitates to call Concerned Women for Progress the "first" feminist group in the country. It may, however, be fair to argue that it was the first group influenced by global second-wave feminism to take an avowedly feminist stance in Trinidad and Tobago. See Patricia Mohammed, "Reflections on the Women's Movement in Trinidad: Calypsos, Changes and Sexual Violence," *Feminist Review* 38 (1991): 42.

208. I certainly do not mean to periodize Caribbean women's writing as emerging for the first time in the 1980s. Evelyn O'Callaghan has demonstrated the difficulties posed by many genealogies of Anglophone Caribbean women's writing, which miss a number of texts from the late nineteenth and early twentieth centuries. See Evelyn O'Callaghan, *Women Writing the West Indies, 1804–1939: "A Hot Place, Belonging to Us"* (New York: Routledge, 2004). After the mid-1980s though, the sheer weight and quality of Caribbean women's literature would have been impossible for James to ignore. By the beginning of the 1980s, given the frailty of his health and surely the exhaustion of decades of activism, James had declared himself retired, though he wrote occasional cricket columns and reviews for the journal *Race Today*, while living above its offices in a small Brixton apartment.

209. James, *Beyond a Boundary*, 41.

210. Wilson Harris, "A Unique Marxist Thinker," in Buhle, *His Life and Work*, 230.

211. Harris, "Unique Marxist Thinker," 230.

212. James, *Beyond a Boundary*, 128.

213. I borrow this phrase from Marcus Garvey's 1915 address "The Future as I See It," in Amy Jacques Garvey, ed., *The Philosophy and Opinions of Marcus Garvey* (Dover, MA: Majority, 1986), 73–78.

214. James, "Birth of a Nation," 19.

215. James, *Modern Politics*, 154–55.

216. James, *Beyond a Boundary*, 210; "On Federation," 123; *Party Politics in the West Indies* (San Juan, Trinidad: Vedic Enterprises, 1962), 140–45.

217. For comments like this from 1962, 1966, and 1971 respectively, see *Party Politics*, 4; "Tomorrow and Today," 86; "Old World," 215.

218. James, "Tomorrow and Today," 86, original italics.

219. James, *Party Politics*, 4, my italics.

220. James's phrase "free creative activity as necessity" emerged from his major work of Marxist theory, *Notes on Dialectics*. See C. L. R. James, *Notes on Dialectics: Hegel, Marx, Lenin* (London: Allison and Busby, 1980 [1948]). His phrase "freedom is creative universality, *not* utility" can be found in *Modern Politics*, 115, original italics.

221. Paul Buhle, "C. L. R. James: West Indian. George Lamming interviewed by Paul Buhle," in Henry and Buhle, *C. L. R. James's Caribbean*, 32–33.

222. Sylvia Wynter, "Beyond the Categories," 63.

5   The Caribbean Beyond

Sylvia Wynter's Black Experience of New World Coloniality and the Human after Western Man

> Human beings are magical. Bios and Logos. Words made flesh, muscle and bone animated by hope and desire, belief materialized in deeds, deeds which crystallize our actualities . . . And the maps of spring always have to be redrawn again, in undared forms.
>
> Sylvia Wynter, "The Pope Must Have Been Drunk, the King of Castile a Madman: Culture as Actuality, and the Caribbean Rethinking Modernity" (1995)[1]

C. L. R. JAMES AND SYLVIA WYNTER, the subjects of my study, were significantly separated by age, distance, and political affiliation, which affected their ability to become the political comrades that James found throughout his life among three generations of Caribbean activist intellectuals. James's intellectual journey was coming to a close when Wynter's, as evidenced by her novel and essays of the 1960s and 1970s, was commencing, and he had not the time to provide a critical interpretation of her work but rather would only marvel at its meaning. In a 1980 interview with Daryl Cumber Dance, he would name Wynter as the most important woman writer in the Caribbean, "an exceptional woman."[2] Nor was this an isolated comment by James. In his scribbled notes on a copy of "The Politics of Black Culture," a 1977 conference paper by Wynter, he wrote that hers is "the greatest mind the Caribbean has ever produced."[3] Wynter, who met James on a number of occasions while both worked in the United States in the 1970s, had the fortune to comment more extensively on his work, and her three essays on James are the most she has written on any Caribbean (or any other) thinker.[4] They are also critical to comprehending Wynter's interpretation of the Caribbean experience, which lies at the heart of this manuscript on the thought of James and Wynter.

I commence this chapter with a discussion of Wynter's unpublished text "Black Metamorphosis: New Natives in a New World."[5] In 1971, after meeting at the ACLALS conference at the University of the West Indies, Mona campus,

Sylvia Wynter wrote African American historian Vincent Harding of her intention to write an essay on the African experience in the Americas for publication by the Institute of the Black World.[6] At the time of ACLALS, Wynter was a lecturer in Spanish in the Department of Modern Languages at the University of the West Indies, a noted novelist and playwright, and considered a significant Caribbean cultural theorist.[7] However, in her proposed essay for the Institute of the Black World, Wynter wanted to try her hand at something new—to move beyond her then Caribbean-centered critical essays toward a hemispheric conception of the weight placed by colonialism on black culture. In a letter clarifying her work written within a month of the conference, she stated that her intention would be to

> explore the Minstrel show as the first Native North American theater—and why Amerika distorted it; why a process of genuine creativity became a process of imitation and degenerated into a power stereotype, a cultural weapon against its creators. I shall relate the Minstrel show to the nineteenth century folk theatre patterns of the Caribbean and Latin America trying to link it to certain archetypal patterns of theater that we find for example among the Yoruba, the Aztecs and the folk English; and the way in which the blacks created a matrix to fuse disparate and yet archetypically related patterns.[8]

This preliminary sketch would expand beyond authorial intention and become Wynter's major project of the 1970s, in its final iteration a 935-page manuscript that never saw publication by the Institute of the Black World. The only part of this manuscript that has been published is her 1979 essay "Sambos and Minstrels," though excerpts and allusions to many of the other texts she wrote in the 1970s can be found in the manuscript, particularly "Jonkonnu in Jamaica" (1970), "Novel and History" (1971), "Ethno or Socio Poetics (1975), "The Politics of Black Culture" (1977) and "In Quest of Matthew Bondman" (1981).[9]

"Black Metamorphosis: New Natives in a New World" is a remarkable manuscript and deserves close study for a number of reasons.[10] It is arguably the most important unpublished nonfiction work by an Anglophone Caribbean intellectual and one major guide to the transition in Wynter's thought between her work mainly on the Caribbean and black America in the 1960s and 1970s and her theory of the human from the early 1980s onward.[11] Those already familiar with some of Wynter's theoretical shift from, through, and with Marxism, Caribbean studies, and Blacks studies toward her theory of the human will find in "Black Metamorphosis" a complex and provocative study, however incomplete. Not only does the manuscript clarify Wynter's reflections on the process of indigenization and black cultural nationalism, but it is her most sustained discussion of the politics of black culture in the United States. In my view it constitutes a highly significant contribution to the black radical tradition and one of the most compelling interpretations of the black experience in the Western hemisphere ever written by a Caribbean intellectual. "Black Metamorphosis" also opens a pathway through which we can trace Wynter's constant preoccupations with the Caribbean, which did not decline after her departure from the region in 1974 and remained the edifice surrounding which her theory of the human would be constructed from the mid-1980s.

The Black Experience of New World Coloniality

> Wright's unrelentingly bleak landscape was not merely that of the Deep South or of Chicago, but that of the world, of the human heart.
>
> James Baldwin on Richard Wright's *Black Boy*[12]

Sylvia Wynter commences "Black Metamorphosis" with the declaration that its intention is "to explore . . . the historical process, the socio-economic sea-change, the cultural metamorphosis by which the multi-tribal African became the native of that area of experience that we term the New World."[13] The daring and breathtaking scope of this statement announces a text devoted to wide-reaching sociohistorical transformation across centuries and a cultural history of the African presence in the New World. The wonder that this might be attempted at all by Wynter can be partially explained by the historical conjuncture during which the work started—within five years of the first programs in black studies at US universities, in which the responsibility to disenchant the fictions of the Eurocentric academy and produce new knowledge in the pursuit of human freedom was the urgent task. "Black Metamorphosis" will undoubtedly give scholars of African diaspora studies much to consider just based on two of its central themes: Wynter's theories of cultural transformation in the Americas and her related perspective on the process of indigenization, through which people of African descent became native to their new land. Yet what gives this text its enduring power is the idea that black experience matters—it is decisive to comprehending that the New World constitutes a distinctive "area of experience," unparalleled in the past history of humankind, a central point to which Wynter would return in her later work.[14] Black experience is here crucial, as without it the ideological fictions of the contemporary world order that consign the vast majority of its population to a subhuman status remain uncontested and grow every generation in weight and power.

Wynter initially intended to "restrict [her]self to the Caribbean with particular reference to Jamaica" with the caveat that she would "draw certain parallels with other New World areas of experience."[15] The expansion of the text resulted in something quite beyond the author's original intent, as "Black Metamorphosis" stands as one of the major interpretations of American society by a West Indian intellectual in the twentieth century. A reflection and brief comparison of the text and another similarly expansive study of the United States, C. L. R. James's *American Civilization*, is a detour worth taking, as it highlights the specific conjuncture in which "Black Metamorphosis" emerged in the 1970s.[16] James and Wynter, coming to the United States in 1938 and 1974 respectively, were aghast at a new experience of racism for which their previous worldliness was an inadequate preparation.[17] Both texts languished for almost forty years before critical attention and publication, with their insights only available to a later generation of scholars, particularly lamentable as they contain perspectives on the popular that would have made their work arresting contributions and potentially decisively influential at the time of composition. James's turn to a study of popular culture was part of a decade-long reorganization of his outlook on the world, occasioned by his disenchantment with Trotskyism and the failure of the end of World War II to usher in a socialist revolution in the United States, which instead underwent an intensification of the bureaucratic totalitarian state.[18] Popular culture became for him a means through which he understood the instinctive self-governing activity of the masses in their most daring revelatory form, which in James's writing would reach its zenith in *Beyond a Boundary*. *American Civilization* is a particularly intriguing text as it represents James's ideas in motion, and one cannot help but be perplexed by what Timothy Brennan astutely terms James's "overestimation of American promise."[19] *American Civilization* represents an original contribution by James to the Marxist interpretation of the politics of culture and a subtle argument that "popular culture provided documentary evidence for an American 'happiness'—an uncompromised hunger for what socialism alone could provide."[20] It is also shadowed by uncritical assumptions throughout the text—best seen in its framing of the United States as a fulfilment of human promise and the absence of any critique of American imperialism.[21]

The quarter century that separated the writing of James's and Wynter's texts appears as a chasm rather than a generation, with the civil rights movement, black power, and the advent of black studies creating conditions of possibility for Wynter that James could not have dreamed of in 1950. It is in audience and theme, though, that these texts part company on the greatest terms. James's concern in *American Civilization*, the working title of which was "The Struggle for Happiness," was part of his decades-long fascination with the Old World and the new, and he wistfully thought that his book might become one read by the leisured class of the United States.[22] Wynter saw hers as part of a creative uprising by a black studies newly present within the academy and an attempt to create a major theoretical text for that movement. Further, despite its discussion of black cultural transformation in the Americas, Wynter was less concerned with the old/new distinction of tradition/modernity than with the black *experience* of coloniality.[23]

"Black Metamorphosis," seen from the perspective of Wynter's entire oeuvre, is the most comprehensive portrayal of "Wynter's black struggle for life itself."[24] What Wynter manages to achieve in this text is one of the most compelling, sustained renditions of the black experience of New World coloniality in African diasporic letters. And even saying this is not quite enough.

Black Experience

Sylvia Wynter's meditation on black experience spans nine hundred pages filled with theoretical speculations on the social, political, and aesthetic features of black life in the Western hemisphere and inaugurates key terms and extends other ideas vital for comprehending black existence. These terms include *niggerbreaking*, the *underlife, indigeneity, non-norms, plantation archipelagos, marginal archipelago*, and the *colonization of consciousness*, which are rendered into a manuscript with a conceptual reach across centuries, leaving no sphere of modern existence—political, social, economic, religious, or cultural—untouched.

In a discussion of the limits of the scholarship of Harold Cruse and E. Franklin Frazier and their assumption of the nonexistence of an African cultural presence in North America, Wynter states that African culture did not disappear in the New World; instead, it metamorphosed.[25] With this succinct comment, Wynter announced her position on a debate that commenced long before her time and to which she was to make a signal contribution. In her article "Jonkonnu in Jamaica," the published article that bears the heaviest responsibility for "Black Metamorphosis," Wynter had already declared her interest in describing the self-fashioning of blacks in the Caribbean as a process of "indigenization" rather than "creolization," where indigenization represented a "secretive process by which the dominated culture survives and resists," and creolization is little more than a false assimilation.[26] "Black Metamorphosis" represents a considerable extension and clarification of Wynter's argument for indigenization and stands as the central theory of her early 250-page version of the manuscript.[27] In making her argument that blacks consider themselves natives of the Americas on an "unconscious level," Wynter turns to Jean-Price Mars, whom she quotes as declaring that "our presence on a spot of that American archipelago which we have 'humanized,' the breach which we made in the process of historical events to snatch our place among men" as indicative of how the process of indigenization manifests itself.[28] Price-Mars's evocative lines here recall the importance of the Haitian revolution and its aftermath on black freedom in the Atlantic world and the sociohistorical features that have fashioned contemporary Caribbean existence. The sheer disruption of the middle passage is figured here as the event that creates a new indigenous experience, as "the extra-African's cultural response to the dehumanizing alienation of the capitalist plantation system of the New World, was to re-root himself, making use of the old cultural patterns which had undergone a true sea-change, in order to *create* the new vocabulary of the new existence"—a process that created a new human in a new land.[29] New World African culture is one "whose crucible of conversion was exile" not just from its original home but from "what was defined as the human condition," resulting in a culture "native to exile."[30]

Yet it is how Wynter theorizes both cultural and political transformation in her text that highlights her distinctive contribution to knowledge on black life. The range of the final text of "Black Metamorphosis" encompasses the transformation of culture wrought within the Caribbean plantation experience and concludes with lengthy meditations on the possibility of social change in the United States. Her early chapters, in which the question of cultural change is omnipresent, are contemporaneous with the well-known scholarship of Kamau Brathwaite, Sidney Mintz, and Richard Price, work enmeshed in a series of debates on the African presence in the Americas.[31] In "Black Metamorphosis," however, perhaps due in part to the restless lavishness of its range, Wynter manages to transcend what David Scott terms a "sustained preoccupation with the corroboration or verification of authentic pasts," which he considers a dominant and limiting feature of African diaspora anthropological thought.[32] It is, in my view, Wynter's resolute focus on black experience that allows her to avoid the narrowness of a vision solely concerned with providing a guarantee of black cultural presence through anthropological determined traces—and it is this that gives the text its power and lasting value. "Black Metamorphosis" turns on the uniquely black experience of embodying the non-norm and the determined struggles to refuse that signification that constitute the history of the black presence in the Americas.

"Ontology . . . does not permit us to understand the being of the black man. For not only must the black man be black; he must be black in relation to the white man. . . . The black man has no ontological resistance in the eyes of the white man."[33] These words are recognizably those of Frantz Fanon from the fifth chapter of *Black Skin, White Masks*, the literal translation of the title of which reads "The Lived Experience of the Black." Fanon's journey of feeling and event in an antiblack world is one of the most searing descriptions of its kind in Africana letters, a reflection on invisibility/hypervisibility and black embodiment rarely surpassed in poignancy or influence. The journey of this idea of "lived experience" to Fanon, as Lewis Gordon has recently shown, came through Simone de Beauvoir, who in turn was in debt to Richard Wright, a path not without significance for "Black Metamorphosis."[34] For of the many texts she consulted, Wynter's discussion of Richard Wright's *Black Boy*, a book she persistently returned to throughout her text, allowed her to theorize a transition away from a Marxist-determined theory of black liberation toward an illuminating (albeit unfinished) schema where black experience determines any conceptualization of black pasts and futures.[35] The moment of *Black Boy* that captured Wynter's attention was the terrible scene of repression and victimization of the young Wright by his white coworkers, Peace and Reynolds. In her initial discussion of this scene, Wynter suggests that Peace and Reynold's racism is secured by economic considerations given force by colonization—"devalued black labor meant a relative over-valuation of theirs."[36] Later in the manuscript, in a development of her argument, the economic motive becomes secondary to a consideration of the "pathology of whiteness," itself a sibling of the pathology of the colonizer and the bourgeoisie.[37] The behavior of Peace and Reynolds is an illustration of their desire for a racial mastery that demands recognition from blacks, recalling Hegel's ideas about lordship and bondage but only if threaded through a Fanonian gaze. For while not disputing Irene Gendzier's assessment of the influence of Hegel's work on Fanon, Wynter argues that "if Hegel's influence is central, even more central is the ground of Fanon's *experience* of being black in a white world."[38] The "non-reciprocity of signification" is the foundation of the settler-native division; "the master-slave model is essentially the Norm/non-Norm model."[39]

The way out of what Fanon called this "infernal cycle" is not the security of négritude, as he so well showed in "The Lived Experience of the Black."[40] Writing in the 1970s, Wynter recognized this well but insisted on the productive resistance négritude proffered to global "cultural blanchitude" and consequently a subversion of the norm/non-norm model, as "it was the pain, the angst of those posited as Non-Norms that compelled examination of the functioning of the Symbolic Order itself."[41] This constant fashioning of blacks as the non-norm, what Richard Iton would call their persistent status as outliers in the modern state, demands centering the *experience* of coloniality rather than class domination as key to the othering practices of societies in the Western Hemisphere.[42] Black suffering is an overlooked phenomena of our contemporary world, angrily denied by many, a victim of a version of historical amnesia and bad faith that we give the term antiblack racism. This "long and sustained agony of black experience" would find its zenith in a contemporary site combining terror and captivity[43]: "The ghettoes and prisons of today's North America are the new forms of the plantation archipelago. The new forms of the plantation archipelago are not, as were the old forms, the sites of a system of industrial colonization, but rather are reservations, where those now inscribed as expendable by the system of production can be herded, to repeat in contemporary terms the protracted agony of the American Indian."[44] Wynter's anticipation of what would two decades later become known in academic and activist circles as the "prison industrial complex" is as prescient and revelatory as her search for a radical anticolonial praxis that could hasten its demise[45]: "It is the natives, all the wretched of the earth, who, breaking out of their reservation, are now called upon to reinvent the very concept of the human, through a restructuring of the world system created by the discovery and conquest of the New World by the West."[46]

We know only too well now that this uprising Wynter saw as possible in the mid-1970s when those words were written never came to pass. The specter of the neocolonial dominance of forty years later was close to unimaginable at the time, and the dreadful reversals in the socioeconomic conditions of people of African descent throughout the world are known too achingly well to rehearse. Wynter had a suspicion of the impending gloom to come, seen in her references to the 1978 *Regents of the University of California v. Bakke* decision of the US Supreme Court, an important early salvo in the reactionary response to civil rights that would reach a crescendo in the following decades.[47] However, "Black Metamorphosis" also gives its readers Wynter's understanding of just how challenging the struggle to effect radical change would be—and central to that is the social dominance of the bourgeoisie.

The Bourgeois Sublime

In the process of writing "Black Metamorphosis," Wynter gives up on her earlier conviction that the primary factor in the consolidation of white supremacy in the United States was a series of economic forces unleashed by colonization and transatlantic slavery. Early in the text, white terror on black bodies is figured as the disguise through which an ideology based on superexploitative labor relations masked itself: "racism was, in the last instance, determined by the profit motive."[48] This preliminary analysis of racism, in which Wynter could state that "cultural racism thus plays an *economic* role," was still filled with caveats—the dialectic of the African as native labor, the status of blacks as property rather than a class excluded from bourgeois property rights.[49] Midway through the manuscript, in an arresting paragraph, Wynter would repudiate her earlier convictions, moving from a theory of the black stereotype as a mechanism to facilitate the production of a superexploited population to this stereotype as intrinsic to domination throughout the system.[50] This requires more than slightly stretching Marx in the colonial situation, as Fanon once observed.[51] Yet Marx is decentered but not abandoned as he is key to the target of Wynter's critique in the last half of her text—the Western bourgeoisie.

For while Wynter cites approvingly Marx's famous dismantling of the legitimation tactics of the bourgeoisie, in Marx's words the "insipid childishness . . . preached to us in defence of property," the drama of coloniality requires a critique beyond even that imagined in Marx's exposure of the social reorderings and upheavals unleashed by capitalism.[52] For Wynter, "the power and effectiveness of the bourgeois order was that ultimately, it allowed for the self-expression of no other group except on the condition that that group expressed itself in bourgeois forms. Its guaranteed freedom of expression was limited to the freedom of bourgeois expression. That is to say, it imposed the form of its expression on every other form in its vicinity."[53] Bourgeois hegemony is not an idle phrase, as "by its nature, the bourgeoisie must be culturally totalitarian or cease to exist."[54] Comprehending race means appreciating that "all racisms are finally bourgeois. It is the bourgeois social order which needs the fixed rigid individuated, separated self."[55] The tactics of force and consent, co-optation, and "vicarious identification" result in blacks, workers, and women being "intimately interlocked" in a system in which their other—respectively white, middle class, and male—constitutes the normative identity, a central feature of the "bourgeois mode of domination."[56] The aspirational quest for whiteness and attendant betrayals of the black bourgeoisie within this system are to be expected. By the conclusion of the text, Wynter's position is practically reversed: "The particular wrong of the Black—his total social exploitation—cannot be fought except it is fought as the general social—rather than merely economic—wrong that it is."[57]

Rather than as an "area of experience" that might give a universal paradigm similar to the proletarian experience, dominant understandings of the black experience in the United States represent it as a "racial experience." This Wynter would argue against, as the black experience shows the "inextricability of the infrastructure and the superstructure" and "the black revolt . . . is the most radical of all revolts as it aims at the code."[58] The black presence in the New World is subterranean but omnipresent, fugitive but hypervisible, condemned as the non-norm and nonperson but the foundation for the concept of free citizenship in the Americas. The monumental importance of "this area of experience that we call the New World" is that "the black/white code is the central inscription and division that generates all the other hierarchies. The secret of capitalism is to be found not in the factory but in the plantation."[59] This allows Wynter to not only resolve a theoretical tension within her argument but to extend her thoughts deeper into the meaning of black experience mediated through culture. She would "propose that we substitute the concept of colonization of consciousness for alienation," as "the black who accepted himself as a *Negro* was not alienated. He was colonized."[60] Here the essential theoretical model for comprehending that "dynamic dialectic of terror and hope" that constitutes the history of blacks in the New World must lie in black experience itself.[61]

Desire plays a crucial role here, both as an analysis of colonization and in presenting the pathways of assimilation and resistance that in different iterations remain the hallmarks of black sociopolitical traditions.[62] The "carefully cultivated sentimental passion of the bourgeois cult of feelings" is the corollary in the realm of desire of the "European humanism" that Frantz Fanon would denounce in his conclusion to *The Wretched of the Earth.*[63] Fanon's *Black Skin, White Masks* "opened theory to the exploration of the central strategy of bourgeois domination—its strategy of the imitation of desire."[64] The coloniality of power through desire is revealed through the following statement: "it is through the totalitarian colonization of desire that bourgeois hegemony activates its strategy of power."[65] Simultaneously though, black culture would produce heretical ways of being capable of dismantling the entire bourgeois mode of being. The yearning of the spirituals that awakened W. E. B. Du Bois to the gift of black culture to humanity is a "powerful expression of uncolonized desire."[66] Black music in the late twentieth century would become a "commercial anodyne, but with its Janus face of subversive desire":[67]

> It is in this decolonization of consciousness, this "degradation" of social fictions that links the collective popular black culture and the theoretical formulations of black intellectuals. Black music from blues to jazz to soul, and its multiple derived variants counters the social fiction of "managed" organizational capitalism that the consumption of more and more consumer goods is the goal-seeking activity of man, one that diminishes pain and increases pleasure.
>
> Rather black popular music sings as it has always done of an absence, a lack, of happiness, an absence, lack, felt in the flesh, and occasioning a radicalization of desire that secularizes utopian longings, the kind that cannot be satisfied by the dominant social order. Under the commercialization of the music it infiltrates this radicalization of desire; and exists as the leaven of the society at a mass-popular level.[68]

Wynter's observation that "it is the 'enthusiasm'—in the religious meaning of the term—secularized by black music and dance that most profoundly undermines bourgeois utilitarianism, and the instrumental rationality of the dominant order" is echoed thirty years later in the work of Timothy Brennan.[69] In a discussion of the "social allegory" that he suggests is fundamental to most New World African music, Brennan states that black popular music's overwhelming popularity resides in the fact that it "offers its listeners a coded revenge on the modern, and that . . . is *why it is popular*."[70] This popular music, based on neo-African forms, "constitutes nothing less than an alternative history of Western civilization."[71] Wynter knew this only too well, as for her "when the black moves out of his place, the entire universe of identity is shaken."[72] The black popular, particularly in the form of music, is where we might see intimations of the human in our present antiblack world. Black music is an "underground reservoir of cultural heresy" through which black reinvention, constitution, and transformation both expresses itself and becomes possible.[73] It engenders the "psychic state of feeling" necessary for black revolt, as "the black oral culture in the Americas . . . has functioned as a sustained and prolonged attempt to reinvent the black as human . . . in the face of intolerable pressures, material and psychic."[74] Yet the secret of black music is beyond its subversive value. Rather, for Wynter, "out of another dispossession, out of another Middle Passage of the spirit, Reggae, like the blues, like jazz, articulates the *revolutionary demand for happiness* on the part of the wretched of the earth—the global natives of all races disrupted from their traditional cultures into twentieth century terror."[75]

Black music is an ethical blueprint for black life. It provides spaces of imagination for other forms of being and is central to the making of the new person beyond coloniality. Black happiness in an antiblack world is an achievement in itself, or as Nikki Giovanni once said in a slightly different accent, "black love is black wealth."[76] At its best, the politics of black culture demand a continual critique in the third world of all "secular Messiahs," exposed as the "new class of the skilled bourgeoisie."[77] There is simply "no revolutionary praxis without revolutionary counter-representation."[78]

Radical social change is inconceivable without anticolonial thought and praxis. Neither Marxism nor black cultural nationalism is the complete answer, as neither can fully address the stigmatization of blackness and deviance as the epitome of the non-norm. Since it is inequality *itself* that defines the non-norms, it is constitutively fruitless to advance integration, this "most terrible form of black alienation," as the solution to problems of racial apartheid in the United States and beyond.[79] The weight of coloniality on black lives is both an unbearable burden and responsibility: "The chain of innovations by which blacks had reconstituted new social identities, new social bodies, has reached the limit of its counter cultural *underlife* existence. Either blacks will be destroyed or blacks will be compelled to impel the social transformation of a chaotic and disintegrating social order."[80]

Here Wynter echoes C. L. R. James's reflections on Fanon's *The Wretched of the Earth*, a passage she knew well. In a January 1967 speech in Detroit, James would say the following:

> Fanon calls his book *Les Damnes de la Terre*; it is translated as "The Wretched of the Earth," but I prefer "The Condemned of the World." I want to end by saying this: the work done by Black Intellectuals, stimulated by the needs of the Black people, had better be understood by the condemned of the earth whether they're in Africa, the United States or Europe. Because if the condemned of the earth do not understand their pasts and know the responsibilities that lie upon them in the future, *all on the earth will be condemned*. That is the kind of world we live in.[81]

The stakes for Wynter and James could never be clearer. The colonial condemnation that has been the lot of blacks will extend to encompass humanity, if the wisdom and experience of African diaspora populations, those forced "to pay the most total psycho-existential price" for the Euro-American West's victory is ignored.[82] This was the simultaneous warning and hope that James and Wynter could announce at the end of the 1960s and 1970s respectively, before the advent of global neoliberalism and the focus on environmental realities that imperil human survival on this planet, both of which would be omnipresent a generation later.

> Angela, there are some people who will never learn new response. . . . Some can never be educated. As a historian you know how long and how fervently we've appealed to these people to take some of the murder out of their system, their economics, their propaganda. And as an intelligent observer you must see how our appeals were received. We've wasted many generations and oceans of blood trying to civilize these elements over here. It cannot be done in the manner we have attempted it in the past. Dialectics, understanding, love, passive resistance, they won't work. (George Jackson, "Letter to Angela Davis" [1970][83])

> It is natural for the imprisoned who see no hope of being released and who know that there is another kind of life, to think in terms of flight. The prison of the African of the diaspora was not a physical structure. *It was a lifestyle.* (Erna Brodber, "Beyond the Boundary—Magical Realism in the Jamaican Frame of Reference" [1997][84])

How can one give voice to the terror and agonizing reversals of the last thirty years, since the conclusion of "Black Metamorphosis"? Wynter's portrayal of the "long black agony" of New World experience has never been more prescient and bitterly evident than in the last generation of state terror, comprador complicity, the accelerating transfer of wealth from the poor to the elites, and the environmental destruction of the planet.[85] Amid this, one wonders if there is anything more that needs to be—or can be—said about the theft of black people's lives in the New World. It is this legacy of trauma, alienation, and disempowerment and the anguish it produces that forces black women, according to Marlene NourbeSe Philip, to "manage the unmanageable" and confronts black subjects of the West, as James Baldwin put it, to "always [be] in the position of having to decide between amputation and gangrene."[86] It is not merely the memory of slavery and the indignity of colonialism that troubles me here. Rather, as Jamaica Kincaid once had one of her characters' utter, "I did not mind my defeat, I only minded that it had to last so long; I did not see the future, and that is perhaps as it should be."[87] The despair here is less over past injustice than over the coloniality of the present and our seemingly potential futures.

Wynter's reply to this moment, in her writings after "Black Metamorphosis," continues the radical daring of her unpublished manuscript and renews the terrain of activism with each succeeding decade, with pressing insights for her Caribbean. In her tribute to C. L. R. James, "Beyond the Categories of the Master Conception: The Counterdoctrine of the Jamesian Poeisis," Sylvia Wynter utilized the term "abduction" as a conceptual tool to assess the nature of existing coloniality.[88] Wynter's use of the term "abduction" is borrowed from Gregory Bateson, for whom it is the "lateral extension of abstract components of description . . . Metaphor, dream, parable, allegory, the whole of art, the whole of science, the whole of religion, the whole of poetry, totemism . . . the organization of facts in comparative anatomy—all these are instances or aggregates of instances of abduction, within the human mental sphere."[89] In her reflections on the lifework of C. L. R. James, the idea of abduction for Wynter becomes a term used to account for the shifting guises of systems of domination that have created the modern colonial world. The phrase "abduction system" is used to refer not merely to the dominance of the West (if we consider the West here, following Edouard Glissant, to be a project and not a place)[90] but the "semiotic foundations of bourgeois thought" and the colonial polis and its system of social rewards and punishments.[91] Abduction systems create "abduction elaboration(s)," which rely on "a differential ratio of distribution of goods and of rewards, which in turn provides additional legitimacy" and simultaneously engender "abductive extension(s)" to keep their founding tropes alive.[92] C. L. R. James's radical journey simultaneously within, through, and beyond coloniality was a "constant and sustained attempt to shift 'the system of abduction' first of colonial Liberalism, later of Stalinist and Trotskyist Marxism, and overall, of the bourgeois cultural model and its underlying head/body, reason/instinct metaphorics."[93]

Sylvia Wynter's use of the term "abduction" to signal our entrapment within the systems of domination that have been the result of the colonial project is not limited to this essay but spans her corpus of writings after "Black Metamorphosis" and appears in her thought on subjects as diverse as the pitfalls of Western feminism and Marxism-Leninism, her speculations on cognitive science and human consciousness, and the condition of the condemned of the earth. Such phrases as the "abductive order of discourse," "abductive terms of inference," and the "abductive schema of Marxism-Leninism" are consistently used to indicate a disquiet with existing coloniality and a concern with the inability of liberation movements in the past to adequately disenchant the schemes by which it asserts its hegemony.[94] When Wynter's concerns move beyond what she terms the "abductive logic of the systems of representation," the potential for abduction as a more universal theory of the colonial condition becomes clear.[95] The offer of assimilation to Francophone Caribbean *départments* saves them from the condemnation that is Haiti's lot but is little more than another form of imprisonment.[96] The condemned of the earth, who live in "Caribbean slums, Brazilian favelas, inner city ghettoes of the US, all now reoccupy the place of the slave ships, quarters of new barracoons no less cramped."[97] The power of abduction systems necessitates, for Wynter, radical disruptions of our hegemonic Western order of knowledge, acts of daring toward which she gestures in her call for heretical knowledge beyond that of Western bourgeois man.[98]

How then might we begin to think of abduction as a concept to describe Wynter's Caribbean and to comprehend the black experience of New World coloniality? A starting point might be the inception of the colonizing mission with Columbus and the Spanish invasion of the Western hemisphere. Historian Anthony Pagden's book *The Fall of Natural Man: The American Indian and the Origins of Comparative Ethnology* opens with a quote from the eighteenth-century Father Pedro Alonso O'Crowley: "the conquest of the Indies . . . filled all the vague diffusion of the imaginary spaces of man"[99]—an incredible comment rich in insights on the nature of the invention of categories of "man" in the Americas, as well as a reminder of the power of imagined spaces and geographies in the colonial project. Pagden's description of the shifts in perspectives of Native Americans—from theories of Aristotelian natural slavery to those that caricatured them as "nature's children"—and attempts to find an "epistemologically persuasive" interpretation of persons under Spanish dominion signal the importance of the conquest of the New World for European understandings of the nature of humanity. In what Wynter might call an abductive elaboration, native people are held within the body of the newly emergent European state, for the purposes of clarifying its own relationship to its subjects, and what it would now consider its colonial (anti)subjects.[100] Stephen Greenblatt would argue in his *Marvellous Possessions* that "from the very first day in 1492, the principal means chosen by the Europeans to establish linguistic contact was kidnapping," a prison house of language far beyond that imagined by Frederic Jameson.[101] Kidnapping, slavery, guerrilla warfare, and genocide all figure prominently here, as well as the movement of native people throughout the Caribbean and beyond both under forced-labor conditions and in search of homes more easily defendable against European aggression.[102]

Abduction as concept also immediately evokes memories of transatlantic slavery—truly theft on the greatest scale in human history. Any reflection on slavery, the pained bodies of the enslaved and the indignity of the indentureship of South Asians that followed, reminds us that Caribbean realities are constituted by the experience of living within the shadow of genocide and unfreedom. Abduction thus centers as a critical philosophical concern the theft of labor from Africa, India, and the Caribbean and the consumption of their wealth, people, and natural resources in an ongoing imperial project.[103] When we consider the kidnapping of Toussaint L'Ouverture by Napoleon Bonaparte and then recall the spiriting away of Jean-Bertrand Aristide on the two hundredth anniversary of his country's birth, the tragedy of the Western-facilitated third-world debt crisis, and the exploitation of Caribbean migrant populations in Europe and North America, the fiction that abduction has ended is made clear.

But is abduction, with its inevitable emphasis in its popular definition on coercive force devoid of agency, anything more than an arresting but misleading metaphor? If every entry into the symbolic order is via abduction—as Gregory Bateson seems to suggest—can abduction be wedded to a specific property called coloniality? As concept, abduction itself has been the scene of incredibly poignant reworkings and mistranslations. In *Representations of the Intellectual*, Edward Said describes the ethical rewards of speaking truth to power as abduction, citing the philosopher C. S. Peirce on the origin of the term and Noam Chomsky on its further elaboration.[104] Yet Peirce's inferential logic and concern with deducing pragmatism as the "logic of abduction" seems far removed from Said's concerns, as does Chomsky's consideration of its merits for the "acquisition of knowledge of language" fifty years later.[105] In the English-language edition of Frantz Fanon's *Black Skin, White Masks*, Charles Markhamm translates Aimé Césaire's famous line from the *Cahier d'un retour au pays natal* as "those who never knew any journey save that of abduction," while standard translations of that line read "those who knew of voyages only when uprooted."[106] Further, if the coloniality of citizenship is key to understanding the contemporary Caribbean predicament, what is the yield of abduction, as a description of a global colonial formation?[107]

The innovation of Wynter's turn to abduction as concept is its *evolution* in concert with the hemispheric conception of black experience articulated in "Black Metamorphosis," toward a global theory of coloniality. Wynter's use of abduction both historicizes black experience in the West and the concomitant agonizing self-fashioning of identities, appropriation, deforming, and claiming of a modernity believed by the West as its sole preserve. What kinds of insights into black experience result if we consider Jan Pieterse's comment that the "west" did not absorb "non-western" cultures but "was constituted by them," Frantz Fanon's observation that "Europe is literally the creation of the Third World," and Hortense Spillers's statement that "My country needs me, and if I was not here, I would have to be invented"?[108] Here, abduction prompts a consideration of colonial condemnation, its consequences of epistemic and physical violence, and the problem of existence posed by the condemned of the earth—manifestly, that these humans *presume* they have the *right* to *exist*.[109] These bodies, given the moniker "no humans involved" by North America's white supremacist state apparatus, as Wynter knew too well, suffer the ultimate dispossession—*condemnation* in our modern antiblack world.[110] The stakes, then, in our contemporary neoliberal world order are the very legitimacy of colonized persons' lives and the right of their bodies to *exist*. At a time in which the United States may well be headed to a culmination of racial insurrection and state-sponsored violence only witnessed in 1919 and 1968 in the last century, Wynter's articulation of the black experience of New World coloniality—written, revised, and extended throughout the 1970s—appears even more prescient and of lasting value.[111] "Black Metamorphosis" is the finest attempt by a Caribbean intellectual of Wynter's generation to consider black struggle in a New World hemispheric perspective, unfettered by the boundaries of the nation-state. It also made possible a pathway to an epistemological uprising that Wynter would later term the demand for the human *after* Western man, a quest for a future beyond coloniality, Césaire's "undared form," in our present tragic times.[112] In her later texts, the invocation of the beyond presses us to disenchant the legacy of coloniality, toward the human *after* Western man.[113] Somewhere between abduction as constant and the "beyond" as possibility lies the black experience of New World coloniality. This potential *beyond* can only be properly apprehended for Wynter through a dismantling of Western reason, a journey through which the Caribbean has played a special part.

Sylvia Wynter's New World

For Sylvia Wynter, the advent of independence in the Caribbean signaled a shift from an imperialism secured by territorial conquest to a "properly epistemological imperialism."[114] A major part of the crisis of the contemporary Caribbean is that while we are aware of and have been engaged in the past with a battle for political and economic sovereignty, we still have not yet come to terms with the need for "ontological sovereignty."[115] It is this crisis, as present today as at the moment of independence, that demands a rethinking of our very understanding of what is the nature of being human.

Wynter's tremendous philosophical enterprise is not, unlike much African diasporic scholarship of the last two decades, indebted to theories of the modern. Rather than tradition/modernity, Wynter deals in such concepts as epistemic ruptures, transumption chains, liminality, symbolic life/death, and genres of the human in her theorization of the processes by which the modern world has come into being. Behind her work are the contributions of a diverse group of scholars, including prominently Gregory Bateson, Zygmunt Bauman, Hans Blumenburg, Aimé Césaire, Frantz Fanon, Michel Foucault, C. L. R. James, Asmarom Legesse, Valentin Mudimbe, Anthony Pagden, and J. G. A. Pocock, to name some of the most frequently cited. A vision of the creation of the modern world emerges from this that centers the history of the last five hundred years and illustrates the coloniality of modernity and the modernity of coloniality in a manner that refuses the separation of one concept from the other. Unlike scholars like Sidney Mintz and Paul Gilroy, who argue for the centrality of slavery to Western modernity, Wynter's work suggests that a gaze further back to the beginnings of the colonization of the New World is needed to fully assess the creation and perpetuation of coloniality/modernity/empire, a perspective shared by Latin Americanists like Enrique Dussel and Walter Mignolo.[116] Wynter studied Spanish literature in London, specializing in the golden age and Renaissance, and this significantly moved her away from the Anglo-centered scholarship of many intellectuals in the Anglophone Caribbean and North America.[117] Jamaica's colonization by

Spain, though almost three centuries past when Wynter was born, fortuitously allowed Wynter to conduct research on New Seville, the third oldest Spanish city in the Western hemisphere and oldest in Jamaica, in 1983–84.[118] Around this time, the coming quincentennial of Columbus's arrival in the Americas stimulated Wynter to start developing a "new interpretation of 1492 . . . outside either the purely celebratory terms of a Western perspective or the purely reactive terms of an anti-Western one . . . to see what it had meant not just within the terms of Western history but at the level of human history as a whole."[119] The aim here is to reconstruct the way that the modern world came into being, which shows it to be wedded to coloniality in a manner that belies the need for a polemical assertion of the terror at modernity's heart.

This retelling of the tale of the creation of the Western world is conducted by Wynter primarily via a tale of the mutation of epistemes, with each epistemic break heralding in a new form of "man," which is the hegemonic representation of what is considered to be a good man or woman of its time. Wynter has frequently retold parts of this elaborate tale of how the West was won in her essays, and it is to three of these that I wish to turn. These are "New Seville and the Conversion Experience of Bartolomé de Las Casas" (1984), "The Ceremony Must Be Found: After Humanism" (1984), and "1492: A New World View" (1995).[120]

The career of Bartolomé de Las Casas is of considerable significance for Wynter, as the debates surrounding his thought on the native people of the Caribbean point to the tragedy that befell them and later people of African descent and also the fundamental shift in Western thought that accompanied the "discovery" of the New World. Las Casas is known today as not only one of the most passionate defenders of the native people against the genocidal conditions that they labored under but as the cleric who originally justified the importation of African labor into the Americas, a position he later recanted with quite extraordinary eloquence.[121] Wynter's concern, however, centers on the debate between Las Casas and the Spanish humanist scholar Ginés de Sepúlveda, at Valladolid in 1550–1551. This debate was an attempt to resolve the question of "what kind of relation—hierarchical or reciprocal—was to be established between the two modes of the human, one argo-artefactual, the other Neolithic, that now confronted each other on the Caribbean islands and mainland territories."[122] It also proposed to answer the question of how to account for people "whose existence now placed in question the very universality of the Euro-Christian figural scheme," who had not had the chance to hear the Christian gospel, in a realm that was thought up to the time of Columbus to be uninhabitable.[123] For Wynter, "the debate at Valladolid can be seen as the official occasion of the conceptual revolution that formerly ushered in the modern world."[124] In his victory, Sepúlveda, "in spite of his still hybrid use of religious terminology and concepts, can be said to have provided the first secular operational self-definition of the human subject," one that was dependent "on a represented essential difference between modes of the human."[125] Relying on ideas about the capacities of reason between different groups of humans, Sepúlveda is symptomatic of a "new humanist and ratiocentric conception of the human . . . the political subject of the state"[126] and could argue that such practices as human sacrifice represented a fundamental lack of reason among the native peoples. This argument, a mutation of the preexisting Christian "theocentric conception of the human," could later be applied to enslaved Africans, who were "disobedient by nature" and thus also lacking natural reason.[127]

Bartolomé de Las Casas "lost that debate because he was at once behind his time and ahead of his time."[128] In response to assertions about the lack of natural reason in the native peoples, Las Casas argued that "to sacrifice innocents for the salvation of the Commonwealth is not opposed to natural reason, is not something abominable and contrary to nature, but it is an error that has its origin in natural reason itself."[129] In short, "all the peoples of the world are men: and all men are rational. It was their rationality which defined them."[130] For Wynter, Las Casas's discovery here is as significant as Columbus's: "Columbus with his empirical voyage made possible a science of geography based on a purely encyclopaedic knowledge of the earth. Las Casas at Valladolid made the same leap (not to be followable up until our own century) *with respect to the possibility of a science of human systems based on the encyclopaedic knowledge of their laws of functioning.*"[131]

The issue here is one of representation and how it figures in conceptual schemes of human systems of thought. Wynter declares that "we think in the mode of the symbolic self-representation. As we act upon the world in the mode of our hands. And both the insights and the oversights—Las Casas' errors—are always governed by our *historically relative* systems of self-representation."[132] Our quest should be to put "an end to the pre-history of the human" and instead "take as the object of our metadisciplinary inquiry . . . the thousand representations out of which the Human has woven itself—and its Others."[133]

The above close reading of Sylvia Wynter's "New Seville and the Conversion Experience of Bartolomé de Las Casas" is necessary as, in its attention to moments of epistemic change and continuity, the partial victories of one regime of thought and the urgent need for new forms of awareness, it shadows the organization of many of the arguments Wynter makes in her other texts from 1984 onward.[134] It also highlights the *Caribbean* provenances of Wynter's argument—we should recall here that Las Casas's conversion experience takes place during his sojourn in Jamaica—as the lesser known essay on Las Casas was published in the same year that the essay typically considered to announce her turn to a theory of the human, "The Ceremony Must Be Found: After Humanism," made its appearance.[135] "The Ceremony Must Be Found" was undoubtedly a landmark in her work, as here for the first time she gives an extensive reading of the legacy of renaissance humanism and its invention of Western man. The heresy of the first humanism was the writing of *secular* knowledge. The epistemological shift of Renaissance humanism invented secular man, an achievement that was inherently flawed, since the human was invented on the basis of one "type"—that of Western bourgeois man: "The heresy of the Studia was, therefore, to lie in its break with the higher system of divinely sanctioned identity and with its absolutized world views or ratiomorphic apparatus; in its release of rhetorical man from the margins, orienting his behaviours by a new ordering secular Logos, the Natural Logos of Humanism which took the place of the Christian Theologos."[136]

The "new men" of this time "struggled for a revaluation of Natural Man in political terms" and came on the term "man" to define themselves, "in opposition to Christian, as the first non-religious definition of the human that was ostensibly universally applicable."[137] This desupernaturalizing of belonging within a community, based on the interests of these city-state dwellers who wished to be "citizens with political rights," required the creation of a new realm of authority beyond the "suprasensory": "The authority of Reason, the Reason coded by the Natural *Logos* of humanism based on the explanatory principle of a Natural Causality verified by the truth of empirical reality, moved into the place of the vanished authority. And the configured macro-concept of Natural Causality now took the place of Divine Causality as the Original Cause, the extra-human source of the new principle of Sameness and Difference, expressed in a new structural opposition, that of Reason and its Lack-state.[138]

The processes that created this newly invented rational, Western man are impossible to understand without reflecting on the conquest of the Americas, as well seen in the debate between Las Casas and Sepúlveda outlined above. In this schema, the order of "spiritual perfection/imperfection" would be replaced by "rational perfection/imperfection," mapped on a distinction made between "Man" and his "Others," which would be the "basis [of] the *coloniality of being,*" and "the *foundational basis of modernity.*"[139] Anthony Pagden's tracing of the changing ways in which native peoples were perceived by the Spaniards, from nature's slaves to nature's children, points not just to the fungibility of categories while in the service of empire, but the ways in which submission to the "rational order of the political state" was now necessitated by the hegemonic order of knowledge.[140] The category of "natural slaves" imposed on the native peoples was dispensed with in favor of a category of "civil slaves" for the arriving enslaved Africans, facilitating the treatment of them as "legal merchandise" and the institutionalization of chattel slavery. Racial difference thus became one of the founding categories of the modern state: "The new order of the secularizing modern state would map its own role-allocating mechanisms and unifying code of symbolic conspecificity onto a new notion of order. This new notion was to be based on a *by-nature difference* between Europeans, on the one hand, and peoples of indigenous and African descent, on the other."[141]

Later on in the nineteenth century, Darwinism would play a crucial role in the invention of secular man, as it would "utterly demolish the argument from divine design."[142] Further, "by re-enacting the Cartesian fallacy of the 'definitive morality' (that is, the premise that scientific knowledge of physical or biological reality could be taken as a guide to what human behaviors should be), it made possible the new mode of adaptive truth that should more properly be defined as metaphysical (rather than social) Darwinism."[143] Race is the fundamental understanding that legitimates Western man's overrepresentation as the human:

> "Man" is not the human, although it represents itself as if it were. It is a specific, local-cultural conception of the human, that of the Judaeo-Christian West, in its now purely secularised form. Its *"Other"* therefore is not *woman*, as I hope to show. Rather because *Man* conceives of itself, through its origin narrative or "official creation story" of Evolution, as having been bio-evolutionarily selected, its *"Other"* and *"Others"* are necessarily those categories of humans who are projected, in the terms of the same Origin narrative, as having been bio-evolutionarily dysselected—i.e. all *native* peoples, and most extremely, to the ultimate zero degree, all peoples of African descent, wholly or partly (i.e. *negroes*) who are negatively marked as *defective humans* within the terms of Man's self-conception, and its related understanding of what it is to *be* human.[144]

The terror of Western colonial reason creates "other subtypes of otherness" out of "this ultimate mode of otherness based on 'race,'" which include "the lower classes as the lack of the normal class, that is the middle class; all other cultures as the lack of the normal culture, that is Western culture; the nonheterosexual as the lack of heterosexuality, represented as a biologically selected mode of erotic preference; women as the lack of the normal sex, the male."[145] This is *not* identical to the privileging of race over class, gender, or sexuality, a heavily criticized (sometimes without adequate nuance) pitfall of some liberation movements.[146] Nor is it a faddish postcolonialism that would seek to meld all four into an ultimately liberal humanism.[147] Instead, Wynter seeks to clarify what David Scott describes well as the *"foundational* epistemological priority of race" in the creation of modernity and the colonial world.[148] The task that Wynter places before us is to effect a transformation of a magnitude similar to that of the Renaissance and create a body of thought that for the first time can result in the birth of the human: "Since what joins all of these challenges, from that of Las Casas to all those of our contemporary order, is . . . their profound challenge to the overrepresentation of Man . . . (and) thereby, the coloniality of being, power, truth, freedom to which such an overrepresentation leads."[149] The crises that man's overrepresentation as the human leads us toward have their origins in European man and the colonial comprador elite, but now, while that center of dominion remains, the genre of the human that requires subversion is beyond even these groups: "This issue is that of the genre of the human, the issue whose target of abolition is the ongoing collective production of our present ethnoclass mode of being human, Man: above all, its overrepresentation of its well-being as that of the human species as a whole, rather than as it is veridically: that of the Western and westernized (or conversely) global middle classes."[150]

The problem with previous humanisms is in part that they were only "partial humanisms," "ethnohumanisms," constructed on the premise that Western-bourgeois man was *the* human and incapable of giving us a "history of the human."[151] Pressed in an interview with David Scott on why we should "re-enchant the human in humanism," Wynter would state that "we have to recognize the dimensions of the breakthroughs that these first humanisms made possible at the level of human cognition, and therefore of the possibility of our eventual emancipation, of our eventual full autonomy, as humans."[152] The West is not just a "local culture" (as Clifford Geertz would put it) like any other but one whose enchantments subvert our autonomy as a species and has resulted in a *genre* of the human that imperils the *habitat* of the human—and the continuation of our species.[153]

Wynter Reading James

In a 1972 conference on the lifework of C. L. R. James at the University of the West Indies, Mona campus, Sylvia Wynter delivered a public consideration of James, with echoes of her own recent essays "Novel and History" and "Jonkonnu in Jamaica" but with an eye toward the global revolutionary sympathies then emerging in her preliminary sketches of "Black Metamorphosis": "James for some 40 years has analysed this crisis, has warned about it, has shown what is to him the only way out, a world revolution in the material basis of existence, in man's view of reality and of himself. A new perspective which will make possible man's *urgent realization of his own humanity* so that in the words of another Caribbean native José Martí, man can live not as he does now as a wolf among wolves, but as a man among men."[154]

The castaway culture of the Caribbean, forever denied legitimacy by the colonial state and its postcolonial quislings, would become for Wynter the crucial link between her work and that of C. L. R. James, and it is here that Wynter's turn to liminality is essential. Wynter borrows the concept of liminality from the anthropologist Asmarom Legesse, who describes a person positioned in the liminal category as one who potentially "generates conscious change by exposing all the injustices inherent in structure."[155] Here we see echoes of Wynter's prior work on black experience, particularly her essay "Sambos and Minstrels," in which she declared that the "pain, the angst of those posited as non-norms . . .

compelled examination of the functioning of the Symbolic order itself."[156] In her essay "After the New Class: James, *Les Damnés*, and the Autonomy of Human Cognition," Wynter provocatively links Legesse's liminality to Fanon's damnés in order to make the claim that the damnés "can alone reveal what the rules that govern the 'Truth' of our present role-allocating and system-integrating Logos, must necessarily *be*."[157] As Wynter puts it, "The starving 'fellah,' (or the jobless inner city N.H.I., the global new poor, or les *damnés*) Fanon pointed out, does not have to *inquire into the truth*. They *are* the truth. It is we who institute this 'truth.' We must now undo their narratively condemned status."[158] The condemned of the earth are a transnational group, more linked by the experience of abjectness than by race, nation, or culture, but the experience of African diasporic populations, those forced "to pay the most total psycho-existential price" for the Euro-American West's victory, may well be decisive.[159]

Beyond coloniality does not exist in a future theory or in a future heaven.[160] It exists in the creative self-activity of the African diasporic masses. As Cedric Robinson, reflecting on the "renegade black intelligentsia," puts it, "we must keep in mind that their brilliance was also derivative. The true genius was in the midst of the people of whom they wrote. There the struggle was more than words or ideas but life itself."[161] James and Wynter knew only too well the profound questions living in an antiblack world raised about the responsibilities of Caribbean and Africana intellectuals. Speaking at a 1968 conference in Cuba, James would reach the position that "intellectuals should prepare the way for the abolition of the intellectuals as embodiment of culture."[162] The key word here may well be "embodiment," through which the authority of intellectuals as legislators and interpreters allows them to attribute meaning and value to cultural phenomena. What James perceives here and is in concert with his work of the 1960s is that the *terrain* of the popular will eclipse the intellectual's ability to explain its meaning. Wynter would go further. Intellectuals, as "grammarians of our present epistemological order," produce and establish the forms of truth that result in the condemned of the earth.[163] As a result of intellectual complicity, the momentous task facing the radical third-world intelligentsia is to have the moral and intellectual courage and *epistemic daring* to demand the human after man.

The intellectual's journey on the road to class power is to be expected and relegates her to a counterhegemonic perhaps, but not a decisively radical rendition of human dreams of emancipation. The Caribbean popular for James and Wynter contained different possibilities, which they both made decisive contributions toward giving an "interpretation of meaning," and became for Wynter the site of her deepest exploration of the legacy of James's work.[164] Today, Caribbean popular culture is the most powerful force that socializes contemporary Caribbean citizens into an understanding of their identities, the limits of their citizenship, and the meaning of their worlds.[165] Wynter's reading of James, threaded through her quest for a radical uprising against bourgeois domination, is a singularly insightful reading of the Caribbean intellectual tradition and popular culture.

In her "In Quest of Matthew Bondman: Some Cultural Notes on the Jamesian Journey," Wynter gives the first of her three readings of the lifework of C. L. R. James and another installment of her ideas on the quest for sovereignty by the condemned of the New World.[166] Matthew Bondman was the first character sketched by James in *Beyond a Boundary*, and he lived next door to James during his childhood. "'His eyes were fierce, his language was violent and his voice was loud', he refused to take a job but 'with a bat in his hand [he] was all grace and style'."[167] Bondman was not one of the "deserving proletariat"; he was, according to James's aunts, *"good for nothing else except to play cricket."*[168] And here Wynter makes her intervention:

> To realize their full powers, to give them full play, the Bondmans had to live in an alternative cosmology, an underground culture which they reconstituted for themselves. In addition, it meant that the total blockage of the realization of their powers, the prevention of their living of their own radical historicity, their subordination, to the historicity of the productive forces would therefore impel the Bondmans of the world (*"Les damnés de la terre,"* as Fanon defines them) to demand, *to desire as that by which alone they can live*, not the liberation of the productive forces (Liberalism and Marxism-Leninism) but the "liberation of Man."[169]

This is a great moment in Caribbean letters. Here the condemned of the earth reject not just coloniality but Eurocentric social theory in both its liberal and radical guises. Affect, resistance, pleasure, play, modernity, power, and desire are transformed into something new. But it is not without its contradictions. One could persuasively argue that Wynter relies here on a version of Marxism that denies the search for human value beyond estranged labor in Marx's *Economic and Philosophic Manuscripts of 1844*, where Marx could say, "If we assume man to be man, and his relation to the world to be a human one, then love can be exchanged only for love, trust for trust, and so on."[170] There is an intricate series of questions, impossible to explore here, about the critical yield of a theory that "redefines Marx's class struggle in terms of a 'politics of being.'"[171] However, Wynter captures well the essence of James's mid-twentieth-century work on culture—his quest to uncover a "properly socialist desire" to fashion a world in which everyone can find an activity that allows them to give their powers full play.[172] Bondman is both the *price* of Western bourgeois man and the key to unlocking the fictions that govern our present mode of being.

In her unpublished contribution to the 1991 Wellesley conference on C. L. R. James, a different aspect of James's thought was considered by Wynter.[173] Here the two key—Wynter refers to them as "scriptural"—texts would be James's *Notes on Dialectics*, his major contribution to Marxist theory, and his lecture "From Dubois to Fanon." The prescience of James's *Notes on Dialectics*, written in 1948, would have been particularly clear to Wynter in 1991, two years after the end of Soviet domination of eastern European countries and mere months away from the collapse of the USSR itself. In *Notes on Dialectics*, James undertakes a philosophical inquiry into how the Soviet Union became not merely a deformed workers' state but a state capitalist regime with the gulag as its natural consequence.[174] For Wynter, the definition of "human emancipation in the terms that empowered your group-interest, representing this interest as that of human emancipation in general," becomes the flaw leading inevitably to "deontological schema, from whose abductive terms of inference, specific behaviours would logically follow—including the behaviours which led to the Gulags of the Soviet Union and Cambodia, to the hardliner's precipitation of the Grenada tragedy."[175] In her reading of "From Dubois to Fanon," Wynter weds James's warning about the fate of society if it ignores those that suffer condemnation within it—in James's words, "all on the earth will be condemned"—to *Beyond a Boundary*'s Matthew Bondman and the concept of the "new poor" in postindustrial Western society.[176] James's work "can enable us to effect . . . [a] rupture with the telos of material redemption" that lies at the heart of both liberalism and orthodox Marxism-Leninism[177]: "The new premise . . . is, that the systemic stifling of the creative powers of the human, whether as individual or group is the worst deprivation of all: that material deprivation is itself only one of the conditions of the effecting of the latter, and that the goal of material redemption is itself only valid, therefore, to the extent that it subserves the telos of the human's full realization of its creative powers."[178]

These critical darts against the elisions of mainstream Marxist theory coupled with an exploration of the popular in James's writing would reach their zenith in Wynter's last published article on James. With the break from Marxism that she first announced in "Black Metamorphosis" assured, Wynter would state that the "capitalist mode of production is a subset of the bourgeois mode of accumulation which constitutes the basis of middle-class hegemony."[179] To the Marxist category of "reserve labor," Wynter presents "lower categories of human lives," in effect "reserve lives" produced through coloniality.[180] The Caribbean popular that James would write about with such brilliance after twenty-five years outside the region is an event with a global presence and significance: "The great unifying forms of our times are no longer, as in the case of cricket, coded, under the hegemony of middle-class cultural mores. What we are experiencing is a cultural shift of historical magnitude, a shift that James pointed to in the lectures on modern politics given in Trinidad. The great unifying cultural forms of our times, beginning with the jazz culture and its derivatives, are popular. This is the significance of calypso and Carnival, of the reggae and Rastafarianism. This is the significance of the Jamesian poiesis."[181]

James gives us "a vision of life that unfurls new vistas on a liveable future, both for ourselves and for the socio-biosphere we inhabit."[182] The secret of James's thought extends beyond the categories advanced to comprehend him. When asked on the tenth anniversary of his death by David Austin what was the most important aspect of James's thought, Wynter would reply with a comment breathtaking in its meaning and economy of words: "It was his tremendous re-vindification of what it means to be human, which is always put down in the bourgeois conception of man."[183] Wynter might easily have been speaking of her own work. Ranging across centuries of black underlife experience, with few aspects of modern existence untouched, it opens the possibility of an encounter with a humanly livable world in our lifetimes. There is simply nothing more we could want.

Notes

1. Sylvia Wynter, "The Pope Must Have Been Drunk, the King of Castile a Madman: Culture as Actuality, and the Caribbean Rethinking Modernity," in *The Reordering of Culture: Latin America, the Caribbean and Canada*, ed. Alvina Ruprecht and Cecilia Taiana (Ottawa: Carleton University Press, 1995): 35.

2. Daryl Cumber Dance, "Interview with C. L. R. James," in *New World Adams* (Leeds, UK: Peepal Tree, 1992), 118. This interview was conducted in 1980.

3. Derrick White, "Black Metamorphosis: A Prelude to Sylvia Wynter's Theory of the Human," *C. L. R. James Journal* 16, no. 1 (Fall 2010): 127. C. L. R. James wrote the quoted words on his copy of "The Politics of Black Culture," which is housed in the library of the Oil Workers Trade Union in Trinidad and Tobago.

4. These three essays are "In Quest of Matthew Bondman: Some Cultural Notes on the Jamesian Journey," *Urgent Tasks* (Summer 1981): 54–69, republished in a slightly changed version in *C. L. R. James: His Life and Work*, ed. Paul Buhle (London: Allison and Busby, 1986); "After the New Class: James, *Les Damnés*, and the Autonomy of Human Cognition," paper prepared for the International Conference C. L. R. James: His Intellectual Legacies, hosted by the Black Studies Department at Wellesley, April 19–21, 1991; "Beyond the Categories of the Master Conception: The Counterdoctrine of the Jamesian Poeisis," in *C. L. R. James's Caribbean*, ed. Paul Buhle and Paget Henry (Durham, NC: Duke University Press, 1992), 63–91.

5. Wynter's "Black Metamorphosis: New Natives in a New World" is currently housed in the Institute of the Black World Papers at the Schomburg Centre for Research in Black Culture, New York. See Aaron Kamugisha, "'That Area of Experience That We Term the New World': Introducing Sylvia Wynter's 'Black Metamorphosis,'" *Small Axe* 49 (2016): 39–46.

6. This conference was the Association for Commonwealth Literature and Language Studies (ACLALS), held on January 3–9, 1971, at the University of the West Indies, Mona campus in Jamaica.

7. Sylvia Wynter's essay, "We Must Learn to Sit Down Together and Discuss a Little Culture: Reflections on West Indian Writing and Criticism," pt. 1, *Jamaica Journal* 2, no. 4 (1968): 24–32; pt. 2, *Jamaica Journal* 3, no. 1 (1969): 27–42, would be hailed by Kamau Brathwaite

as "one of our great critical landmarks: a major essai into literary *ideas*, and the first to be written *in* the West Indies." See Kamau Brathwaite, "The Love Axe/l: Developing a Caribbean Aesthetic," in *Reading Black: Essays in the Criticism of African, Caribbean and Black American Literature*, ed. Houston Baker (Ithaca, NY: Africana Studies and Research Center, Cornell University, 1976), 27 (original emphasis), republished in *Caribbean Cultural Thought: From Plantation to Diaspora*, ed. Yanique Hume and Aaron Kamugisha (Kingston: Ian Randle, 2013). In addition to this and other essays, she had published "Jonkonnu in Jamaica: Towards the Interpretation of Folk Dance as a Cultural Process," *Jamaica Journal* 4, no. 2 (June 1970): 34–48, a similarly pathbreaking critical essay on Jamaican culture.

8. This letter by Wynter, dated February 15, 1971, is quoted in Derrick White, "'Black Metamorphosis': A Prelude to Sylvia Wynter's Theory of the Human," *C. L. R. James Journal* 16, no. 1 (Fall 2010): 129.

9. "Jonkonnu in Jamaica"; "Novel and History, Plot and Plantation," *Savacou* 5 (June 1971): 95–102; "Ethno Or Socio Poetics," *Alcheringa: Ethnopoetics* 2, no. 2 (1976): 78–94; "'We Know Where We Are From': The Politics of Black Culture from Myal to Marley," paper presented at the joint meeting of the African Studies Association and the Latin American Studies Association in Houston, Texas, November 1977; "In Quest of Matthew Bondman: Some Cultural Notes on the Jamesian Journey," *C. L. R. James: His Life and Work*, ed. Paul Buhle (London: Allison and Busby, 1986), 131–45.

10. For a first collection of critical responses to the manuscript, see the special issue of *Small Axe* 49 (March 2016) "Sylvia Wynter's Black Metamorphosis: A Discussion," edited by myself with essays by Demetrius Eudell, Greg Thomas, Katherine McKittrick, Tonya Haynes, and Nijah Cunningham.

11. This point is made well by Derrick White, in his essay "Black Metamorphosis: A Prelude to Sylvia Wynter's Theory of the Human." To my knowledge, prior to *Small Axe* 49, this was the only existing published critical commentary on "Black Metamorphosis."

12. James Baldwin, front page blurb on Richard Wright, *Black Boy* (New York: Signet, 1951).

13. Wynter, "Black Metamorphosis," 1.

14. See especially here Sylvia Wynter, "1492: A New World View," in *Race, Discourse and the Origin of the Americas*, ed. Vera Hyatt and Rex Nettleford (Washington, DC: Smithsonian, 1995), 5–57.

15. Wynter, "Black Metamorphosis," 3. Wynter still refers to the text as an "essay" at this point, and it is clear that this introduction was not rewritten subsequent to the addition of the majority of the text.

16. C. L. R. James, *American Civilization*, ed. Anna Grimshaw and Keith Hart (London: Blackwell, 1993). This manuscript was written in 1950.

17. For Wynter's comments on this, see David Scott, "The Re-Enchantment of Humanism: An Interview with Sylvia Wynter," *Small Axe* 8 (2000): 171–73. For James's anger after he had traveled in the Jim Crow South for the first time, see Scott McLemee, "Introduction," in *C. L. R. James on the "Negro Question"* (Jackson, Mississippi: University of Mississippi Press, 1996), xi–xxxvii. Years after his fifteen years in the United States, James would say the following: "In America, a West Indian learns for the first time what the race question really is." C. L. R. James, "A Convention Appraisal: Dr. Eric Williams, First Premier of Trinidad and Tobago, a Biographical Sketch," in *Eric Williams Speaks: Essays on Colonialism and Independence*, ed. Selwyn Cudjoe (Wellesley, MA: Calaloux, 1993), 338. In an interview, Wynter

would state that "had I not come to the United States, I could have never have come to think like this." Greg Thomas, *"Proud Flesh* Inter/views Sylvia Wynter," *Proudflesh: New Afrikan Journal of Culture, Politics and Consciousness* 4 (2006): 27.

18. C. L. R. James, *Beyond a Boundary* (Durham, NC: Duke University Press, 1993), 19, 151.

19. Timothy Brennan, "Cosmopolitan's American Base: C. L. R. James in New York, 1950," in *At Home in the World: Cosmopolitanism Now* (Cambridge, MA: Harvard University Press, 1997), 219. Brennan's chapter remains the best reading of James's *American Civilization* to date.

20. Brennan, *At Home in the World*, 221, 233.

21. Andrew Ross, "Civilization in One Country? The American James," in *Rethinking C. L. R. James*, ed. Grant Farred (Cambridge, MA: Blackwell, 1996), 75–84.

22. See Brennan, *At Home in the World*, 221, 231; C. L. R. James, "The Old World and the New," in *At the Rendezvous of Victory* (London: Allison and Busby, 1984), 202–17.

23. Scholarship on black modernity has been central to the intellectual production of Africana intellectuals in the Euro-American academy over the last two decades. Wynter's work allows us to consider the idea that debates on black modernity are merely a subset of an inquiry into black experience—and likely not the most productive one.

24. Greg Thomas, "Sex/Sexuality and Sylvia Wynter's *Beyond . . .*: Anti-Colonial Ideas in 'Black Radical Tradition,'" *Journal of West Indian Literature* 10, nos. 1 and 2 (November 2001): 111.

25. Wynter, "Black Metamorphosis," 455.

26. Wynter, "Jonkonnu in Jamaica." For more on this argument, see Carole Boyce Davies, "From Masquerade to Maskarade: Caribbean Cultural Resistance and the Rehumanizing Project," in *Sylvia Wynter: On Being Human as Praxis*, ed. Katherine McKittrick (Durham, NC: Duke University Press, 2015), 203–25. On pp. 228–29 of "Black Metamorphosis," Wynter would state, "Creolization leads to the philosophy of integration. Marronage leads to the principle of separation. Indigenization must lead to the principle of liberation."

27. For more on the development and different versions of "Black Metamorphosis," see my introduction to this issue.

28. See Wynter, "Jonkonnu in Jamaica," 35; "Black Metamorphosis," 17.

29. Wynter, "Black Metamorphosis," 18, 243–44. Wynter's use of "indigenization" has recently come under criticism by Shona Jackson and Melanie Newton, who have both shown, relying on "Jonkonnu in Jamaica," that this essay assumes native absence in order to claim black nativity to the land. The more extended argument on nativity in "Black Metamorphosis" will undoubtedly be a prominent feature of future discussions of this theme in Wynter's work but is not my focus in this essay. See Shona Jackson, *Creole Indigeneity: Between Myth and Nation in the Caribbean* (Minneapolis: University of Minnesota Press, 2012), 43–44, 244n7; Melanie Newton, "Returns to a Native Land: Indigeneity and Decolonization in the Anglophone Caribbean," *Small Axe* 41 (2013): 117–18.

30. Wynter, "Black Metamorphosis," 56.

31. The wider body of work here is substantial. To restrict myself to two key texts and critical responses to Brathwaite, Mintz, and Price, see the following: Kamau Brathwaite, *Contradictory Omens: Cultural Diversity and Integration in the Caribbean* (Kingston: Savacou, 1974); Sidney Mintz and Richard Price, *An Anthropological Approach to the Afro-American Past: A Caribbean Perspective* (Philadelphia: Institute for the Study of Human Issues, 1976); David Scott, "That Event, This Memory: Notes on the Anthropology of African Diasporas in the New World," *Diaspora* 1, no. 3 (1991): 261–84; David Scott, "'An Obscure Miracle of

Connection': Discursive Tradition and Black Diaspora Criticism," *Small Axe* 1 (1997): 19–38; Richard Price, "The Miracle of Creolization: A Retrospective," *New West India Guide* 75, no. 1/2 (2001): 35–64.

32. David Scott, "That Event," 278.

33. Frantz Fanon, *Black Skin, White Masks* (New York: Grove, 1967), 110.

34. Lewis R. Gordon, *What Fanon Said: A Philosophical Introduction to His Life and Thought* (New York: Fordham University Press, 2015), 47.

35. For Wynter on *Black Boy*, see "Black Metamorphosis," 37–38, 404–8, 415–25, 778.

36. Wynter, "Black Metamorphosis," 38.

37. Wynter, "Black Metamorphosis," 407.

38. Wynter, "Black Metamorphosis," 421, my emphasis. See also especially Wynter's reading of Hegel and Fanon on the desires of the master on p. 425.

39. Wynter, "Black Metamorphosis," 393, 421.

40. Frantz Fanon, *Black Skin*, 116; on negritude, see 122–40.

41. Wynter, "Black Metamorphosis," 428. For a later essay in which Wynter would make a similar argument in defense of Aimé Césaire and in criticism of the créolistes of Martinique, see "'A Different Kind of Creature': Caribbean Literature, the Cyclops Factor, and the Second Poetics of the Propter Nos," *Annals of Scholarship* 12, nos. 1–2 (1997): 153–72.

42. Richard Iton, *In Search of the Black Fantastic: Politics and Popular Culture in the Post-Civil Rights Era* (New York: Oxford University Press, 2008), 30.

43. Wynter, "Black Metamorphosis," 627.

44. Wynter, "Black Metamorphosis," 372.

45. Amid a now voluminous literature, for an important early statement on this, see Avery F. Gordon, "Globalism and the Prison Industrial Complex: An Interview with Angela Davis," *Race and Class* 40, nos. 2 and 3 (1998): 145–57.

46. Wynter, "Black Metamorphosis," 249–50.

47. For Wynter's mention of the decision by the US Supreme Court in the *Regents of the University of California v. Bakke*, see "Black Metamorphosis," 391, 393, 782, 824–25.

48. Wynter, "Black Metamorphosis," 37–38. See also the convictions expressed on p. 33.

49. Wynter, "Black Metamorphosis," 39–40 (original emphasis), 43–44, 46. See also here Paget Henry's careful reading of Wynter on the question of her engagement with Marxist thought, in "Wynter and the Transcendental Spaces of Caribbean Thought," in *After Man, Towards the Human: Critical Essays on Sylvia Wynter*, ed. Anthony Bogues (Kingston: Ian Randle, 2006), especially 274–80.

50. The passage reads as follows: "I would like at this point to contradict an earlier formulation. At the beginning of the monograph, I defined the Sambo stereotype as the mechanism by which more surplus value could be extracted from relatively devalued labour . . . I would tend now, however, to see the Sambo stereotype as a mechanism which is far more central to capitalism's functioning as a mode of domination. That is, I would see its function in extracting surplus as secondary to its function of permitting a mode of domination to be generalized at all levels of the system." "Black Metamorphosis," 429. Also see p. 589, "Earlier on in this manuscript, I had accepted the Marxist . . . privileging of the economic . . . But that was to take a central effect for a cause . . . nigger-breaking was directed towards an essentially social purpose." See also Demetrius Eudell, "From Mode of Production to Mode of Auto-Institution: Sylvia Wynter's Black Metamorphosis of the Labor Question," *Small Axe* 49 (2016): 47–61; and White, "Prelude."

51. I refer to Frantz Fanon's well-known comment that "Marxist analysis should always be slightly stretched every time we have to do with the colonial problem." *The Wretched of the Earth*, trans. Constance Farrington (London: Penguin Books, 1990), 31.

52. Wynter, "Black Metamorphosis," 710–12. The passage by Marx is from *Capital: A Critique of Political Economy*, trans. Samuel Moore and Edward Aveling (New York: Random House, 1906), 785.

53. Wynter, "Black Metamorphosis," 535. See here Wynter's argument about how bourgeois expression discursively legitimated itself in the West, in "Beyond the Categories."

54. Wynter, "Black Metamorphosis," 572–73.

55. Wynter, "Black Metamorphosis," 846.

56. Wynter, "Black Metamorphosis," 578, 773–74. The journey from Wynter's thoughts here to her theory of the human after Western man can be clearly seen. See especially here "Unsettling the Coloniality of Being/Power/Truth/Freedom: Towards the Human, After Man, Its Overrepresentation: An Argument," *CR: The New Centennial Review* 3, no. 3 (Fall 2003): 257–337; and White, "Prelude."

57. Wynter, "Black Metamorphosis," 919.

58. Wynter, "Black Metamorphosis," 691, 615.

59. Wynter, "Black Metamorphosis," 582.

60. Wynter, "Black Metamorphosis," 571. In the original text, "Negro" is underlined.

61. Wynter, "Black Metamorphosis," 225.

62. See here Bernard Boxill, "Two Traditions in African American Political Philosophy," *Philosophical Forum* 24, nos. 1–3 (1992–1993): 119–35; and Peter Hudson and Aaron Kamugisha, "On Black Canadian Thought," *C. L. R. James Journal* 20 (Fall 2014): 1–18.

63. Wynter, "Black Metamorphosis," 765; Fanon, *Wretched of the Earth*.

64. Wynter, "Black Metamorphosis," 578.

65. Wynter, "Black Metamorphosis," 439. Also see p. 798 on the "colonization of black desire" and p. 402 on "the central strategy of the system is the colonization of desire." The latter line, along with other parts of this section of "Black Metamorphosis" were directly incorporated into Wynter's one publication taken from this manuscript, see "Sambos and Minstrels," *Social Text* 1 (Winter 1979): 152.

66. Wynter, "Black Metamorphosis," 476. Let us listen to Du Bois: "the Negro folk song—the rhythmic cry of the slave—stands today not simply as the sole American music, but as the most beautiful expression of human *experience* born this side of the seas . . . It remains as the singular spiritual heritage of the nation and the greatest gift of the Negro people." W. E. B. Du Bois, *The Souls of Black Folk* (New York: Signet, 1995), 265, emphasis added.

67. Wynter, "Black Metamorphosis," 607.

68. Wynter, "Black Metamorphosis," 817.

69. Wynter, "Black Metamorphosis," 545.

70. Timothy Brennan, *Secular Devotion: Afro-Latin Music and Imperial Jazz* (London: Verso, 2008), 2, 4, original emphasis.

71. Brennan, *Secular Devotion*, 9.

72. Wynter, "Black Metamorphosis," 646.

73. Wynter, "Black Metamorphosis," 245, 666–67.

74. Wynter, "Black Metamorphosis," 245.

75. Wynter, "Black Metamorphosis," 205, my emphasis.

76. Nikki Giovanni, "Nikki-Rossa," in *The Collected Poetry of Nikki Giovanni, 1968–1998* (New York: HarperCollins, 2003), 53.

77. Sylvia Wynter, "'We Know Where,'" 45.

78. Wynter, "Black Metamorphosis," 917.

79. Wynter, "Black Metamorphosis," 824; for the quoted passage, see Wynter's paper "Natives in a New World: The African Transformation in the Americas," Institute of the Black World Papers at the Schomburg Center for Research in Black Culture, New York, 30.

80. Wynter, "Black Metamorphosis," 849. The wonder of this text is the abundance of paragraphs of a similar power. For another one on p. 918: "blacks by the nature of their experience must delegitimate the cultural signification systems; the cultural hegemonic imperialism, by which all modes of expropriation of wealth and power are legitimated and carried out."

81. C. L. R. James, "From Du Bois to Fanon," Radical America 2, no. 4 (July–August 1968): 29. This document is an excerpt from a speech given in Detroit in January 1967. See "Black Metamorphosis," 251, for a paraphrase of this quote from James by Wynter.

82. Wynter, "Unsettling the Coloniality," 306.

83. George Jackson, Soledad Brother: The Prison Letters of George Jackson (Chicago: Lawrence Hill Books, 1994), 282–83.

84. Erna Brodber, "Beyond the Boundary—Magical Realism in the Jamaican Frame of Reference," Annals of Scholarship 12, nos. 1 and 2 (1997): 44, my italics.

85. Wynter, "Black Metamorphosis," 615–16.

86. Marlene NourbeSe Philip, "Managing the Unmanageable," in Caribbean Women Writers: Essays from the First International Conference, ed. Selwyn Cudjoe (Wellesley, MA: Calaloux, 1990), 295–300. James Baldwin as cited in David Marriott, On Black Men (New York: Columbia University Press, 2000), 66.

87. Jamaica Kincaid, The Autobiography of My Mother (New York: Farrar, Straus, Giroux, 1996), 139. The entire passage reads as follows: "For to me history was not a large stage filled with commemoration, bands, cheers, ribbons, medals, the sound of fine glass clinking and raised high in the air; in other words, the sound of victory. For me history was not only the past: it was the past and it was also the present. I did not mind my defeat, I only minded that it had to last so long; I did not see the future, and that is perhaps as it should be."

88. Wynter, "Beyond the Categories."

89. Gregory Bateson, Mind and Nature (New York: E. P. Dutton, 1979), 142.

90. Edouard Glissant, Caribbean Discourse: Selected Essays, trans. Michael Dash (Charlottesville: University Press of Virginia, 1989), 2.

91. Wynter, "Beyond the Categories," 65, 72–73, 78.

92. Wynter, "Beyond the Categories," 82, 66.

93. Wynter, "Beyond the Categories," 67.

94. See Wynter, "After the New Class," 14, 16; "Beyond Liberal and Marxist Leninist Feminisms: Towards an Autonomous Frame of Reference," unpublished paper, prepared for the session "Feminist Theory at the Crossroads," American Sociological Association, San Francisco, September 1982, 18. See also Wynter's use of abduction in "The Ceremony Must Be Found: After Humanism," Boundary 2 vol. 12, no. 3 / vol. 13, no. 1 (1984): 44, 48, 49, 55, 56, 64n54.

95. Wynter, "Beyond Liberal," 15

96. Wynter, "Beyond the Word of Man: Glissant and the New Discourse of the Antilles," World Literature in Review 63, no. 4 (1989): 638

97. Wynter, "'Different Kind of Creature,'" 154.

98. See here especially "Ceremony Must Be Found," 21, 25; and Sylvia Wynter, "Afterword: Beyond Miranda's Meanings: Un/silencing the 'Demonic Ground' of Caliban's 'Woman,'"

in *Out of the Kumbla: Caribbean Women and Literature*, ed. Carole Boyce Davies and Elaine Savory Fido (Trenton, NJ: Africa World Press, 1990): 364.

99. Anthony Pagden, *The Fall of Natural Man: The American Indian and the Origins of Comparative Ethnology* (Cambridge: Cambridge University Press, 1986), 10. This comment by O'Crowley was made in 1774. Pagden goes on to note that travelers from Europe at that time "went to America with precise ideas about what they could expect to find there. They went looking for wild men and giants, Amazons and pygmies. They went in search of the Fountain of Eternal Youth, of cities paved with goal, of women whose bodies, like those of the Hyperboreans, never aged, of cannibals and of men who lived to be a hundred years or more."

100. I allude here to the title of Joan Dayan's essay "Held in the Body of the State: Prisons and the Law," in *History, Memory, and the Law*, ed. Austin Sarat and Thomas R. Kearns (Ann Arbor: University of Michigan Press, 1999), 183–247.

101. Stephen Greenblatt, *Marvellous Possessions: The Wonder of the New World* (Chicago: University of Chicago Press, 1991), 106. Greenblatt later states that "in the absence of any secure grasp of the native language or culture, the little that the English learn from their captive seems overwhelmed by all that they do not understand, and when they do not understand, they can only continue to entrap, kidnap, and project vain fantasies." *Marvellous Possessions*, 117.

102. Luis N. Rivera-Pagán, "Freedom and Servitude: Indigenous Slavery and the Spanish Conquest," in *General History of the Caribbean Vol. 1: Autochthonous Societies*, ed. Jalil Sued-Badillo (Paris: UNESCO; London: Macmillan Caribbean, 2003), 316–61.

103. See Mimi Sheller, *Consuming the Caribbean: From Arawaks to Zombies* (London: Routledge, 2003).

104. Edward W. Said, *Representations of the Intellectual: The 1993 Reith Lectures* (New York: Vintage Books, 1993), 99–100.

105. Noam Chomsky, *Language and Mind* (Cambridge: Cambridge University Press, 2006), 79–81.

106. Aimé Césaire, *Cahier d'un retour au pays natal* (Paris: Présence Africaine, 1968), 95. The line reads, "ceux qui n'ont connu de voyages que de déracinements." Clayton Eshleman and Annette Smith translate the line as "those who have known voyages only through uprootings." Aimé Césaire, *Notebook of a Return to the Native Land*, trans. and ed. Clayton Eshleman and Annette Smith (Middletown, CT: Wesleyan University Press, 2001).

107. For the term "coloniality of citizenship," see chapter 2 above and Aaron Kamugisha, "The Coloniality of Citizenship in the Contemporary Anglophone Caribbean," *Race and Class* 49, no. 2 (2007): 20–40.

108. Jan Pieterse, as cited in Ella Shohat and Robert Stam, *Unthinking Eurocentrism: Multiculturalism and the Media* (London: Routledge, 1994), 14; Fanon, *Wretched of the Earth*, 81; Hortense J. Spillers, "Mama's Baby, Papa's Maybe: An American Grammar Book," *Diacritics* 17, no. 2 (1987): 65.

109. I borrow this formulation in part from Elaine Brown. See her *The Condemnation of Little B* (Boston: Beacon, 2002), 9.

110. Sylvia Wynter, "*No Humans Involved*: An Open Letter to My Colleagues," *Voices of the African Diaspora* 8, no. 2 (Fall 1992): 13–16.

111. This chapter was largely written during the summer of 2015.

112. Césaire, *Notebook*, 34.

113. For Wynter's use of the idea of the "beyond," see "Afterword: Beyond Miranda's"; "Beyond the Word"; "Beyond the Categories."

114. David Scott, "The Re-enchantment of Humanism: An Interview with Sylvia Wynter," *Small Axe* 8 (2000): 159.

115. Scott, "Re-enchantment," 136.

116. For a discussion of these arguments, see Nelson Maldonado-Torres, "The Topology of Being and the Geopolitics of Knowledge: Modernity, Empire, Coloniality," *City* 8, no. 1 (2004): 29–56.

117. See here Wynter's comments in Scott, "Re-enchantment," 190–92.

118. See here Sylvia Wynter, *New Seville: Major Facts, Major Questions* (Kingston: JIS Press, 1984).

119. Scott, "Re-enchantment," 191.

120. It is quite impossible to do justice to the complex and overlapping themes through which Wynter has mapped out her retelling of the modern world. What follows can only be a provisional assessment/summary.

121. Las Casas would remark in book 3 of his *History of the Indies*:

> The priest Casas having at the time no knowledge of the unjust methods which the Portuguese used to obtain slaves, advised that permission should be given for the import of slaves into the islands, an advice which, once he became informed about these methods, he would not have given for the world . . . The remedy which he proposed to import Black slaves in order to liberate the Indians was not a good one, even though he thought the Black slaves, at the time to have been enslaved with a just title; and it is not at all certain that his ignorance at the time or even the purity of his motive will sufficiently absolve him when he finds himself before the Divine Judge.

Quoted in Sylvia Wynter, "New Seville and the Conversion Experience of Bartolomé de Las Casas," part 1, *Jamaica Journal* 17, no. 2 (1984): 25.

122. Sylvia Wynter, "New Seville and the Conversion Experience of Bartolomé de Las Casas," part 2, *Jamaica Journal* 17, no. 3 (1984): 52.

123. Wynter, "Bartolomé de Las Casas," part 2, 52.

124. Wynter, "Bartolomé de Las Casas," part 2, 53.

125. Wynter, "Bartolomé de Las Casas," part 2, 53, 52.

126. Wynter, "Unsettling the Coloniality," 269.

127. Wynter, "Unsettling the Coloniality," 269; "Bartolomé de Las Casas," part 2, 52. See also Wynter's comments on Sepúlveda in "Ceremony Must Be Found," 34–35.

128. Wynter, "Bartolomé de Las Casas," part 2, 53.

129. Las Casas as cited in Wynter, "Bartolomé de Las Casas," part 1, 25.

130. Wynter, "Bartolomé de Las Casas," part 2, 54.

131. Wynter, "Bartolomé de Las Casas" part 2, 53, original italics.

132. Wynter, "Bartolomé de Las Casas" part 2, 54, original italics.

133. Wynter, "Bartolomé de Las Casas" part 2, 54. Wynter has also argued that Las Casas represents "one of the earliest attempts at a transcultural mode of thinking"; see "Unsettling the Coloniality," 298.

134. These arguments, however, are not premised solely on a model of epistemic change borrowed from Michel Foucault but find their original inspiration in anticolonial thought, her earlier work of the 1960s and 1970s, and in "Black Metamorphosis." Wynter gives priority to the Caribbean intellectual tradition over Foucault in her essay "Beyond the Word," 640.

135. Wynter, "Ceremony Must Be Found."

136. Wynter, "Ceremony Must Be Found," 25.

137. Wynter, "Ceremony Must Be Found," 29–30.

138. Wynter, "Ceremony Must Be Found," 30, 33.

139. Wynter, "Unsettling the Coloniality," 287–88, my italics.

140. Wynter, "Pope Must Have Been Drunk," 28; Pagden, *Fall of Natural Man.*

141. Wynter, "1492," 38.

142. Wynter, "1492," 38.

143. Wynter, "Columbus, the Ocean Blue, and Fables That Stir the Mind: To Reinvent the Study of Letters," in *Poetics of the Americas: Race, Founding, and Textuality,* ed. Bainard Cowan and Jefferson Humphries (Baton Rouge: Louisiana State University Press, 1997), 159. See also Wynter's comments on Darwin in Scott, "Re-enchantment," 176–78.

144. Sylvia Wynter, "Africa, the West and the Analogy of Culture: The Cinematic Text after Man," in *Symbolic Narratives / African Cinema: Audiences, Theory and the Moving Image,* ed. June Givanni (London: British Film Institute, 2000), 25. All italics in the passages are Wynter's.

145. Wynter, "1492," 42.

146. For Wynter on gender, see especially Tonya Haynes, "The Divine and the Demonic: Sylvia Wynter and Caribbean Feminist Thought Revisited," in *Love and Power: Caribbean Discourses of Gender,* ed. Eudine Barriteau (Kingston: University of the West Indies Press, 2012), 54–71; and Tonya Haynes, "Sylvia Wynter's Theory of the Human and the Crisis School of Caribbean Heteromasculinity Studies," *Small Axe* 49 (2016): 92–112.

147. Bruce Robbins, "Race Gender, Class, Postcolonialism: Toward a New Humanistic Paradigm?" in *A Companion to Postcolonial Studies,* ed. Henry Schwarz and Sangeeta Ray (Malden, MA: Blackwell, 2000), 556–73. Wynter has spoken against "the present faddist and deceptive term of 'postcolonial,' one that conflates the ending of political colonialism with that of the more proud and continuing cultural, and therefore epistemological, 'imperialism' as enforced by academia and its disciplinary apparatuses." Wynter, "Is Development a Purely Empirical Concept or Also Teleological: A Perspective from 'We the Underdeveloped,'" in *Prospects for Recovery and Sustainable Development in Africa,* ed. Aguibou Yansane (Westport, CT: Greenwood, 1996), 315.

148. Scott, "Re-enchantment," 183, original italics.

149. Wynter, "Unsettling the Coloniality," 327.

150. Wynter, "Unsettling the Coloniality," 313.

151. Scott, "Re-enchantment," 196, 198.

152. Scott, "Re-enchantment," 195.

153. The influence of anthropologists like Clifford Geertz, Stanley Diamond, and Asmarom Legesse on Wynter's thought is evident here.

154. Sylvia Wynter, "James and the Castaway Culture of the Caribbean," paper delivered at the conference Symposium on the Life and Work of C. L. R. James, February 3, 1972, University of the West Indies, Mona Campus, audio recording in author's possession, the italicized emphasis is mine.

155. This quote is from Asmarom Legesse, *Gada: Three Approaches to the Study of an African Society* (New York: Free Press, 1973): 271, as quoted in Wynter, "Beyond Liberal," 36. For Wynter on liminality, see also, "Ceremony Must Me Found," 38–39; "Towards the Sociogenic Principle: Fanon, the Puzzle of Conscious Experience, of 'Identity' and What It's Like to Be 'Black,'" in *National Identity and Sociopolitical Change: Latin America Between Marginalization and Integration,* ed. Mercedes Durán-Cogan and Antonio Gómez-Moriana (New York: Garland, 2000), 58; and the essay by Nelson Maldonado-Torres, "Notes on the

Current Status of Liminal Categories and the Search for a New Humanism," in Bogues, *After Man*, 190–208.

156. Wynter, "Sambos and Minstrels," 150. This essay makes it clear that black peoples' struggle against coloniality is a struggle against the symbolic order of Western man.

157. Wynter, "After the New Class," 110.

158. Wynter, *"No Humans Involved,"* 16. This letter was written in the aftermath of the Los Angeles rebellion of 1992, in which, according to Wynter, it was revealed that "public officials of the judicial system of Los Angeles routinely used the acronym NHI (no humans involved) to refer to any case involving a breach of the rights of young, jobless black males living in the inner city ghetto."

159. Wynter, "Unsettling the Coloniality," 306.

160. I am alluding here to Frantz Fanon's comment that "the Algerian nation is no longer in a future heaven." See Frantz Fanon, *A Dying Colonialism* (Middlesex, UK: Penguin Books, 1970), 18.

161. Cedric Robinson, *Black Marxism: The Making of the Black Radical Tradition* (Chapel Hill: University of North Carolina Press, 2000), 184.

162. C. L. R. James, "The Responsibility of Intellectuals," unpublished talk at the Congress on Intellectuals, Cuba, 1968.

163. Sylvia Wynter, *"No Humans Involved,"* 13–16.

164. The phrase "interpretation of meaning" is from Wynter's "Jonkonnu in Jamaica."

165. Yanique Hume and Aaron Kamugisha, eds., *Caribbean Popular Culture: Power, Politics and Performance* (Kingston: Ian Randle, 2016).

166. Wynter, "In Quest of Matthew Bondman."

167. Wynter, "In Quest of Matthew Bondman." The quoted sections within this passage are from C. L. R. James's *Beyond a Boundary*.

168. Wynter, "In Quest of Matthew Bondman," 136, original italics.

169. Wynter, "In Quest of Matthew Bondman," 137.

170. Karl Marx, "Economic and Philosophical Manuscripts," *Karl Marx: Early Writings*, trans. Rodney Livingstone and Gregory Benton (Harmondsworth, UK: Penguin, 1975), 379.

171. Wynter, "Unsettling the Coloniality," 319.

172. The phrase a "properly socialist desire" to describe James's quest at midcentury is Timothy Brennan's; see Timothy Brennan, *At Home in the World: Cosmopolitanism Now* (Cambridge, MA: Harvard University Press, 1997), 208.

173. Wynter, "After the New Class."

174. C. L. R. James, *Notes on Dialectics: Hegel, Marx, Lenin* (London: Allison and Busby, 1980 [1948]).

175. Wynter, "After the New Class," 16.

176. C. L. R. James, "From Du Bois to Fanon," 29.

177. Wynter, "After the New Class," 99.

178. Wynter, "After the New Class," 100.

179. Wynter, "Beyond the Categories," 81.

180. Wynter, "Beyond the Categories," 78, 79.

181. Wynter, "Beyond the Categories," 87.

182. Wynter, "Beyond the Categories," 89.

183. David Austin, "Interview with Sylvia Wynter," May 1999, copy of CD in author's possession.

Conclusion

A Caribbean Sympathy

There is potential in this reality. What is missing from the notion of Caribbeanness is the transition from the shared experience to conscious expression; the need to transcend the intellectual pretensions dominated by the learned elite and to be grounded in collective affirmation, supported by the activism of the people.

Edouard Glissant, *Caribbean Discourse* (1989)[1]

We already know who brought us here
And who created this confusion
And so I'm begging, begging my people please

David Rudder, *Rally Round the West Indies* (1988)[2]

IN MY DISCUSSION of Sylvia Wynter's life work, I reflected on her use of the concept of abduction, meant to signify the spectacular drama of existing coloniality in the Caribbean and the world today. Abduction suggests the most wrenching of dislocations but also simultaneously signifies "marronage, insurrection, rebellion, revolution, and fugitive escape."[3] It also engenders wonder, at the ability of subaltern populations to survive coloniality and in the case of the African diaspora to create forms of expressive culture that have had a decisive impact on twentieth-century Western popular culture. This wonder, approaching incredulity, and concomitant vision of the diaspora is well described by one of Aimé Césaire's commentators as "a sprawling dynamic landscape with its cultures arranged like 'an incomprehensible rain of stars' all spread out against a black sky."[4] However, as Wynter once asked in a different context, what does wonder do?[5] What, beyond celebration and lament, does the recognition of multiple diasporas and the power of black expressive culture give to us in our battle to move beyond coloniality?[6] And where does diaspora as concept leave our insights on discourses of Caribbeanness and the related issue of regional integration?

In 1998, the *Journal of Eastern Caribbean Studies* published a special issue titled "Eastern Caribbean Integration: A Rekindling of the Little Eight?"[7] The issue was in part inspired by the recent election of political leaders in St. Lucia and

Barbados who seemed determined to put the issue of Caribbean political integration back on the agenda forty years after the birth of the ill-fated West Indies Federation and also included an article by the soon-to-be prime minister of St. Vincent and a reprint of Arthur Lewis's famous essay from 1965, "The Agony of the Eight."[8] The miniaturizing of the goal of regional integration was evident in the journal, with a wider discussion of a Caribbean state that could include Jamaica and Trinidad and Tobago, the two largest Anglophone territories not on the agenda, and a simultaneous warning of insularity through an article on the secessionist movement in St. Kitts–Nevis. Regional unity, in effect, had boiled down to Barbados's relationship to the Organisation of Eastern Caribbean States and the possibility of the political integration of those countries.[9] Five years later, in a response to statements from the prime ministers of St. Vincent and Trinidad and Tobago that they were committed to immediately engaging in talks leading to regional integration, both Barbados and Jamaica decisively declared their disinterest in a political union at this time.[10] In his comments on St. Vincent and Trinidad and Tobago's proposals, the then Barbadian prime minister Owen Arthur stated, "In the absence of a clear concept of what is being advocated for this new form of governance within the Community, it is like having a song with an enchanting melody but no lyrics."[11]

One is sadly reminded here of Eric Williams's infamous "ten minus one equals zero" comment from another time and Michael Manley's resigned observation about the ability of Caribbean politicians to mix humor and tragedy.[12] Or alternatively, one is led to simply consider the sheer number of songs, with enchanting melody *and* lyrics, by Caribbean musicians who have testified to the "oneness" of the Caribbean people and urged its political unity.[13] This though, as I have been arguing in this work, is the condition of our time—one in which the Anglophone Caribbean stumbles along, buffeted by the neoliberal imperial agenda that seeks to encircle the globe, with its Caricom Single Market and Economy (CSME) acting as a prelude for other global neoliberal trade arrangements, and in which new Caribbean institutions and articulations of Caribbean citizenship emerge from elite opinion with little concern for the lived experiences of Caribbean people.[14]

Within the last decade, the Caribbean has been enmeshed in one of its greatest experiments in postcolonial citizenship, with the formation of the Caribbean Court of Justice, designed to replace Britain's Privy Council as the final court of appeal for the Anglophone Caribbean, and the Caricom Single Market and Economy (CSME), which aims to facilitate the free movement of goods and people throughout the region.[15] The CSME's stated intention—to facilitate the free movement of goods, capital, and people across national boundaries—has had a curious effect on the Caribbean Left. It is accepted that, despite its vast implementation problems, its fundamental premise is sound—as the ability of Caribbean people to move freely and live and work in different jurisdictions facilitates regional integration and the movement toward sovereignty as one people. The language of the 2001 Revised Treaty of Chaguaramas CSME says something somewhat different though—it declares that the "market-driven industrial development in the production of goods and services is essential for the economic and social development of the peoples of the Community." Rather than development, market efficiency is the prize. As Clare Newstead and others have shown, Caricom embodies a series of practices wedded to neoliberal rule that include the previous mentioned emphasis on market rule, "individual and corporate freedoms, entrepreneurialism and self-determination."[16] The entrepreneurial subject is privileged, as are elite actors able to move easily across national boundaries. The Caricom secretariat renders political decisions nonideological choices that merely require technical solutions.[17] There is a real and legitimate doubt about its benefit for the majority of people in the Caribbean. While a future Caribbean union remains a hallmark of Caribbean political thought, as it still proffers a compelling and never discredited solution to the aching dilemmas of sovereignty and survival that the region faces, the question remains whether the current approach, which is beholden to an assemblage of unelected technocrats, can usher in a sovereign Caribbean. What is the likely longevity of a regionalism driven by an elite component of its middle classes?

There is, however, a different vision of the Caribbean that emerges from the lived realities of its citizens and the work of its most distinguished thinkers. This is the dream of the Caribbean *as* diaspora. Diaspora as concept and method pays scrupulous attention not just to a tracing of the routes by which the Caribbean people have come into being, a people for C. L. R. James "more than any other people constructed by history," but also poses acute questions about our contemporary moment, as we cannot conceive of contemporary Caribbean citizenship without it.[18] As Michelle Cliff once said, "the Caribbean doesn't exist as an entity; it exists all over the world. It started in diaspora and it continues in diaspora."[19] The language of diaspora gives a powerful discursive arrangement to an attempt to articulate the complexity of cultural life and identity construction in the Caribbean and hopes of a future free of coloniality to come. Diasporic identifications do not diminish the wrenching effects of incarceration, exploitation, and disempowerment that are pervasive in the present. However, though abduction is constant, diaspora signals *possibility*.

Studies of diasporas and the development of diasporic methodologies or reading practices have gained considerable popularity in African diaspora intellectual circles over the last twenty-five years, a not inconsiderable amount of it in response to the most influential book in the field in that time, Paul Gilroy's *The Black Atlantic*.[20] The Caribbean response to this text has been more muted, likely partly due to the metropolitan-focused nature of Gilroy's argument, which consists of a conversation between black Britain and African America, in which

Caribbean theory is used while its history and contemporary condition are forgotten. Moreover, for Norval Edwards, the text articulates a "somewhat romanticized investment in the emancipatory and transgressive potential of creolization and cultural syncretism," which a knowledge of the region's history would have disavowed.[21] Paget Henry would similarly be critical of the "racial semioticism" of Gilroy's work, arguing persuasively that his postnational turn and diminution of a class perspective leaves it unable to address any of the wrenching political-economy or nation-state questions faced by Caribbean countries.[22]

At its best though, the style and the ethics of diaspora, the structure of feeling it promotes, offers a discourse that could support the continuation of emancipatory sociopolitical projects in the region unencumbered by the often microcolonial nationalism of its elites. It is telling that the region's most distinguished economists of the last two generations have consistently argued for the creation of a discourse about a shared sense of cultural and historical identity as an indispensable part of the process of deepening regionalism.[23] This commonly shared position is articulated by Norman Girvan as follows: "the regional option is a survival imperative, a development imperative, the only means of realizing the 'national project'—in the *spirit* of those who dreamed it and conceptualized [it] throughout our history."[24] But given that Caribbean elites, devoid of the commitment to Caribbean sovereignty of a Girvan, will gesture to "Caribbean unity" so easily, as this performance gives them cultural capital and a sense of patriotism similar to that gained by African elites in their recourse to "African unity," what kind of idea of the Caribbean can survive the blandishments of such an incarcerated discourse? Is a turn to envisage the Caribbean as diaspora simply a reiteration of one of the most popular trends in African diaspora criticism of the last two decades? Since both policy elites and the radical intelligentsia are in apparent agreement on the necessity of Caribbean solidarity and unity yet have been unable to achieve it over the last two generations, is it time to give it up as an achievable future? The dream of Caribbean unity predates the postcolonial state, and its faltering still haunts the region. The struggle here is not merely the difficulty of coordinating the social, economic, and political arrangements of a number of territories but the problem of *vision*. It suggests, further, the necessity of understanding its antithesis.

The Life and Death of a Nation: The Mood on Intraregional Migration

In November 1961, while convalescing in Barbados from a car accident that almost took his life in Jamaica, C. L. R. James wrote the following words to his friend Carl La Corbinière:

> Physically burdened as I am, I feel impelled to overcome my difficulties to the extent that that is possible and tell you what are my political views in the

present crisis. It is the most desperate that the WI [West Indies] have faced since the emancipation from slavery. The idea of a West Indian nation cannot dissolve. . . . For me this is not a question of governments but of people, of what world the young people will grow up into, what spirit they will have. . . . But what I fear is that the whole conception and organization of a WI nation is on the way to being destroyed or corrupted. . . . This is a matter of the life and death of a nation.

James's anguish at the slow demise of the federation, which he foresaw in a letter to George Padmore on his departure for Trinidad in 1958, is as difficult a read as any document of its time in its realization of the crushing forces preventing a radical alternative to the colonial status quo, its resignation at the vacuity of the new middle classes who were to lead the Caribbean nations into independence, and doubts of the future. Just two years before his accident, in a major speech on federation in Guyana, he declared, "Federation is the means and the only means whereby the West Indies and British Guiana can accomplish the transition from colonialism to national independence, can create the basis of a new nation; and by reorganizing the economic system and the national life give us our place in the modern community of nations."[25] James was not just a committed regionalist, but like so many Caribbeans abroad, he spoke with true poignancy about the disenchantments of exile: "The majority of us [writers in exile] keep on talking about the only subject which really explodes in our hearts—our native land. But as it becomes more and more of a dream its contours fade, and when our people at home read what we have written about them, they cannot recognize themselves any more . . . I, who am old, have lived through this calvery, but they who are young, are only now undergoing theirs. Until my last breath, I shall refuse to accept that this exile will not have an end."[26]

His letter of November 1961 was written in Barbados, a country that fascinated him throughout his life for reasons both idiosyncratic to him and shared by a wider Caribbean community. For James, Barbadians had to negotiate such a predatory colonial order that he would not condemn, though not ignore, the conservative turn of the first and only premier of the West Indies Federation, Grantley Adams, who James couldn't help admire despite his antisocialist politics and support for British colonialism in the 1950s.[27] Yet far from reproducing the standard stereotype of the conservative Bajan, James's admiration of the island's legendary cricket culture, sutured as this was to a disciplinary coloniality, meant he never thought of them as less than quintessentially West Indian.

One cannot walk within the second decade of the twenty-first-century Caribbean without being haunted by the catastrophic consequences of the 2010 earthquake in Haiti, the greatest tragedy a Caribbean people have had to bear since slavery, or reflect on the culmination of a predatory political culture in Jamaica.[28] James knew only too well that it was in the Haitian revolution that

Caribbean people announced themselves to the world as a people[29] and that every historical-cultural movement and political conundrum in the wider region since—neocolonialism, black consciousness, and the debt burden—first announced itself there. However, it is another seemingly less compelling tragedy that I wish to discuss here. This is the current moment in Barbados, often considered the most "successful" Anglophone Caribbean independent state, and the mood around the presence of Caribbean nationals in that country.

There is a particular tale, told at the beginning of the second decade of this century by state managers in Barbados that I wish to repeat here, in order to contest it. In it, the administration that demitted office in January 2008 turned a blind eye to the presence of large numbers of undocumented workers in the country, a situation that is now causing considerable problems for the Barbadian state. While these workers have contributed immensely to the country, the burden on state services (particularly health, education, and transport) is simply too great and, unmanaged, poses serious questions about the state's ability to deliver these services. Yet also of worry is the exploitation of members of these immigrant populations by employers and the public who know of their uncertain status, and which the government supposedly abhors as it will not allow the creation of a pool of persons with second-class status in Barbados. There is also a real security risk attached to the inability of the country to adequately secure its borders, determine who enters and for what purpose, increasingly relevant due to the incredible explosion in violent crime and the smuggling of weapons and narcotics in the region in the last two decades. This anti-immigrant rhetoric would be familiar to many in the North Atlantic, and one of the many ironies is that most of these social services, in heavily managed and policed Barbados, are inaccessible without government-issued identification anyway. It also conveniently omits the tremendous contribution that many workers, undocumented and documented, are making to the economy of the country *and*, through compulsory national insurance contributions, to the social services they are actively being denied.

However, one of the greatest indictments of the current administration and civil society is their inability to adequately critique the sturdy ethnic chauvinism that underlies the most pervasive anti-immigrant sentiments in Barbados and lingers not far behind public discussions of the immigrant question. The horrifying sexual assaults on Caribbean women in police and immigration custody remind us that the current mood on immigration intensifies the exploitation of vulnerable communities within the reach of the state—the border becomes a prison. In the everyday public sphere, we are bombarded with crass comments that compare an illegal immigrant to an unregistered weapon that similarly needs to be turned over to the police or the usual erroneous claims that much of the crime in the country is committed by those without citizenship or permanent residence status. These more vulgar comments are often dismissed by public figures. The subtler claims mouthed by government ministers, though, revolve around the idea that Barbados cannot solve the social problems of other Caribbean countries. The state tells us that other Caricom countries have been unwilling to extend certain contingent rights that Barbados allows, hence its seemingly strict positions, as according to the late prime minister David Thompson, at a town hall meeting on March 25, 2010, "there is no reason for us to be more generous than anyone else."[30] Other Caribbean citizens are seemingly aliens in Barbados, who must be "protected" from exploitation but also from the temptation of believing that they should have the rights of full citizens in an apparently foreign land.

I wonder, are we committed to finding Caribbean solutions for Caribbean problems? Are the concerns of the region our concerns? Do we wish to continue to be microstates with independence but no sovereignty? Or do we long, as Lloyd Best once said, to be part of a massive Caribbean *sou-sou*?[31] One of the greatest indictments of this story by Barbadian state managers is the fact that their new tightened immigration policies only target Caricom citizens—who by virtue of their membership in the Caribbean community should have greater access to any country in the region than North American or European citizens. British and American nationals have through their real estate purchases in the last fifteen years in collusion with local white elites and the government made arguably the greatest changes in the living standards of Barbadians, with land and building costs priced out of the reach of many families and with no clear end to this in sight. Yet their right to enter and exist within the country is assured. I am reminded of Frantz Fanon's statement in *The Wretched of the Earth* that European minorities in the postcolonial state would demand a twofold citizenship, and it is clear how easily this is accommodated without question by postcolonial elites.[32] That Barbados, which has always historically exported persons to the Anglophone Caribbean and beyond, should be prey to such assumptions about the value of Caribbean immigrants shows the sheer global reach and seductions of anti-immigrant discourse, with its arguments secured by ethnic chauvinism and elite manipulation of working-class anxieties about their economic disempowerment.[33]

Yet in this complex region, depictions of Barbadians as constitutively anti-regional or more xenophobic than others do not ring true.[34] And parallels of this relationship, with practical identical rhetoric, exist throughout the region. The 2013 decision by the Constitutional Court of the Dominican Republic, which has led to a policy decision to exile citizens of its country deemed to be of Haitian descent, is the most prominent and wrenching case of its kind, with generations of citizens rendered stateless. However, when we consider the injustices faced by Jamaicans at the Trinidad border, citizens of the Dominican Republic in Antigua, and Haitians and Guyanese everywhere—we see more dreary examples of the repeating logic of ethnic chauvinism wrapped in the garb of territorial security.[35] The idea, however, that Caribbean people's movements can be reduced to questions of labor, an arithmetic of jobs available, sought, protected, or denied, is simply false. We don't only move in the Caribbean for work; we do so to have a life—because there are different experiences we crave, people we love in another location, a world of experience we desire. The splitting of Caribbean bodies by the dry calculus of immigration figures, of how many bodies can this country support, predictably ignores this. The surrender that we see throughout the region to *realpolitik* and affairs of the state is more than a flawed and antiregional immigration strategy. It represents a growing abandonment of what so many of us ultimately yearn for—a Caribbeanness unrestrained by microcolonial nationalisms. This quest, as James was not afraid to examine, is not felt by governments but by people who want their children to grow up into a different Caribbean and world.[36] This version of Caribbeanness is long on the way to being destroyed and corrupted. And if it continues, it will end the possibility of a Caribbean nation.

A Caribbean Sympathy

> Politics is the only ground for a universal Negro sympathy.
>
> George Lamming, "The Negro Writer and His World"[37]

> Recognizing the power of the erotic within our lives can give us the energy to pursue genuine change within our world, rather than merely settling for a shift of characters in the same weary drama.
>
> Audre Lorde, "Uses of the Erotic: The Erotic as Power"[38]

Against the defeat so evident in the aforementioned tale of interisland political suspicion, immigration anxieties, and ethnic chauvinism, I wish to proffer a different view, secured by the vision of the radical Caribbean intelligentsia. George Lamming has in his seven decades of intellectual work in the region and on its diaspora engaged deeply with the meaning of Caribbeanness. For Lamming, the natural impulse to exile by Caribbean people results in a moment in which "migration is going to be very central to the psychology of that whole generation of people."[39] Lamming's central place within that generation of Caribbean people who journeyed to London in the 1950s is too well known to recount here. His collection of essays, *The Pleasures of Exile* (1960), claims the creation of a sense of Caribbeanness as a diasporic activity: "no islander from the West Indies sees himself as a West Indian until he encounters another islander in foreign territory . . . the category West Indian, formerly understood as a geographical term, now assumes cultural significance."[40] This movement was, as it could only be at the time, naive of what was to come; Caribbean people were experiencing a "journey to an expectation . . . going to a more elaborate extension of something you thought you knew," but their suffering, isolation, and the need to forge com-munity created a new people.[41] This idea has achieved some popularity in Carib-bean diasporic circles, due to how well it captures the lived experiences of new waves of migrants from the region to the metropolis, who when faced with the pressures of minoritization and loneliness, often (though crucially not always) shed their interisland rivalries for a regional solidarity.

A longer historical pause gives us some doubts about this argument. It for-gets the Antilleanism of the nineteenth century in the Greater Antilles, which at its best proposed a unity of the Caribbean islands beyond its colonial-linguistic divisions, though the difficult terrain of race and the naïveté of the pronounce-ments on this would collapse this movement into a species of mestizaje.[42] It is also innocent of the early twentieth-century history of the federal idea in the Anglophone territories, in which black political actors in the region and its di-aspora seized on the idea as a means toward further black self-determination.[43] Shalini Puri's collection *Marginal Migrations* is a particularly welcome and stud-ied attempt to come to terms with the meaning of internal migrations within the Caribbean, well known to historians and migration specialists but obscured amid the scale and recent vintage of the migrations to the metropolis.[44] A focus on the multiple migrations between different islands in the Caribbean potentially guides theorists toward a closer examination of the social history of the region and the decisive impact that migrants had on the sociohistorical development of territories other than their birthplaces. It also makes it difficult to conceive of the question of diaspora without considering the centrality of labor to discourses of diaspora.[45] Puri's "circulation of cultures" does not take place only via the movement of laboring bodies throughout the region, but it is impossible to ser-iously consider these intraregional migrations without emphasizing the question of labor.

Lamming's reflections on his first sojourn outside Barbados provide an in-teresting contrast to his meditations on displacement in *The Pleasures of Exile*. On his arrival in Trinidad in 1946, in house after house that he visited, he en-countered the region through the assemblage of islands that constituted each family—"father Grenada, mother St. Vincent, one grandfather from Barbados."[46] So struck was he by this regionalism in the intimate sphere of the family that he would note that his "Caribbeanness begins in Trinidad, not in Barbados."[47] This lived "existential reality" of Caribbeanness, coupled with the influence of Eric Williams, whose introduction to the work of Aimé Césaire and Nicholás Guil-lén he never forgot, resulted in Lamming's location of all of his novels after his first outside of one discernible territory in the region. A Caribbean sensibility emerges from the "peculiarities of its historical formulation," similar to James's claim that we are "more than any other people constructed by history," but com-prehending this sensibility demands a careful attention to the place of feeling in our imaginations.[48] Lamming would famously call for the "sovereignty of the imagination" in which "cultural sovereignty" would be "the free definition and articulation of the collective self, whatever the rigor of external constraints."[49] This is hardly a disavowal of the forces of colonialism, white supremacy, and economic exploitation that roar through the past and present Caribbean experience but a recognition that a sovereignty of the imagination is the amalgam of the pursuit of a *style* and freedom: "what I'm claiming that is *not* limited is another kind of sovereignty, and that is the capacity you have for *choosing* and making and remaking that self which you discover is *you*, is distinctly you. And which in a way is always unfinished, but it has a very special essence that is you, and its power is that it allows you to create the meanings that are to be given to what happens to you."[50]

In a 1982 address on the island of Carriacou in the midst of the Grenada revolution, Lamming's address gave an answer to the conundrums posed by aesthetic decolonization. The "education of feeling" is vital to revolutionary artistic expression, as the "central and seminal value of the creative imagination is that it functions as a civilizing and a humanizing force in a process of struggle . . . It offers an experience through which feeling is educated. Through which feeling is deepened. Through which feeling can increase its capacity to accommodate a great variety of knowledge."[51] The tiny island of Carriacou, which inspired Lamming to make one of his finest speeches, was also the setting of a great novel of African diaspora feeling, experience, and desire, Paule Marshall's *Praisesong for the Widow*. It was also the birthplace of one of the parents of a theorist whose remarkable work would go beyond Lamming's yearning for a decolonized aesthetic of feeling. Audre Lorde's "Uses of the Erotic," read in concert with Lamming's "The Education of Feeling," alerts us to the depth of the colonization of feeling by patriarchal control. It demands a revolution in human relations that C. L. R. James, as I have shown above, could only hazily perceive.[52]

For Lorde, "every oppressor must corrupt or distort those various sources of power within the culture of the oppressed that can provide *energy* for change."[53] The "horror" of the capitalist, inhumane system that we live within, predicated on the "exclusion of the psychic and emotional components" that *are* human needs, is that it "robs our work of its erotic value, its erotic power and life appeal and fulfillment."[54] It is not a wonder that men instinctively recoil against the erotic, as they "fear this . . . depth too much to examine the possibilities of it within themselves."[55] The erotic as the "lifeforce of women," this "measure between the beginnings of our sense of self and the chaos of our strongest feelings," is the capacity that women possess, which James discerned men have got to learn.[56] The erotic as "creative energy empowered," "the nurturer . . . of all our deepest knowledge"—some of Lorde's signal contributions—shows a strange moment of commonality between two very different theorists, as Lamming too knows that change will occur through "making the body speak feeling."[57] Lorde and Lamming might well agree on the statement "to educate in love is really the function of the creative imagination."[58]

The epigraph with which I began this section by Lamming proffers the seemingly unexceptional claim that politics is the only ground on which black solidarity might be achieved, and the 1956 First Congress of Negro Writers and Artists conference at which this paper was delivered could be seen as an extended meditation on the possibilities of precisely the form that black kinship might take in a rapidly decolonizing world.[59] Aimé Césaire, in an address that elicited some controversy at that conference, provided the following declaration on the basis of black solidarity: "all who have met here are united by a double solidarity; on the one hand a *horizontal solidarity*, that is a solidarity created for us by the colonial, semi-colonial or para-colonial condition imposed on us from without; and on the other a vertical solidarity, a *solidarity in time*, due to the fact that we started from an original unity, the unity of African civilization, which has become diversified into a whole series of cultures, all of which, in varying degrees, owe something to that civilization."[60] The link to a Caribbean solidarity known by Lamming and expressed by so many before and since is clear—a kinship forged by experience, politics, and sympathy.[61]

In 1950, Césaire published a volume of poetry titled *Corps Perdu*, or *Lost Body*. *Lost Body* is a very different text than his incomparable *Notebook of a Return to the Native Land*, with the latter's slow building to a triumphal conclusion. His translators, Clayton Eshleman and Annette Smith, capture well Césaire's mood in writing *Lost Body*, in which he "seems to have realized that in certain ways the black would remain in exile from himself and, in effect, not enter the house called negritude that Césaire had built for him . . . The tragic roots of being black in a world governed for the most part by whites are deeper and more embedded than the poet of the *Notebook* had calculated."[62] The answer is a poignant revolt, which requires quoting the title poem, "Lost Body" at some length:

I who Krakatoa
I who everything better than a monsoon

. . . I who outside the musical scale
I who Zambezi or frantic or rhombus or cannibal
I would like to be more and more humble

and more lowly
always more serious

without vertigo or vestige
to the point of losing myself falling
into the live semolina

of a well-opened earth

. . .

The wind alas I will continue to hear it
nigger nigger nigger from the depths
of the timeless sky
a little less loud than today
but still too loud
and this crazed howling of dogs and horses
which it thrusts at our *forever fugitive heels*
but I turn in the air
shall rise a scream so violent
that I shall splatter the whole sky
and with my branches torn to shreds

. . .

I shall command the islands to be[63]

Césaire's despair at coloniality's persistence, the constant echo of its most humiliating term for black bodies, results in a resignation that black people will be "forever fugitive" in a world whose fundamental premises remain colonial. His command is less an order than an entreaty, David Rudder's plea for a full self-actualization of his native land.[64] The poet has a responsibility that he cannot disown with a flourish, as his prayer is to become the "lover of this unique people," an ambition forged in diaspora but with the self-determination of Caribbean people at its heart.[65]

Césaire's work stands in contrast to the dull, unimaginative call for a "Caribbean civilization" by some of the contemporary Caribbean political elites, a call that simply lists the Caribbean's accomplishments over the last couple generations with no perspective to offer on how to counter the wrenching dislocations and legacy of colonialism that bedevil us today.[66] In his essay "Calling the Magician: A Few Words for a Caribbean Civilization," Césaire declares, "The true manifestation of civilization is myth. Social organization, religion, partnerships, philosophies, morals, architecture and sculpture are the representations and expressions of myth. . . . Civilization is an absurd idea which, felt and lived in its entirety, by that very fact and by that fact alone, becomes true."[67] In his challenge to the absurdity of a concept of "civilization" dependent on a Western epistemological order, Césaire daringly attests that "true civilizations are poetic shocks."[68] The call *beyond* the sterility of our times and the "exploitative nonsense that is our bourgeois" is to a "great mad sweep of renewal," for which Césaire declares that he is "calling upon the Enraged."[69] These enraged are the condemned of the earth self-mobilized to fight against their oppression and to call into question what Sylvia Wynter terms the coloniality of being/power/truth/freedom.[70]

The moment of African independence would find Césaire again preoccupied with the question of the affective bases of black transnational solidarity. "A Salute to the Third World/ for Léopold Sedar Senghor" was fittingly published in 1960, the year seventeen African countries gained their independence from European rule. In this poem to his friend Leopold Senghor, with whom he cofounded the négritude movement in 1930s Paris, Césaire's wonder at the unfolding spectacle of third-world independence is evident:

Ah!
my half-sleep of an island so indistinct
on the sea!

And here from all the corners of peril
history makes the sign that I am waiting for
I see nations grow.
Banners, green and red,
I salute you, throats of ancient wind,
Mali, Guinea, Ghana . . .

Listen!
from my remote island
from my watchful island
I cry Hoo! to you
And your voices answer me

and what they are saying means:
"There is plenty of light here." . . .

Hatred, yes, either ban or bar
and the grunting array, yet
in a stiff wind, once we were bruised, I saw
the slave master's mug recede! . . .

Look:
Africa is no longer
a black heart scratched
at by the diamond of misfortune;

Our Africa is a hand free of the cestus,
it is a right hand, palm forward,
the fingers held tight;

it is a swollen hand,
a-wounded-open-hand,
extended to

all hands, brown, yellow
white, to all the wounded hands
in the world.[71]

Césaire's sympathy for "all hands . . . all the wounded hands / in the world" finds its place in a long genealogy of Francophone Caribbean thought, including Jacques Roumain and Frantz Fanon.[72] His work also represents, along with other members of the radical Caribbean intelligentsia that I have considered in this manuscript, particularly C. L. R. James, Sylvia Wynter, and Frantz Fanon, the best of a radical cosmopolitan humanist tradition, internationalist in its scope and vision and one of the gifts of Caribbean thought to humanity. Poetry, Césaire declared, "is born in the great silence of scientific knowledge."[73] Scientific knowledge may have led to the invention of Western man, but poetic knowledge is what will create the human *after* man.

The Caribbean, partly due to its unique history of colonialism and the intimacy of the size of its polities, has the potential to create that "free community of valid persons" that Martin Carter yearned for. Carter knew that the time of crisis (his own Burnham's dictatorship in Guyana) could not be the excuse for anomie and "paralysis of the spirit."[74] But the search for this community will remain elusive if our state managers remain in thrall to the dictates of global capital and deny a style of thinking that places at the center of its reflection the evolution of individual and community. This is not to suggest that the overturning of the realities of colonial citizenship that I have detailed in this work can be done without a concerted effort to engage in and win political struggles. The Caribbean Left, with a memory of, but not burdened by Grenada, must find its way back to revolutionary socialism. Or have the Caribbean's neocolonial status continue until imperial globalization formally dismisses even the fiction of national sovereignty.

The stakes of our struggle, the disappointment of past failures by the Caribbean Left sharpen the need to have a clear understanding of the new socialist society we wish to create, founded on the destruction of capitalism without which there will never be any social justice, a demand for reparatory justice for the crimes of colonialism, a voice to the world for peace, a resolute commitment to gender justice, and an end of the march toward the planet's environmental destruction. Rather than sorrow, our history illuminates our chance: to proffer a mode of existence and human sociality that the world continues to desperately need, from one small part of it—small perhaps in its territorial expanse, but vast in the size of its heart.[75] The venture of *Beyond Coloniality* has been to show the Caribbean intellectual tradition at its finest, especially a group of thinkers who are vanishing from this sphere of existence every year and who have produced a remarkably insightful body of thought that in its denunciation of exploitation and quest for truly human (in Wynter's sense, *after* Western man) relations has global resonance and appeal.

From its opening sentence and even more in this conclusion, *Beyond Coloniality* has been a quest to remake the Caribbean anew and also about that most elusive of human emotions—love. Love, as June Jordan once wrote Alice Walker, is the "single, true prosperity of any moment."[76] Love, as Richard Iton knew, is a "subversive gift, is an important public good, and loving is a significant political act, particularly among those stigmatized and marked as unworthy of love and incapable of deep commitment."[77] Césaire would entreat his "heart [to] preserve me from all hatred" in his quest to be a "lover of this unique people."[78] Che Guevara would remark that "the true revolutionary is guided by a great feeling of love. . . . We must strive every day so that this love of living humanity will be transformed into actual deeds."[79] Lamming says politics is the ground for that universal sympathy. Yet in "The Education of Feeling" he cannot help but face the unavoidable question of the awareness that will create the resolve that will make political and personal sacrifice possible. The case for Caribbean freedom through a regionalism anchored to an anticolonial will has now been made for a century. What impulses, what species of desire, might make its pull too irresistible to forfeit yet again?

My reading of Caribbean thought suggests that its urgent belief is that the Caribbean must recreate itself anew. This transformation will mean a different political economy, political arrangements beyond the reification of petty bourgeois dominance, and an entirely different structure of feeling in the realm of our public and private citizens' lives. Caribbean solidarity in the interests of self-determination and human freedom, like its sibling black solidarity, has never existed outside a labyrinth of contradictions, persistently troubled by the ongoing reproduction of coloniality. We are reminded, though, that the black survival of coloniality is the ultimate beyond. It is a future dreamed of and struggled toward by the black radical tradition that each generation has to learn anew.[80] When one considers the African and Caribbean experience through a diasporic lens, one great truth emerges: a people not *meant* to survive have consistently *needed each other* in order to survive.[81] This applies whether we consider the Haitian revolutionaries ending slavery for the first time in the Western hemisphere, the Jamaicans of 1832 precipitating the end of slavery for all in the British-colonized West Indies, or the Africana world in uproar over the invasion of Ethiopia by Italy in 1935. It is impossible to imagine Caribbean spirituality without Africa, the humanization of the Caribbean landscape without Indian indentured labor, Kwame Nkrumah without C. L. R. James or George Padmore, *négritude* without the Harlem Renaissance, or Garvey without the entire diaspora. This is the diasporic sensibility that rings out clearly from centuries of Caribbean history. It may well be a mobilizing principle for future sociopolitical movements yet to come. A great poet, Kamau Brathwaite, has already summoned these contradictions toward political purpose in a statement as compelling as anything scribed in New World letters:

> Know that . . . the middle passage with its tears of ancestors
> Sometimes wonderfully shared
> Is not only a voyage from death to life
> Or if you prefer a journey from life to death
> The middle passage of our years
> *Beyond* hopefully the Caribbean auction block
> It is above all a continuing tidalectical not dialectical experience and process
> From home to whom, from home to *whom*
> From origin to continuum
> From love my beloveds
> to love.[82]

Notes

1. Edouard Glissant, *Caribbean Discourse: Selected Essays*, trans. Michael Dash (Charlottesville: University Press of Virginia, 1989), 222.

2. David Rudder, "Rally Round the West Indies," *Haiti* (Sire: October 1990).

3. I borrow the list of terms "marronage, insurrection, rebellion, revolution, and fugitive escape" from Greg Thomas, "Sex/Sexuality and Sylvia Wynter's *Beyond . . .*: Anti-Colonial Ideas in 'Black Radical Tradition,'" *Journal of West Indian Literature* 10, nos. 1 and 2 (November 2001): 94.

4. Louis Chude-Sokei, "The Incomprehensible Rain of Stars: Black Modernism, Black Diaspora," dissertation submitted to UCLA, 1995. UMI Dissertation Services No. 9601378.

5. Sylvia Wynter, "But What Does 'Wonder' Do? Meanings, Canons, Too? On Literary Texts, Cultural Contexts, and What It's Like to Be One/Not One of Us," in "Bridging the Gap: Where Cognitive Science Meets Literary Criticism," ed. Guven Guzeldere and Stefano Franchi, special supplement, *Stanford Humanities Review* 4, no. 1 (Spring 1994): 124–28.

6. On the limits of celebration and lament, see here Aisha Khan, "Journey to the Center of the Earth: The Caribbean as Master Symbol," *Cultural Anthropology* 16, no. 3 (2001): 277.

7. "Eastern Caribbean Integration: A Rekindling of the Little Eight?," special issue, *Journal of Eastern Caribbean Studies* 23, no. 1 (March 1998).

8. Then prime ministers Owen Arthur (Barbados) and Kenny Anthony (St. Lucia) authored articles, while Ralph Gonsalves would become prime minister of St. Vincent in March 2001.

9. The Organisation of Eastern Caribbean States (OECS) is composed of seven full members: Antigua and Barbuda, Commonwealth of Dominica, Grenada, Montserrat, St. Kitts and Nevis, St. Lucia, and St. Vincent and the Grenadines. Anguilla and the British Virgin Islands are associate members.

10. Rickey Singh, "Not Now!" *Daily Nation* (Barbados) February 16, 2003; for an acerbic critique of this antiregionalist trend, see David Commissiong, "Conspire to Unite," *Daily Nation* (Barbados) March 10, 2003.

11. Singh, "Not Now!"

12. Michael Manley, *A History of West Indies Cricket* (London: Andre Deutsch, 1988). Manley was referring here to Eric Williams's "ten minus one equals zero" jibe and the demise of the West Indies Federation.

13. The classics here would be the Mighty Sparrow's "Federation," Black Stalin's "Caribbean Man," and David Rudder's "Rally Round the West Indies." See here Gordon Rohlehr, "A Scuffling of Islands: The Dream and Reality of Caribbean Unity in Poetry and Song," in *New Caribbean Thought: A Reader*, ed. Brian Meeks and Folke Lindahl (Mona, Jamaica: University of the West Indies Press, 2001), 265–305.

14. For the long-awaited birth of CSME, see Peter Richards, "Common Market Opens, sans Eastern Caribbean States," Inter Press Service News Agency, January 2, 2006; Michael Williams, "Caribbean Nations Sign Single Market Instrument," Caribbeannetnews.com, February 2, 2006. For the full text of the Revised Treaty of Chaguaramas, see https://caricom.org/documents/4906-revised_treaty-text.pdf.

15. Tracy Robinson, "A Caribbean Common Law," *Race and Class* 49, no. 2 (2007): 118–24; Kamari Clarke, "Assemblage of Experts: The Caribbean Court of Justice and the Modernity of Caribbean Postcoloniality," *Small Axe* 41 (2013): 88–107.

16. Clare Newstead, "Regional Governmentality: Neoliberalisation and the Caribbean Community Single Market and Economy," *Singapore Journal of Tropical Geography* 30 (2009): 158–73.

17. Newstead, "Regional Governmentality."

18. C. L. R. James, "The West Indian Intellectual," introduction to J. J. Thomas, *Froudacity: West Indian Fables by James Anthony Froude* (London: New Beacon Books, 1969), 46. This is not to deny how important this work, which traces the movement of people into the region and into its extraterritorial diaspora, continues to be.

19. Meryl F. Schwartz, "An Interview with Michelle Cliff," *Contemporary Literature* 34, no. 4 (1993): 597.

20. Paul Gilroy, *The Black Atlantic: Modernity and Double Consciousness* (Harvard University Press, 1993). On the term "diaspora" in African diaspora thought, see Brent Hayes Edwards, "The Uses of Diaspora," *Social Text* 66 (Spring 2001): 45–73.

21. Norval Edwards, "Roots, and Some Routes not Taken: A Caribcentric Reading of The Black Atlantic," *Found Object* 4 (1994): 27–35.

22. Paget Henry, *Caliban's Reason: Introducing Afro-Caribbean Philosophy* (London: Routledge, 2000), 216–20, 272.

23. William G. Demas, *West Indian Nationhood and Caribbean Integration* (Bridgetown, Barbados: CCC, 1974); Havelock Ross-Brewster, "Identity, Space and the West Indian Union," in *Caribbean Political Thought: Theories of the Post-Colonial State*, ed. Aaron Kamugisha (Kingston: Ian Randle, 2013), 374–79.

24. Norman Girvan, "Existential Threats in the Caribbean: Democratising Politics, Regionalising Governance," C. L. R. James Memorial Lecture, May 11, 2011, Oil Workers Trade Union, Cipriani College of Labour and Cooperative Studies, Valsayn, Trinidad and Tobago, p. 26.

25. C. L. R. James, "On Federation," in *At the Rendezvous of Victory: Selected Essays* (London: Allison and Busby, 1984), 90. In the original text, this entire quote is italicized.

26. C. L. R. James, "Interview in *Le Monde*," as quoted in Sylvia Wynter, "We Must Learn to Sit Down Together and Discuss a Little Culture: Reflections on West Indian Writing and Criticism," part 1, *Jamaica Journal* 2, no. 4 (1968): 25.

27. See here C. L. R. James, "The Making of the Caribbean People," in *Spheres of Existence: Selected Writings* (London: Allison and Busby, 1980), 189.

28. I refer here to the "Dudus affair"; see Brian Meeks, "The Dudus Events in Jamaica and the Future of Caribbean Politics," in *Critical Interventions in Caribbean Politics and Theory* (Jackson: University Press of Mississippi, 2014), 169–82.

29. C. L. R. James, "Appendix: From Toussaint L'Ouverture to Fidel Castro," in *The Black Jacobins: Toussaint L'Ouverture and the San Domingo Revolution* (New York: Vintage, 1963), 391.

30. I attended this meeting.

31. Lloyd Best's line was "I dream myself of participating in a massive Caribbean sousou." "Wither New World," *New World Quarterly* 4, no. 1 (Dead Season, 1967): 5.

32. Frantz Fanon, *The Wretched of the Earth* (London: Penguin Books, 1967), 35.

33. Dennis Conway, "Why Barbados Has Exported People?: International Mobility as a Fundamental Force in the Creation of Small Island Society," in *Ethnicity, Race and Nationality in the Caribbean*, ed. Juan Manuel Carrion (San Juan, Puerto Rico: Institute of Caribbean Studies, 1997), 274–308; Winston James, *Holding Aloft the Banner of Ethiopia: Caribbean Radicalism in Early Twentieth Century America* (London: Verso, 1999). On Barbados and migration to Guyana, see Walter Rodney, "Barbadian Immigration into British Guiana, 1863–1924," paper delivered at the ninth annual conference of the Association of Caribbean Historians, April 3–7, 1977, University of the West Indies, Cave Hill campus.

34. Barbadians, by and large, do not wish to imagine their country as one that denies the rights of free citizenship to its neighbors or stymies progress toward greater Caribbean integration. But their public utterances far too often belie a regional sentiment. The moment described here had dissipated substantially by the end of the second decade of the twenty-first century, in which Barbadians find themselves amid the worst financial crisis in their postindependence history, with little end to it in sight. A new administration, swept to power in a historic landslide victory in May 2018, has already signaled its firm commitment to reversing these anti-immigration and antiregional policies.

35. For a devastating critique of this nationalism, see Hilbourne Watson, "Beyond Ronald Mason's Diatribe," *Stabroek News*, May 20, 2013, https://www.stabroeknews.com/2013/features/in-the-diaspora/05/20/beyond-ronald-masons-diatribe/.

36. In the contemporary moment in Barbados, James's long stay would likely have been "illegal," and he would have been denied access to state health services.

37. George Lamming, "The Negro Writer and His World," *Présence Africaine* 8–10 (June–November 1956): 320.

38. Audre Lorde, "The Uses of the Erotic," in *Sister/Outsider* (Freedom, CA: Crossing, 1984), 59.

39. George Kent, "'A Future They Must Learn': An Interview," in *The George Lamming Reader: The Aesthetics of Decolonisation*, ed. Anthony Bogues (Kingston: Ian Randle, 2011), 168. Lamming is here referring to his second book, *The Emigrants* (1954).

40. George Lamming, *The Pleasures of Exile* (Ann Arbor: University of Michigan Press, 1992 [1960]), 215.

41. Anthony Bogues, "The Aesthetics of Decolonization—Anthony Bogues and George Lamming in Conversation," in Bogues, *George Lamming Reader*, 188; also see page 199 for Lamming's idea of the journeys of Caribbean literature.

42. Antonio Gaztambide-Geigel, "The Rise and Geopolitics of Antilleanism," in *The UNESCO General History of the Caribbean Volume IV: The Long Nineteenth Century*,

Nineteenth Century Transformations, ed. K. O. Laurence and Jorge Cuesta (Paris: UNESCO, 2012), 430–52.

43. See here the work of Eric Duke, "The Diasporic Dimensions of Caribbean Federation in the Early Twentieth Century," *New West Indian Guide* 83, nos. 3–4 (2009): 219–48; and *Building a Nation: Caribbean Federation in the Black Diaspora* (Gainsville: University of Florida Press, 2016).

44. Shalini Puri, "Theorizing Diasporic Cultures: The Quiet Migrations," in *Marginal Migrations: The Circulation of Cultures within the Caribbean* (Oxford: Macmillan Caribbean, 2003), 1–16.

45. Thanks to cultural historian Lyndon Philip for making this point to me.

46. Bogues, "Aesthetics of Decolonization," 192.

47. David Scott, "The Sovereignty of the Imagination: An Interview with George Lamming," *Small Axe* 12 (September 2002): 87.

48. Bogues, "Aesthetics of Decolonization," 202; James, "West Indian Intellectual," 46.

49. George Lamming, *The Sovereignty of the Imagination* (Kingston: Arawak, 2004), 37.

50. Scott, "Sovereignty of the Imagination," 147.

51. George Lamming, "The Education of Feeling," in Bogues, *George Lamming Reader*, 20.

52. See chapter 4.

53. Lorde, "Uses of the Erotic," 53, my italics.

54. Lorde, "Uses of the Erotic," 53.

55. Lorde, "Uses of the Erotic," 54.

56. Lorde, "Uses of the Erotic," 55, 54.

57. These quotes are from, respectively, Audre Lorde, "Uses of the Erotic," 55, 56; Lamming, "Education of Feeling," 20.

58. Lamming, "Education of Feeling," 20.

59. For a discussion of this conference, see Catherine John, "Paris 1956," in *Clear Word and Third Sight: Folk Groundings and Diasporic Consciousness in African Caribbean Writing* (Durham, NC: Duke University Press, 2003).

60. Aimé Césaire, "Culture and Colonisation," *Présence Africaine* 8–10 (June–November 1956): 195.

61. Alaí Reyes-Santos, *Our Caribbean Kin: Race and Nation in the Neoliberal Antilles* (New Brunswick, NJ: Rutgers University Press, 2015).

62. Clayton Eshleman and Annette Smith, "Introduction," in Aimé Césaire, *Lost Body*, trans. Clayton Eshleman and Annette Smith (New York: George Braziller, 1986), xii–xiii.

63. Aimé Césaire, "Lost Body," in *Lost Body*, 55–63, my italics.

64. I am recalling here David Rudder's lines from his cricketing anthem titled "Rally Round the West Indies": "We already know who brought us here / And who created this confusion / So I'm begging, begging my people please."

65. Aimé Césaire, *Notebook of a Return to the Native Land*, trans. Clayton Eshleman and Annette Smith (Middletown, CT: Wesleyan University Press, 2001), 37.

66. Ralph Gonsalves, "Our Caribbean Civilization: Retrospect and Prospect," *Journal of Eastern Caribbean Studies* 23, no. 1 (March 1998): 51–74. Calls of this nature for a "Caribbean civilization" are disconcertingly unaware of the invented nature of the term "civilization" itself. Among many counters to this, see Thomas Patterson, *Inventing Western Civilization* (New York: Monthly Review Press, 2009).

67. Aimé Césaire, "Calling the Magician: A Few Words for a Caribbean Civilization," in *Refusal of the Shadow: Surrealism and the Caribbean*, ed. Michael Richardson. (London: Verso, 1996), 120, 121.

68. Césaire, "Calling the Magician," 119.

69. Césaire, "Calling the Magician," 122.

70. Sylvia Wynter, "Unsettling the Coloniality of Being/Power/Truth/Freedom: Towards the Human, After Man, Its Overrepresentation—an Argument," *CR: The New Centennial Review* 3, no. 3 (Fall 2003): 257–337.

71. Aimé Césaire, "A Salute to the Third World/for Léopold Sedar Senghor," in *Aimé Césaire, the Collected Poetry*, trans. Clayton Eshleman and Annette Smith (Berkeley: University of California Press, 1983), 351, 353. This poem appeared under the title "For the Third World," trans. G. R. Coulthard, in "Guyana Independence Issue," special issue, *New World Quarterly* 2, no. 3 (1966): 120.

72. See especially here Jacques Roumain, "Sales Nègres," in *Ebony Wood: Poems by Jacques Roumain*, trans. Sidney Shapiro (New York: Interworld, 1972), 43–45.

73. Aimé Césaire, "Poetry and Knowledge," in *Aimé Césaire, Lyric and Dramatic Poetry 1946–1982*, trans. Clayton Eshleman and Annette Smith, introduction by A. James Arnold (Charlottesville: University of Virginia Press, 1990), xlii.

74. Martin Carter, "A Free Community of Valid Persons," *Kyk-Over-Al* 44 (May 1993): 31.

75. I borrow here from the opening line of *The Bridge of Beyond*: "A man's country may be cramped or vast according to the size of his heart." Simone Schwarz-Bart, *The Bridge of Beyond*, trans. Barbara Bray (Oxford: Heinemann, 1982), 2.

76. June Jordan cited in Alice Walker, *Her Blue Body Everything We Know: Earthling Poems 1965–1990* (Toronto: Women's Press, 1991), 214.

77. Richard Iton, *In Search of the Black Fantastic: Politics and Popular Culture in the Post-Civil Rights Era* (New York: Oxford University Press, 2008).

78. Césaire, *Notebook*, 37.

79. Ernesto Che Guevara, *Notes on Man and Socialism in Cuba* (New York: Merit Publishers, 1968), 20

80. The allusion here is to Fanon's comment in his essay "On National Culture" that "each generation must, out of relative obscurity, discover its mission, fulfill it, or betray it." See Fanon, *Wretched of the Earth*, 166.

81. For a poignant comment on the expendability of black lives, see Audre Lorde, "The Transformation of Silence into Language and Action," in *I Am Your Sister*, ed. Rudolph P. Byrd, Johnnetta Betsch Cole, and Beverly Guy Sheftall (Oxford: Oxford University Press, 2011), 39–43.

82. Kamau Brathwaite, *Middle Passages*, lecture at the Caribbean Migrations conference at Ryerson University, Toronto, Canada, July 2005.

Bibliography

Archives and Unpublished Manuscripts

C. L. R. James Archive, University of the West Indies,
Saint Augustine Campus, Trinidad and Tobago

James, C. L. R. Unpublished autobiography.
James, C. L. R. "My experiences with women and sex." Unpublished autobiography.
James, C. L. R. "Autobiography, 1932–38."
James, C. L. R. Letter to George Padmore. March 17, 1958. Box 5, folder 105.
James, C. L. R. Letter to Carl (La Corbinière). November 6, 1961 Box 5, Folder 105.
Lamming, George. Letter to C. L. R. James. June 27, 1961. Box 3, folder 76.

C. L. R. James Papers, Columbia University

James, C. L. R. Letter to Eric Williams. December 10, 1957 Box 3, Folder 4.
Williams, Eric. Letter to C. L. R. James. March 17, 1958. Box 3, folder 4.

Institute of the Black World Papers at the Schomburg Center for Research
in Black Culture, New York

Wynter, Sylvia. "Black Metamorphosis: New Natives in a New World." Unpublished
    manuscript.
Wynter, Sylvia. "Natives in a New World: The African Transformation in the Americas."
    Unpublished manuscript.

Secondary Sources

Abraham, Sara. *Labour and the Multiracial Project in the Caribbean: Its History and Its
    Promise.* Lanham, MD: Lexington Books, 2007.
———. "Multiracialism as More Than the Sum of Ethnicities." *Race and Class* 49, no. 2
    (2007): 91–100.
Alexander, M. Jacqui. "Redrafting Morality: The Postcolonial State and the Sexual Offences
    Bill of Trinidad and Tobago." In *Third World Women and the Politics of Feminism,*
    edited by Chandra Talpade Mohanty, Ann Russo, and Lourdes Torres, 133–52.
    Bloomington: Indiana University Press, 1991.
———. "Not Just (Any)Body Can Be a Citizen: The Politics of Law, Sexuality and Postco-
    loniality in Trinidad and Tobago and the Bahamas." *Feminist Review* 48 (Autumn
    1994): 6–23.
———. "Erotic Autonomy as a Politics of Decolonization: An Anatomy of Feminist and State
    Practice in the Bahamas Tourist Economy." In *Feminist Genealogies, Colonial Legacies,
    Democratic Futures,* edited by M. Jacqui Alexander and Chandra Talpade Mohanty,
    63–100. New York: Routledge, 1997.

——. *Pedagogies of Crossing: Meditations on Feminism, Sexual Politics, Memory, and the Sacred*. Durham, NC: Duke University Press, 2005.

Allahar, Anton, ed. *Caribbean Charisma: Reflections on Leadership, Legitimacy and Populist Politics*. Kingston: Ian Randle, 2001.

Allen, Carolyn. "Creole: The Problem of Definition." In Shepherd and Richards, *Questioning Creole*, 47–63.

Andaiye and Richard Drayton, eds. *Conversations: George Lamming, Essays, Addresses and Interviews 1953–1990*. London: Karia House, 1992.

Anthony-Welch, L. "Wisdom: An Interview with C. L. R. James." In *Sturdy Black Bridges: Visions of Black Women in Literature*, edited by Roseann P. Bell, Bettye J. Parker, and Beverly Guy-Sheftall. New York: Anchor Books, 1979.

Arnold, A. James. "The Erotics of Colonialism in Contemporary French West Indian Literary Culture." *Annals of Scholarship* 12, nos. 1 and 2 (1997): 173–86.

Austin, David. "Interview with Sylvia Wynter." May 1999. CD in author's possession.

Austin, David. "In Search of a National Identity: C. L. R. James and the Promise of the Caribbean." In *You Don't Play with Revolution: The Montreal Lectures of C. L. R. James*, edited by David Austin, 1–26. Oakland: AK, 2009.

——, ed. *You Don't Play with Revolution: The Montreal Lectures of C. L. R. James*. Oakland, California: AK, 2009.

Austin, Diane J. "Culture and Ideology in the English-Speaking Caribbean: A View from Jamaica." *American Ethnologist* 10, no. 2 (May 1983): 223–40.

Awkward, Michael. "Black Feminism and the Challenge of Black Heterosexual Male Desire." *Souls* 2, no. 4 (Fall 2000): 32–37.

——. "A Black Man's Place in Black Feminist Criticism." In *The Black Feminist Reader*, edited by Tracey Denean Sharpley-Whiting and Joy James, 88–108. Malden, MA: Blackwell, 2000.

Bailey, Barbara, and Elsa Leo-Rhynie, eds. *Gender in the Twenty-First Century Caribbean: Perspectives, Visions and Possibilities*. Kingston, Jamaica: Ian Randle Publishers, 2014.

Baldwin, James. *The Evidence of Things Not Seen*. New York: Holt, Rinehart and Winston, 1985.

Balutansky, Kathleen, and Marie-Agnes Sourieau, eds. *Caribbean Creolization: Reflections on the Cultural Dynamics of Language, Literature and Identity*. Gainsville: University of Florida Press, 1998.

Banyan, "Interview with C. L. R. James." OWTU Guest House, San Fernando, Trinidad and Tobago, September 5, 1980.

Barrett, Lindon. "Black Men in the Mix: Badboys, Heroes, Sequins, and Denis Rodman." *Callaloo* 20, no. 1 (1997): 106–26.

Barriteau, Eudine, ed. *Confronting Power, Theorizing Gender: Interdisciplinary Perspectives in the Caribbean*. Kingston: University of the West Indies Press, 2003.

——. "Requiem for the Male Marginalization Thesis in the Caribbean: Death of a Non-Theory." In Barriteau, *Confronting Power*, 324–55.

Barrow, Christine, Marjan de Bruin, and Robert Carr, eds. *Sexuality, Social Exclusion and Human Rights* Kingston: Ian Randle, 2009.

Barrow-Giles, Cynthia, and Don D. Marshall, eds. *Living at the Borderlines: Issues in Caribbean Sovereignty and Development*. Kingston: Ian Randle, 2003.

Bateson, Gregory. *Mind and Nature*. New York: E. P. Dutton, 1979.

Baugh, Edward. "Confessions of a Critic." *Journal of West Indian Literature* 15, nos. 1 and 2 (November 2006): 15–28.

Beckford, George. *Persistent Poverty: Underdevelopment in Plantation Economies of the Third World.* New York: Oxford University Press, 1972.

Beckles, Hilary. *Corporate Power in Barbados: The Mutual Affair.* Bridgetown, Barbados: Lighthouse, 1989.

Beckles, Hilary, and Verene Shepherd, eds. *Caribbean Freedom: Economy and Society from Emancipation to the Present.* Kingston: Ian Randle, 1993.

Benitez-Rojo, Antonio. "The Repeating Island." Translated from the Spanish by James Maraniss. *New England Review and Bread Loaf Quarterly* 7, no. 4 (Summer 1985): 430–52.

———. "The Polyrhythmic Paradigm: The Caribbean and the Postmodern Era." In *Race, Discourse and the Origin of the Americas: A New World View,* edited by Vera Hyatt and Rex Nettleford, 255–67. London: Smithsonian Institution Press, 1995.

Benn, Dennis. *The Growth and Development of Political Ideas in the Caribbean, 1774–1983.* Kingston: Institute of Social and Economic Research, University of the West Indies, 1987.

——— *The Caribbean: An Intellectual History, 1774–2003.* Kingston: Ian Randle, 2004.

Bernabé, Jean, Patrick Chamoiseau, and Raphaël Confiant. "In Praise of Creoleness." Translated by Mohamed B. Taleb Khyar. *Callaloo* 13 (1990): 886–909.

Besson, Jean. "Reputation and Respectability Reconsidered: A New Perspective on Afro-Caribbean Peasant Women." In *Women and Change in the Caribbean: A Pan-Caribbean Perspective,* edited by Janet Momsen, 15–37. Bloomington: Indiana University Press, 1993.

Best, Lloyd. "Independent Thought and Caribbean Freedom." *New World Quarterly* 3, no. 4 (1967): 13–34.

———. "Whither New World." *New World Quarterly* 4, no. 1 (Dead Season 1967): 1–6.

———. "West Indian Society 150 Years after Abolishment: A Re-examination of Some Classical Theories." In *Out of Slavery: Abolishment and After,* edited by Jack Hayward, 132–58. London: Frank Cass, 1985.

Best, Lloyd, and Kari Polanyi Levitt. *Essays on the Theory of Plantation Economy: A Historical and Institutional Approach to Caribbean Economic Development.* Kingston: University of the West Indies Press, 2009.

Best, Robert. "Controlling Sex Results." *Daily Nation* (Barbados), August 5, 2003.

Best, Yvette. "Roll Tumbles." *Daily Nation* (Barbados) August 27, 2014, 3A.

Bhagwan, Rose. "Unemployment Rate Decreasing," *NOW Grenada,* April 22, 2016. http://nowgrenada.com/2016/04/unemployment-rate-decreasing/.

Birbalsingh, Frank. "The Literary Achievement of C. L. R. James." *Journal of Commonwealth Literature* 19, no. 1 (1984): 108–21.

"Black Election 2000." Special issue, *Black Scholar* 31, no. 2 (2001).

Bogues, Anthony. "Politics, Nation and Postcolony: Caribbean Inflections." *Small Axe* 11 (2002): 1–30.

———, ed. *After Man, Towards the Human: Critical Essays on Sylvia Wynter.* Kingston: Ian Randle, 2006.

———. "The Aesthetics of Decolonization—Anthony Bogues and George Lamming in Conversation." In Bogues, *George Lamming Reader,* 183–240.

———. *The George Lamming Reader: The Aesthetics of Decolonisation.* Kingston: Ian Randle, 2011.

Bolland, O. Nigel. *The Politics of Labour in the British Caribbean: The Social Origins of Authoritarianism and Democracy in the Labour Movement*. Kingston: Ian Randle, 2001.

——. "Creolisation and Creole Societies: A Cultural Nationalist View of Caribbean Social History." In Shepherd and Richards, *Questioning Creole*, 15–46.

——. "Reconsidering Creolization and Creole Societies." *Shibboleths: Journal of Comparative Theory* 1, no. 1 (2006): 1–14.

Bolland, O. Nigel, ed. *The Birth of Caribbean Civilization: A Century of Ideas about Culture and Identity, Nation and Society*. Kingston, Jamaica: Ian Randle Publishers, 2004.

Bolles, A. Lynn. "Michael Manley in the Vanguard towards Gender Equality." *Caribbean Quarterly* 48, no. 1 (March 2002): 45–56.

Boxill, Bernard. "Two Traditions in African American Political Philosophy." *Philosophical Forum* 24, no. 1–3 (1992–1993): 119–35.

Boyce Davies, Carole. *Left of Marx: The Political Life of Black Communist Claudia Jones*. Durham, NC: Duke University Press, 2008.

Boyce Davies, Carole, and Elaine Savory Fido, eds. *Out of the Kumbla: Caribbean Women and Literature*. Trenton, NJ: Africa World Press, 1990.

Braithwaite, Lloyd. *Social Stratification in Trinidad*. Kingston: Institute of Social and Economic Research, University of the West Indies, Mona Campus, 1975. Originally published in *Social and Economic Studies* 2, nos. 2 and 3 (1953).

Brathwaite, Edward Kamau. *The Development of Creole Society in Jamaica, 1770–1820*. Oxford: Oxford University Press, 1971.

——. *The Arrivants*. London: Oxford University Press, 1973.

——. *Contradictory Omens: Cultural Diversity and Integration in the Caribbean*. Mona, Jamaica: Savacou, 1974.

——. "Timehri." In Coombs, *Is Massa Day Dead?*, 29–44.

——. "Caribbean Man in Space and Time," *Savacou* 11/12 (1975): 1–11.

——. "The Love Axe (l): Developing a Caribbean Aesthetic 1962–1974." In *Reading Black: Essays in the Criticism of African, Caribbean, and Black American Literature*, edited by Houston A. Baker Jr., 20–36. University of Pennsylvania: Africana Studies and Research Center Monograph Series no. 4, 1976. Reprinted in Hume and Kamugisha, *Caribbean Cultural Thought*, 354–76.

——. *History of the Voice: The Development of Nation Language in Anglophone Caribbean Poetry*. London: New Beacon Books, 1984.

——. *Barabajan Poems*. New York: Savacou North, 1993.

——. *The Zea Mexican Diary*. Madison: University of Wisconsin Press, 1994.

——. *Middle Passages*. A lecture given at the Caribbean Migrations conference at Ryerson University, Toronto, Canada, July 2005.

Brathwaite, Edward Kamau, and Edouard Glissant. "A Dialogue: Nation Language and Poetics of Creolization." In *Presencia criolla en el Caribe y América Latina / Creole Presence in the Caribbean and Latin America*, edited by Ineke Phaf, 19–35. Madrid: Iberoamericana, 1996.

Brathwaite, Edward Kamau, and Timothy Reiss, eds. "Sisyphus and Eldorado: Magical and Other Realisms in Caribbean Literature." Special issue, *Annals of Scholarship* 12, nos. 1 and 2 (1997).

Breiner, Laurence A. *An Introduction to West Indian Poetry*. Cambridge University Press, 1998.

Breitman, George, ed. *Leon Trotsky on Black Nationalism and Self-Determination.* New York: Pathfinder, 1978.

Brennan, Timothy. "Black Theorists and Left Antagonists." *Minnesota Review* 37 (Fall 1991): 89–113.

———. *At Home in the World: Cosmopolitanism Now.* Cambridge, MA: Harvard University Press, 1997.

———. *Secular Devotion: Afro-Latin Music and Imperial Jazz.* London: Verso, 2008.

Brereton, Bridget. "The Development of an Identity: The Black Middle Class of Trinidad in the Later Nineteenth Century." In Beckles and Shepherd, *Caribbean Freedom,* 274–83.

Brereton, Bridget, and Kevin A. Yelvington, eds. *The Colonial Caribbean in Transition: Essays on Postemancipation Social and Cultural History.* Kingston: University of the West Indies Press, 1999.

Britton, Celia. "Identity and Change in the Work of Edouard Glissant." *Small Axe* 52 (2017): 169–79.

Brodber, Erna. "Beyond the Boundary—Magical Realism in the Jamaican Frame of Reference." *Annals of Scholarship* 12, nos. 1 and 2 (1997): 41–48.

———. "Re-engineering Blackspace." *Caribbean Quarterly* 43, no. 1 (1997): 1–12.

Brown, Elaine. *The Condemnation of Little B.* Boston: Beacon, 2002.

Brown-Glaude, Winnifred. "The Fact of Blackness? The Bleached Body in Contemporary Jamaica." *Small Axe* 11, 3 (2007): 34–51.

Bryan, Patrick. "The Black Middle Class in Nineteenth Century Jamaica." In Beckles and Shepherd, *Caribbean Freedom,* 284–95.

Bucknor, Michael A., and Alison Donnell, eds. *The Routledge Companion to Anglophone Caribbean Literature.* London: Routledge, 2011.

Buhle, Paul, ed. *C. L. R. James: His Life and Work.* London: Allison and Busby, 1986.

———. *C. L. R. James: The Artist as Revolutionary.* London: Verso, 1988.

———. "C. L. R. James: West Indian. George Lamming interviewed by Paul Buhle." In Henry and Buhle, *C. L. R. James's Caribbean,* 28–36.

———. "The Making of a Literary Life: C. L. R. James Interviewed by Paul Buhle." In Henry and Buhle, *C. L. R. James's Caribbean,* 56–60.

Bundy, Andrew, ed. *Selected Essays of Wilson Harris: The Unfinished Genesis of the Imagination.* New York: Routledge, 1999.

Buisseret, David, and Steven G. Reinhardt, eds. *Creolization in the Americas.* College Station: Texas A&M University Press, 2000.

Burton, Richard. "Ki Moun Nou Ye? The Idea of Difference in Contemporary French West Indian Thought." *New West Indian Guide* 67, nos. 1 and 2 (1993): 5–32.

Campbell, James. *Talking at the Gates: A Life of James Baldwin.* Berkeley: University of California Press, 2002.

Carby, Hazel V. "Proletarian or Revolutionary Literature: C. L. R. James and the Politics of the Trinidadian Renaissance." *South Atlantic Quarterly* 87, no. 1 (Winter 1988): 39–52.

———. *Race Men.* Cambridge, MA: Harvard University Press, 1998.

Carrion, Juan Manuel, ed. *Ethnicity, Race and Nationality in the Caribbean.* San Juan, Puerto Rico: Institute of Caribbean Studies, 1997.

Carter, Martin. "I Come from the Nigger Yard." In *Poems of Succession,* 38–40. London: New Beacon Books, 1977.

———. "A Free Community of Valid Persons." *Kyk-Over-Al* 44 (May 1993): 30–32.

———. *Poesias Escogidas / Selected Poems*. Edited by David Dabydeen and translated by Salvador Ortiz-Carboneres. Leeds, UK: Peepal Tree, 1999.

Césaire, Aimé. "Culture and Colonisation." *Présence Africaine* 8–10 (June–November 1956): 193–207. Reprinted in Hume and Kamugisha, *Caribbean Cultural Thought*, 28–39.

———. *Cahier d'un retour au pays natal*. Paris: Présence Africaine, 1968.

———. *Aimé Césaire, the Collected Poetry*. Translated, with an introduction and notes by Clayton Eshleman and Annette Smith. Berkeley: University of California Press, 1983.

———. "A Salute to the Third World / for Léopold Sedar Senghor." In *Aimé Césaire, the Collected Poetry*, 350–53. Translated by Clayton Eshleman and Annette Smith. Berkeley: University of California Press, 1983.

———. *Lost Body*. Translated by Clayton Eshleman and Annette Smith. New York: George Braziller, 1986.

———. "Lost Body." In *Lost Body*, 242–45.

———. "Poetry and Knowledge." In *Aimé Césaire, Lyric and Dramatic Poetry 1946–1982*, xlii–lvi. Translated by Clayton Eshleman and Annette Smith. Introduction by A. James Arnold. Charlottesville: University of Virginia Press, 1990. Originally published in *Tropiques* 12 (January 1945).

———. "Calling the Magician: A Few Words for a Caribbean Civilization." In *Refusal of the Shadow: Surrealism and the Caribbean*, 119–22. Edited by Michael Richardson. London: Verso, 1996.

———. *Discourse on Colonialism*. Translated by Joan Pinkham. New York: Monthly Review Press, 2000.

———. *Notebook of a Return to the Native Land*. Translated and edited by Clayton Eshleman and Annette Smith. Middletown, CT: Wesleyan University Press, 2001.

Chambers, Iain, and Lidia Curti, eds. *The Post-Colonial Question: Common Skies, Divided Horizons*. London: Routledge, 1996.

Chomsky, Noam. *Language and Mind*. Cambridge: Cambridge University Press, 2006.

Chude-Sokei, Chude. "The Incomprehensible Rain of Stars: Black Modernism, Black Diaspora." Dissertation, submitted to UCLA, 1995. UMI Dissertation Services No. 9601378.

C. L. R. James at 100: Global Capitalism, Culture and the Politics of World Revolution, September 20–23, 2001. Audio proceedings of conference panels.

Clarke, Kamari. "Assemblage of Experts: The Caribbean Court of Justice and the Modernity of Caribbean Postcoloniality." *Small Axe* 41 (2013): 88–107.

Collis-Buthelezi, Victoria. "Caribbean Regionalism, South Africa, and Mapping New World Studies." *Small Axe* 46 (2015): 37–54.

Comaroff, Jean, and John Comaroff, eds. *Modernity and Its Malcontents: Ritual and Power in Postcolonial Africa*. Chicago: University of Chicago Press, 1993.

Commissiong, David. "Conspire to Unite." *Daily Nation* (Barbados) March 10, 2003.

Condé, Maryse, and Madeleine Cottenet-Hage, eds. *Penser la créolité*. Paris: Karthala, 1995.

Condé, Maryse. "Order, Disorder, Freedom, and the West Indian Writer." *Yale French Studies* 83 (1993): 121–35.

Condé, Maryse. "Créolité without the Creole Language?" In Balutansky and Sourieau, *Caribbean Creolization*, 101–9.

Constantine, Learie. *Cricket and I*. London: Phillip Allan, 1933.

Conway, Dennis. "Why Barbados Has Exported People?: International Mobility as a Fundamental Force in the Creation of Small Island Society." In Carrion, *Ethnicity*, 274–308.

Coombs, Orde, ed. *Is Massa Day Dead? Black Moods in the Caribbean*. New York: Anchor Books, 1974.

Cottias, Myriam. "Gender and Republican Citizenship in the French West Indies, 1848–1945." *Slavery and Abolition* 26, no. 2 (2005): 233–45.

Cox, Oliver. "Introduction." In Hare, *The Black Anglo-Saxons*. New York: Marzani and Munsell, 1965.

Crenshaw, Kimberlé, and Neil Gotanda, eds. *Critical Race Theory: The Key Writings That Formed the Movement*. New York: New Press, 1996.

Critic, "Review of Party Politics in the West Indies." *West Indian Gazette*, December 1962, 10.

Cudjoe, Selwyn. "C. L. R. James Misbound." *Transition* 58 (1992): 124–36.

———. "'As Ever, Darling, All My Love, Nello': The Love Letters of C. L. R. James." In Cudjoe and Cain, *His Intellectual Legacies*, 215–43.

———, ed. *Caribbean Women Writers: Essays from the First International Conference*. Wellesley, MA: Calaloux, 1990.

Cudjoe, Selwyn R., and William E. Cain, eds. *C. L. R. James: His Intellectual Legacies*. Amherst: University of Massachusetts Press, 1995.

Curtin, Philip. *Two Jamaicas: The Role of Ideas in a Tropical Colony 1830–65*. New York: Atheneum, 1955.

Dance, Daryl Cumber. "Conversation with C. L. R. James." In *New World Adams: Conversations with Contemporary West Indian Writers*. Leeds, UK: Peepal Tree Books, 1992.

———. "Conversation with Sylvia Wynter." In *New World Adams: Conversations with Contemporary West Indian Writers*. Leeds, UK: Peepal Tree, 1992.

Davies, Carole Boyce. "Deportable Subjects: U.S. Immigration Laws and the Criminalizing of Communism." *South Atlantic Quarterly* 100, no. 4 (2001): 949–66.

———. *Left of Karl Marx: The Political Life of Black Communist Claudia Jones*. Durham, NC: Duke University Press, 2008.

———. "From Masquerade to Maskarade: Caribbean Cultural Resistance and the Rehumanizing Project." In McKittrick, *Sylvia Wynter*, 203–25.

Dayan, Joan. "Held in the Body of the State: Prisons and the Law." In *History, Memory, and the Law*, edited by Austin Sarat and Thomas R. Kearns, 183–247. Ann Arbor: University of Michigan Press, 1999.

"Declaration of Rights of the Negro Peoples of the World." In *The Philosophy and Opinions of Marcus Garvey, or Africa for the Africans, Vol. 1 and 2*, edited by Amy Jacques Garvey. Dover, MA: Majority, 1986.

Demas, William G. *West Indian Nationhood and Caribbean Integration*. Bridgetown, Barbados: CCC, 1974.

Depestre, René. "Interview with Aimé Césaire." In Césaire, *Discourse on Colonialism*, 81–94.

Dessalines, Jean-Jacques. "Liberty or Death, Proclamation." In Kamugisha, *Caribbean Political Thought*, 21–23.

Dube, Saurabh. "Introduction: Enchantments of Modernity." *South Atlantic Quarterly* 101, no. 4 (2002): 729–55.

Du Bois, W. E. B. *The Souls of Black Folk*. New York: Signet, 1995.

Du Bois, W. E. B. "The Study of Negro Problems." *Annals of the American Academy of Political and Social Science* 11 (January 1898): 1–23.

DuBois, Laurent. *A Colony of Citizens: Revolution and Slave Emancipation in the French Caribbean, 1787–1804*. Chapel Hill: University of North Carolina Press, 2004.

Duke, Eric. "The Diasporic Dimensions of Caribbean Federation in the Early Twentieth Century." *New West Indian Guide* 83, nos. 3–4 (2009): 219–48.

———. *Building a Nation: Caribbean Federation in the Black Diaspora*. Gainsville: University of Florida Press, 2016.

"Eastern Caribbean Integration: A Rekindling of the Little Eight?" Special issue, *Journal of Eastern Caribbean Studies* 23, no. 1 (March 1998).

Edie, Carlene. *Democracy by Default: Dependency and Clientelism in Jamaica*. Boulder, CO: Lynne Rienner, 1990.

———, ed. *Democracy in the Caribbean: Myths and Realities*. Westport, CT: Praeger, 1994.

Edmondson, Belinda. *Caribbean Middlebrow: Leisure Culture and the Middle Class*. Ithaca, NY: Cornell University Press, 2009.

Edwards, Brent Hayes. "The Uses of Diaspora." *Social Text* 66 (Spring 2001): 45–73.

Edwards, Norval. "Roots, and Some Routes Not Taken: A Caribcentric Reading of *The Black Atlantic*." *Found Object* 4 (1994): 27–35.

———. "The Foundational Generation: From *The Beacon* to *Savacou*." In *The Routledge Reader in Anglophone Caribbean Literature*, edited by Michael Bucknor and Alison Donnell, 111–23. New York: Routledge, 2011.

Enwezor, Okwui, Carlos Basualdo, Ute Meta Bauer, Susanne Ghez, Sarat Maharaj, Mark Nash, and Octavio Zaya, eds. *Créolité and Creolization: Docmenta11_Platform3*. Ostfildern-Ruit, Germany: Hatje Cantz, 2003.

Eshleman, Clayton, and Annette Smith. "Introduction." In Césaire, *Lost Body*, vii–xxvii.

Essed, Philomena. "Everyday Racism." In Goldberg and Solomos, *Companion*, 202–16.

Essed, Philomena, and David Theo Goldberg, eds. *Race: Critical Theories*. Malden, MA: Blackwell, 2002.

Eudell, Demetrius. "From Mode of Production to Mode of Auto-Institution: Sylvia Wynter's Black Metamorphosis of the Labor Question." *Small Axe* 49 (2016): 47–61.

Fanon, Frantz. *Black Skins, White Masks*. Translated by Charles Lam Markmann. New York: Grove, 1967.

———. "Racism and Culture." In *Towards the African Revolution: Political Essays*, 31–44. Translated by Haakon Chevalier. New York: Grove, 1967.

———. *Towards the African Revolution: Political Essays*. Translated by Haakon Chevalier. New York: Grove, 1967.

———. *The Wretched of the Earth*. Translated by Constance Farrington. London: Penguin, 1967.

———. *A Dying Colonialism*. Translated by Haakon Chevalier. Middlesex, UK: Penguin Books, 1970.

Farred, Grant, ed. *Rethinking C. L. R. James*. Cambridge, MA: Blackwell, 1996.

———. *What's My Name? Black Vernacular Intellectuals*. Minneapolis: University of Minnesota Press, 2003.

Foley, Barbara. *Spectres of 1919: Class and Nation in the Making of the New Negro*. Urbana: University of Illinois Press, 2003.

Fischer, Sibylle. *Modernity Disavowed: Haiti and the Cultures of Slavery in the Age of Revolution*. Durham, NC: Duke University Press, 2004.

Francis, Wigmore. "Nineteenth and Early Twentieth Century Perspectives on Women in the Discourses of Radical Black Caribbean Men." *Small Axe* 13 (March 2003): 116–39.

Fraser, Cary. "Lloyd Best: 1934–2007," *Race and Class* 49, 2 (2007): n.p.

Garvey, Amy Jacques, ed. *The Philosophy and Opinions of Marcus Garvey; or, Africa for the Africans, Vol. 1 and 2*. Dover, MA: Majority, 1986.

Garvey, Marcus. "The Future as I See It." In *The Philosophy and Opinions of Marcus Garvey; or, Africa for the Africans, Vol. 1 and 2*, edited by Amy Jacques Garvey, 73–78. Dover, MA: Majority, 1986.

Gaspar, Barry. "With a Rod of Iron: Barbados Slave Laws as a Model for Jamaica, South Carolina, and Antigua, 1661–1697." In *Crossing Boundaries: Comparative History of Black People in Diaspora*, edited by Darlene Clark Hine and Jacqueline McLeod, 343–66. Bloomington: Indiana University Press, 1999.

Gaztambide-Geigel, Antonio. "The Rise and Geopolitics of Antilleanism." In *The UNESCO General History of the Caribbean Volume IV: The Long Nineteenth Century, Nineteenth Century Transformations*, edited by K. O. Laurence and Jorge Cuesta, 430–52 (Paris: UNESCO, 2012).

Gifford, Sheryl. "'This Is How I Know Myself': A Conversation with Sandra Pouchet Paquet." *Small Axe Salon*, May 28, 2012. http://smallaxe.net/wordpress3/interviews/2012/05/28/this-is-how-i-know-myself/#more-102.

Gikandi, Simon. "Paule Marshall and the Search for the African Diaspora." *New West Indian Guide* 73 nos. 1 and 2 (1999): 83–88.

Gilroy, Paul. *The Black Atlantic: Modernity and Double Consciousness*. Cambridge, MA: Harvard University Press, 1993.

Giovanni, Nikki. *The Collected Poetry of Nikki Giovanni, 1968–1998*. New York: HarperCollins, 2003.

Girvan, Norman. "Aspects of the Political Economy of Race in the Caribbean and the Americas: A Preliminary Interpretation." Institute of Social and Economic Research, University of the West Indies, Mona Campus, working paper no. 7, 1975.

———. *Corporate Imperialism: Conflict and Expropriation*. New York: Monthly Review Press, 1976.

———. "New World and Its Critics." In *The Thought of New World: The Quest for Decolonisation*, edited by Brian Meeks and Norman Girvan, 3–29. Kingston: Ian Randle, 2010.

———. "Existential Threats in the Caribbean: Democratising Politics, Regionalising Governance." C. L. R. James Memorial Lecture, May 11, 2011, Oil Workers Trade Union, Cipriani College of Labour and Cooperative Studies, Valsayn, Trinidad and Tobago.

Glissant, Edouard. *Caribbean Discourse: Selected Essays*. Translated by Michael Dash. Charlottesville: University Press of Virginia, 1989.

Goldberg, David Theo. *Racist Culture: Philosophy and the Politics of Meaning*. Oxford: Blackwell, 1993.

———. *The Racial State*. Malden, MA: Blackwell, 2002.

———. "Racial States." In Goldberg and Solomos, *Companion*, 233–57.

———. "Reflections on 'Modernity, Race, and Morality.'" In Essed and Goldberg, *Race: Critical Theories*, 422–25.

Goldberg, David Theo, and John Solomos, eds. *A Companion to Racial and Ethnic Studies*. Malden, MA: Blackwell, 2002.

Gonsalves, Ralph. "Our Caribbean Civilization: Retrospect and Prospect." *Journal of Eastern Caribbean Studies* 23, no. 1 (March 1998): 51–74.

Gordon, Avery F. "Globalism and the Prison Industrial Complex: An Interview with Angela Davis." *Race and Class* 40, nos. 2 and 3 (1998): 145–57.

Gordon, Lewis R. *Bad Faith and Anti-Black Racism.* Atlantic Highlands, NJ: Humanities Press, 1995.

———. *Fanon and the Crisis of European Man: An Essay on Philosophy and the Human Sciences.* New York: Routledge, 1995.

———, ed. *Existence in Black: An Anthology of Black Existential Philosophy.* London: Routledge, 1997.

———. *Her Majesty's Other Children: Sketches of Racism from a Neocolonial Age.* Lanham, MD: Rowman and Littlefield, 1997.

———. "Race, Biraciality, and Mixed Race—in Theory." In *Her Majesty's Other Children,* 51–71.

———. "Du Bois' Humanistic Philosophy of Human Science." *Annals of the American Academy of Political and Social Science* 568 (March 2000): 265–80.

———. *Existentia Africana: Understanding Africana Existential Thought.* London: Routledge, 2000.

———. *What Fanon Said: A Philosophical Introduction to His Life and Thought.* New York: Fordham University Press, 2015.

Goveia, Elsa. *A Study of the Historiography of the British West Indies to the End of the Nineteenth Century.* Washington, DC: Howard University Press, 1980. Originally published 1956.

———. "New Shibboleths for Old." *New Beacon Reviews* 1 (1968): 48–54.

———. "The Social Framework." *Savacou* 2 (September 1970): 7–15.

Gray, Obika. *Radicalism and Social Change in Jamaica, 1960–1972.* Knoxville: University of Tennessee Press, 1997.

———. "Predation Politics and the Political Impasse in Jamaica." *Small Axe* 13 (March 2003): 72–94.

———. *Demeaned but Empowered: The Social Power of the Urban Poor in Jamaica.* Kingston: University of the West Indies Press, 2004.

Green, Cecilia. "Disciplining Boys: Labor, Gender, Generation and the Penal System in Barbados, 1880–1930," *Journal of the History of Childhood and Youth* 3, no. 3 (2010): 366–90.

Greenblatt, Stephen. *Marvellous Possessions: The Wonder of the New World.* Chicago: University of Chicago Press, 1991.

Grimshaw, Anna, ed. *Cricket.* London: Allison and Busby, 1986.

———. *The C. L. R. James Archive: A Reader's Guide.* New York: C. L. R. James Institute, 1991.

———, ed. *The C. L. R. James Reader.* Oxford: Blackwell, 1992.

Grimshaw, Anna, and Keith Hart. "*American Civilization*: An Introduction." In James, *American Civilization,* 1–25.

Guardian Staff. "Chilcot Report: Key Points from the Iraq Inquiry." *Guardian* (UK), July 6, 2016. https://www.theguardian.com/uk-news/2016/jul/06/iraq-inquiry-key-points-from-the-chilcot-report.

Guevara, Ernesto Che. *Notes on Man and Socialism in Cuba.* New York: Merit Publishers, 1968

Hall, Stuart. "Cultural Studies and its theoretical legacies." In Morley and Chen, *Stuart Hall,* 262–75.

———. "Interview with David Scott." *Bomb* 90 (2005): 54–59.

———. "New Ethnicities." In Morley and Chen, *Stuart Hall,* 441–49.

———. "Old and New Identities, Old and New Ethnicities." In *Culture, Globalization and the World-System: Contemporary Conditions for the Representation of Identity*, edited by Anthony King, 41–68. Minneapolis: University of Minnesota Press, 1997.

———. "When Was 'The Post-Colonial'? Thinking at the Limit." In *The Post-Colonial Question: Common Skies, Divided Horizons*, edited by Iain Chambers and Lidia Curti, 242–60. London: Routledge, 1996.

Hanchard, Michael. "Afro-Modernity: Temporality, Politics, and the African Diaspora." *Public Culture* 11, no. 1 (1999): 245–68.

Hannerz, Ulf. "The World in Creolization." In *Readings in African Popular Culture*, edited by Karin Barber, 12–18. Bloomington: Indiana University Press, 1997.

Hare, Nathan. *The Black Anglo-Saxons*. New York: Marzani and Munsell, 1965.

Harney, Stefano. *Nationalism and Identity: Culture and the Imagination in a Caribbean Diaspora*. Kingston: University of the West Indies Press, 1996.

Harris, Wilson. *Tradition, the Writer and Society*. London: New Beacon, 1967.

———. "A Unique Marxist Thinker." In Buhle, *His Life and Work*, 230–31.

———. "Creoleness: The Crossroads of a Civilization?" In Bundy, *Selected Essays*, 237–47.

———. "History, Fable and Myth in the Caribbean and Guianas." In Bundy, *Selected Essays*, 152–66.

Harrison, Faye V. "The Gendered Politics and Violence of Structural Adjustment: A View from Jamaica." In *Situated Lives: Gender and Culture in Everyday Life*, edited by Louise Lamphere, Helena Ragone, and Patricia Zavella, 451–68. New York: Routledge, 1997.

Hartman, Saidiya V. *Scenes of Subjection: Terror, Slavery and Self-Making in Nineteenth-Century America*. New York: Oxford University Press, 1997.

———. "The Time of Slavery." *South Atlantic Quarterly* 101, no. 4 (2002): 757–77.

Haynes, Tonya. "The Divine and the Demonic: Sylvia Wynter and Caribbean Feminist Thought Revisited." In *Love and Power: Caribbean Discourses of Gender*, edited by Eudine Barriteau, 54–71. Kingston: University of the West Indies Press, 2012.

———. "Sylvia Wynter's Theory of the Human and the Crisis School of Caribbean Heteromasculinity Studies." *Small Axe* 49 (2016): 92–112.

Head, Bessie. *A Question of Power*. Oxford: Heinemann, 1974.

Headley, Bernard. "Man on a Mission: Deconstructing Jamaica's Controversial Crime Management Head." *Social and Economic Studies* 51, no. 1 (2002): 179–91.

Henke, Holger. "Ariel's Ethos: On the Moral Economy of Caribbean Experience." *Cultural Critique* 56 (2004): 33–63.

Henke, Holger, and Fred Reno, eds. *Modern Political Culture in the Caribbean*. Kingston: University of the West Indies Press, 2003.

Henke, Holger, and Don Marshall. "The Legitimacy of Neo-Liberal Trade Regimes in the Caribbean: Issues of 'Race', Class and Gender." In Barrow-Giles and Marshall, *Living at the Borderlines*, 118–64.

Henry, Paget. "C. L. R. James and the Caribbean Economic Tradition." In Henry and Buhle, *C. L. R. James's Caribbean*, 145–73.

———. *Caliban's Reason: An Introduction to Afro-Caribbean Philosophy*. London: Routledge, 2000.

———. "Globalization and the Deformation of the Antiguan Working Class." Paper presented at the University of the West Indies, Antigua and Barbuda Country Conference,

November 13–15, 2003. http://www.open.uwi.edu/sites/default/files/bnccde/antigua/conference/papers/henry.html.

———. "Wynter and the Transcendental Spaces of Caribbean Thought." In Bogues, *After Man*, 258–89.

———. "Caribbean Sociology, Africa and the African Diaspora." In *The African Diaspora and the Disciplines*, edited by Tejumola Olaniyan and James H. Sweet, 145–60. Bloomington: Indiana University Press, 2010.

———. "C. L. R. James, Walter Rodney and the Rebuilding of Caribbean Socialism." In *Journeys in Caribbean Thought: The Paget Henry Reader*, edited by Jane Gordon, Lewis Gordon, Aaron Kamugisha, and Neil Roberts, 199–223. Lanham, MD: Rowman and Littlefield, 2016.

Henry, Paget, and Paul Buhle, eds. *C. L. R. James's Caribbean*. Durham, NC: Duke University Press, 1992.

Higman, Barry. *Writing West Indian Histories*. London: Macmillan, 1999.

Hintzen, Percy. *The Costs of Regime Survival: Racial Mobilization, Elite Domination, and Control of the State in Guyana and Trinidad*. Cambridge: Cambridge University Press, 1989.

———. "Democracy and Middle-Class Domination in the Anglophone Caribbean." In *Democracy in the Caribbean: Myths and Realities*, edited by Carlene J. Edie, 9–23. Westport, CT: Praeger, 1994.

———. "Structural Adjustment and the New International Middle Class." *Transition* (Guyana) 24 (February 1995): 52–74.

———. "Reproducing Domination: Identity and Legitimacy Constructs in the West Indies." *Social Identities*, 3, no. 1 (1997): 47–75.

———. "Afro-Creole Nationalism as Elite Domination: The English-Speaking West Indies." In *Foreign Policy and the Black (Inter)National Interest*, edited by Charles P. Henry, 185–215. New York: State University of New York Press, 2000.

———. "Rethinking Democracy in the Postnationalist State." In Meeks and Lindahl, *New Caribbean Thought*, 104–24.

———. "The Caribbean: Race and Creole Ethnicity." In Goldberg and Solomos, *Companion*, 475–94.

———. "Race and Creole Ethnicity in the Caribbean." In Shepherd and Richards, *Questioning Creole*, 92–110.

———. "Race, Ideology, and International Relations: Sovereignty and the Disciplining of Guyana's Working Class." In Barrow-Giles and Marshall, *Living at the Borderlines*, 414–40.

———. "Rethinking Democracy in the Postnationalist State: The Case of Trinidad and Tobago." In *Modern Political Culture in the Caribbean*, edited by Holger Henke and Fred Reno, 395–423. Kingston: University of the West Indies Press, 2003.

———. "Creoleness and Nationalism in Guyanese Anticolonialism and Postcolonial Formation." *Small Axe* 15 (2004): 106–22.

Hodge, Merle. "Peeping Tom in the Nigger Yard." *Tapia*, April 2, 1972, 11–12.

Høgsbjerg, Christian. "'A Thorn in the Side of Great Britain': C. L. R. James and the Caribbean Labour Rebellions of the 1930s." *Small Axe* 35 (2011): 24–42.

———. *C. L. R. James in Imperial Britain*. Durham, NC: Duke University Press, 2014.

Hope, Donna. "From *Browning* to *Cake Soap*: Popular Debates on Skin Bleaching in the Jamaican Dancehall." *Journal of Pan-African Studies* 4, no. 4 (June 2011): 165–94.

Hosein, Gabrielle Jamela, and Lisa Outar eds. *Indo-Caribbean Feminist Thought: Genealogies, Theories, Enactments.* London: Palgrave Macmillan, 2016.

Hudson, Peter, and Aaron Kamugisha, "On Black Canadian Thought." *C. L. R. James Journal* 20 (Fall 2014): 1–18.

Hyatt, Vera, and Rex Nettleford, eds. *Race, Discourse and the Origin of the Americas: A New World View.* London: Smithsonian Institution Press, 1995.

Idahosa, Pablo. *The Populist Dimension to African Political Thought: Critical Essays in Reconstruction and Retrieval.* Trenton, NJ: Africa World Press, 2004.

Interview, C. L. R. James with James Early, Ethelbert Miller, Paul Buhle, and Noel Ignatin. In Buhle, *His Life and Work*, 164–67.

"Interview with C. L. R. James." In *Visions of History by MARHO the Radical Historians Organization*, edited by Henry Abelove, Betsy Blackmar, Peter Dimock, and Johnathan Schneer, 265–77. Manchester: Manchester University Press, 1983.

"Interview with C. L. R. James." In *Kas-Kas: Interviews with Three Caribbean Writers in Texas*, edited by Ian Munro and Reinhard Sander, 23–42. Austin: African and Afro-American Research Institute, University of Texas at Austin 1972.

Iton, Richard. *In Search of the Black Fantastic: Politics and Popular Culture in the Post-Civil Rights Era.* New York: Oxford University Press, 2008.

Jackson, Esther Merle. "The American Negro and the Image of the Absurd." *Phylon* 23, no. 4 (1962): 359–71.

Jackson, George. *Soledad Brother: The Prison Letters of George Jackson.* Chicago: Lawrence Hill Books, 1994.

Jackson, Shona. *Creole Indigeneity: Between Myth and Nation in the Caribbean.* Minneapolis: University of Minnesota Press, 2012.

James, C. L. R. *The Life of Captain Cipriani: An Account of British Government in the West Indies.* Nelson, UK: Coulton, 1932.

———. "The Woman Question: An Orientation." A discussion held on September 3, 1951, no location given. Accessed 22, July 2017. https://www.marxists.org/archive/james -clr/works/1951/09/woman-question.htm.

———. *Party Politics in the West Indies.* San Juan, Puerto Rico: Vedic Enterprises, 1962.

———. "The West Indian Middle Classes." In *Party Politics in the West Indies*, 130–39. San Juan, Puerto Rico: Vedic Enterprises, 1962.

———. "Appendix: From Toussaint L'Ouverture to Fidel Castro." In *The Black Jacobins: L'Ouverture and the San Domingo Revolution*, 391–418. New York: Vintage, 1963.

———. *The Black Jacobins: Toussaint L'Ouverture and the San Domingo Revolution.* 2nd edition. New York: Vintage, 1963.

———. "The West Indians and the Vote." *New Society* 49 (September 5, 1963): 6–7.

———. "Lenin, Trotsky and the Vanguard Party: A Contemporary View." Detroit: Facing Reality, January 1964.

———. "Race Relations in the Caribbean." *Newsletter*, Institute of Race Relations, London (April/May 1964): 19–23.

———. "On Wilson Harris," in *Spheres of Existence* (London: Allison and Busby, 1980 [1964]), 157–72.

———. "Introduction." In *Caribbean Plays*, vol. 2, edited by Errol Hill, v–viii. St. Augustine, Trinidad and Tobago: Extra Mural Department, University of the West Indies, 1965.

———. "Marxism for the Sixties." *Speak Out*, no. 2 (May 1965) (Detroit: Bulletin of the Facing Reality Publishing Committee): 1–23.

——. "Tomorrow and Today: A Vision." *New World Quarterly* 2, no. 3 (1966): 86–88.

——. "From Du Bois to Fanon." Speech delivered in Detroit, January 1967. *Radical America* 2, no. 4 (July–August 1968): 20–29.

——. "The Responsibility of Intellectuals." Unpublished talk at the Congress on Intellectuals, Cuba, 1968.

——. *A History of Pan-African Revolt.* Washington, D.: Drum and Spear, 1969. Originally published 1938.

——. "The West Indian Intellectual." Introduction to J. J. Thomas, *Froudacity: West Indian Fables by James Anthony Froude*, 23–49. London: New Beacon Books, 1969.

——. "The Atlantic Slave Trade and Slavery: Some Interpretations of Their Significance in the Development of the United States and the Western World." In *The Future in the Present: Selected Writings*, 235–64.

——. "Sir Frank Worrell." In *Cricket: The Great Captains, Studies of Eight Great Captains of Cricket History*, edited by John Arlott, 135–52. Newton Abbot, UK: Sportsmans Book Club, 1972.

——. "The West Indian." *Bim* 14, 55 (July–December 1972): 121–24.

——. *Modern Politics.* Detroit: Bewick, 1973. Originally published 1960.

——. "Beyond the Boundary." *Race Today* 7, no. 7 (1975): 152–53.

——. "The Artist in the Caribbean." In James, *Future in the Present: Selected Writings*, 183–90.

——. "C. L. R. James on Walter Rodney." *Race Today* 12 no. 2 (1980): 28–30.

——. *The Future in the Present: Selected Writings.* London: Allison and Busby, 1977.

——. "The Making of the Caribbean Peoples." In James, *Spheres of Existence*, 173–90.

——. "The Mighty Sparrow." In James, *Future in the Present*, 191–201.

——. *Notes on Dialectics: Hegel, Marx, Lenin.* London: Allison and Busby, 1980. Originally published 1948.

——. "Parties, Politics and Economics in the Caribbean." In James, *Spheres of Existence*, 151–56.

——. *Spheres of Existence.* London: Allison and Busby, 1980.

——. "I'm a Poet." *Race Today* 14, no. 1 (1980/81): 2–6.

——. "Life on the Hill." Review of *The Dragon Can't Dance* by Earl Lovelace. *Race Today* 13 (1980/81): 84.

——. "The Birth of a Nation." In *Contemporary Caribbean: A Sociological Reader Vol. 1*, edited by Susan Craig, 3–35. Maracas, Trinidad and Tobago: College Press, 1981.

——. "Sexual Relations." Review of *You Can't Keep a Good Woman Down* by Alice Walker. *Race Today* 14, no. 3 (1982): 111–12.

——. "Zenith." Review of *Meridian* by Alice Walker. *Race Today* 14, no. 4 (1982): 140–41.

——. "Mama Was There." Review of *Sassafrass, Cypress and Indigo* by Ntozake Shange. *Race Today* 14, no. 6 (1983): n.p.

——. *At the Rendezvous of Victory.* London: Allison and Busby, 1984.

——. "Kanhai: A Study in Confidence." In James, *At the Rendezvous*, 166–71.

——. "The Old World and the New." In James, *At the Rendezvous*, 202–17.

——. "On Federation." In James, *At the Rendezvous*, 85–128.

——. "A National Purpose for Caribbean Peoples." In James, *At the Rendezvous*, 143–58.

——. "Presence of Blacks in the Caribbean and Its Impact on Culture." In James, *At the Rendezvous*, 218–35.

———. "Towards the Seventh: The Pan-African Congress—Past, Present and Future." In James, *At the Rendezvous*, 236–50.

———. "West Indian Personality." *Caribbean Quarterly* 35, no. 4 (December 1989): 11–13.

———. "A New View of West Indian History." *Caribbean Quarterly* 35, no. 4 (December 1989): 49–70.

———. "The Case for West Indian Self-Government." In Grimshaw, *James Reader*, 49–62.

———. "Dialectical Materialism and the Fate of Humanity." In Grimshaw, *James Reader*, 153–81.

———. "Garfield Sobers." In Grimshaw, *James Reader*, 379–89.

———. "Letters to Constance Webb." In Grimshaw, *James Reader*, 127–52.

———. "Letter to Maxwell Geismar, 11 April 1961." In Grimshaw, *James Reader*, 277–80.

———. "The Revolutionary Answer to the Negro Problem in the United States." In Grimshaw, *James Reader*, 182–89 .

———. "Three Black Women Writers: Toni Morrison, Alice Walker, Ntozake Shange." In Grimshaw, *James Reader*, 411–17.

———. *American Civilization*. Edited by Anna Grimshaw and Keith Hart. Cambridge, MA: Blackwell, 1993.

———. *Beyond a Boundary*. Durham, NC: Duke University Press, 1993. Originally published 1963.

———. "A Convention Appraisal: Dr. Eric Williams, First Premier of Trinidad and Tobago, a Biographical Sketch." In *Eric Williams Speaks: Essays on Colonialism and Independence*, edited by Selwyn Cudjoe, 327–51. Wellesley, MA: Calaloux, 1993.

———. *World Revolution 1917–1936: The Rise and Fall of the Communist International*. Atlantic Highlands, NJ: Humanities Press International, 1993. Originally published 1937.

———. *A History of Pan-African Revolt*. Chicago: Charles H. Kerr, 1995. Originally published 1938.

———. "On *The Negro in the Caribbean* by Eric Williams." in *C. L. R. James on the "Negro Question,"* edited by Scott McLemee, 117–25. Jackson: University Press of Mississippi, 1996.

———. "Africans and Afro-Caribbeans: A Personal View." In *Writing Black Britain: 1948–1998*, 60–63. Manchester: Manchester University Press, 2000.

———. "Lectures on *The Black Jacobins*." *Small Axe* 8 (2000): 65–112. Lectures delivered June 14–18, 1971.

———. *Mariners, Renegades and Castaways: The Story of Herman Melville and the World We Live In*. Hanover, NH: University Press of New England, 2001. Originally published 1953.

———. *Letters from London*. Port of Spain, Trinidad and Tobago: Prospect, 2003.

James, C. L. R., Grace Lee Boggs, and Raya Dunayevskaya. *State Capitalism and World Revolution*. Chicago: Charles Kerr, 2013. Originally published 1950.

James, C. L. R., Grace C. Lee, and Pierre Chaulieu. *Facing Reality*. Detroit: Bewick, 1974. Originally published 1958.

James, Selma. "A Woman's Place." Introduction to Mariarosa Della Costa, *The Power of Women and the Subversion of the Community*, 55–77. Bristol, UK: Falling Wall, 1972.

James, Winston. *Holding Aloft the Banner of Ethiopia: Caribbean Radicalism in Early Twentieth Century America*. London: Verso, 1998.

John, Catherine. "Paris 1956." In *Clear Word and Third Sight: Folk Groundings and Diasporic Consciousness in African Caribbean Writing*, 21–42. Durham: Duke University Press, 2003.

Johnson, Buzz. "I Think of My Mother": Notes on the Life and Times of Claudia Jones. London: Karia, 1985.

Johnson, Michele, and Brian Moore. Neither Led nor Driven: Contesting British Cultural Imperialism in Jamaica, 1865–1920. Kingston: University of the West Indies Press, 2004.

Jones, Claudia. "An End to the Neglect of the Problems of Negro Women!" In "I Think of My Mother": Notes on the Life and Times of Claudia Jones, edited by Buzz Johnson, 103–20. London: Karia, 1985.

Joseph, Tennyson. "'Old Expectations, New Philosophies': Adjusting State-Society Relations in the Post-Colonial Anglophone Caribbean." Journal of Eastern Caribbean Studies 22, no. 4 (1997): 31–67.

Kamugisha, Aaron. "The Coloniality of Citizenship in the Contemporary Anglophone Caribbean." Race and Class 49, no. 2 (2007): 20–40.

———. "The Survivors of the Crossing and the Impossibility of Late Colonial Revolt." Introduction to Austin Clarke, The Survivors of the Crossing, 2nd edition, 7–22. Leeds, UK: Peepal Tree, 2012.

———, ed. Caribbean Political Thought: The Colonial State to Caribbean Internationalisms. Kingston: Ian Randle, 2013.

———, ed. Caribbean Political Thought: Theories of the Post-Colonial State. Kingston: Ian Randle, 2013.

———. "On the Idea of a Caribbean Cultural Studies." In "Caribbean Studies." Special issue, Small Axe 41 (2013): 43–57.

———. "C. L. R. James's The Black Jacobins and the Making of the Modern Atlantic World." In 10 Books That Shaped the British Empire: Creating an Imperial Commons, edited by Antoinette Burton and Isabel Hofmeyr, 190–215. Durham, NC: Duke University Press, 2014.

———. "'That Area of Experience That We Term the New World': Introducing Sylvia Wynter's 'Black Metamorphosis.'" Small Axe 49 (2016): 37–46.

Kamugisha, Aaron, and Yanique Hume, eds. Caribbean Cultural Thought: From Plantation to Diaspora. Kingston: Ian Randle, 2013.

———. "Caribbean Cultural Thought in the Pursuit of Freedom." Kamugisha and Hume, Caribbean Cultural Thought, xiii–xxiv.

———, eds. Caribbean Popular Culture: Power, Politics and Performance. Kingston: Ian Randle, 2016.

Kamugisha, Aaron, and Alissa Trotz, eds. "Editorial." Special issue, "Caribbean Trajectories: 200 Year On" Race and Class 49, no. 2 (2007): i–iv.

Kane, Cheikh Hamidou. Ambiguous Adventure. London: Heinemann, 1972.

Kanhai, Rosanne, ed. Matikor: The Politics of Identity for Indo-Caribbean Women. St. Augustine, Trinidad and Tobago: University of the West Indies School of Continuing Studies, 1999.

Kelley, Robin D. G. "Introduction." Introduction to C. L. R. James, A History of Pan-African Revolt, 1–33. Chicago: Charles H. Kerr, 1995.

Kempadoo, Kamala, ed. Sun, Sex and Gold: Tourism and Sex Work in the Caribbean. Lanham, MD: Rowman and Littlefield, 1999.

Kent, George. "'A Future They Must Learn': An Interview." In Bogues, George Lamming Reader, 149–70.

Khan, Aisha. "Journey to the Center of the Earth: The Caribbean as Master Symbol." Cultural Anthropology 16, no. 3 (2001): 271–302.

———. *Callaloo Nation: Metaphors of Race and Religious Identity among South Asians in Trinidad*. Durham, NC: Duke University Press, 2004.

———. "Sacred Subversions? Syncretic Creoles, the Indo-Caribbean, and 'Culture's In-between.'" *Radical History Review* 89 (Spring 2004): 165–84.

Knauft, Bruce M., ed. *Critically Modern: Alternatives, Alterities, Anthropologies*. Bloomington: Indiana University Press, 2002.

Kwayana, Eusi. *The Bauxite Strike and the Old Politics*. N.p.: On Our Own Authority, 2014. Originally published 1972.

Lamming, George. "The Negro Writer and His World," *Présence Africaine* 8–10 (June–November 1956): 318–25.

———. *The Pleasures of Exile*. Ann Arbor: University of Michigan Press, 1992. Originally published 1960.

———. *The Sovereignty of the Imagination*. Kingston: Arawak, 2004.

———. "The Education of Feeling." In Bogues, *George Lamming*, 13–22.

———. "The Honourable Member." In Bogues, *The George Lamming Reader: The Aesthetics of Decolonization*, 101–9.

Larsen, Neil. "Negativities of the Popular: C. L. R. James and the Limits of 'Cultural Studies.'" In Farred, *Rethinking C. L. R. James*, 85–102.

Lazarus, Neil. *Nationalism and Cultural Practice in the Postcolonial World*. Cambridge: Cambridge University Press, 1999.

Legesse, Asmarom. *Gada: Three Approaches to the Study of an African Society*. New York: Free Press, 1973.

Lemelle, Sidney J. "The Politics of Cultural Existence: Pan-Africanism, Historical Materialism and Afrocentricity." *Race and Class* 35, no. 1 (1993): 93–112.

Lemons, Gary L. *Womanist Forefathers: Frederick Douglass and W. E. B. Du Bois*. Albany: State University of New York Press, 2009.

Lenin, V. I. "Will the Sweep of the Democratic Revolution Be Diminished if the Bourgeoisie Recoils from It?" In *Two Tactics of Social Democracy in the Democratic Revolution* (1905). Accessed July 5, 2016. https://www.marxists.org/archive/lenin/works/1905/tactics/ch12.htm.

Lewis, Arthur. "The Agony of the Eight." In Kamugisha, *Caribbean Political Thought*, 346–60.

Lewis, Gordon. *Main Currents in Caribbean Thought: The Historical Evolution of Caribbean Society in Its Ideological Aspects, 1492–1900*. Baltimore: John Hopkins University Press, 1983.

Lewis, Linden, ed. *The Culture of Gender and Sexuality in the Caribbean*. Gainesville: University Press of Florida, 2003.

Lewis, Rupert. *Walter Rodney's Intellectual and Political Thought*. Kingston: University of the West Indies Press, 1998.

———. "Reconsidering the Role of the Middle Class in Caribbean Politics." In Meeks and Lindahl, *New Caribbean Thought*, 127–43.

Locke, Alain. "The New Negro." In *The New Negro*, edited by Alain Locke, 3–16. New York: Antheum, 1969. Originally published 1925.

Look-Lai, Walton. "C. L. R. James and Trinidadian Nationalism." In Henry and Buhle, *C. L. R. James's Caribbean*, 174–209.

Lorde, Audre. "The Uses of the Erotic." In *Sister/Outsider*, 53–59. Freedom, CA: Crossing, 1984.

———. "The Transformation of Silence into Language and Action." In *I Am Your Sister*, edited by Rudolph P. Byrd, Johnnetta Betsch Cole, and Beverly Guy Sheftall, 39–43. Oxford: Oxford University Press, 2011.

Lowenthal, David. *West Indian Societies*. Oxford: Oxford University Press, 1972.

Luis-Brown, David. *Waves of Decolonization: Discourses of Race and Hemispheric Citizenship in Cuba, Mexico, and the United States*. Durham, NC: Duke University Press, 2008.

Lynn-Evanson, Heather. "Not All Gloom." *Daily Nation* (Barbados) August 29, 2015, 3.

Macey, David. *Frantz Fanon: A Life*. London: Granta Books, 2000.

Maldonado-Torres, Nelson. *Against War: Views from the Underside of Modernity*. Durham, NC: Duke University Press, 2008.

Maldonado-Torres, Nelson. "The Topology of Being and the Geopolitics of Knowledge: Modernity, Empire, Coloniality." *City* 8, no. 1 (2004): 29–56.

———. "Notes on the Current Status of Liminal Categories and the Search for a New Humanism." In Bogues, *After Man*, 190–208.

———. "On the Coloniality of Being: Contributions to the Development of a Concept." *Cultural Studies* 21, nos. 2 and 3 (2007): 240–70.

Manley, Michael. *A History of West Indies Cricket*. London: Andre Deutsch, 1988.

Marriott, David. *On Black Men*. New York: Columbia University Press, 2000.

Mars, Perry. *Ideology and Change: The Transformation of the Caribbean Left*. Kingston: University of the West Indies Press, 1998.

Marshall, Don. "Academic Travails and a Crisis-of-Mission of UWI Social Sciences: From History and Critique to Anti-Politics." In *Higher Education in the Caribbean: Past, Present and Future Directions*, edited by Glenford Howe, 59–84. Kingston: University of the West Indies Press, 2000.

Marx, Karl. *Capital: A Critique of Political Economy*. Translated by Samuel Moore and Edward Aveling. New York: Random House, 1906.

Matthews, Kimmo. "Bread Sold by the Slice." *Jamaica Observer*, October 7, 2013. http://www .jamaicaobserver.com/news/Bread-sold-by-the-slice-_15053101.

McClendon, John H. *C. L. R. James's Notes on Dialectics: Left Hegelianism or Marxism-Leninism?* Lanham, MD: Lexington, 2005.

McKittrick, Katherine, ed. *Sylvia Wynter: On Being Human as Praxis*. Durham, NC: Duke University Press, 2015.

McLemee, Scott. *C. L. R. James on the "Negro Question."* Jackson: University of Mississippi Press, 1996.

Meeks, Brian. *Radical Caribbean: From Black Power to Abu Bakr*. Kingston: University of the West Indies Press, 1993.

———. *Narratives of Resistance: Jamaica, Trinidad, the Caribbean*. Kingston: University of the West Indies Press, 2000.

———. "On the Bump of a Revival." In Meeks and Lindahl, *New Caribbean Thought*, viii–xx.

———. *Critical Interventions in Caribbean Politics and Theory*. Jackson: University Press of Mississippi, 2014.

Meeks, Brian, and Folke Lindahl, eds. *New Caribbean Thought: A Reader*. Kingston: University of the West Indies Press, 2001.

Meeks, Brian, and Norman Girvan, eds. *The Thought of New World: The Quest for Decoloni-sation.* Kingston: Ian Randle, 2010.

Mehta, Brinda. "Addressing Marginality through the 'Coolie/Dougla' Stereotype in C. L. R. James's *Minty Alley.*" *C. L. R. James Journal* 9, no. 1 (2002/03): 37–66.

Mehta, Brinda, and Paget Henry. "From the Editors." In "Indo-Caribbean/Afro-Caribbean Thought." Special issue, *C. L. R. James Journal* 9, no. 1 (Winter 2002/03): 2.

Mignolo, Walter D. *The Idea of Latin America.* Malden, MA: Blackwell, 2005.

———. "Sylvia Wynter: What Does It Mean to Be Human." In McKittrick, *Sylvia Wynter,* 106–23.

Mill, John Stuart. *On Liberty.* Indianapolis: Hackett, 1978.

Miller, Daniel. *Modernity: An Ethnographic Approach, Dualism and Mass Consumption in Trinidad.* Oxford: Berg, 1994.

Mills, Charles. *The Racial Contract.* Ithaca, NY: Cornell University Press, 1999.

Mintz, Sidney W. "The Caribbean as a Socio-Cultural Area." *Journal of World History* 9, no. 4 (1966): 912–37.

———. "Enduring Substances, Trying Theories: The Caribbean Region as *Oikoumene.*" *Jour-nal of the Royal Anthropological Institute* 2, no. 2 (1996): 289–311.

Mintz, Sidney, and Richard Price. *An Anthropological Approach to the Afro-American Past: A Caribbean Perspective.* Philadelphia: Institute for the Study of Human Issues, 1976.

Mohammed, Farahnaz. "Guyana: Mental Illness, Witchcraft and the Highest Suicide Rate in the World." *Guardian* (UK), June 3, 2015. http://www.theguardian.com/global-devel-opment-professionals-network/2015/jun/03/guyana-mental-illness-witchcraft-and-the-highest-suicide-rate-in-the-world.

Mohammed, Patricia. "Reflections on the Women's Movement in Trinidad: Calypsos, Changes and Sexual Violence." *Feminist Review* 38 (1991): 33–47.

———. "Midnight's Children and the Legacy of Nationalism." *Small Axe* 2 (1997): 19–37.

———. "The Future of Feminism in the Caribbean." *Feminist Review* 64 (Spring 2000): 116–19.

———. "The 'Creolisation' of Indian Women in Trinidad." In Shepherd and Richards, *Ques-tioning Creole,* 130–47.

Mohammed, Patricia, ed. *Gendered Realities: Essays in Caribbean Feminist Thought.* Kings-ton, Jamaica: University of the West Indies Press, 2002.

Mohammed, Patricia, and Catherine Shepherd, eds. *Gender in Caribbean Development.* Kingston, Jamaica: University of the West Indies School of Continuing Studies, 1988.

Moore, Brian. *Cultural Power, Resistance and Pluralism: Colonial Guyana 1838–1900.* Kings-ton: University of the West Indies Press, 1995.

Morley, David, and Kuan-Hsing Chen, eds. *Stuart Hall: Critical Dialogues in Cultural Stud-ies.* London: Routledge, 1996

Morrison, Toni. *Sula.* New York: Knopf, 1976.

Moses, Wilson. *Afrotopia: The Roots of African American Popular History.* Cambridge: Cam-bridge University Press, 1998.

Mosse, George. *Nationalism and Sexuality: Respectability and Abnormal Sexuality in Modern Europe.* New York: Howard Fertig, 1985.

Mudimbe, Valentin. *The Invention of Africa: Gnosis, Philosophy and the Order of Knowledge.* Bloomington: Indiana University Press, 1988.

Murray, David. *Flaming Souls: Homosexuality, Homophobia and Social Change in Barbados.* Toronto: University of Toronto Press, 2012.

Naipaul, V. S. *The Mimic Men.* London: André Deutsch, 1967.

——. *The Middle Passage*. Harmondsworth, UK: Penguin, 1969.

Nettleford, Rex. "The Melody of Europe, the Rhythm of Africa." In *Carifesta Forum: An Anthology of 20 Caribbean Voices*, edited by John Hearne, 139–54. Kingston: Institute of Jamaica, 1976.

——. "The Battle for Space." In *Inward Stretch, Outward Reach: A Voice from the Caribbean*, 80–90. Basingstoke, UK: Macmillan, 1993.

Newstead, Clare. "Regional Governmentality: Neoliberalisation and the Caribbean Community Single Market and Economy." *Singapore Journal of Tropical Geography* 30 (2009): 158–73.

Newton, Melanie. *The Children of Africa in the Colonies: Free People of Color in Barbados in the Age of Emancipation*. Baton Rouge: State University of Louisiana Press, 2008.

——. "Returns to a Native Land: Indigeneity and Decolonization in the Anglophone Caribbean." *Small Axe* 41 (2013): 108–22.

Nielsen, Aldon Lynn. *C. L. R. James: A Critical Introduction*. Jackson: University Press of Mississippi, 1997.

O'Callaghan, Evelyn. *Women Writing the West Indies, 1804–1939: "A Hot Place, Belonging to Us."* New York: Routledge, 2004.

O'Connell Davidson, Julia, and Jacqueline Sanchez Taylor. "Fantasy Islands: Exploring the Demand for Sex Tourism." In *Sun, Sex and Gold: Tourism and Sex Work in the Caribbean*, edited by Kamala Kempadoo, 37–54. Lanham, MD: Rowman and Littlefield, 1999.

Oxaal, Ivar. *Black Intellectuals Come to Power: The Rise of Creole Nationalism in Trinidad and Tobago*. Cambridge, MA: Schenkman, 1968.

Pagden, Anthony. *The Fall of Natural Man: The American Indian and the Origins of Comparative Ethnology*. Cambridge: Cambridge University Press, 1986.

Palmié, Stephan. *Wizards and Scientists: Explorations in Afro-Cuban Modernity and Tradition*. Durham, NC: Duke University Press, 2002.

——. "Creolization and Its Discontents." *Annual Review of Anthropology* 35 (2006): 433–56.

Paton, Diana. *No Bond but the Law: Punishment, Race and Gender in Jamaican State Formation, 1780–1870*. Durham, NC: Duke University Press, 2004.

Patterson, Thomas. *Inventing Western Civilization*. New York: Monthly Review Press, 2009.

Patullo, Polly. *Last Resorts: The Cost of Tourism in the Caribbean*. Kingston: Ian Randle, 1996.

Paul-Emile, Barbara. "Gender Dynamics in James's *Minty Alley*." In Cudjoe and Cain, *His Intellectual Legacies*, 72–78.

Pépin, Ernest, and Confiant, Raphael. "The Stakes of Créolité." In Balutansky and Sourieau, *Caribbean Creolization*, 96–100.

Philip, Marlene NourbeSe. "Discourse on the Logic of Language." In *She Tries Her Tongue, Her Silence Softly Breaks*, 30–33. Charlottetown, Canada: Ragweed, 1989.

——. "Managing the Unmanageable." In *Caribbean Women Writers: Essays from the First International Conference*, edited by Selwyn Cudjoe, 295–300. Wellesley, MA: Calaloux, 1990.

Pierre, Jemima. *The Predicament of Blackness: Postcolonial Ghana and the Politics of Race*. Chicago: University of Chicago Press, 2013.

Plantation Systems of the New World: Papers and Discussion Summaries of the Seminar Held in San Juan, Puerto Rico. Washington, DC: Pan American Union, 1959.

Powrie, Barbara. "The Changing Attitude of the Colored Middle Class towards Carnival." *Caribbean Quarterly* 4, nos. 3 and 4 (March/June 1956): 224–32.

Price, Richard. "The Miracle of Creolization: A Retrospective." *New West Indian Guide* 75, nos. 1 and 2 (2001): 35–64.

Price, Richard, and Sally Price. "Shadowboxing in the Mangrove." *Cultural Anthropology* 12, no. 1 (1997): 3–36.

Puri, Shalini. "Beyond Resistance: Notes towards a New Caribbean Cultural Studies." *Small Axe* 14 (2003): 23–38.

———, ed. *Marginal Migrations: The Circulation of Cultures within the Caribbean.* Oxford: Macmillan Caribbean, 2003.

———. *The Caribbean Postcolonial: Social Equality, Post-Nationalism, and Cultural Hybridity.* New York: Palgrave, 2004.

———. *The Grenada Revolution in the Caribbean Present: Operation Urgent Memory.* New York: Palgrave MacMillan, 2014.

Quest, Matthew. "Review of Christian Høgsbjerg, C. L. R. James in Imperial Britain." *Insurgent Notes*, May 2014. http://insurgentnotes.com/2014/05/review -christian-hogsbjerg-c-l-r-james-in-imperial-britain-2014/.

Quijano, Aníbal. "Coloniality of Power, Eurocentrism, and Latin America." *Nepantla* 1, no. 3 (2000): 533–80.

Reddock, Rhoda. "'Douglarisation' and the Politics of Gender Relations in Contemporary Trinidad and Tobago: A Preliminary Exploration." *Contemporary Issues in Social Science: A Caribbean Perspective* 1 (1994): 98–124.

———. "Jahaji Bhai: The Emergence of a Dougla Poetics in Trinidad and Tobago." *Identities* 5, no. 4 (April 1999): 569–601.

———, ed. *Interrogating Caribbean Masculinities: Theoretical and Empirical Analyses.* Mona, Jamaica: University of the West Indies Press, 2004.

Reid, Stanley. "An Introductory Approach to the Concentration of Power in the Jamaican Corporate Economy and Notes on Its Origin." In *Essays on Power and Change in Jamaica*, edited by Carl Stone and Aggrey Brown, 15–44. Kingston: Jamaica Publishing House, 1982.

Reyes-Santos, Alaí. *Our Caribbean Kin: Race and Nation in the Neoliberal Antilles.* New Brunswick: Rutgers University Press, 2015.

Richards, Peter. "Common Market Opens, Sans Eastern Caribbean States." Inter Press Service News Agency, January 2, 2006. http://www.ipsnews.net/news.asp?idnews =31655

Richardson, Bonham C., and Joseph L. Scarpaci. "The Quality of Life in the Twentieth Century Caribbean." In *General History of the Caribbean Volume V: The Caribbean in the Twentieth Century*, edited by Bridget Brereton, 627–66. Paris: UNESCO; London: Macmillan, 2004.

Richardson, Michael, ed. *Refusal of the Shadow: Surrealism and the Caribbean.* London: Verso, 1996.

Rivera-Pagán, Luis N. "Freedom and Servitude: Indigenous Slavery and the Spanish Conquest." In *General History of the Caribbean Vol. 1: Autochthonous Societies*, edited by Jalil Sued-Badillo, 316–61. Paris: UNESCO; London: Macmillan Caribbean, 2003.

Robbins, Bruce. "Race Gender, Class, Postcolonialism: Toward a New Humanistic Paradigm?" In *A Companion to Postcolonial Studies*, edited by Henry Schwarz and Sangeeta Ray, 556–73. Malden, MA: Blackwell, 2000.

Robinson, Cedric. *Black Marxism: The Making of the Black Radical Tradition.* Chapel Hill: University of North Carolina Press, 2000.

Robinson, Tracy. "Fictions of Citizenship, Bodies without Sex: The Production and Effacement of Gender in the Law." *Small Axe* 7 (March 2000): 1–27.

———. "Beyond the Bill of Rights: Sexing the Citizen." In Barriteau, *Confronting Power*,
231–61.

———. "A Caribbean Common Law." *Race and Class* 49, no. 2 (2007): 118–24.

———. "A Loving Freedom: A Caribbean Feminist Ethic." *Small Axe* 24 (2007): 118–29.

———. "Authorized Sex: Same Sex Sexuality and Law in the Caribbean." In *Sexuality, Social
Exclusion and Human Rights*, edited by Christine Barrow, Marjan de Bruin, and Robert Carr, 3–22. Kingston: Ian Randle, 2009.

Robotham, Don. "Blackening the Jamaican Nation: The Travails of a Black Bourgeoisie in a
Globalized World." *Identities* 7, no. 1 (March 2000): 1–37.

———. "Two Views on Grenada." *Social and Economic Studies* 65, no. 1 (2016): 189–99.

Rodney, Walter. *The Groundings with My Brothers*. London: Bogle-L'Ouverture, 1969.

———. "Contemporary Political Trends in the English-Speaking Caribbean." *Black Scholar* 7,
1 (September 1975): 15–21.

———. "Barbadian Immigration into British Guiana, 1863–1924." Paper delivered at the ninth
annual conference of the Association of Caribbean Historians, April 3–7, 1977, University of the West Indies, Cave Hill campus.

———. *Walter Rodney Speaks: The Making of an African Intellectual*. Trenton, NJ: Africa
World Press, 1990.

Rohlehr, Gordon. "Sparrow and the Language of Calypso," *Savacou* 2 (1970): 87–99.

———. "History as Absurdity," in Coombs, *Is Massa Day Dead?*, 69–108.

———. "Articulating a Caribbean Aesthetic: The Revolution in Self-Perception." In *My
Strangled City and Other Essays*, 1–16. Port-of-Spain, Trinidad: Longman, 1992.

———. "The Dilemma of the West Indian Academic in 1970." In *Power: The Black Power
Revolution 1970, a Retrospective*, edited by Selwyn Ryan and Taimoon Stewart,
381–402. St. Augustine, Trinidad and Tobago: Institute of Social and Economic
Research, 1995.

———. "The Culture of Williams: Context, Performance, Legacy." *Callaloo* 20, no. 4 (Fall
1997): 849–88.

———. "A Scuffling of Islands: The Dream and Reality of Caribbean Unity in Poetry and
Song." In Meeks and Lindahl, *New Caribbean Thought*, 265–305.

Rosengarten, Frank. *Urbane Revolutionary: C. L. R. James and the Struggle for a New Society*.
Jackson: University Press of Mississippi, 2008.

Ross, Andrew. "Civilization in One Country? The American James." In Farred, *Rethinking
C. L. R. James*, 75–84.

Ross-Brewster, Havelock. "Identity, Space and the West Indian Union." In Kamugisha, *Caribbean Political Thought*, 374–79.

Roumain, Jacques. "Sales Nègres." In *Ebony Wood: Poems by Jacques Roumain*, 32–45. Translated by Sidney Shapiro. New York: Interworld, 1972.

Rudder, David. "Rally Round the West Indies." *Haiti*. Sire: October 1990.

Ryan, Selwyn. *The Jihandi and the Cross: The Clash of Cultures in Post-Creole Trinidad and
Tobago*. St. Augustine, Trinidad and Tobago: Sir Arthur Lewis Institute of Social and
Economic Studies, University of the West Indies, 1999.

———. "Democratic Governance in the Anglophone Caribbean: Threats to Sustainability." In
Meeks and Lindahl, *New Caribbean Thought*, 73–103.

———. *Deadlock: Ethnicity and Electoral Competition in Trinidad and Tobago 1995-2002*. St. Augustine, Trinidad and Tobago: Sir Arthur Lewis Institute of Social and Economic Studies, University of the West Indies, 2003.

Ryan, Selwyn, and Lou Ann Barclay. *Sharks and Sardines: Blacks in Business in Trinidad and Tobago*. St. Augustine, Trinidad and Tobago: Institute of Social and Economic Research, 1992.

Sagás, Ernesto. "The Development of *Antihaitianismo* into a Dominant Ideology during the Trujillo Era." In Carrion, *Ethnicity*, 96–121.

Said, Edward. *Representations of the Intellectual: The 1993 Reith Lectures*. New York: Pantheon Books, 1994.

Sartre, Jean-Paul. "Black Orpheus." *Massachusetts Review* 6, 1 (Autumn/Winter 1964/65): 13–52.

Saunders, Patricia. *Alienation and Repatriation: Translating Identity in Anglophone Caribbean Literature*. Lanham, MD: Lexington Books, 2008.

Schwarz, Bill. "C. L. R. James and George Lamming: The Measure of Historical Time." *Small Axe* 14 (2003): 39–70.

Schwartz, Meryl F. "An Interview with Michelle Cliff," *Contemporary Literature* 34, no. 4 (1993): 594–619.

Schwarz-Bart, Simone. *The Bridge of Beyond*. Oxford: Heinemann, 1982.

Scott, David. "That Event, This Memory: Notes on the Anthropology of African Diasporas in the New World." *Diaspora* 1, no. 3 (1991): 261–84.

———. "'An Obscure Miracle of Connection': Discursive Tradition and Black Diaspora Criticism." *Small Axe* 1 (1997): 19–38.

———. "The Vocation of an Intellectual: An Interview with Lloyd Best," *Small Axe* 1 (1997): 119–39.

———. "Memories of the Left: An Interview with Richard Hart," *Small Axe* 3 (1998): 65–114.

———. "The Archaeology of Black Memory: An Interview with Robert A. Hill," *Small Axe* 5 (1999): 81–151.

———. *Refashioning Futures: Criticism after Postcoloniality*. Princeton, NJ: Princeton University Press, 1999.

———. "The Re-enchantment of Humanism: An Interview with Sylvia Wynter." *Small Axe* 8 (2000): 119–207.

———. "The Dialectic of Defeat: An Interview with Rupert Lewis," *Small Axe* 10 (2001): 85–177.

———. "The Sovereignty of the Imagination: An Interview with George Lamming." *Small Axe* 12 (2002): 72–200.

———. "Political Rationalities of the Jamaican Modern," *Small Axe* 14 (2003): 1–22.

———. *Conscripts of Modernity: The Tragedy of Colonial Enlightenment*. Durham, NC: Duke University Press, 2004.

———. "Counting Women's Caring Work: An Interview with Andaiye." *Small Axe* 15 (2004): 123–217.

———. *Omens of Adversity: Tragedy. Time, Memory, Justice*. Durham, NC: Duke University Press, 2014.

Searle, Chris. *Words Unchained: Language and Revolution in Grenada*. London: Zed, 1984.

———. "Language and the Seizure of Power: An Interview with C. L. R. James." *Race and Class* 50, no. 1 (2008): 79–97.

Sekyi-Otu, Ato. *Fanon's Dialectic of Experience*. Cambridge: Harvard University Press, 1996.

Shange, Ntozake. *The Love Space Demands: A Continuing Saga*. New York: St. Martin's, 1991.

Sheller, Mimi. *Consuming the Caribbean: From Arawaks to Zombies*. London: Routledge, 2003.

———. "Towards a Caribbean Cultural Political Economy." *New West Indian Guide* 80, nos. 1 and 2 (2006): 91–95.

———. *Citizenship from Below: Erotic Agency and Caribbean Freedom*. Durham, NC: Duke University Press, 2012.

Shepherd, Verene, and Glen Richards, eds. *Questioning Creole: Creolisation Discourses in Caribbean Culture*. Kingston: Ian Randle, 2002.

Shepherd, Verene, Bridget Brereton, and Barbara Bailey, eds. *Engendering History: Caribbean Women in Historical Perspective*. London: Palgrave Macmillan, 1995.

Sheridan, Richard. "Eric Williams and Capitalism and Slavery: A Biographical and Historiographical Essay." In *British Capitalism and Caribbean Slavery: The Legacy of Eric Williams*, edited by Barbara L. Solow and Stanley L. Engerman, 317–45. Cambridge: Cambridge University Press, 1987.

Sherwood, Marika. *Claudia Jones: A Life in Exile*. London: Lawrence and Wishart, 1999.

Shohat, Ella, and Robert Stam. *Unthinking Eurocentrism: Multiculturalism and the Media*. London: Routledge, 1994.

Singh, Rickey. "Not Now!" *Daily Nation* (Barbados) February 16, 2003.

Singham, A. W., and N. L. Singham. "Cultural Domination and Political Subordination: Notes towards a Theory of the Caribbean Political System." *Comparative Studies in Society and History* 15, no. 3 (June 1973): 258–88.

Singham, Archie. "Three Cases of Constitutionalism and Cuckoo Politics: Ceylon, British Guyana and Grenada." *New World Quarterly* 2, no. 1 (1965): 23–33.

———. *The Hero and the Crowd in a Colonial Polity*. New Haven, CT: Yale University Press, 1968.

Smith, Faith. "Coming Home to the Real Thing: Gender and Intellectual Life in the Anglophone Caribbean." *South Atlantic Quarterly* 93, no. 4 (Fall 1994): 895–923.

Smith, M. G. *The Plural Society in the British West Indies*. Berkeley: University of California Press, 1965.

Spillers, Hortense J. "Mama's Baby, Papa's Maybe: An American Grammar Book." *Diacritics* 17, no. 2 (1987): 65–81.

Stoler, Ann. "Racial Histories and Their Regimes of Truth." *Political Power and Social Theory* 11 (1997): 183–206.

———. "Reflections on 'Racial Histories and Their Regimes of Truth.'" In Essed and Goldberg, *Race: Critical Theories*, 417–21.

Stone, Carl. *Democracy and Clientelism in Jamaica*. New Brunswick, NJ: Transaction Books, 1980.

Taylor, Lucien. "Créolité Bites." *Transition* 74 (1997): 124–61.

———. "Mediating Martinique: The 'Paradoxical Trajectory' of Raphael Confiant." In *Cultural Producers in Perilous States: Editing Events, Documenting Change*, edited by George E. Marcus, 259–329. Chicago: University of Chicago Press, 1997.

Taylor, Patrick. *The Narrative of Liberation: Perspectives on Afro-Caribbean Literature, Popular Culture, and Politics*. Ithaca, NY: Cornell University Press, 1989.

"The *Black Scholar* Interviews C. L. R. James." *Black Scholar* 2, no. 1 (September 1970): 35–43.

"The *Black Scholar* Interviews Walter Rodney." *Black Scholar* 6, no. 3 (1975): 38–47.

Thomas, Clive. *The Poor and the Powerless: Economic Policy and Change in the Caribbean.* New York: Monthly Review Press, 1988.

Thomas, Deborah A. *Modern Blackness: Nationalism, Globalization and the Politics of Culture in Jamaica.* Durham, NC: Duke University Press, 2004.

———. "Public Bodies: Virginity Testing, Redemption Songs and Racial Respect in Jamaica." *Journal of Latin American Anthropology* 11, no. 1 (2006): 1–31.

Thomas, Greg. "Sex/Sexuality and Sylvia Wynter's *Beyond . . .*: Anti-Colonial Ideas in 'Black Radical Tradition.'" *Journal of West Indian Literature* 10, nos. 1 and 2 (November 2001): 92–118.

———. "*Proud Flesh* Inter/views Sylvia Wynter." *Proudflesh: New Afrikan Journal of Culture, Politics and Consciousness* 4 (2006): 1–35.

———. *The Sexual Demon of Colonial Power: Pan-African Embodiment and Erotic Schemes of Empire.* Bloomington: Indiana University Press, 2006.

Thomas, J. J. *Froudacity: West Indian Fables by James Anthony Froude.* London: New Beacon, 1969. Originally published 1889.

Torres-Saillant, Silvio. *An Intellectual History of the Caribbean.* New York: Palgrave Macmillan, 2006.

Trotz, Alissa, and Beverley Mullings. "Transnational Migration, the State, and Development: Reflecting on the 'Diaspora Option.'" *Small Axe* 41 (2013): 154–71.

Trouillot, Michel-Rolph. *Haiti: State against Nation: The Origins and Legacy of Duvalierism.* New York: Monthly Review Press, 1989.

———. *Silencing the Past: Power and the Production of History.* Boston: Beacon Books, 1995.

———. "Culture on the Edges: Creolization in the Plantation Context." *Plantation Society in the Americas* 5, no. 1 (Spring 1998): 8–28.

———. "The Otherwise Modern: Caribbean Lessons from the Savage Slot." In Knauft, *Critically Modern*, 220–37.

Tucker, Robert C., ed. *The Marx-Engels Reader.* London: W. W. Norton, 1978.

United Nations 1514 (XV), "Declaration on the Granting of Independence to Colonial Countries and Peoples." 947th plenary meeting, December 14, 1960.

United Nations Office on Drugs and Crime and the World Bank. *Crime, Violence and Development: Trends, Costs and Policy Options in the Caribbean* (March 2007).

Walcott, Derek. "The Muse of History." In Coombs, *Is Massa Day Dead?*, 1–27.

Walker, Alice. *Her Blue Body Everything We Know: Earthling Poems 1965–1990.* Toronto: Women's Press, 1991.

Watson, Hilbourne. "Caribbean Options under Global Neoliberalism." In *The Caribbean: New Dynamics in Trade and Political Economy*, edited by Anthony T. Bryan, 165–206. New Brunswick, NJ: Transaction Books, 1995.

———. "Beyond Ronald Mason's Diatribe." *Stabroek News*, May 20, 2013. https://www.stabroeknews.com/2013/features/in-the-diaspora/05/20/beyond-ronald -masons-diatribe/.

Webb, Constance. "C. L. R. James: The Speaker and His Charisma." In Buhle, *His Life and Work*, 168–76.

Weis, Tony. "Agrarian Reform and Breadbasket Dependency in the Caribbean: Confronting Illusions of Inevitability." *Labour, Capital and Society* 36, no. 2 (November 2003): 174–99.

———. "Small Farming and Radical Imaginations in the Caribbean Today." *Race and Class* 49, no. 2 (2007): 112–17.

White, Derrick. "'Black Metamorphosis': A Prelude to Sylvia Wynter's Theory of the Human." *C. L. R. James Journal* 16, no. 1 (Fall 2010): 127–48.

Wilder, Gary. *Freedom Time: Negritude, Decolonization, and the Future of the World.* Durham, NC: Duke University Press, 2015.

Williams, Brackette. *Stains on My Name, War in My Veins: Guyana and the Politics of Struggle.* Durham, NC: Duke University Press, 1991.

Williams, Michael. "Caribbean Nations Sign Single Market Instrument." Caribbeannetnews. com, February 2, 2006. http://www.caribbeannetnews.com.

Wilson, Peter. "Reputation and Respectability: A Suggestion for Caribbean Ethnology." *Man* 4, no. 1 (1969): 70–84.

———. *Crab Antics: The Social Anthropology of English-Speaking Negro Societies of the Caribbean.* New Haven, CT: Yale University Press, 1973.

Worcester, Kent. *C. L. R. James: A Political Biography.* Albany: State University of New York Press, 1995.

Worrell, Frank. *Cricket Punch.* London: Stanley Paul, 1959.

Wright, Richard. *Black Boy.* New York: Signet Books, 1951.

Wylie, Hal. "Metellus, Diasporism and Créolité." In *Penser la créolité,* edited by Maryse Condé and Madeleine Cottenet-Hage, 251–62. Paris: Karthala, 1995.

Wynter, Sylvia. "Lady Nugent's Journal," *Jamaica Journal* 1, no. 1 (December 1967): 23–34.

———. "We Must Learn to Sit Down Together and Discuss a Little Culture: Reflections on West Indian Writing and Criticism," part 1. *Jamaica Journal* 2, no. 4 (1968): 24–32; part 2, *Jamaica Journal* 3, no. 1 (1969): 27–42.

———. "Jonkonnu in Jamaica." *Jamaica Journal* 4, no. 2 (June 1970): 34–48.

———. "Novel and History, Plot and Plantation." *Savacou* 5 (June 1971): 95–102.

———. "Creole Criticism—a Critique." *New World Quarterly* 5, no. 4 (1972): 12–37.

———. "James and the Castaway Culture of the Caribbean." Paper delivered at the conference Symposium on the Life and Work of C. L. R. James, February 3, 1972, University of the West Indies, Mona campus.

———. "One Love—Rhetoric or Reality? Aspects of Afro-Jamaicanism." *Caribbean Studies* 12, no. 3 (1972): 64–97.

———. "Ethno or Socio Poetics." *Alcheringa: Ethnopoetics* 2, no. 2 (1976): 78–94.

———. "'We Know Where We Are From': The Politics of Black Culture from Myal to Marley." Paper presented at the joint meeting of the African Studies Association and the Latin American Studies Association in Houston, Texas, November 1977.

———. "Sambos and Minstrels." *Social Text* 1 (1979): 149–56.

———. "A Utopia from the Semi-Periphery: Spain, Modernization, and the Enlightenment." *Science Fiction Studies* 6, 1 (1979): 100–107.

———. "Beyond Liberal and Marxist Leninist Feminisms: Towards an Autonomous Frame of Reference." Unpublished paper, prepared for the session "Feminist Theory at the Crossroads," American Sociological Association, San Francisco, September 1982.

———. "The Ceremony Must Be Found: After Humanism." In "Humanism and the University." Special issue, *Boundary 2* 12, no. 3/13, no. 1 (Spring/Fall 1984): 359–78.

———. "New Seville and the Conversion Experience of Bartolomé de las Casas," part 1, *Jamaica Journal* 17, no. 2 (May 1984): 25–32; part 2, *Jamaica Journal* 17, no. 3 (August/October 1984): 46–55.

———. "In Quest of Matthew Bondman: Some Cultural Notes on the Jamesian Journey." In Buhle, *His Life and Work,* 131–45.

——. "On Disenchanting Discourse: 'Minority' Literary Criticism and Beyond." *Cultural Critique* 7 (Fall 1987): 207–44.

——. "Beyond the Word of Man: Glissant and the New Discourse of the Antilles." *World Literature in Review* 63, no. 4 (1989): 637–47.

——. "Afterword: Beyond Miranda's Meanings: Un/silencing the 'Demonic Ground' of Caliban's 'Woman.'" In *Out of the Kumbla: Caribbean Women and Literature*, edited by Carole Boyce Davies and Elaine Savory Fido, 355–70. Trenton, NJ: Africa World Press, 1990.

——. *"Do Not Call Us Negroes": How "Multicultural" Textbooks Perpetuate Racism.* Introduction by Joyce King. San Francisco: Aspire Books, 1990.

——. "After the New Class: James, *Les Damnés*, and the Autonomy of Human Cognition." Paper prepared for the international conference C. L. R. James: His Intellectual Legacies and hosted by the Black Studies Department at Wellesley, April 19–21, 1991.

——. "Columbus and the Poetics of the Propter Nos." *Annals of Scholarship* 8, no. 2 (Spring 1991): 251–86.

——. "Beyond the Categories of the Master Conception: The Counterdoctrine of the Jamesian Poiesis." In Buhle and Henry, *C. L. R. James's Caribbean*, 63–91.

——. *"No Humans Involved*: An Open Letter to My Colleagues." *Voices of the African Diaspora* 8, no. 2 (Fall 1992): 13–16.

——. "Rethinking 'Aesthetics': Notes towards a Deciphering Practice." In *Ex-iles: Essays on Caribbean Cinema*, edited by Mbye B. Cham, 237–79. Trenton, NJ: Africa World Press, 1992.

——. "But What Does 'Wonder' Do? Meanings, Canons, Too? On Literary Texts, Cultural Contexts, and What It's Like to Be One/Not One of Us." In "Bridging the Gap: Where Cognitive Science Meets Literary Criticism," edited by Guven Guzeldere and Stefano Franchi. Special supplement, *Stanford Humanities Review* 4, no. 1 (Spring 1994): 124–28.

——. "1492: A New World View." In *Race, Discourse, and the Origin of the Americas*, edited by V. L. Hyatt and R. Nettleford, 5–57. Washington, DC: Smithsonian, 1995.

——. "The Pope Must Have Been Drunk, the King of Castile a Madman: Culture as Actuality, and the Caribbean Rethinking Modernity." In *The Reordering of Culture: Latin America, the Caribbean and Canada*, edited by Alvina Ruprecht and Cecilia Taiana, 17–41. Ottawa: Carleton University Press, 1995.

——. "Is Development a Purely Empirical Concept or Also Teleological: A Perspective from 'We the Underdeveloped.'" In *Prospects for Recovery and Sustainable Development in Africa*, edited by Aguibou Yansane, 299–316. Westport, CT: Greenwood, 1996.

——. "Columbus, the Ocean Blue, and Fables That Stir the Mind: To Reinvent the Study of Letters." In *Poetics of the Americas: Race, Founding, and Textuality*, edited by Bainard Cowan and Jefferson Humphries, 141–63. Baton Rouge: Louisiana State University Press, 1997.

——. "'A Different Kind of Creature': Caribbean Literature, the Cyclops Factor, and the Second Poetics of the Propter Nos." *Annals of Scholarship* 12, nos. 1–2 (1997): 153–72.

——. "'Genital Mutilation' or 'Symbolic Birth'? Female Circumcision, Lost Origins, and the Aculturalism of Feminist/Western Thought." *Case Western Reserve Law Review* 47, no. 2 (1997): 501–52.

——. "Africa, the West and the Analogy of Culture: The Cinematic Text after Man." In *Symbolic Narratives / African Cinema: Audiences, Theory and the Moving Image*, edited by June Givanni, 25–76. London: British Film Institute, 2000.

———. "Towards the Sociogenic Principle: Fanon, the Puzzle of Conscious Experience, of 'Identity' and What It's Like to Be 'Black.'" In *National Identity and Sociopolitical Change: Latin America Between Marginalization and Integration*, edited by Mercedes Durán-Cogan and Antonio Gómez-Moriana, 30–66. New York: Garland, 2000.

———. "Unsettling the Coloniality of Being/Power/Truth/Freedom: Towards the Human, after Man, Its Overrepresentation—an Argument." *CR: The New Centennial Review* 3, no. 3 (Fall 2003): 257–337.

———. "On How We Mistook the Map for the Territory, and Re-imprisoned Ourselves in Our Unbearable Wrongness of Being, of *Désêtre*: Black Studies towards the Human Project." In *Not Only the Master's Tools: African-American Studies in Theory and Practice*, edited by Lewis R. Gordon and Jane Anna Gordon, 107–69. Boulder, CO: Paradigm, 2006.

Yelvington, Kevin. "The Anthropology of Afro-Latin America and the Caribbean: Diasporic Dimensions." *Annual Review of Anthropology* 30 (2001): 227–60.

Yelvington, Kevin A., Jean-Pierre Sainton, Michel Hector, and Jean Casimir. "Caribbean Social Structure in the Nineteenth Century." In *UNESCO General History of the Caribbean Vol. 4: The Long Nineteenth Century; Nineteenth Century Transformations*, edited by K. O. Laurence, 283–333. Paris: UNESCO, 2011.

Young, Robert. *Colonial Desire: Hybridity in Theory, Culture and Race*. New York: Routledge, 1995.

———. *Postcolonialism: An Historical Introduction*. Malden, Massachusetts: Blackwell, 2001.

Zack, Naomi. *Race and Mixed Race*. Philadelphia: Temple University Press, 1993.

Index

abduction, 177–80, 200, 202
Abeng (journal), 14
abjectness, 187
Abraham, Sara, 102
absurdity, 61–65, 122–23
Achebe, Chinua, *Things Fall Apart*, 15
ACLALS (Association for Commonwealth Literature and Language Studies), 14–15, 30n74, 166–67
Adams, Grantley, 204
aesthetic decolonization, 209
African countries: elites in, 139, 203; independence, 47, 97, 212; modernity and, 128
African culture: C. L. R. James and, 127–28; influence on Caribbean culture, 65, 78–79, 84, 87–89, 95, 101, 108n97; influence on Western popular culture, 200; in North America, 170
African diaspora, 78, 176; abjectness and, 187; black survival of colonialism, 200, 214; criticism, 202–3; historicism, 32n103; intellectuals on class formation, 48; modernity and, 18–19
African languages, 127
Afro-Caribbeans, 101
Afro-creole nationalism, 41–46
Afro-Indian solidarity, 138
Alexander, M. Jacqui, 9, 19, 44–46, 58, 69n64; *Pedagogies of Crossing*, 7, 159n123
Algeria, 97, 199n160
alienation, 177
Allen, Carolyn, 79
alterity status, 99, 111n179
American Indian Movement (AIM), 2
American Indians, 172; conquest of, 179. *See also* indigenous people
Americanness, 85
Americas: black citizenship in, 62–63; creolization in, 95; cultural transformation in, 168. *See also* New World; United States
Anglo-centered scholarship, 181
Anglophone Caribbean: antiblack racism in, 100–103; class-stratification in, 5; creolization in, 78, 86; independence, 23, 47, 120, 151; Leftist politics, 4, 12; neoliberalism and neocolonialism in, 201–2; new society in, 126–29, 151–52; politics in, 1–2, 9; rights of colonial subjects, 39–41, 77; social and economic conditions, 24n4, 54–55 (*see also* political economy); social transformation in, 40–41; tourism, 57–59
Anguilla, 215n9
Anthony, Kenny, 215n8
Anthony, Michael, 127
Anthony-Welch, L., 145
anthropology, 78, 95, 123, 171
antiblack racism, 20–21, 77–78, 91–92, 98–103, 109n120, 112n188, 176, 180, 187; sources of, 172–73
anticapitalist political theory, 6. *See also* Marxism
anticolonial nationalism, 41–46
anticolonial romance, 119
anticolonial thought, 6, 22, 50, 172–73, 176, 197n134
Antigua and Barbuda, 215n9; associated state status, 68n38; Caribbean immigrants in, 206; independence, 29n55, 68n38; patronage, 55; tourism, 72n130
anti-immigrant sentiment, 205–7
anti-imperialism, 12, 97–98
Antilleanism, 208
Aristide, Jean-Bertrand, 179
Arnold, A. James, 87
Arnold, Thomas, 133–34
Arthur, Owen, 201, 215n8
articulation, 8

in, 167–68; black experience in, 174; black women in, 141–43; compared to Europe, 122; "Negro question," 141–42; post-WWII dominance, 42–43, 122; racism in, 169
universal adult suffrage, 40, 45, 73n142
universalism, 86, 99
Universal Negro Improvement Association, 62
University of the West Indies, 8; Mona campus, 12–14, 166–67; tuition fees, 54
USSR, 189

vindicationism, 18, 32n103, 38, 50
violence: crime and, 55, 63, 205; state-sponsored, 71n116
vision, 203
Visions of History (1983), 146

Wages for Housework, 145, 149
Walcott, Derek, 32n114; "The Muse of History," 31n78
Walker, Alice, 22, 145–46, 148, 150, 162n179, 214; *Meridian*, 162n177
Walzer, Michael, 19
Warner, Pelham, 157n76
Watts, Raymond, 12
Webb, Constance, 137, 143, 150
Western culture: consumption patterns in, 43; ideals, 49; modernity and, 8, 15–20, 31n89; rationality and reason, 184–85; "universal," 99–100
Western man, 23, 61, 181, 184–86, 194n56, 199n156, 213
Western/non-Western, Caribbean as, 126–27, 129, 157n71
Western white tourists, 57–59
West Indian exceptionalism, 152
West Indian Federal Parliament, 124–25
West Indian personality, 126, 130–36
West Indies Cricket Board of Control, 130
West Indies Federal Labour Party, 124
West Indies Federation, 42, 201, 204; end of, 47, 56
White, Derrick, 191n11
whiteness, 50, 83; pathology of, 172
white supremacy, 45, 92, 97, 173, 180, 209; colonialism and, 98; criticism of, 49

Wilder, Gary, 9
Williams, Eric, 10–11, 28n50, 28n53, 63–65, 74n168, 201, 208; *Capitalism and Slavery*, 6, 124; *The Negro in the Caribbean*, 124; People's National Movement and, 29n56
Wilson, Peter: *Crab Antics*, 52–53; "Reputation and Respectability," 52
Witter, Michael, 63
women: in Caribbean society, 22; cricket culture and, 136, 158n113; as a future, 138–40, 151; legal rights, 59–60; new society and, 136–38; sexual commodification of, 58–59, 83–84, 146. *See also* black women; feminism; gender; women writers
Women in the Caribbean Project, 25n11, 150, 165n207
women's liberation, 120, 142, 162n168; as social movement, 147
women writers: black, 137, 145–46, 148, 162n177, 162n179; Caribbean, 3, 164–65n206, 165n208; Francophone, 87. *See also names of individual writers*
Worcester, Kent, 148
Workers and Farmers Party, 124
working classes, 138–39; women's equality and, 144. *See also* masses
World Bank, 2
Worrell, Frank Mortimer, 130–33, 157n78, 157n85, 163n190
Wright, Richard, *Black Boy*, 168, 171–72
Wynter, Sylvia, 7, 9, 14–16, 21, 166–90, 213; on abduction, 177–80, 200; on American racism, 191–92n17; on black experience of New World coloniality, 167–73, 180–81, 192n23; on bourgeoisie, 61, 157n91, 173–77; on Caribbean women writers, 164–65n206; on C. L. R. James, 117–19, 130, 152, 166, 177–78, 186–90; on colonization of desire, 150; on conquest of New World, 179–83; on creolization, 82, 111n179, 111n182; on freedom, 211; human, theory of, 167–68, 181–90, 194n56, 213; importance of, 166; liminality and, 186–87; meetings with C. L. R. James, 166; on popular culture, 187–89; on postcolonial as term, 198n147; on power, 79; on racism, 99–100

AARON KAMUGISHA is Senior Lecturer in Cultural Studies at the University of the West Indies, Cave Hill Campus. He is editor of *Caribbean Political Thought: The Colonial State to Caribbean Internationalisms, Caribbean Political Thought: Theories of the Post-Colonial State,* (with Yanique Hume) *Caribbean Cultural Thought: From Plantation to Diaspora* and *Caribbean Popular Culture: Power, Politics and Performance,* and (with Jane Gordon, Lewis Gordon, and Neil Roberts) *Journeys in Caribbean Thought: The Paget Henry Reader.*

CPSIA information can be obtained
at www.ICGtesting.com
Printed in the USA
LVHW040430170223
739516LV00005B/64